Economic Transition and Labor Market Reform in China

Xinxin Ma

Economic Transition and Labor Market Reform in China

palgrave
macmillan

Xinxin Ma
Hitotsubashi University
Tokyo, Japan

ISBN 978-981-13-1986-0 ISBN 978-981-13-1987-7 (eBook)
https://doi.org/10.1007/978-981-13-1987-7

Library of Congress Control Number: 2018953333

Cover Design by Emma J. Hardy

This Palgrave Macmillan imprint is published by the registered company Springer Nature Singapore Pte Ltd.
The registered company address is: 152 Beach Road, #21-01/04 Gateway East, Singapore 189721, Singapore

To my family and friends

Preface

China has experienced rapid economic development and huge economic growth since 1978. The main reason for this is that the Chinese government promoted transition of the economic system from a planned economy to a market-oriented economy. The Chinese government enforced gradualism reform in which the government retains and controls the public sector (e.g. state-owned enterprises), and simultaneously promotes the private sector (e.g. privately owned enterprises, foreign-owned enterprises, and the self-employed sector). No other country with a transition economy, including Russia and the Central and Eastern European states, followed this path. This uniquely gradual reform led to the mixed ownership system in China and to new segmentation problems in the Chinese labor market. For example, the labor market is segmented into both public and private sectors; into the monopoly industry sector and competitive industry sector; into migrant and local urban resident groups; and into the formal sector and informal sector.

This is a significant area of academic debate. There is a set of unique issues in these labor market segmentations that only occurred in China: they generate valuable research questions to help us understand an imperfect competitive market and transition economics. The government could usefully address the segmentation problems in the Chinese labor market that may contribute to severe income inequality and harm social fairness and welfare in China. Thus Part I of this book focuses on these special issues related to the segmentation of the Chinese labor market during the economic transition period from 1978. The overarching purpose of this book is to investigate the causes and consequences of Chinese labor market segmentations.

As well as the transition from a planned economy to a market economy, the government implemented a set of new policies to address problems related to segmentation of the labor market and to enforce system reforms, for example, the minimum wage system implemented from 1993, the public pension system reformed from the 1990s, and the higher education expansion policy promoted from 1999. Did these policy changes influence labor market outcomes? Part II of this book analyzes the influence of these policies on household and individual behaviors. The results provide reliable evidence to evaluate these policies and generate some suggestions for reform. This policy evaluation not only contributes to academic debate but also provides evidence on which to base new governmental policy.

This research was supported by the Japan Society for the Promotion of Science (JSPS) with its grant-in-aid for scientific research (grant numbers: 25243006 and 16K03611) from 2012 to 2018, and the Joint Usage and Research Center, Institute of Economic Research, Hitotsubashi University from 2015 to 2018. I am grateful to Professor Li Shi (Beijing Normal University) for providing the CHIPs data, and giving so many valuable suggestions and comments since 2004. I acknowledge Professor Atsushi Seike (Keio University), Professor Yoshio Higuchi (Keio University), Professor Ryoshin Minami (Hitotsubashi University), and Professor Katsuji Nakagane (The University of Tokyo) for their teaching and coaching that opened the world of labor economics, development economics, and transition economics and led me to become an Economics researcher. I would like to thank Professor Jun Zhang (Fudan University), Professor Go Yano (Kyoto University), Professor Kazufumi Yugami (Kobai University), Professor Kai Kajitani (Kobai University), and Professor Quheng Deng (Chinese Academy of Social Sciences) and the conference participants for their many helpful comments in 2015 First World Congress of Comparative Economics (WCCE) at Roma Tre University; the 2015 International Conference titled "Economic Transition and Income Inequality in China" at Kyoto University; the Annual Conference of the Japanese Association for Chinese Economy and Management Studies, Tokyo; the 2015 6th Biennial International Conference on Transition and Economic Development (TED) at Fudan University; the 27th CEA (UK) and 8th CEA (Europe) Annual Conference held at the University of Duisburg-Essen; and the 2016 14th European Association of Comparative Economic Studies (EACES) Conference at the University of Regensburg, Germany. I would like to express my gratitude to my colleagues and friends, Professor Ichiro Iwazaki and Professor Kazuhiro Kumo, for their helpful suggestions and encouragement for my research, and colleagues at the Institute of Economic Research (IER), Hitotsubashi University, for giving me such an excellent research environment and support. I greatly appreciate the staff at Palgrave Macmillan for their interest in my research work. Particularly, I acknowledge Dreyer Jacob, Nirmal Kumar Gnana Prakasam, and Jasper Asir for their encouragement and editing work.

Finally, I am deeply grateful to my family for their warm and strong support of my life and work.

Tokyo, Japan
May 30, 2018

Xinxin Ma

Contents

List of Figures

List of Tables

CHAPTER 1

Introduction

1.1 Background: Economic Transition and Change in Labor Policies and Labor Market Structures in China

The level of economic development, production resources, ownership, and economic policies and systems has been transformed since 1949 when the People's Republic of China was established. Economic historians usually divide the Chinese economy into the planned economy period (1949–1977) and the economic transition period (post 1978) (see Table 1.1).

In the planned economy period, the economic development level was poor, capital was scarce, and there was a lot of surplus labor. "Socialist remodeling" (*Sherhui Zhuyi Gaizao*) was introduced to enforce central government control and management for the national economy. All ownership types were transferred into the public sector. By 1956 this included government organizations, state-owned enterprises (SOEs), and collectively owned enterprises (COEs). Figure 1.1 shows the proportions of various ownership types in China from 1949 to 1956. The share of privately owned enterprises (POEs) and foreign-owned enterprises (FOEs) decreased dramatically from 55.8% in 1949 to 0.0% in 1956, whereas the share of public sector (government organizations, SOEs, COEs, and joint-owned enterprises[1]) increased from 44.2% in 1949 to 100.0% in 1956. From 1956 to 1977 the government managed production, capital, and wage/employment of labor in the public sector. In addition, to promote the "Heavy

X. Ma, *Economic Transition and Labor Market Reform in China*,
https://doi.org/10.1007/978-981-13-1987-7_1

Table 1.1 Economic transition and changes of labor policies in China

Period	*Economic development level*	*Production factor*	*Ownership type*	*Labor policy and system*
The planned economy period	Low-income country	*Labor*: a lot of surplus labor	SOEs, COEs	• *Employment*: the employment managed by the government, and long-term employment system
		Capital: scare		• *Wage*: the Unified Management Wage System (UMWS), the wage level, and promotion were controlled by the central government
The economic transition period	Middle-income country	*Labor*: surplus labor decreased	SOEs, COEs, FOEs, POEs, self-employed, others	• *Employment*: labor contract system is implemented in both the public sector and private sector.
		Capital: to become more		• *Wage*: total wage bill is determined by the government for the public sector, whereas the wage level is determined based on the market mechanism in the private sector. • Minimum wage system is implemented in both public and private sectors

Industry Development" policy, the *Hukou* system (population registration system for rural and urban regions) was implemented from 1958, and migration from the rural regions to the urban regions was discouraged. Thus, it can be said that there was no competitive labor market in China in the planned economy period.

From 1978, the government began economic reform and gradualism system transition. In the rural regions the government implemented the Household Land Contract System and from the 1980s reformed the agriculture production price determination system, and the market mechanism for agricultural production began to influence prices. Urban labor market reform commenced from the 1980s and may be divided into four main movements as follows.

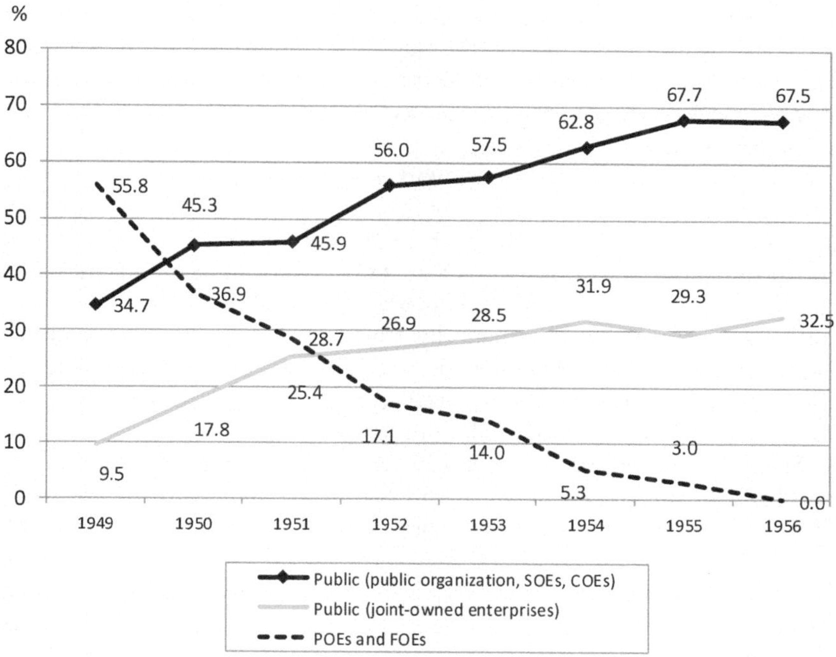

Fig. 1.1 Proportions of public sector and private sector from 1949 to 1956 in China. *Source*: Data based on National Bureau of Statistics (1959), page 32

First, the government promoted SOEs reform. In the 1980s the government delegated some production and profit distribution authorities to enterprises. The government implemented the reform of separating the ownership and management of enterprises, and it only remained as the owner of SOEs at the beginning of the 1990s. In the latter half of the 1990s, the government carried out a policy "to control large SOEs, and to release small-sized SOEs" (*Zhuada Fangxiao*), and promoted the privatization of small and medium-sized SOEs. From the 2000s the government implemented policy so the SOEs became listed enterprises and controlled these large SOEs through the State-owned Assets Supervisory Committee (SASAC). The government promoted foreign direct investment (FDI), and FOEs were permitted from the 1980s. From the 1980s the government also promoted the self-employed sector and POEs. During the economic transition period SOEs, COEs, FOEs, POEs, and the self-employed sector were the predominate ownership types. Even though the government still manages and controls the wage and employment of labor for the large SOEs and government organizations, they remain influenced by labor market mechanisms in the private sector (FOEs, POEs, and the self-employed sector).

Figure 1.2 shows the shares of worker numbers by ownership types. It is clear that the workers in the public sector (government organizations and SOEs) decreased dramatically from 1978 to 2016, and the workers in the private sector, including COEs, POEs, and FOEs, and the self-employed sector, increased. Particularly, the number of workers in the public sector decreased dramatically from 1998 when the government enforced SOEs reform. It is also observed that the increase of workers in the informal sector, the self-employed sector, is marked: it increased from 150,000 in 1978 to 128.62 million in 2016.

Second, although the Chinese government promoted privatization for middle- and small-sized SOEs, it still controlled and managed the large SOEs related to the country's security and economy. The government

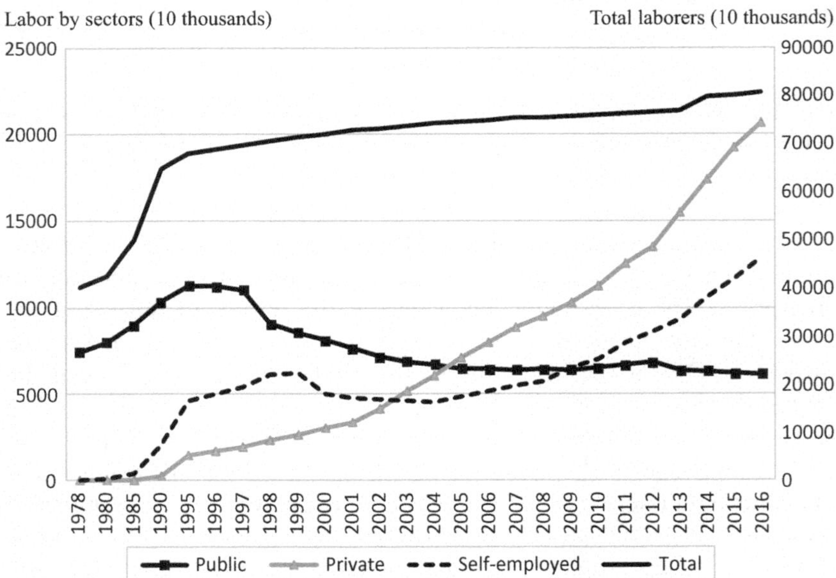

Fig. 1.2 Changes of worker numbers by ownership sectors from 1978 to 2016 in China. *Note*: Data based on National Bureau of Statistics *China Statistical Yearbook 2017*. *Source*: author

published regulations to prohibit entry to some industry sectors for the POEs and FOEs, and provided financial preferential treatment to these protected sectors. Thus, it is thought there is segmentation of the public sector and the private sector. As a result, wage gaps formed between various ownership sectors. Figure 1.3 shows the wage levels by ownership sectors. It is observed that the average annual wage level is higher for the private sector including POEs and FOEs than for the public sector, including SOEs, from 1995 to 2004; it is higher for the public sector than for the private sector after 2005, and the wage gap between the public sector and the private sector increased from 2014.

Third, since the *Hukou* system was deregulated in the 1980s, much surplus labor moved from the urban to the rural regions and the number of workers in the primary industry sector decreased. Figure 1.4 summarizes

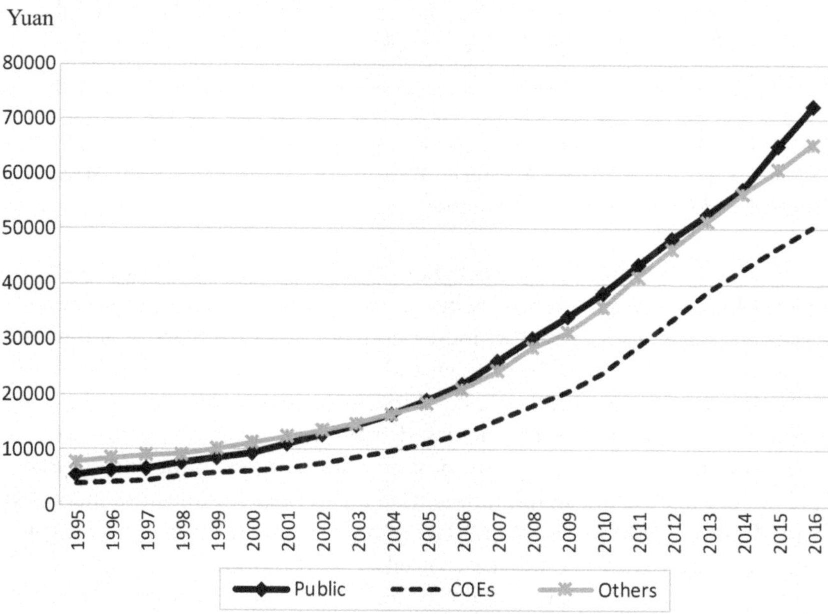

Fig. 1.3 Changes of average wages by ownership sectors from 1995 to 2016 in urban China. *Note*: (1) Data based on National Bureau of Statistics *China Statistical Yearbook 2017*. (2) The values are average annual wages. They are nominal wages. (3) Public includes government organizations and SOEs; Others are composed of FOEs, POEs, and other ownership-type enterprises. *Source*: author

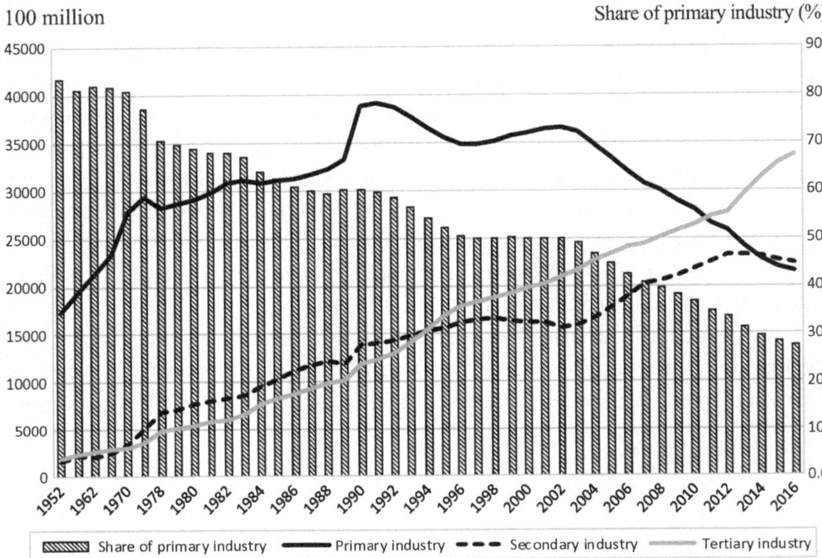

Fig. 1.4 Changes of labor numbers by industry sector from 1952 to 2016 in China. *Note*: Data from National Bureau of Statistics *China Statistical Yearbook 2017* Table 4–3. *Source*: author

the change in the number of workers by industry sectors. Labor in the primary industry sector decreased, whereas the amount of labor in the secondary and tertiary industry sectors increased from 1952 to 2016. Notably, the proportion of workers in the primary industry sector decreased greatly after 2004, from 49.1% in 2003 to 27.7% in 2016. Figure 1.5 shows the total numbers of migrant workers increased from 121 million in 2000 to 282 million in 2016, and the proportion of migrant workers to the total workers in rural regions, including migrant workers with rural registration, increased from 19.8% in 2000 to 43.8% in 2016. It may be that the amount of surplus labor decreased with the decrease of labor in the primary industry sector and the increase of migrants. Even though the number of migrant workers has greatly increased, the *Hukou* system still influences wage, employment, and social security. Work conditions are worse for migrants than for local urban residents. For example, most migrants who work in the POEs, FOEs, and the self-employed sector earn low wages, whereas most of the workers in the public sector, including government organizations and SOEs, are local urban residents and they earn a higher wage (Ma 2018).

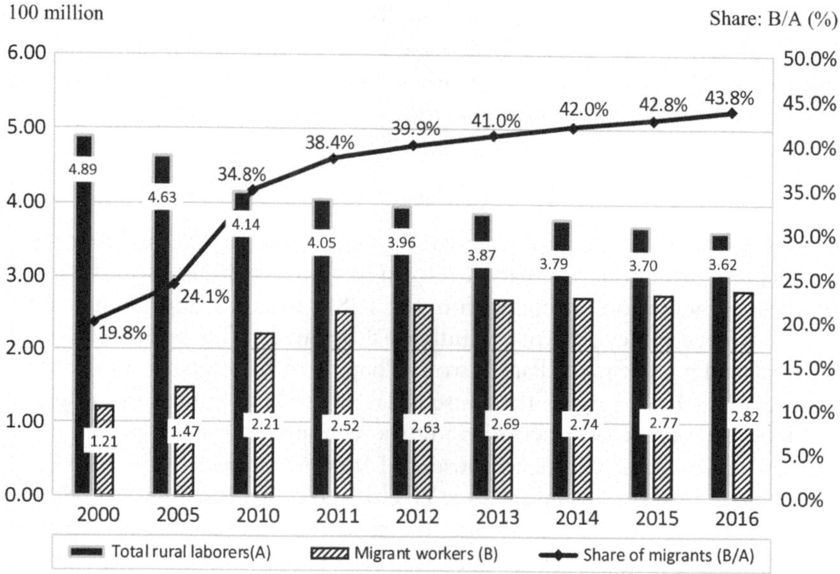

Fig. 1.5 Changes of numbers of migrant workers from 2000 to 2016 in China. *Note*: (1) Data from National Bureau of Statistics *2016 Migrants Monitoring Report*. http://www.stats.gov.cn/tjsj/zxfb/201704/t20170428_1489334.html (accessed on April 16, 2018). (2) Migrants (B) is the total number of migrant workers. (3) Share of migrant workers = migrant workers/total workers including migrant workers and workers in rural regions. *Source*: author

As previously described, during the period of economic transition the Chinese labor market appears segmented by the public sector and the private sector, the informal sector and formal sector, and migrants and local registration residents. It is thought that this labor market segmentation may be the cause of income inequality in China, and it is the main feature of the Chinese labor market during the period of economic transition. Thus, Part I of this book will focus on labor market segmentation issues.

Fourth, during the economic transition period the government implemented a set of new policies that may have affected labor market outcomes. For example, the minimum wage system was implemented from 1993; the higher education expansion system was implemented from 1999; and the social security systems including the pension system were reformed and the new public pension systems (New Rural Social Pension

Program, Basic Pension Insurance for Rural and Urban Residents) were implemented in the 2000s. Did these policies influence household and individual behavior and labor market outcomes? Part II of this book employs quasi-natural experiments to find evidence for these issues.

1.2 The Main Arguments of the Book

This study provides an empirical investigation of the changes in labor market structure due to labor market reform in China. It focuses on the labor market segmentation problems from the 1980s to 2013, and examines the effect of labor policy reform on individual behavior. This book consists of two parts. The first part (Part I, from Chap. 2 to Chap. 6) comprises five chapters which investigate the cause of labor market segmentation during the labor market reform period using the Chinese national repeated cross section survey data (Chinese Household Income Project Survey: CHIPs) and longitudinal survey data (China Health and Nutrition Survey: CHNS). The focus is on the change of wage structure in urban China; the wage gap between the public sector and private sector; the wage gap between the monopolistic industry sector and its influence on wage gaps between migrants and local urban residents; labor market segmentation by ownership types and its impact on gender wage gap; and the determinants of labor supply for the formal sector and informal sector. The second part comprises four chapters that provide evidence about the impact of labor market policy reform on labor market outcomes.

The second part (Part II, from Chap. 7 to Chap. 10) investigates the effect of minimum wage policy on wage distribution and wage gap, the impact of China's higher education expansion policy on youth employment, the impact of the public pension system on the labor supply, and the influence of social security insurance premium based on wage, which can be thought as a kind of payroll tax on wage. The second part is based on CHNS data from 1989 to 2011, CHIPs data from 1995 to 2013, and enterprise panel data from 2004 to 2007. Quasi-natural experiment analysis methods and the panel data analysis method are employed to examine the causal relations between these labor policy reforms and their impact on labor market outcomes in both the short term and the long term.

Chapter 2 considers how wage structure changed during the economic transition. Wage determining mechanisms in China transformed over its planned economy period (1949–1977) and economic transition period (post 1978). It is known that market mechanisms did not function during the earlier period, when the government set the price of both labor and capital. After 1978, the Chinese government enforced market-oriented reform and the SOEs could partly determine the wage and employment independently. According to human capital theory, wages are mainly determined by labor productivity in a perfect competitive market. It is thought that a highly educated worker may show higher productivity, and thus more years of schooling may positively affect the wage level. This chapter examines the effect of years of school on wages and the effect of the market mechanism on wage determination. This is known as the internal return rate (IRR) of education. It compares the long-term changes using CHNS data from 1989 to 2011. It is found that in general the years of schooling positively affects wage level: the marginal effect is 1.5–3.3% during the period from 1989 to 2011. To compare the education effect over three periods (1989–1997, 2000–2007, and 2009–2011), the impact of education on earnings is largest for the period 2009–2011. When the education effect for each survey year is compared, it is found that the education effect increased in recent survey years. In the 1989–1997 period education affects the wage level for the low-wage group; in 2000–2006, education does not influence the wage level for the low-, middle-, and high-wage groups; and in the period 2009–2011 education positively affects the wage for the low-, middle-, and high-wage groups. These results indicate that the impact of market mechanism on wage determination increases with the progress of labor market reform.

Chapter 3 explores the wage gap between the public sector and private sector. It investigates in detail the influence of ownership reform on wage structure. As China shifted to a market-oriented economy, reforms to wage determination lagged behind price reforms for production and consumption goods. It is argued that China's economic reform was incomplete. For example, most small-sized SOEs were privatized, but the governance of large-sized SOEs scarcely changed. Did ownership reforms influence the wage structure in SOEs? Chapter 3 examines changes in wage structures and the determinants of wage gaps between the public sector and private sector during the economic transition period, using three periods of CHIPs datasets (CHIPs 1995, CHIPs 2007, CHIPs 2013). According to the empirical study results, it is clear that with the progress of economic system transition, the wage gap between the public sector (SOEs, government organizations) and COEs decreased, but wage gaps between the public sector and FOEs/POEs increased.

Human capital influenced wage level in both the public sector and the private sector in 1995 and 2013. However, differentials of human capital influences between the public sector and private sector became slighter. The results of decomposition show a wage gap endowment effect, explained by differences in labor productivity characteristics (education attainment, work experience year), and a price effect, partly caused by institutional factors. From 1995 to 2013 the endowment effect increased while the price effect decreased. These results reveal that with the progress of market-oriented economic reform, labor productivity characteristics based on individual human capital were more highly rewarded. These results demonstrate that market mechanisms began to function and correct the distortion of wage levels during the period of economic transition.

From the end of the 1990s the Chinese government promoted the privatization of SOEs in industries related to the country's security and economic stability. The Chinese government has enforced management and control by using preferential financing policies and industry entry regulations. Thus, the government supported segmentation of the monopoly industry sector and competitive industry sector. Second, there is segmentation of rural migrants and local urban residents related to the *Hukou* system. Chapter 4 examines these two kinds of labor market segmentation. It investigates how industry sector segmentation influences the wage gap between the migrants and local urban residents. Using CHIPs 2002 and CHIPs 2013 data, Chap. 4 employs an empirical study. It indicates that the influence of intra-industrial differentials is greater than the influence of inter-industry differentials in both 2002 and 2013. The influence of the explained component of the intra-industry differentials is larger than the influence of inter-industry differentials in both 2002 and 2013, and the influence of the unexplained component of the intra-industrial differentials rises steeply from 2002 to 2013. These results show that the individual productivity characteristic differentials, like human capital, in the same industry sector is the main factor causing the wage gap in both 2002 and 2013, and the problem of discrimination against migrants in the same industry sector became more serious from 2002 to 2013.

The gender wage gap increased with the economic transitions in China. What factors can explain the gender wage gaps in China in the 2000s? It is thought that if the wage determinant mechanism differs between the public and private sectors, or if the human capital endowments of men and women workers differ between these two sectors, segmentation by ownership type may affect the gender wage gap. Chapter 5 utilizes CHIPs 2002 and CHIPs 2013 data to provide empirical evidence about the influence of labor market segmentation by ownership type on the gender wage gap. The decomposition analysis results based on the Brown et al. model indicate that both inter-sector differentials and intra-sector differentials affect the gender wage gap, but the intra-sector differentials are greater in both 2002 and 2013, and the influence of intra-sector differentials is greater for 2013 than for 2002. The influence of unexplained components of the effect of intra-sector differentials is greater than the explained components in both 2002 and 2013, and it is greater for 2013 than for 2002. The results indicate that when other factors, like human capital, are constant, the problem of discrimination against female workers in a given ownership sector, whether public or private, is increasingly serious, and is the main factor associated with the widening of the gender wage gap in China from 2002 to 2013.

Chapter 6 considers formal and informal labor market segmentation in urban China. The self-employed sector is a representative informal sector of the employment market, and it has influence on income inequality as noted in previous studies. The number of self-employed workers ("*Geti Gongshang Hu*") in urban regions increased greatly during the period of economic transition and economic development. Why was there a large growth in self-employment in urban China during the economic transition period? Two hypotheses are proposed to answer this question. First, the disguised unemployment hypothesis suggests there was little opportunity to access the formal sector to obtain better work. Second, the business creation hypothesis suggests successful business owners created new jobs for others, new business opportunities, and many innovative new products for society. Empirical studies for other transition countries have been published but there is no study on the issue for China and it is not clear which mechanisms influence the choice to enter the self-employment sector. The two hypotheses are tested using CHIPs 2007 and the latest survey data, CHIPs 2013. It is found that in general, utilizing the imputed wage premiums used in previous studies, the business creation hypothesis is rejected. The disguised unemployment hypothesis is supported for both the local urban residents' group and the migrant group in 2007 and 2013. The results that utilized the new wage premiums based on the imputed employee wages in the private sector show that the business creation hypothesis is supported when a worker chooses to become an employer for both the migrant group and the local urban resident group in 2013. Finally, the business creation hypothesis is relevant for the older generation group of local urban residents in 2013.

The rationale behind the minimum wage policy is to increase the wage level for the low-income group, reduce poverty, and reduce income inequality between the high-wage group and the low-wage group. Thus, minimum wage implementation is an important labor policy in both developing and developed countries. In China the first minimum wage legislation the Enterprise's Minimum Wage Regulations, was promulgated in 1993. In 2004, central government promoted the implementation of a minimum wage policy across China. Chapter 7 analyzes the effects of minimum wage policy on the average wage, the wage percentile groups, and the wage gap between rural and urban resident groups in China using CHNS data from 1991 to 2011. It is found that the 1997 minimum wage implementation positively affected the average wage for both the rural group and the urban group, but the implementation of 2004 minimum wage policy may have decreased the average wage for the urban group and the enforcement of the minimum wage policy since 2008 does not affect the average wage for either the rural or urban group. In the policy promulgation period the effect of the minimum wage policy on the low-wage group is greater for the urban group than for the rural group. The minimum wage policy affected the middle- and high-wage groups during 1991–1997 and 2006–2011 for the rural and the urban groups. The spillover effect is greater for the minimum wage policy promulgation period (1991–1997) than for other periods. The minimum wage policy may have increased the wage gap between the rural and urban groups in the minimum wage policy promulgation period but not in other periods.

Chapter 8 investigates the impact of China's higher education expansion policy on youth employment. The higher education expansion policy was introduced in 1999. The number of college graduates increased from 108 million in 1998 to 638.1 million in 2013. It is thought the increase of college graduate labor supply in the short term may affect college graduate employment. Based on a natural experiment model (DID model and DDD model), an empirical study using CHNS longitudinal survey data from 1989 to 2011 provides evidence on whether the higher education expansion policy has affected the employment of new college graduates. It indicates that the higher education expansion policy reduces the employment prospects of young college graduates. The negative effect of the policy on employment was greater for 2006 and 2009 than for 2004 and 2011. The higher education expansion policy decreases the likelihood of young college graduates gaining either regular or irregular work. It is found policy implementation decreases the proportion of young college graduates in a desirable sector. The differences of policy impact on employment in the Eastern, Central, and Western regions are small. The negative effect of the policy on employment is greater for the group with urban registration than the group with rural registration.

To address the social and economic problems caused by the aging population, many governments around the world sought to establish a set of social security systems, for example a universal public pension scheme, to provide security for the elderly. However, according to empirical studies for developed countries a public pension may reduce the labor supply; therefore, a public pension scheme may negatively affect economic growth in the long term. The Chinese government implemented a public pension, the New Rural Pension Scheme (NRPS), in 2009 for rural residents. For the elderly in China does the NRPS change the choice whether to work or not? Chapter 9 attempts to answer this question with empirical analysis to provide evidence using the natural experiment models (DID model) and the CHNS longitudinal survey data. Several major conclusions emerge. In general, the NRPS decreases the probability of labor force participation. The negative policy effect decreases from 2000 to 2011. The NRPS may increase the probability of people choosing to become a regular worker. However, the difference of probability between the irregular worker, self-employed, and no-work group is not statistically significant. It is also found that the influence of the NRPS differs by various groups. For example, the impact of the NRPS is greater for the Western region than for the Eastern and Central regions; it is greater for women than for men. Finally, the robustness checks, including the use of various treatment and control groups, and the Placebo test, confirm again that the NRPS may decrease labor force participation of the elderly in rural China.

The Chinese government enforces the public security system reform during the economic transition period; the insurance premium, which can be considered a kind of payroll tax, is nearly 40% of total wage. It is thought the enterprises may transfer the social insurance contributions to the worker by reducing the worker's wage. Do the social insurance contributions influence wage? Chapter 10 employs an empirical study using the enterprise panel survey data. It is found that in general, the enterprise's social insurance contributions do negatively affect the worker's wage level—the enterprise may transfer the social insurance contributions rise to the worker. Moreover, even though the social insurance contributions rise may decrease the worker wage level for both the public sector and private sector, the negative effect is greater for the private sector (FOEs, HTOEs, POEs, and COEs) than for the public sector (SOEs). It should be noted that the social security coverage scale spreading from the public sector to the private sector may increase the welfare of workers in the private sector; the harm by the social security system reform is greater for the workers in the private sector than those in the public sector, which is a new inequality problem to be considered.

1.3 Significance of the Book

This book investigates the changes in labor market structure during the economic transition period. It considers problems associated with labor market segmentation resulting from the incomplete delivery of marketization or progressive reforms that caused the wage gaps between various sectors. It analyzes the influence of new labor policies on wage gaps and labor force participation behaviors. A strength of the method of this book is the use of empirical studies based on the theories in labor economics, transition economics, and development economics. Three valuable features of the book can be summarized as follows.

First, using Chinese national long-term repeated cross section survey data (CHIPs) and longitudinal survey data (CHNS), a set of econometric analyses is used to investigate the changes in labor market structure from the 1980s to the 2000s. The most recent survey data, like CHIPs 2013, provides the newest information. Comparison of the changes from the short-term and long-term perspective provides valuable new insights.

Second, in order to investigate the cause and consequence of labor market reform, this book focuses on the problems associated with labor market segmentation, particularly on the wage gaps between various sectors and groups (the wage gap between the public sector and private sector, wage gap between migrants and local urban residents, wage gap between informal sector and formal sector, and the gender wage gap). It examines the determinants of these wage gaps developing empirical studies using Chinese national survey data that covers all representative districts, provinces, and regions in China. These econometric analyses investigate the relation between the unique segmentation of the Chinese labor market and its influence on various wage gaps. These results help us to better understand the complex income inequality problems in China related to the economic transition period.

Third, this book evaluates the causal relations between the impacts of labor policy change on labor market outcomes, including wage level, income inequality, labor employment, and labor force participation behavior, which are not adequately addressed in the published literature. This study provides academically sound evidence that may support the policy reforms of the Chinese government. It provides a point of reference for countries attempting economic transition and for developing countries.

Note

1. A joint-owned enterprise is an enterprise that is owned by the government and private or foreign owners. The government is the majority owner, and therefore the joint-owned enterprise is managed and controlled by the government and is in the public sector.

References

Ma, X. (2018). Labor market segmentation by industry sectors and wage gaps between migrants and local urban residents in urban China. *China Economic Review, 47*, 96–115.

National Bureau of Statistics (NBS) of China. (2017). *China statistical yearbook*. Beijing: Chinese Statistics Press (In Chinese).

PART I

Labor Market Reform in China: Consequence and Cause

CHAPTER 2

Economic Transition and Change of Wage Structure

2.1 Introduction

Given that labor is a necessary factor of production, the wage determination mechanism attracts attention for its role in setting the price of labor properly. Neoclassical economics asserts that wages in perfectly competitive markets are decided by labor demand and supply, and by the principles of profit maximization for firms and labor productivity.[1] In addition, the government establishes wage policies, for example, the Minimum Wage Act,[2] to rectify inequalities, and trade unions influence wages through collective bargaining. Thus it is can be said that the wage policies and systems coincide with market mechanisms to determine wages.

Wage determining mechanisms in China transformed between its planned economy period (1949–1977) and economic transition period (post 1978). Market mechanisms did not function during the earlier period, when the government priced both labor and capital. In the planned economy period, the Chinese government enacted its united management wage policy to set wage levels and control wage growth ranges. During the economic transition period, the reasons for change of wage determinate mechanism can be considered as follows. First, even as China shifted to a market-oriented economy, reforms to wage determination were late compared to price reforms of production, and consumption goods, and it is pointed out that China's economic reform was incomplete[3] For example, most small state-owned enterprises (SOEs) were privatized, but the governance of large SOEs scarcely changed. It is thought the SOE reform

X. Ma, *Economic Transition and Labor Market Reform in China*,
https://doi.org/10.1007/978-981-13-1987-7_2

should influence the wage determinant in China. Second, since the end of the 1980s, foreign direct investment (FDI) policy was enforced by the Chinese government, the foreign-owned enterprises (FOEs) were drawn to the Chinese market, and the FOEs increased since the 1990s. Third, with the deregulation of the *Hukou* system (registration system), the rural residents moved to the urban regions as "migrants". With the increase of migrants, the workers in the informal sector (e.g. the self-employed sector, small-sized enterprises) in urban China increased. It is thought the influence of the market mechanism on wage determination is greater for FOEs and informal sectors than for the public sector (e.g. government organizations, SOEs). Thus it is thought with the progress of economic transition, the impact of market mechanism on wage determination should become great.

Based on the neoclassical economics theory (e.g. the human capital theory), in a perfect competitive market, wage is determined by labor productivity. It is thought that the high education group may have high productivity, and thus the years of schooling may positively affect wage level. To indicate the effect of market mechanism on wage, this chapter of the book aims to examine the effect of years of schooling on wage level, which is named as internal return rate (IRR) of education and compares their changes for the long term using Chinese Health and Nutrition Survey (CHNS) longitudinal survey data from 1989 to 2011.

This chapter is structured as follows. Section 2.2 provides the background of changes in China's wage policies and systems during the period of economic transition. Section 2.3 introduces the framework of the empirical analysis, including datasets and models. Section 2.3 is the literature review about the channel of the effect of education on wage and empirical studies on the estimation of IRR of education. Section 2.5 introduces and explains estimation results. Section 2.6 gives a summary of conclusions.

2.2 Institutional Background: Changes in China's Wage Policy and Wage System

To promote priority development of heavy manufacturing during the planned economy period, China's government enforced low-wage labor policies to increase employment in urban regions, and established a unified-management wage system in the public sector (Meng and Kidd 1997; Bowles and White 1998; Yamamoto 2000; Marugawa 2002; Li and Zhao

2003; Ma 2018a, b). In 1956, the self-employment sector,[4] privately owned enterprises (POEs), and foreign-owned enterprises (FOEs) disappeared under the "socialism remodeling" campaign enforced by the government. The entirety of the government organizations, SOEs, and collectively owned enterprises (COEs) became the state-owned sector, forming only one sector named "the public sector".

Along with the corporate governance reform, China's government reformed wage systems in 1951 and 1956 and established the grade wage system in the public sector. The government controlled wage levels and wage rise ranges. Wage determinations were essentially based on factors such as education, occupation, and seniority (Li and Zhao 2003). The individual worker's labor input and productivity did not affect his wage level and promotion. Thus, the wage disparity was small during the early period of economic reform in the late 1970s. However, these wage policies and systems did not incentivize work efforts, and both labor productivity and enterprise effectiveness were low. To solve these problems, the Chinese government reformed wage systems after the 1980s.

Changes in wage policies and systems during the economic transition period (after 1978) can be summarized as follows.

During the 1980s, China's government rescinded policies that had been in effect more than 10 years and permitted firms to pay bonuses and piece rates. The State Council promulgated the enforcement of bonus and piece wage in 1978 and established policies concerning the upper limits of and tax rates applicable to bonuses in 1983 and 1984.

As a second major change, the government linked a firm's efficiency and profit to wage bill. In 1985 and 1986, the State Council promulgated the notification about problems of SOEs wage system reform and the rules about promoting enterprise reform and enhancing enterprise vitality. They specified that "government does not prescribe a unified payment system for enterprises, and enterprises themselves can decide payment systems within a range of total wage accounts decided by government".

Wage policies for linking enterprise efficiency to wage bill and promoting this were published in 1987 and 1989. SOEs gained some autonomy of wage and employment decisions on the basis of hard budget constraints from the government. Overall, during the 1980s, mechanisms for deciding workers' wages became better aligned with enterprise efficiency and profit, and individual human capital based on education was more highly rewarded (Meng and Kidd 1997).

Corporate governance reforms were ongoing throughout SOEs during the 1990s. The government published new policies extending SOEs' autonomy in determining labor employment and individual wage level. For example, in 1990 and 1992, the Chinese government promulgated the regulations for the transition to modern management systems in SOEs.

However, with the government's control over wage determination waning, wage levels of workers in SOEs increased greatly while enterprise profits paid to the government declined dramatically. To address this situation, the notification strengthening macro-control of enterprises' wage bill was published in July 1993, and the rule for the constitution of wage bill was promulgated in November 1995. The government again inserted itself into determining enterprise wage bill and individual wage levels, and enforced the unified-management wage system again.

During the 2000s, China's government has promoted establishment and enforcement of labor policy and strengthened its macro-control over the labor market. The tenth five-year plan for labor and social security in January 2002 noted the expansion of wage differentials between monopolistic and competitive sectors of the economy. To settle the discrepancy, the government established the modern enterprise wage system, set the rate of sustainable wage growth and wage-level adjustments based on market mechanisms mainly, and granted autonomy over wage determination to enterprises while permitting workers to participate in wage decisions.

At the same time, the government promoted wage determination based on both market mechanisms and enterprise profit, and proposed a collective wage determination system for SOEs and non-SOEs. The government also promulgated the Minimum Wage Act in January 2004 and the notification about improvements in the Minimum Wage Act in June 2007. The Labor Contract Act and the Arbitration and Conciliation of Labor Disputes Act were published in January and May 2008. These laws defined conditions of governing wage determination, employment, and labor disputes.

During the current period of economic transition, in the public sector, the government has reformed wage systems and promoted wage determination based on market mechanisms, but it has retained control over enterprise wage bill and individual basic wage levels. On the other hand, in the private sector (FOEs and POEs), wages are primarily decided by market mechanisms. How did wage policies changes affect wage structures during the economic transition period in China? How did the effect of education on wage change along with the economic transition progress? The following empirical analysis will answer these questions.

2.3 The Channels and Empirical Studies on the Influence of Education on Wage

2.3.1 The Channels of the Influence of Education on Wage

How can education influence an individual wage? Two channels of influence can explain it. First, based on human capital theory (Becker 1964; Mincer 1974), the individual wage is determined by individual labor productivity. Educational attainment is thought to be a part of human capital. High-level education expresses high labor productivity, which causes a high individual wage (schooling model). Second, based on the signaling model (or screening model), the "halo effect" of educational attainment (such as graduation from university or graduate school) signals a worker's potential quality to employers. From this viewpoint, the positive effect of education on wages is not because of the worker's high labor productivity, it just certifies that the worker may have an ability to do high-level skilled work. Educational attainment can play a signaling role when it is difficult for employers to estimate the worker's potential ability which is not easily observed.

However, some factors may affect the influence of education on wages. For example, the implementation by firms of a set of human resource management systems to improve the workers' motivation based on the internal labor market and the efficient wage hypotheses. Another factor is that in China the wage determination system is different for the public sector (e.g. the government organizations, SOEs) and the private sector (e.g. POEs, FOEs). For example, in the public sector, the government controls the basic wage, whereas in the private sector the wage level is decided by the market mechanism. Thus the effect of educational level on wages might be different in these two sectors. Based on the discrimination hypothesis (Becker 1957), even though the labor productivity of group A (e.g. women, migrants) is similar to group B (e.g. men, local urban residents), because there is discrimination for group A, which may come from employers, customers, counterpart colleagues, or others, the wage level is set lower for group A than that for group B. Therefore, the influence of educational level on wages may differ between various groups (women vs. men, migrant workers vs. local urban resident workers).

2.3.2 Previous Empirical Studies on the Return to Education in China

Wage function is estimated based on Mincer (1974). The coefficient of years of schooling in Mincer's wage function expresses the return to education; the estimated value is approximate to the private internal rate of return to years of schooling (which is abbreviated as "IRR"). The Ordinary Least Square (OLS) model and wage function based on the sample selection bias correction model are usually used in previous studies (Psacharopoulos 1981; Byron and Manaloto 1990; Johnson and Chow 1997; Liu 1998, 2008; Lai 1998; Trostel et al. 2002; Li 2003; Li and Ding 2003; Psacharopoulos and Patrinos 2004; Bishop and Chiou 2004; Heckman and Li 2004; Zhang et al. 2005; Qian and Smyth 2008; Chen and Hamori 2009; Qiu and Hudson 2010; Ge and Yang 2011; Kang and Peng 2012; Ren and Miller 2012; Deng and Ding 2012; Wang 2013; and Mishra and Smyth 2014; Ma 2018a, b). In addition, in order to address the endogenous problem, the instrument variable (IV) method is also utilized (Fleisher et al. 2004; Heckman and Li 2004; Li and Luo 2004; Giles et al. 2008; Chen and Hamori 2009; Kang and Peng 2012; Fang et al. 2012; Mishra and Smyth 2013; Wang 2012a, 2013; and Gao and Smyth 2015). The estimated results in these studies are different in the analyzed periods, and the utilized data and methods. It is observed that the estimated IRR values range from 1.4 (Byron and Manaloto 1990) to 44.0 (Wang 2012a) from 1988–2011 (see Appendix Table 2.8).

The contributions of this chapter are as follows. First, this chapter analyzes the changes in return to education from 1989 to 2011, using the long-term panel survey data (CHNS 1989–2011) which provides new evidence on the issue. Second, in order to investigate the change of effects of education on wage during the economic transition period, the IRRs are calculated by periods and survey years. Third, to consider how the effect of education on wage might differ throughout wage distribution (e.g. low-wage, middle-wage, and high-wage groups), the IRRs by wage percentiles are also estimated.

2.4 Methodology and Data for Estimation of Return to Education

2.4.1 Models

First, to measure wage structure based on variable means, the OLS model is utilized, which is expressed as Eq. (2.1).

$$\ln W_i = \alpha + \beta_s S_i + \beta_X X_i + u_i \tag{2.1}$$

In Eq. (2.1), ln W indicates the dependent variable (as a logarithm of the wage rate), i denotes workers, S is the years of schooling, X are the other factors (e.g. experience year, occupation) affecting wages, β_s is the return to education, β_X are the estimated coefficients of X, α is a constant, and u is the error term.

Second, to address the sample selection bias problem, the Heckman two-step model is used. It is expressed as follows. ln W_i can be observed only when

$$\begin{gathered} Y_i = \text{Prob}(y_i = 1) = \gamma_H H_i + v_i > 0 \\ u \sim N(0,\sigma) \\ v \sim N(0,1) \\ \text{corr}(u,v) = \rho \end{gathered} \tag{2.2a}$$

In Eq. (2.2a), Y_i = Prob(y_i = 1) is the individual probability of labor force participation (it is equal to 1 when the individual is in work), H is the factors affecting the labor force participation decision, γ_H are the estimated coefficients of H, v is the error term. corr (u, v) = ρ is the correlation coefficient of u and v. The correct item λ can be calculated ($\lambda = \rho\sigma$) based on the probit regression function (select function) expressed by Eqs. (2.2). Then, the Heckman two-step model can be expressed as Eq. (2.2b).

$$\ln W_i = \alpha + \beta_s S_i + \beta_X X_i + \beta_\lambda \lambda_i + u_i \tag{2.2b}$$

Third, when Corr(S, u) $\neq 0$, there might exist the endogenous problem in the results based on Eqs. (2.1) and (2.2b). In order to address the problem, the instrument variable method (IV) is used in the study; it can be expressed as Eqs. (2.3a) and (2.3b).

$$\ln W_i = \alpha + \beta_s S_i + \beta_X X_i + u_i \tag{2.3a}$$

$$\begin{gathered} S_i = b + \kappa_z Z_i + \kappa_X X_i + \varepsilon_i \\ \mathrm{Corr}(S,u) \neq 0 \\ \mathrm{Corr}(Z,u) = 0 \end{gathered} \tag{2.3b}$$

In Eq. (2.3b), S is the years of schooling, X are the other factors (e.g. experience year, occupation) which are similar in Eqs. (2.3a) and (2.3b), Z indicates the instrument variable, κ are the estimated coefficients, b is a constant, and ε is the error term. In previous studies (Fleisher et al. 2004; Chen and Hamori 2009; Fang et al. 2012; Kang and Peng 2012; Mishra and Smyth 2013; Wang 2012a, b, 2013; Gao and Smyth 2015), Kang and Peng 2012, spouse's education and parent's education are usually used as the instrument variable. Based on the CHNS data, the parent's education attainment (the total years of schooling of parent) is used as the instrument variable in this study.

Finally, the quantile regression model (Koenker and Bassett 1978) is also utilized to investigate the effect of education on wage throughout the wage distributions, which is expressed as:

$$\min \begin{bmatrix} \sum\limits_{h_1:\ln W_i >= \beta(\theta)_s S_i + \beta(\theta)_X X_i} \theta \left| \ln W_i - \beta(\theta)_s S_i - \beta(\theta)_X X_i \right| \\ + \sum\limits_{h_0:\ln W_i < \beta(\theta)_s S_i + \beta(\theta)_X X_i,\ \rho(\theta)\in(0\sim1)} (1-\theta) \left| \ln W_i - \beta(\theta)_s S_i - \beta(\theta)_X X_i \right| \end{bmatrix} \tag{2.4}$$

In Eq. (2.4), θ is an index indicating the wage percentiles, and $\beta(\theta)_s$, $\beta(\theta)_X$ are the estimated coefficients of years of schooling and X at various wage percentiles.

2.4.2 *Data*

This chapter employs nine waves (1989, 1991, 1993, 1997, 2000, 2004, 2006, 2009, and 2011) of CHNS survey data. CHNS is a nationwide longitudinal survey conducted by the Carolina Population Center at the University of North Carolina and the National Institute for Nutrition and Health (NINH, former National Institute of Nutrition and Food Safety) at the Chinese Center for Disease Control and Prevention (CCDC). The survey was conducted by an international team of researchers whose backgrounds include nutrition, public health, economics, sociology, Chinese studies, and demography. The survey took place over a 7-day period using a multistage, random cluster process to draw a sample of about 7,200 households with over 30,000 individuals in 12 provinces and municipal cities (Beijing, Liaoning, Heilongjiang, Shanghai, Jiangsu, Shandong, Henan, Hubei, Hunan, Guangxi, Guizhou, Chongqing) that vary substantially in geography, economic development, and government public resources. The information on wage, work status, and individual and household characteristics (e.g. age, education, gender, marriage, number of children, children's ages) used in the analysis can be obtained from the CHNS. Because CHNS is a survey in the long term, the analysis by periods can be employed, which can provide the evidence for the wage determination mechanism change from a long-term perspective.

Table 2.1 displays the description statistics of the analysis variables. The logarithm of the wage rate (ln *W*) is the dependent variable. Monthly wage includes base salary and allowance. Bonus, financial assets, and public transfer payments are excluded. The consumption price index (CPI) from 1989 to 2011 is used to adjust the nominal wage. Monthly working hours are calculated using daily working hours and monthly working days. Wage rate calculations are based on total wage and working hours.

Independent variable settings are as follows. In wage functions, (1) as indexes of human capital, I use education (years of schooling), experience year,[5] the occupation dummy (technician, manager, clerk, agriculture worker, high-skilled manufacturing worker (H), low-skilled manufacturing worker (L), service worker, and others),[6] and mental health score.

(2) Male dummy variable is used to control the wage gap by gender.

(3) To consider the labor market segmentation by sectors, the employment status and public sector dummy variables are used in the analysis.[7] Employment status is composed of the regular worker, the irregular worker I, the irregular worker II, the self-employed I, the self-employed II, and other dummy variables.[8] Public dummy variable is equal to 1 if the worker is in a government organization or SOE.

(4) It is likely that labor market situations such as labor supply and demand, and the labor policy implementation, such as minimum wage system, are different among provinces (Li and Ma 2015). Region dummy variables (Western, Central, and Eastern Region) are used to control these regional disparities.

Table 2.1 Descriptive statistics by four periods

	1989–2011		*1989–1997*		*2000–2006*		*2009–2011*	
	Mean	*SD*	*Mean*	*SD*	*Mean*	*SD*	*Mean*	*SD*
ln wr	1.169	1.279	0.390	1.152	1.328	1.034	1.991	1.086
Years of schooling	11	4	10	4	11	4	12	4
Experience years	26	12	23	11	27	11	30	11
Experience years squared	820	663	640	595	862	655	1004	694
Male	0.574	0.495	0.560	0.496	0.560	0.496	0.607	0.489
Mental health score	6.629	2.891	6.828	2.754	6.519	3.039	6.495	2.881
Occupation								
Technician	0.159	0.365	0.130	0.337	0.164	0.371	0.188	0.391
Manager	0.097	0.295	0.097	0.296	0.091	0.288	0.102	0.302
Clerk	0.114	0.318	0.091	0.287	0.119	0.324	0.138	0.345
Agriculture worker	0.082	0.275	0.104	0.306	0.080	0.271	0.056	0.230
Manufacturing worker (H)	0.144	0.351	0.167	0.373	0.144	0.352	0.114	0.317
Manufacturing worker (L)	0.166	0.372	0.213	0.410	0.151	0.358	0.121	0.326
Service worker	0.128	0.334	0.100	0.300	0.124	0.330	0.169	0.375
Others	0.111	0.314	0.097	0.297	0.126	0.331	0.112	0.316
Employment status								
Regular worker	0.625	0.484	0.717	0.450	0.601	0.490	0.535	0.499
Irregular worker I	0.120	0.324	0.049	0.217	0.125	0.331	0.202	0.402
Irregular worker II	0.097	0.296	0.073	0.259	0.111	0.314	0.114	0.317
Self-employed I	0.029	0.168	0.020	0.142	0.033	0.177	0.037	0.188
Self-employed II	0.118	0.322	0.135	0.342	0.118	0.322	0.096	0.295
Others	0.011	0.104	0.005	0.073	0.012	0.110	0.016	0.127

(*continued*)

Table 2.1 (continued)

	1989–2011		*1989–1997*		*2000–2006*		*2009–2011*	
	Mean	*SD*	*Mean*	*SD*	*Mean*	*SD*	*Mean*	*SD*
Ownership types								
Public sector	0.330	0.470	0.174	0.379	0.378	0.485	0.478	0.500
Regions								
East	0.383	0.486	0.339	0.473	0.358	0.480	0.466	0.499
Central	0.399	0.490	0.416	0.493	0.453	0.498	0.317	0.465
West	0.218	0.413	0.245	0.430	0.189	0.392	0.217	0.412
Survey year								
y1989	0.093	0.290						
y1991	0.091	0.287						
y1993	0.085	0.279						
y1997	0.109	0.312						
y2000	0.114	0.318						
y2004	0.102	0.303						
y2006	0.111	0.314						
y2009	0.105	0.306						
y2011	0.191	0.393						
Observations	12,418		4,689		4,059		3,670	

Source: Calculated based on CHNS from 1989 to 2011

Analysis objects are limited to employees aged 16–60. Sample sizes are 12,418 for the whole period, 4,689 for the 1989–1997 period, 4,059 for the 2000–2006 period, and 3,670 for the 2009–2011 period.

The descriptive statistics of variables is shown in Table 2.1. Years of schooling increased from 10 years (the 1989–1997 period) to 12 years (the 2006–2009 period). It is shown that along with the implementation of the higher-education expansion policy since 1999, the average years of schooling increased. It is thought that the changes of labor supply of high-level education might affect the return of education. The proportion of regular worker decreased from 71.7% (the 1989–1997 period) to 53.5% (the 2006–2009 period). The proportion of irregular worker I (the contactor with other people or enterprise) increased from 4.9% (the 1989–1997 period) to 20.2% (the 2006–2009 period).

2.5 Estimated Results of Wage Structure

2.5.1 Results of Wage Function at Mean Wage Level

First, Table 2.2 summarizes wage function results at mean values of wage levels in the whole period (the 1989–2011 period) based on the OLS. They are distinguished into model1–model4 by using various independent variables. Model1 is the basic model which only controls the human capital variables; model2 adds the male and health dummy variables to model1; model3 adds occupation variables to model2; and model4 is the one which uses all independent variables. The coefficients of years of schooling in both model1 and model2 are 0.033, which are statistically significant at the 1% level. When the occupation is controlled in model3, the coefficients of years of schooling decrease to 0.13; when all the variables are controlled in model4, the coefficients of years of schooling in model4 become 0.015. It indicates that the logarithm of the wage level might increase 1.5–3.3% when years of schooling increase by one year. In addition, it is shown that the education level influences the occupation selection (e.g. the probability to occupy the manager or professional work is higher for high-education group). In other words, the education might affect wage level throughout its influence on occupation (or job) selection. The result is consistent with Byron and Manaloto (1990), Johnson and Chow (1997), Liu (1998), Li and Ding (2003), Bishop and Chiou (2004), Ma (2018a, b), and Kang and Peng (2012), which estimate the effect of education on wage by the OLS.

Second, it is thought that an endogenous problem and sample selection bias problem might exist in the results by the OLS shown in Table 2.3. To

Table 2.2 Results of wage function (OLS)

	(1) Basic		*(2): (1) + male, health*		*(3): (2) + occupation*		*(4): (3) + sectors*	
	Coeff.	*SE*	*Coeff.*	*SE*	*Coeff.*	*SE*	*Coeff.*	*SE*
Years of schooling	0.033***	0.003	0.033***	0.003	0.013***	0.003	0.015***	0.003
Experience years	−0.010***	0.003	−0.009	0.003	−0.009**	0.003	−0.004***	0.003
Experience years squared	0.000	0.000	0.000***	0.000	0.000	0.000	0.000***	0.000
Male			0.037***	0.019	0.032*	0.019	0.029**	0.018
Mental health score			−0.015***	0.003	−0.010***	0.003	−0.006*	0.003
Occupation								
Technician					0.177***	0.036	0.230***	0.036
Manager					0.171***	0.041	0.158***	0.040
Agriculture worker					0.053	0.045	0.103*	0.059
Manufacturing worker (H)					−0.202***	0.037	−0.139***	0.037
Manufacturing worker (L)					−0.341***	0.037	−0.268***	0.037
Service worker					−0.194***	0.039	−0.232***	0.039
Others					0.102***	0.039	0.116***	0.042
Employment status								
Irregular worker I							0.262***	0.031
Irregular worker II							0.049	0.036
Self-employed I							0.169***	0.056
Self-employed II							0.085*	0.044
Others							0.154*	0.089
Ownership type								
Public sector							0.304***	0.021

(*continued*)

Table 2.2 (continued)

	(1) Basic		*(2): (1) + male, health*		*(3): (2) + occupation*		*(4): (3) + sectors*	
	Coeff.	*SE*	*Coeff.*	*SE*	*Coeff.*	*SE*	*Coeff.*	*SE*
Regions								
Central							−0.058***	0.022
West							−0.205***	0.025
Year	Yes		Yes		Yes		Yes	
Constants	0.077	0.060	0.153***	0.064	0.418***	0.073	0.273***	0.074
Observations	12,418		12,418		12,418		12,418	
Adj R-squared	0.338		0.083		0.339		0.378	

Source: Calculated based on CHNS from 1989 to 2011

Note:

(1) *, **, ***: statistically significant levels are 10%, 5%, and 1%

(2) Reference variables are clerk, regular worker, private sector, Eastern region

Table 2.3 Results of wage function (OLS, Heckman two-step, and IV)

	(1) OLS		*(2) Selection model*		*(3) IV*	
	Coeff.	*SE*	*Coeff.*	*SE*	*Coeff.*	*SE*
Years of schooling	0.015***	0.003	0.005	0.005	0.016*	0.010
Experience years	−0.004***	0.003	−0.013***	0.004	−0.036***	0.011
Experience years squared	−1.208E-04***	5.980E-05	5.350E-05	8.150E-05	2.957E-04	1.916E-04
Male	0.029**	0.018	0.025	0.019	−0.006	0.057
Mental health score	−0.006*	0.003	−0.010***	0.004	−0.012	0.011
Occupation						
Technician	0.230***	0.036	0.227***	0.036	0.312**	0.135
Manager	0.158***	0.040	0.163***	0.040	0.373**	0.150
Agriculture worker	0.103*	0.059	0.107*	0.059	−0.053	0.158
Manufacturing worker (H)	−0.139***	0.037	−0.135***	0.037	−0.163	0.126
Manufacturing worker (L)	−0.268***	0.037	−0.264***	0.037	−0.162	0.125
Service worker	−0.232***	0.039	−0.228***	0.039	−0.186	0.130
Others	0.116***	0.042	0.121***	0.042	0.111	0.139
Employment status						
Irregular worker I	0.262***	0.031	0.259***	0.031	0.380***	0.101
Irregular worker II	0.049	0.036	0.053	0.036	0.206*	0.111
Self-employed I	0.169***	0.056	0.172***	0.056	0.393***	0.146
Self-employed II	0.085*	0.044	0.088**	0.044	0.327***	0.114
Others	0.154*	0.089	0.155*	0.089	0.179	0.233
Ownership type						
Public sector	0.304***	0.021	0.307***	0.021	0.363***	0.064

(*continued*)

Table 2.3 (continued)

	(1) OLS		*(2) Selection model*		*(3) IV*	
	Coeff.	*SE*	*Coeff.*	*SE*	*Coeff.*	*SE*
Regions						
Central	−0.058***	0.022	−0.022	0.025	−0.172**	0.073
West	−0.205***	0.025	−0.142***	0.033	−0.126	0.082
Year						
y1991	−0.001	0.042	−0.006	0.043	0.001	0.131
y1993	−0.049	0.043	−0.067	0.044	0.054	0.129
y1997	0.678***	0.041	0.644***	0.043	0.599***	0.127
y2000	0.891***	0.041	0.866***	0.042	0.735***	0.124
y2004	1.128***	0.043	1.108***	0.043	0.984***	0.133
y2006	1.096***	0.042	1.084***	0.043	1.071***	0.129
y2009	1.329***	0.044	1.313***	0.044	1.159***	0.134
y2011	1.829***	0.040	1.812***	0.041	1.506***	0.127
Mill's ratio			−0.230***	0.074		
Constants	0.273***	0.074	0.678***	0.150	0.862***	0.241
Observations	12,418		29,262		1,467	
Censored observations			16,871			
Uncensored observations			12,391			
Prob > chi2			0.000			
Adj R-squared	0.377				0.277	
Hausman test					chi2(28) = 81.02, Prob > chi2 = 0.000	

Source: Calculated based on CHNS from 1989 to 2011

Note:

(1) *, **, ***: statistically significant levels are 10%, 5%, and 1%

(2) Reference variables are clerk, regular worker, private sector, Eastern region, 1989 survey year dummy

consider these econometric problems, the empirical studies are employed as follows.

In order to address the endogenous problem, the instrument variable method (IV) is also used in the previous studies (Fleisher et al. 2004; Chen and Hamori 2009; Fang et al. 2012; Kang and Peng 2012; Mishra and Smyth 2013; Wang 2012a, b, 2013; Gao and Smyth 2015). In the previous studies, spouse's education and parent's education are usually used as the instrument variable. Based on the CHNS data, the parent's education attainment (the total years of schooling of parent) is used as the instrument variable in this study. Then, the Heckman two-step model (Heckman 1979) is utilized to correct the sample selection bias. Table 2.3 summarizes the results using the OLS, IV, and Heckman two-step model.

In the results based on model2, the coefficient of adverse Mill's ratio is −0.230, and it is statistically significant at 1% level. It indicates that when the sample selection bias is not considered, there may exist an overestimation problem in results. In the results based on model3, the Hausman test shows that there exists the endogenous problem in the OLS estimation, and the instrument variable is proper.

Next are the estimated values by these models. The coefficients of years of schooling is 0.015 for model1(OLS), 0.005 for model1 (Heckman two-step model), and 0.016 for model3 (IV). The values of return to education based on the OLS and IV are similar. In addition, the coefficients of years of schooling are statistically significant for model1 and model3, whereas the effect of education on wage is not statistically significant when one considers the sample selection bias in model2. For the results based on model2, the first step estimation results show that education positively affects the individual's labor force participation. It indicates that education might affect wage throughout its influence on the work status selection behavior.

Third, as described above, to consider the change of the influence of the market mechanism on wage determination, return to education by periods is examined. The main findings are as follows.

(1) The effects of education on wage are examined by three periods; they are the periods of 1989–1997 and 2000–2007 in which the SOE reform was enforced by the Chinese government, and the 2009–2011 period (post-world financial crisis period) based on the Heckman two-step model. The results are summarized in Table 2.4. When the other factors are constant, the education positively affects wage level for the 2009–2011 period; concretely, the return to education is 3.3%, whereas the coeffi-

Table 2.4 Results of wage function by three periods (Heckman two-step model)

	1989–1997		*2000–2007*		*2009–2011*	
	Coeff.	*SE*	*Coeff.*	*SE*	*Coeff.*	*SE*
Years of schooling	−0.010	0.007	0.006	0.007	0.032***	0.007
Experience years	0.008	0.007	−0.026***	0.007	−0.040***	0.008
Experience years squared	−4.460E-05	1.535E-04	1.662E-04	1.260E-04	4.518E-04***	1.358E-04
Male	−0.017	0.032	0.039	0.031	0.035	0.032
Mental health score	−0.009	0.007	0.006	0.006	−0.023***	0.006
Occupation						
Technician	0.130*	0.067	0.282***	0.060	0.260***	0.057
Manager	0.253***	0.071	0.144**	0.069	0.073	0.066
Agriculture worker	0.231**	0.097	0.050	0.100	−0.109	0.107
Manufacturing worker (H)	−0.060	0.064	−0.105*	0.062	−0.144**	0.066
Manufacturing worker (L)	−0.176***	0.062	−0.216***	0.063	−0.272***	0.067
Service worker	−0.153**	0.072	−0.281***	0.067	−0.173***	0.061
Others	0.191**	0.078	0.146**	0.068	0.046	0.067
Employment status						
Irregular I	0.590***	0.073	0.180***	0.051	0.068	0.044
Irregular II	0.293***	0.069	0.037	0.058	−0.137**	0.057
Self-employed I	0.192*	0.110	0.114	0.091	0.100	0.087
Self-employed II	0.270***	0.074	0.041	0.074	−0.123	0.077
Others	0.238	0.210	0.335**	0.143	−0.098	0.126
Ownership type						
Public sector	0.483***	0.043	0.293***	0.034	0.185***	0.033
Regions						
Central	0.257***	0.044	−0.054	0.041	−0.297***	0.042
West	−0.017	0.063	−0.187***	0.055	−0.159***	0.048
Year	Yes		Yes		Yes	
Mill's ratio	−0.633***	0.159	0.064	0.096	−0.143	0.094
Constants	0.543**	0.249	1.697***	0.216	2.795***	0.236
Observations	11,552		9,504		8,206	
Censored observations	6,869		5,457		4,535	
Uncensored observations	4,683		4,047		3,661	
Prob > chi2	0.000		0.000		0.000	

Source: Calculated based on CHNS from 1989 to 2011

Note:

(1) *, **, ***: statistically significant levels are 10%, 5%, and 1%

(2) Reference variables are clerk, regular worker, private sector, Eastern region, survey year dummy

Table 2.5 Results of wage function by every survey year (OLS, Heckman two-step, IV)

	(1) OLS		*(2) Selection model*		*(3) IV*	
	Coeff.	*SE*	*Coeff.*	*SE*	*Coeff.*	*SE*
1989	0.024***	0.010	0.034***	0.011	0.058*	0.035
1991	0.024**	0.011	0.017	0.012	0.033	0.035
1993	−0.008	0.012	−0.022*	0.013	0.006	0.033
1997	−0.002	0.010	−0.015	0.015	−0.029	0.033
2000	−0.006	0.009	−0.003	0.013	−0.029	0.028
2004	−0.002	0.009	−0.002	0.012	−0.019	0.030
2006	0.017*	0.009	0.021*	0.013	0.061**	0.030
2009	0.023**	0.010	0.009	0.014	0.050*	0.028
2011	0.048***	0.006	0.041***	0.008	0.048*	0.023

Source: Calculated based on CHNS from 1989 to 2011

Note:

(1) *, **, ***: statistically significant levels are 10%, 5%, and 1%

(2) Only the results of schooling are shown in the table

(3) Experience years, male, health, occupation, employment status, ownership sector, and region are estimated; the results are not shown in the table

cients of years of schooling are not statistically significant for both the 1989–1997 and 2000–2007 periods. It indicates that with the economic transition progress, the influence of market mechanism on wage determination recently became great.

(2) To see the change of the effects of education on wage in detail, the estimations by every survey year are employed (Table 2.5). The OLS, instrument variable method, and Heckman two-step model are used in these analyses. It is clear that in the economic reform prior period (e.g. 1989, 1991) and the recent period (e.g. 2006, 2009, 2011), education positively affects the wage level, whereas in the SOEs reform enforcement period (e.g. 1993, 1997, 2000, 2004), the effect of education on wage is not statistically significant. The reason for the results can be considered as follows. First, in the period prior to economic reform (e.g. 1989, 1991), since the end of the 1980s, the government enforced the FDI policy and the FOEs increased. It is thought that in the FOEs, the wage level is determined by the labor productivity based on the neoclassical economics theory, and thus the effect of education on wage is significant in the period. Second, it can be thought that with the progress of the economic transi-

tion from the planned economy to the market-oriented economy, the influence of education on wage should become great recently. Moreover, since the end of the 2000s, the Chinese government has promoted the industry and technology upgrading. Therefore the effect of education on wage became more significant in 2009 and 2011.

Fourth, for the other factors, (1) the results in Table 2.3 based on model3 (IV) show general wage-level decrease with longer experience years during the period from 1989 to 2011. It indicates that the effect of seniority wage system on wage is small during the period. The wage of the professional worker and manager is higher than the others, for example, they are 31.2%, 37.3% higher than the clerk worker. The wage level is higher for irregular worker I (contact worker), self-employed worker I (the self-employed employer), and self-employed worker II (the own-account workers who work on their own) than the regular worker. The results might be caused by the fact that the average age of the regular worker group is higher than the irregular worker group, and with the SOEs reform, when the influence of seniority wage system on wage becomes small, the wage might be lower for the elderly worker. When the other factors are constant, the wage is higher for the public sector than the private sector. In other words, there remains a wage gap between these two sectors during the period from 1989 to 2011.

(2) To compare the wage structure by three periods, the results shown in Table 2.4 indicate that in 1989–1997, the influence of experience on wage is not statistically significant, whereas the experience year negatively affects wage for both the 2000–2007 and 2009–2011 periods. Health status does not affect wage for both the 1989–1997 and 2000–2007 periods, whereas the worker with poor health might gain lower than the healthy worker recently. The wage is higher for the professional worker and manager groups than the others in the three periods. The influence of employment status on wage differs by periods. Concretely, the wage is higher for the irregular worker and the self-employed worker groups than for the regular worker in the 1989–1997 and 2000–2007 periods, whereas the wage is lower for the irregular worker than for the regular worker during the period from 2009 to 2011. Because of the fact that after the global financial crisis, the government provided public investment to large SOEs, the problem of public sector monopoly might have become severe recently. Moreover, the government is promoting technology upgrading in the public sector recently. Along with the increase of the public financial support, and the technology upgrading in the SOEs in which most regular

Table 2.6 Results of wage function by wage distribution and four periods

	(1) 10%		*(2) 30%*		*(3) 60%*		*(4) 90%*	
	Coeff.	*SE*	*Coeff.*	*SE*	*Coeff.*	*SE*	*Coeff.*	*SE*
1989–2011								
Years of schooling	0.013**	0.006	0.017***	0.004	0.016***	0.004	0.016***	0.005
Experience years	0.001	0.006	−0.006	0.004	0.000	0.005	−0.001	0.005
Experience years squared	0.000	0.000	0.000	0.000	0.000**	0.000	0.000	0.000
Pseudo R_squared	0.198		0.284		0.233		0.165	
1989–1997								
Years of schooling	0.021***	0.006	0.021***	0.005	−0.004	0.008	−0.013	0.010
Experience years	0.027***	0.006	0.033***	0.005	0.018**	0.008	0.034***	0.011
Experience years squared	0.000***	0.000	0.000***	0.000	0.000***	0.000	−0.001***	0.000
Pseudo R_squared	0.084		0.148		0.143		0.0915	
2000–2006								
Years of schooling	−0.004	0.007	−0.001	0.007	0.005	0.005	0.011	0.008
Experience years	−0.082***	0.008	−0.033***	0.008	−0.008	0.006	−0.005	0.010
Experience years squared	0.001***	0.000	0.000*	0.000	0.000	0.000	0.000	0.000
Pseudo R_squared	0.125		0.066		0.060		0.057	
2009–2011								
Years of schooling	0.034***	0.012	0.043***	0.008	0.031***	0.005	0.038***	0.008
Experience year	−0.067***	0.015	−0.029***	0.009	−0.009	0.006	−0.014	0.009
Experience year squared	0.001***	0.000	0.000**	0.000	0.000	0.000	0.000	0.000
Pseudo R_squared	0.210		0.164		0.155		0.123	

Source: Calculated based on CHNS 1989–2011

Note:

(1) *, **, ***: statistically significant levels are 10%, 5%, and 1%

(2) The results of schooling are shown in the table

(3) Male, health, occupation, employment status, ownership sector, region, and survey year dummy variables are estimated; the results are not shown in the table

Table 2.7 Results of wage function by wage distribution and by every survey year

	1989	*1991*	*1993*	*1997*	*2000*	*2004*	*2006*	*2009*	*2011*
10th	0.035***	0.036***	0.026***	−0.005	0.009	−0.019	−0.013	−0.004	0.053***
20th	0.031***	0.023***	0.019*	0.008	0.002	−0.016	−0.011	0.012	0.063***
30th	0.032***	0.020**	0.012	0.022	0.001	−0.003	0.006	0.021	0.047***
40th	0.033***	0.019*	0.010	0.019	−0.007	0.005	0.015	0.021*	0.048***
50th	0.029***	0.013	0.003	0.006	−0.009	0.006	0.022**	0.018*	0.037***
60th	0.017***	0.001	−0.007	−0.011	−0.004	0.002	0.016	0.016	0.038***
70th	0.020***	0.017	−0.036	−0.006	−0.015	0.008	0.026**	0.024**	0.034***
80th	0.043***	0.027	−0.043**	−0.017	−0.015	0.003	0.028***	0.031***	0.038***
90th	0.030***	0.038*	−0.063*	−0.016	−0.007	0.001	0.016	0.042***	0.034***

Source: Calculated based on CHNS from 1989 to 2011

Note:

(1) *, **, ***: statistically significant levels are 10%, 5%, and 1%

(2) The results of years of schooling are shown in the table

(3) Experience years, male, health, occupation, employment status, ownership sector, and region dummy variables are estimated; the results are not shown in the table

workers are working, the average wage might become higher for the regular worker group. When the other factors are constant, there remains the wage gap between the public sector and private sector in the three periods, and the wage gap decreases from 48.3% to 18.5% from 1989 to 2011. It indicates that with the economic transition progress, the influence of market mechanism on wage determination becomes greater, which causes the decrease of wage gap between the public sector and private sector. Finally, there remains the regional wage disparity in three periods. For example, the wage is lower for the worker in the Western region than in the Eastern region.

2.5.2 *Results of Return to Education by Wage Percentiles*

Tables 2.3, 2.4, and 2.5 show the change of effect of education on the mean value of wage (average wage). It is thought the effect of education on wage might differ for the low-, middle-, and high-wage groups. Therefore the effect of education throughout the wage distributions should be investigated. These results are shown in Tables 2.6 and 2.7.

First, Table 2.6 summarizes the effect of education on wage by wage percentiles and by three periods. (1) Generally, in the period during 1989–2011, the education positively affects wage for low-wage, middle-wage, and high-wage groups; when the years of schooling increases one year, the logarithm of wage increase 1.3% for the 10th wage percentile group, 1.7% for the 30th wage percentile group, 1.6% for the 60th wage percentile group, and 1.6% for the 90th wage percentile group. The differences of the effects of education on wage by various wage percentile groups are small. (2) To compare three periods, in the period 1989–1997, education positively affected the wage for the low-wage group (10th and 20th wage percentile groups), and the logarithm of wage increase was 2.1% when the years of schooling increased one year for the low-wage group. In the period during 2000–2006, the effects of education on wage are not statistically significant for all wage percentile groups. In the period 2009–2011, the education positively affects wage for low-wage, middle-wage, and high-wage groups; when the years of schooling increases one year, the logarithm of wage increases 3.4% for the 10th wage percentile group, 4.3% for the 30th wage percentile group, 3.1% for the 60th wage percentile group, and 3.8% for the 90th wage percentile group. It is shown that the effect of education on wage is greater for the low-wage group and high-wage group than the middle-level wage group.

Second, Table 2.7 summarizes the effect of education on wage by wage percentiles and by every survey year. (1) In 1989 and 2011, the education positively affected wage significantly for the whole wage percentile (for low-, middle-, and high-wage groups). In 1989, the difference of the education effect by wage percentiles is small, whereas in 2011, the education effect is higher for the low-wage group than for the middle- and high-wage groups. (2) In 1991 and 1993, education positively affected wage for the low-wage group; in 1993, education negatively affected the wage for the high-wage group. (3) In 2006 and 2009, education positively affected the wage for middle- and high-wage groups. It is clear that the education effect decreased for the low-wage group, whereas it increased for the middle- and high-wage groups during the period from 1997 to 2009. However, the education effect for the low-wage group increased in 2011. It indicates that even though education seems to expand the wage gap between low- and high-education groups, the effect is becoming smaller recently. The following reason can be considered. Since 1999, the government has implemented the higher-education expansion policy, and it is thought when the labor demand is constant, the increase of higher-education labor supply may decrease the wage for middle- and high-wage groups in the long term.[9]

2.6 Conclusions

Since 1978, the Chinese government has enforced the economy system reform. The Chinese economy transferred from the planned economy to the marketization economy. With the dramatic change by the economy system transition, it is thought that the wage determining mechanisms in China might change greatly. Based on neoclassical economic theory, when the influence of market mechanism on wage determination becomes great, the education effect on wage should exist and increase. In other words, the education effect should change with the wage determination mechanism change. This chapter of the book aims to examine the change of the effect of education on wage, particularly the return to education in the long term by using CHNS longitudinal survey data from 1989 to 2011.

The interesting findings are as follows. First, generally, the years of schooling positively affected wage; the marginal effect is 1.5–3.3% in urban China during the period from 1989 to 2011 based on OLS and IV methods. Second, to compare the education effect by three periods (1989–1997 period, 2000–2007 period, 2009–2011 period), the impact of education on wage is largest for the 2009–2011 period. When comparing the education effect by every survey year, it is shown that the education effect increased for recent survey years. Third, in the 1989–1997 period, education affects the wage level for low-wage group; in 2000–2006, education does not influence the wage level for low-, middle-, and high-wage groups; in the 2009–2011 period, education positively affects the wage for the low-, middle-, and high-wage groups. These results indicate that the impact of market mechanism on wage determination becomes greater with the progress of labor market reform.

Appendix

Table 2.8 Summary of previous studies on the IRR in China

Previous studies	*Analysis objects*	*Published year*	*Model*	*Estimated IRR (%)*
Byron and Manaloto (1990)	Urban China	1986	OLS	1.4
Johnson and Chow (1997)	Urban China	1988	OLS	3.3
Liu (1998)	Urban China	1988	OLS	2.9–3.6
Lai (1998)	Urban China	1995	OLS	5.14–5.99
Li (2003)	Urban China	1995	OLS	4.7–5.4
Li and Ding (2003)	Urban China	1990–1999	OLS	1.19–4.75
Bishop and Chiou (2004)	Urban China	1988, 1995	OLS	2.8, 5.6
Fleisher et al. (2004)	Urban China	1988–2002	IV	16.9–38.6
Heckman and Li (2004)	Urban China	2000	OLS IV	7.3–23.2
Zhang et al. (2005)	Urban China	1988–2001	OLS OLS	M: 2.9–8.4 F: 5.2–13.2
Zhang et al. (2007)	Urban China	2002	Twins	3.8–9.8
Giles et al.(2008)	Urban China	2000	IV	8.3–9.6
Qian and Smyth (2008)	Urban China	2005	OLS	12.0–13.0
Liu (2008)	Urban China	2004	OLS	5.43–10.93
Chen and Hamori (2009)	Urban China	2004, 2006	OLS IV	OLS: 7.7–8.1 IV: 12.6–14.5
Qiu and Hudson (2010)	Urban China	1989, 1993, 1997, 2000	OLS	5.1–6.9
Ma (2018a, b)	Urban China	1988–2002	OLS	Total: 3.24–11.07 M: 2.45–9.21 F: 3.34–12.09

(*continued*)

Table 2.8 (continued)

Previous studies	*Analysis objects*	*Published year*	*Model*	*Estimated IRR (%)*
Ge and Yang (2011)	Urban China	1988–2011	OLS	3.6–11.4
Kang and Peng (2012)	Urban China	1989–2009	OLS	OLS: 2.2–10.3
			IV	IV: 6.2–11.0
Ren and Miller (2012)	Urban China	2004, 2006	OLS	7.0–8.0
Fang et al. (2012)	Urban China	1997–2006	IV	20.0
Mishra and Smyth (2013)	Ethnic Koreans in urban China	2009–2010	IV	21.0–23.0
Wang (2012a)	Urban China	1995, 2002	IV	9.5–44.0
Wang (2013)	Urban China	1995, 2002	OLS	OLS: 3.6–8.1
			IV	IV: 4.4–11.8
Deng and Ding (2012)	Chin	2010	OLS	9.3–11.7
Mishra and Smyth (2014)	Shanghai	2007	OLS	6.9–7.4
Chen and Ju (2004)	Urban China	1996	OLS	M: 4.7, F: 6.5
		1997	OLS	M: 5.0, F: 9.1
		1998	OLS	M: 6.1, F: 9.8
		1999	OLS	M: 4.9, F: 8.2
		2000	OLS	M: 6.7, F: 10.3
Gao and Smyth (2015)	Urban China	2001, 2005, 2010	OLS	2001: 6.78
			OLS	2005: 7.81
			OLS	2010: 8.60
			IV	2001: 8.24
			IV	2005: 8.72
			IV	2010: 9.00

Source: By author based on Sun (2004), Gao and Smyth (2015)

Note:

(1) OLS: ordinary least square analysis; IV: instrument variable estimation method

(2) M: male; F: female

Notes

1. According to internal labor market theory (Piore 1970), in institutional economics, wage decisions are also related to firms' internal practices (e.g. payment and employment systems). However, it is believed that firms set wage levels by referring to market wages.
2. For more information on the Minimum Wage Act in China, please refer to Chap. 7 of the book; for the empirical studies of the effect of the Minimum Wage Act on the male and female wage levels in China, please see Li and Ma (2015).
3. Lin et al. (1996) and Nakagane (1999) pointed out that state-owned enterprises (SOEs) reform was promoted after the 1990s, but it was "an incom-

pleteness reform" (radical restructuring did not occur) because government retained ownership of large SOEs.

4. The Urban Self-employment Management Ordinance (USMO) published in August 1987. Based on the USMO, the self-employment sector is defined as a privately owned business unit that employs one or two helpers and four or five workers.
5. Experience year = age-6-years of schooling.
6. Based on the questionnaire of CHNS, manufacturing worker (H) is high-skilled manufacturing worker, manufacturing worker (L) is low-skilled manufacturing worker.
7. For the wage gap between the public sector and private sector, please refer to Meng and Kidd (1997), Chen et al. (2005), Xing (2006), Zhang and Xue (2008), Ye et al. (2011), Demurger et al. (2012), Lu et al. (2012), and Ma (2009, 2014, 2016).
8. Regular worker is an individual who works for another person or enterprise as a permanent employee; irregular worker (I) is a contractor with other people or an enterprise; irregular worker (II) is a temporary worker; the self-employed (I) is self-employed, owner-manager with employees; the self-employed (II) is self-employed, independent operator with no employee; others composes the paid family worker, unpaid family worker, and others.
9. He (2009), Wu and Zhao (2010), Chang and Xiang (2013), Yao et al. (2014), Gao and Smyth (2015), Xia et al. (2016), and Ma (2018a, b) employed empirical studies and indicated that the higher-education expansion policy reduced the wage level of higher-education graduates.

References

Becker, G. S. (1957). *The economics of discrimination*. Chicago: University of Chicago Press.

Becker, G. S. (1964). *Human capital: A theoretical and empirical analysis, with special reference to education*. New York: Columbia University Press.

Bishop, J. A., & Chiou, J. R. (2004). Economic transformation and earnings inequality in China and Taiwan. *Journal of Asian Economics, 15*(3), 549–562.

Bowles, P., & White, G. (1998). Labor systems in transitional economies: An analysis of China's township and village enterprises. *Labor markets in transition: International dimensions. International Review of Comparative Public Policy, No. 10*. Stamford, CT: JAI Press.

Byron, R., & Manaloto, E. (1990). Returns to education in China. *Economic Development and Cultural Change, 38*(4), 783–796.

Chang, J., & Xiang, J. (2013). Higher education expansion and returns to college education. *Chinese Journal of Population Science, 3*, 104–111 (In Chinese).

Chen, L., & Ju, G. (2004). An empirical study on the gender differentials of return to schooling by Mincer model. *Peking University Education Review, 2*(3), 40–45 (in Chinese).

Chen, G., Demurger, S., & Fournier, M. (2005). Wage differentials and ownership structure of China's enterprises. *World Economic Paper, 6*, 11–31 (In Chinese).

Chen, G., & Hamori, S. (2009). Economic returns to schooling in urban China: OLS and instrumental variables approach. *China Economic Review, 20*(2), 143–152.

Demurger, S., Li, S., & Yang, J. (2012). Earning differentials between the public and private sectors in China: Exploring changes for urban local residents in the 2002s. *China Economic Review, 23*, 138–153.

Deng, F., & Ding, X. (2012). Human capital, labor market segmentation and gender income gap. *Sociological Studies, 5*, 24–46 (In Chinese).

Fang, H., Eggleston, K., Rizzo, J., Rozelle, S., & Zeckhauser, R. J. (2012). The returns to schooling: Evidence from the 1986 compulsory education law. *NBER Working Paper, No. 18189.*

Fleisher, B., Li, H., Li, S., & Wang, X. (2004). Sorting, selection and transformation of return to college education in China. *IZA Discussion Paper, No. 1446.*

Gao, W., & Smyth, R. (2015). Education expansion and returns to schooling in urban China, 2001–2010: Evidence from three waves of the China urban labor survey. *Journal of the Asia Pacific Economy, 20*(2), 178–201.

Ge, S., & Yang, D. T. (2011). Labor market developments in China: A neoclassical view. *China Economic Review, 22*(4), 611–625.

Giles, J., Park, A., & Wang, M. (2008). The great proletarian cultural revolution, disruptions to education and returns to schooling in urban China. *World Bank Policy Research Working Paper, No. 4729.*

He, Y. (2009). The changes of the rate of return to education: An empirical study based on the data of CHNS. *Chinese Journal of Population Science, 2*, 44–54 (In Chinese).

Heckman, J. J. (1979). Sample selection bias as a specification error. *Econometrica, 47*(1), 153–161.

Heckman, J., & Li, X. (2004). Selection bias, comparative advantage, heterogeneous returns to education: Evidence from China in 2000. *Pacific Economic Review, 9*(3), 155–171.

Johnson, E. N., & Chow, G. (1997). Rates of return to schooling in China. *Pacific Economic Review, 2*(2), 101–113.

Kang, L., & Peng, F. (2012). Siblings, public facilities and education returns in China. *MPRA Paper, No. 38922.*

Koenker, R. W., & Bassett, G. J. (1978). Regression quantile. *Econometrica, 46*(1), 33–50.

Lai, D. (1998). Education, labor market, and income distribution. *Economic Research Journal, 5*, 42–49 (In Chinese).

Li, H. (2003). Economic reform and returns to education in China. *Economics of Education Review, 22*(3), 317–328 (In Chinese).

Li, H., & Luo, Y. (2004). Reporting errors, ability heterogeneity and returns to schooling in China. *Pacific Economic Review, 9*(3), 191–207.

Li, S., & Ding, S. (2003). Long-term change in private returns to education in urban China. *Social Sciences in China, 6*, 58–72 (In Chinese).

Li, S., & Ma, X. (2015). Impact of minimum wage on gender wage gaps in urban China. *IZA Journal of Labor and Development, 4*, 20.

Li, S., & Zhao, R. (2003). The decline of in-kind wage payments in urban China. *Journal of Chinese Economic and Business Studies, 1*, 245–258.

Lin, Y., Cai, F., & Li, Z. (1996). *Miracle development strategy and economic reform in China*. Shanghai: Shanghai People Publishing (In Chinese).

Liu, Z. (1998). Earnings, education and economic reforms in urban China. *Economic Development and Cultural Change, 46*(4), 697–725.

Liu, Z. (2008). Why are returns to education higher for the women than for men: An analysis based on gender wage discrimination. *Economic Science, 2*, 119–128 (In Chinese).

Lu, Z., Wang, X., & Zhang, P. (2012). Do Chinese state-owned enterprises pay high wage? *Economic Research, 3*, 28–39 (In Chinese).

Ma, X. (2009). The enterprise ownership reforms and the change of wage structure in China: Comparison of gender wage profiles differentials by ownership. *Journal of Chinese Economic Studies, 6*(1), 48–64 (In Japanese).

Ma, X. (2014). Wage policy: Economy transition and wage differentials of sectors. In K. Nkagane (Ed.), *How did Chinese economy changed? Evaluation of economic systems and policies in post-reform period*. Tokyo: Kokusai Shoin Co., Ltd (in Japanese).

Ma, X. (2016). Changes of wage structures in Chinese public and private sectors: 1995–2007. *Management Studies, 4*(6), 1–13.

Ma, X. (2018a). Labor market segmentation by industry sectors and wage gaps between migrants and local urban residents in urban China. *China Economic Review, 47*, 96–115.

Ma, X. (2018b). Ownership sector segmentation and gender wage gap in urban China during the 2000s. *Post-Communist Economies*, June 2018, 1–30.

Marugawa, T. (2002). *Series contemporary Chinese economy 3: Crustal change in the labor market*. Nagoya: Nagoya University Publishing (In Japanese).

Meng, X., & Kidd, M. P. (1997). Labor market reform and the changing structure of wage determination in China's state sector during the 1980s. *Journal of Comparative Economics, 25*, 403–421.

Mincer, J. (1974). *Schooling, experience and earning*. New York: Columbia University Press.

Mishra, V., & Smyth, R. (2013). Economic returns to schooling for China's Korean minority. *Journal of Asian Economics, 24*, 89–102.

Mishra, V., & Smyth, R. (2014). Returns to schooling in China's urban labour market: Evidence from matched employer-employee data for Shanghai. In Z. Cheng, M. Wang, & J. Chen (Eds.), *Chinese cities in the new era: Market reform, current state, and the road forward* (pp. 169–183). Berlin: Springer.

Nakagane, K. (1999). *Economic development in China*. Tokyo: Yuhikaku Publishing (In Japanese).

Piore, M. J. (1970). Job and training. In S. H. Beer & R. Barringer (Eds.), *The state and the poor* (pp. 53–83). Cambridge, MA: Winthrop.

Psacharopoulos, G. (1981). Return to education: An updated international comparison. *Comparative Education, 17*(3), 321–341.
Psacharopoulos, G., & Patrinos, H. A. (2004). Returns to investment in education: A further update. *Education Economics, 12*(2), 111–134.
Qian, X., & Smyth, R. (2008). Measuring regional inequality of education in China: Widening coast–inland gap or widening rural–urban gap? *Journal of International Development, 20*(2), 132–144.
Qiu, T., & Hudson, J. (2010). Private returns to education in urban China. *Economic Change and Restructuring, 43*(2), 131–150.
Ren, W., & Miller, P. (2012). Changes over time in the return to education in urban China: Conventional and ORU estimates. *China Economic Review, 23*(1), 154–169.
Trostel, P., Walker, I., & Woolley, P. (2002). Estimates of the economic return to schooling for 28 countries. *Labour Economics, 9*(1), 1–16.
Wang, L. (2012a). Economic transition and college premium in urban China. *China Economic Review, 23*(2), 238–252.
Wang, L. (2012b). Social exclusion and education inequality: Towards an integrated analytical framework for the urban–rural divide in China. *British Journal of Sociology of Education, 33*(3), 409–430.
Wang, L. (2013). How does education affect the earnings distribution in urban China? *Oxford Bulletin of Economics and Statistics, 75*(3), 435–454.
Wu, Y., & Zhao, Q. (2010). Higher education expansion and employment of university graduates. *Economic Research, 9*, 93–108 (In Chinese).
Xia, Q., Wang, X., Li, X., & Zhou, H. (2016). The effects of China's higher education expansion on income distribution. *Social Science Front, 7*, 54–65 (In Chinese).
Xing, C. (2006). Wage decision and returns to education by ownerships in China based on quantile regression. *World Economic Papers, 1*, 1–25.
Yamamoto, T. (2000). *Labor economics in modern China: From rational low wage system to modern labor market*. Tokyo: Sotosya Press (In Japanese).
Yao, X., Fang, X., & Qian, X. (2014). The effects of higher education expansion on wage of college graduates. *Population & Economics, 202*(1), 67–79 (In Chinese).
Ye, L., Li, S., & Luo, C. (2011). Industrial monopoly, ownership and enterprises wage inequality: An empirical research based on the first national economic census of enterprises data. *Management World, 4*, 26–36 (In Chinese).
Zhang, J., & Xue, X. (2008). State and non-state sector wage differentials and human capital contribution. *Economic Research, 4*, 15–25 (In Chinese).
Zhang, J., Liu, P. W., & Yung, L. (2007). The cultural revolution and returns to schooling in China: Estimates based on twins. *Journal of Development Economics, 84*(2), 631–639.
Zhang, J., Zhao, Y., Park, A., & Song, X. (2005). Economic returns to schooling in urban China, 1988 to 2001. *Journal of Comparative Economics, 33*(4), 730–752.

CHAPTER 3

Determinants of Wage Gap Between Public Sector and Private Sector

3.1 Introduction

As it is described in Chap. 2, along with the economy marketization reform, the wage determining mechanisms in China changed in the economic transition period (post 1978). However, even though the wage determination is based on market mechanism in the private sector (e.g. FOEs, POEs), the basic wage and employment is still managed by the Chinese government in the public sector (e.g. SOEs, government organizations). Then, considering the changes in wage gap between the public and private sectors in the economic transition period, the ratios of average annual wages in both sectors from 1952 to 2011 are represented in Fig. 3.1. The ratios reveal that average wages in the private sector were higher from the 1980s to the early 1990s. However, wage differentials declined from 1993 to 2003, and the average wage levels in the public sector exceeded that in the private sector after 2004.

Does the wage determination differ by the public and private sectors? How does the difference of wage determination system affect the wage gap between the public and private sectors? These are important issues for a deep understanding of the features of the labor market in China. This chapter examines the changes in wage structures and determinants of wage gap between the public sector and private sector during the economic transition period. Previous empirical studies have investigated this issue. For example, Dong and Bowles (2002), Xing (2006), Demurger et al. (2007), Yin and Gan (2009), Ma (2009, 2014), Xing and Li (2012), and Lu, Wang, and

X. Ma, *Economic Transition and Labor Market Reform in China*,
https://doi.org/10.1007/978-981-13-1987-7_3

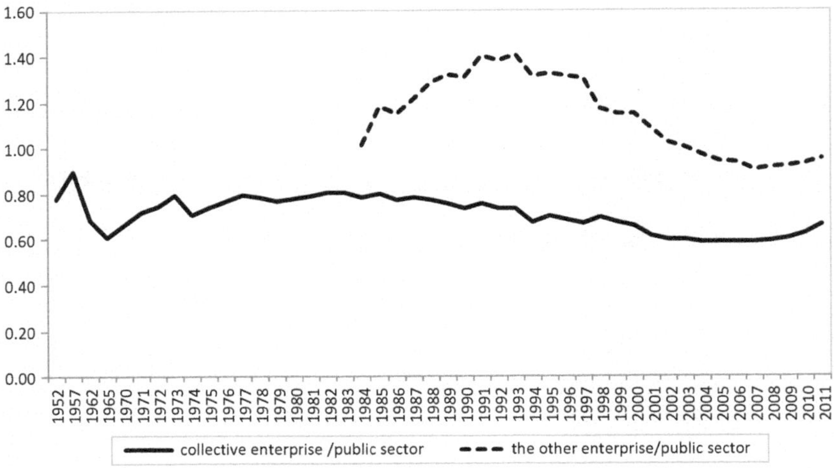

Fig. 3.1 Wage gaps between public and private sectors. *Note*: (1) Public sector includes SOEs, government organizations, and units related to government organizations. (2) The other enterprise includes privately owned enterprises (POEs) and foreign-owned enterprises (FOEs). *Source*: Based on data from Tables 4–12 in National Bureau of Statistics *Chinese Statistical Yearbook 2011*

Zhang (2012) pointed out that the wage structure is different between SOEs and non-SOEs (e.g. FOEs, POEs), and indicated that human capital exerts greater influence on wages among non-SOEs. Chen et al. (2005), Zhang and Xue (2008), Ye et al. (2011), Demurger et al. (2012), and Zhang (2012) decomposed the determinants of wage gaps between the public and private sectors (or between SOEs and non-SOEs), and showed that the main determinants of wage gaps are the individual human capital factors.

However, these studies use annual and monthly wages as dependent variables and ignore working hours. If working hours are longer in the private sector, using annual and monthly wages rather than hourly wages (wage rates) might underestimate differentials. In addition, there was no empirical study on wage gaps from the early 1990s to the late 2000s, and information is lacking about the changes in wage gaps over that extended period.

In this chapter, using two waves (1995 and 2007) of Chinese Household Income Project Survey (CHIPs) data for urban residents, three questions are investigated. They are (1) How large are the public-private sector wage gaps in China? (2) Are there wage structure differences between the two sectors, and (3) What determines the wage gaps between the public and private sectors? Using two period survey data, changes in wage structure and determinants of wage gaps can be estimated.

This chapter is structured as follows. Section 3.2 introduces the framework of the empirical analysis, including datasets and models. Section 3.3 presents estimation results. Section 3.4 gives a summary of conclusions and policy implications.

3.2 Methodology and Data

3.2.1 Models

To measure wage structure, the OLS model based on variable means and the quantile regression model (Koenker and Bassett 1978) derived from the wage distribution are utilized. These models are expressed as Eqs. (3.1a and 3.1b).

$$\ln W_i = \alpha + \beta_p \text{Pub}_i + \beta_X X_i + u_i \tag{3.1a}$$

$$\ln W_{\theta i} = \alpha_\theta + \beta_{\theta(p)} \text{Pub}_{\theta i} + \beta_{\theta X} X_{\theta i} + u_{\theta i} \tag{3.1b}$$

In (3.1a) and (3.1b), i denotes workers, θ is an index indicating the wage percentile, and $\ln W$ indicates the dependent variable (as a logarithm of the wage rate). X are factors affecting wages and β are the estimated coefficients of X. Further, α is a constant and u is the error term. β_p and $\beta_{\theta(p)}$ express public-private sector wage differentials.

To clarify differences in wage structure between the two sectors, wage functions by sector groups are estimates. To overcome sample selection bias, this study uses the selectivity-bias corrected wage function model (Heckman 1979) shown by Eqs. (3.2a–3.2c). Equation (3.2a) expresses the probability that a worker chooses employment in the public or private sector.[1] The choice of employment in the public sector is expressed as $I^* = 1$, and the choice of employment in the private sector is expressed as $I^* = 0$. X shows factors identical to those expressed in Eqs. (3.1a and 3.1b). Z is an identification variable (resembling an instrument variable). Job research routes dummy and the married dummy are used as an identification variable.[2] Using the estimated results of the distribution function and the density function of the sector selection probability, correct item-named adverse Mill's ratio (λ) is calculated. The selectivity-bias corrected wage functions expressed by Eqs. (3.2b and 3.2c) can be estimated using correct items.

$$E\left(\varepsilon_{pub_i} | I_i^* = 1\right) \quad \text{or} \quad E\left(\varepsilon_{pri_i} | I_i^* = 0\right) \tag{3.2a}$$
$$I_i^* = b_i + \gamma_X X_i + \gamma_Z Z_i + \varepsilon_i$$

$$\ln W_i = \alpha + \beta_X X_i + \beta_\lambda \lambda_i + u_i \tag{3.2b}$$

$$\ln W_{\theta i} = \alpha_\theta + \beta_{\theta i} X_{\theta i} + \beta_{\theta\lambda} \lambda_{\theta i} + u_{\theta i} \tag{3.2c}$$

Two decomposition methods are used to estimate determinants of wage differentials. The first is Blinder–Oaxaca decomposition based on variable means (Blinder 1973; Oaxaca 1973). It is expressed by Eqs. (3.3a and 3.3b). X_{pub} and X_{pri} are variable means of the public and private sectors. β_{pub} and β_{pri} are estimated coefficients. Public-private sector wage differentials are decomposed into two parts as characteristics effects $((\beta_{\text{pub}}(X_{\text{pub}}-X_{\text{pri}})$ or $\beta_{\text{pri}}(X_{\text{pri}}-X_{\text{pub}}))$ and price effects $((\beta_{\text{pub}}-\beta_{\text{pri}})X_{\text{pri}}$ or $(\beta_{\text{pri}}-\beta_{\text{pub}})X_{\text{pub}})$.[3] Oaxaca (1973) and Blinder (1973) divide wage differentials into two factors: characteristics effects (differences in human capital endowments) and price effects (differences in wage determination systems, discrimination, and capabilities not presently measurable). The larger the estimated price effect, the greater the influence of wage determination systems on wage gaps.

$$\ln W_{\text{pub}} - \ln W_{\text{pri}} = \beta_{\text{pub}}\left(X_{\text{pub}} - X_{\text{pri}}\right) + \left(\beta_{\text{pub}} - \beta_{\text{pri}}\right) X_{\text{pri}} \tag{3.3a}$$

$$\ln W_{\text{pub}} - \ln W_{\text{pri}} = \beta_{\text{pri}}\left(X_{\text{pri}} - X_{\text{pub}}\right) + \left(\beta_{\text{pri}} - \beta_{\text{pub}}\right) X_{\text{pub}} \tag{3.3b}$$

The second decomposition is based on Machado and Mata (2005). Concrete procedures are as follows.

- First, n samples are randomly selected from the wage distribution $(\theta_i(\theta_1, \theta_2, \theta_3, \ldots)\ (i = 1, \ldots, n))$ for the public sector datasets.
- Second, $\beta_{\theta(\text{pub})}$ are calculated using the public sector datasets.
- Third, n samples are randomly selected from the wage distribution $(\theta_i(\theta_1, \theta_2, \theta_3, \ldots)\ (i = 1, \ldots, n))$ of the private sector. Labor productivity characteristics in the private sector are expressed as X.

- Fourth, counterfactual sector, for example the public sector wages are calculated as $\ln W_{cpub} = \beta^*_{\theta(\mathrm{pub})} X_{\theta(\mathrm{pri})}$, $i = 1, \ldots, n$ (for the density that results in the public sector group, if all covariates parallel the distribution of the private sector), and new datasets are built by pooling the samples of counterfactual public and actual public sector. We also conduct new datasets by pooling the samples of counterfactual private and actual private sector. Using the actual dataset and counterfactual dataset, the result of the characteristics effect, the price effect, and the residual on wage gaps are calculated according to wage percentiles.

3.2.2 Data

This chapter employs two waves of CHIPs data for urban residents: CHIPs 1995 and CHIPs 2007. These surveys were conducted by the Economic Research Institute of the Chinese Academy of Social Sciences (CASS), Beijing Normal University, and the National Bureau of Statistics (NBS) in 1996 and 2008. CHIPs 1995 covers 11 provinces and CHIPs 2007 covers 9 provinces; the common provinces in these two period surveys are used in this study. CHIPs 1995 encompasses 27,694 individuals and 5003 households and CHIPs 2007 19,748 individuals and 6931 households. Samples in six provinces (Jiangsu, Anhui, Henan, Hubei, Guangdong, and Sichuan) that are surveyed in both 1995 and 2007 are used. Based on CHIPs (1995, 2007) questionnaires, the samples can be divided into two subsamples: (1) the public sector, which contains SOEs, government organizations, and units related to government organizations (*Shiye Danwei*); (2) the private sector, which contains collectively owned enterprises (COEs), foreign-owned enterprises (FOEs), and privately owned enterprises (POEs).

Table 3.1 displays analysis variables. The logarithm of the wage rate is the dependent variable. Monthly and annual wages include base salary, bonuses, and allowance; financial assets and public transfer payments are excluded. Monthly working hours are calculated using daily working hours and monthly working days. Wage rate calculations are based on total wage and working hours.

Independent variable settings are as follows. In wage functions, ownership dummy variables are divided into four categories: the public sector, COEs, FOEs and POEs (hereafter FOEs–POEs), and others. As indexes of human capital, we use education, tenure, age, occupation dummy (managerial, technology, clerical, manufacturing, and others), and industry dummy (agriculture, manufacturing, traffic and communication, commerce, finance-public, and others) variables. It is pointed out that the effect of work experience on wages includes an age effect and the firm-specific human capital effect results from tenure years increase (Ono 1989; Ma 2007, 2009). This study considers both effects.

Employment status is divided into regular worker (a worker with the long-term employment contract), irregular worker (a worker employed under a contract lasting less than one year and non-contract workers), and others. Dummy variables for male, Han race, and married are used as individual attributes. In addition, it is likely that labor market situations, such as labor supply and demand, and the labor policy implementation, such as minimum wage system, are different among provinces (Li and Ma 2015). Six province dummy variables (Jiangsu, Anhui, Henan, Hubei, Guangdong, and Sichuan) are used to control for these regional disparities.

Analysis objects are limited to employees aged 16–59, and self-employed and family workers are excluded. Sample sizes are 4285 for CHIPs (1995)—4679 in the public sector, 1233 in the private sector, and 5912 for CHIPs (2007)—2619 in the public sector, and 1666 in the private sector.

Table 3.1 provides descriptive statistics and shows that worker characteristics are different between public and private sectors. For example, years of schooling and tenure are longer and percentages of managerial and regular workers are higher among public sector workers. Table 3.1 also shows that wage gaps ($\ln \bar{W}_{pub} - \ln \bar{W}_{pri}$) rose from 0.284 in 1995 to 0.291 in 2007.

Figure 3.2 shows Kernel density distribution of the logarithm of wage rate in 1995 and 2007. Wage distributions in 1995 and 2007 resemble normal distribution, and arithmetic means of the logarithm of wage rate in the public sector are higher than that in the private sector. In addition, variances increase from 1995 to 2007 in both sectors, which shows that wage gaps within sectors rose during the economic transition period.

Figure 3.3 displays the logarithm of public and private sector wage rates and wage gaps between the two sectors. Across all wage percentiles (10th–90th percentile), public sector wages exceeded private sector wages in 1995 and 2007. Moreover, 1995 and 2007 wage gaps are larger in the low-wage percentiles than that in the middle- and high-wage percentiles. Although wage gaps appear across all wage percentiles, they are larger for low-wage (i.e. lesser skilled and educated) groups.

Table 3.1 Descriptive statistics for 1995 and 2007

	1995		*2007*	
	Public sector	*Private sector*	*Public sector*	*Private sector*
Logarithm of wage rate	1.001	0.717	2.434	2.143
Years of schooling	11	9	12	11
Tenure years	15	14	18	12
Age	39	37	37	36
Male	55.8%	40.2%	50.3%	50.4%
Han race	98.0%	98.1%	98.8%	98.9%
Married	87.8%	85.2%	67.8%	64.9%
Occupation				
Manager job	13.7%	6.8%	11.1%	2.5%
Technology job	23.8%	11.1%	28.0%	19.0%
Clerk job	23.3%	16.0%	28.4%	17.5%
Manufacturing job	35.7%	56.8%	15.6%	16.2%
Others	3.5%	9.3%	15.9%	43.8%
Employment status				
Regular	98.6%	88.9%	89.7%	62.9%
Non-regular	1.2%	8.4%	9.8%	36.3%
Others	0.2%	2.7%	0.5%	0.8%
Industrials				
Agriculture	2.9%	0.9%	21.5%	39.1%
Manufacturing	43.9%	61.3%	18.6%	28.9%
Traffic and communication	4.8%	4.2%	15.2%	16.0%
Commerce	2.7%	2.9%	1.1%	0.5%
Finance and public organization	19.6%	9.1%	33.1%	9.9%
Others	26.2%	21.6%	10.5%	5.6%
Province				
Jiangsu	16.8%	26.8%	13.3%	18.9%
Anhui	11.7%	15.9%	17.5%	13.1%
Hernan	16.1%	10.7%	19.8%	11.7%
Hubei	19.8%	11.7%	11.2%	10.0%
Guangdong	14.0%	18.3%	20.7%	30.3%
Xichuan	21.6%	16.6%	17.5%	16.0%
Observations	4,679	1,233	2,619	1,666

Source: Calculated based on CHIPs 1995 and CHIPs 2007

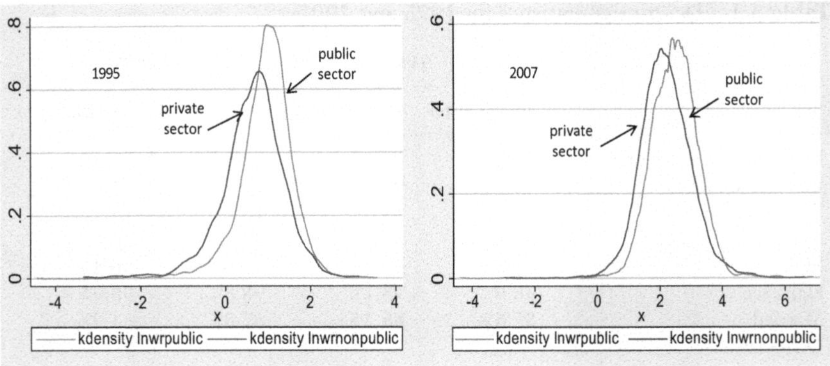

Fig. 3.2 Kernel density distribution in public and private sector wages for 1995 and 2007. *Source*: Calculated based on CHIPs 1995 and CHIPs 2007

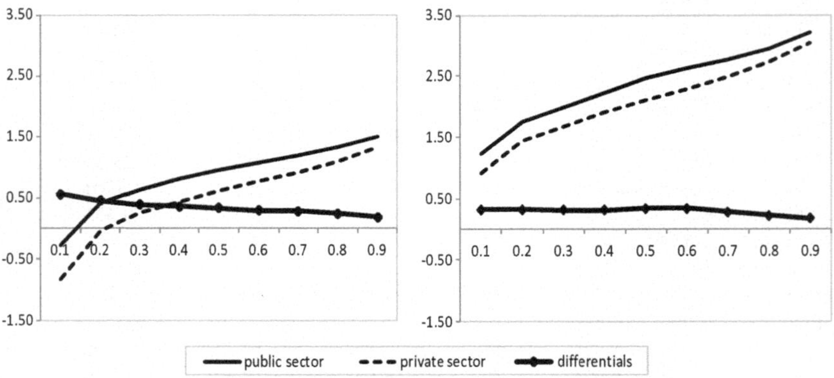

Fig. 3.3 Wage gaps between public and private sectors by wage percentiles for 1995 and 2007. *Note*: Differential = logarithm of wage rate in public sector-logarithm of wage rate in private sector. *Source*: Calculated based on CHIPs 1995 and CHIPs 2007

3.3 Econometric Analysis Results

3.3.1 How Large Are the Wage Gaps Between the Public Sector and Private Sector?

Estimated results of the wage function are summarized in Table 3.2 (OLS model) and Fig. 3.4 (QR model). The main findings are as follows.

Table 3.2 Results of wage gaps between public and private sectors for 1995 and 2007

	1995		*2007*	
	Coeff.	t *value*	*Coeff.*	t *value*
Ownerships (Public sector)				
COEs	−0.221***	−10.59	−0.089**	−2.35
FOEs–POEs	0.141**	2.07	−0.040*	−1.78
Others	0.023	0.24	−0.291***	−6.11

Source: Calculated based on CHIPs 1995 and CHIPs 2007

Note:

(1) ***$p < 0.01$, **$p < 0.05$, *$p < 0.10$

(2) Years of schooling, tenure, tenure squared, age, age squared, male, race, married, occupation dummy, industry dummy, and province dummy variables are estimated, but these are omitted by publication in the table

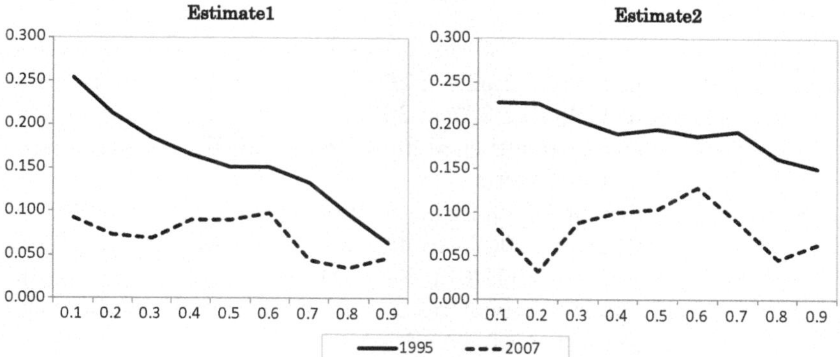

Fig. 3.4 Estimated wage gaps between public and private sectors by wage distribution for 1995 and 2007. *Note*: (1) Estimate 1: education, tenure, tenure square, age, age square, occupation, and industry dummy are used as variables. (2) Estimate 2: added sex, race, employment status, and province dummy as variables to estimate 1. *Source*: Calculated based on CHIPs 1995 and CHIPs 2007

First, in 1995, compared with the public sector, the wage level is 22.1% lower for COEs, but it is 14.1% higher for FOEs–POEs. The wage level in the private sector (FOEs–POEs) is higher than that in the public sector. In 2007, the wage level is 8.92% lower for COEs and 3.95% lower for FOEs–POEs. These results reveal that wage gaps existed between the public and private sectors in 1995 and 2007. In addition, even though China's economic transition reduced wage gaps between the public sector and COEs, the wage gaps between the public sector and FOEs–POEs expanded.

Second, Fig. 3.4 displays wage gaps between the public and private sectors by wage percentiles. The analysis is divided in to estimate 1 and estimate 2 according to the variables used. Results of both estimates 1 and 2 for 1995 indicate that the lower the wage distribution, the larger the wage gap. On the other hand, 2007 wage gaps in the middle-wage group are largest.

3.3.2 *Are There Wage Structure Differences Between the Public and Private Sectors?*

The estimated results of wage functions based on variable means are reported in Table 3.3 (OLS model). The main conclusions are as follows.

- First, the internal rates of return to education in public sector rise from 0.97% in 1995 to 2.32% in 2007. In the private sector, they rise from 1.46% in 1995 to 2.22% in 2007. The influence of human capital on wage levels strengthened from 1995 to 2007 in both the public sector and private sector.
- Second, coefficients of tenure in the public sector rise from 0.0092 in 1995 to 0.0125 in 2007. In the private sector they rise from 0.0039 in 1995 to 0.0228 in 2007. Market-oriented reforms and firm-specific human capital became more important in the wage determination mechanism.
- Third, 1995 coefficients of age are statistically significant in the public and private sectors, but in 2007 age shows no significant effect on wages in either sector. China's public sector wage reforms might explain these results. For example, the seniority wage system was reformed after the 1980s, and the previously described performance payment systems were established for SOEs. Therefore, age became less of a factor in public sector wages, while human capital (education and tenure) were rewarded more in 2007.

Table 3.4 provides the estimated results from the QR model. The wage structures by wage percentiles become apparent as follows.

Table 3.3 Estimated results of wage function by public and private sectors for 1995 and 2007

	1995				*2007*			
	Public sector		*Private sector*		*Public sector*		*Private sector*	
	Coeff.	t *value*	*Coeff.*	t *value*	*Coeff.*	t *value*	*Coeff.*	t *value*
Years of schooling	0.010**	2.54	0.015	1.48	0.023***	5.85	0.022***	4.57
Tenure years	0.009**	2.47	0.004	0.44	0.013***	9.23	0.023***	4.00
Tenure years squared	−1.369E-04	−1.38	−1.064E-04	−0.41	−7.300E-06***	−10.69	−0.001***	−3.59
Age	0.048***	5.76	0.093***	4.96	0.006	0.61	−0.008	−0.73
Age squared	−4.579E-04***	−4.46	−0.001***	−4.64	−1.258E-04	−1.09	7.390E-05	0.56
Male	0.061***	3.56	0.035	0.85	3.299E-04	0.01	0.003	0.11
Han race	0.159***	2.97	−0.011	−0.09	0.153	1.27	0.189	1.33
Married	0.115***	3.46	−0.005	−0.07	0.104**	2.10	0.068	1.31
Occupation (Manager)								
Technician	0.028	1.06	0.060	0.71	−0.178***	−3.97	0.030	0.31
Clerk	−0.070***	−2.63	−0.027	−0.34	0.615*	1.87	−0.184	−0.42
Manufacturing worker	−0.172***	−6.19	−0.097	−1.30	−0.470	−1.32	−0.310	−0.55
The others	−0.148***	−3.18	−0.199**	−2.17	0.354	1.10	−0.401	−0.92
Employment (Regular)								
Nonregular	−0.248***	−3.61	−0.055	−0.81	−0.371***	−8.03	−0.382***	−11.07
Others	0.036	0.19	−0.119	−1.08	−0.211	−1.21	−0.540***	−3.08
Industry (Manufacturing)								
Agriculture	0.034	0.74	0.306*	1.68	0.983***	2.98	−0.077	−0.17
Traffic and communication	0.135***	3.82	0.145*	1.70	0.933***	6.11	−0.114	−0.32
Commerce	−0.112**	−2.42	0.012	0.12	1.505***	6.47	0.075	0.19
Finance and public organization	0.130***	6.01	−0.021	−0.34	0.091	1.34	−0.009	−0.17
The others	0.101***	4.31	0.128	1.36	0.849**	2.40	−0.301	−0.65

(*continued*)

Table 3.3 (continued)

	1995				*2007*			
	Public sector		*Private sector*		*Public sector*		*Private sector*	
	Coeff.	t *value*	*Coeff.*	t *value*	*Coeff.*	t *value*	*Coeff.*	t *value*
Province (Jiangsu)								
Anhui	−0.317***	−11.1	−0.350***	−6.45	−0.184***	−4.03	−0.360***	−6.42
Henan	−0.512***	−17.1	−0.596***	−8.30	−0.394***	−8.53	−0.288***	−4.83
Hubei	−0.247***	−8.47	−0.385***	−5.49	−0.215***	−4.22	−0.038	−0.64
Guangdong	0.339***	12.31	0.553***	10.25	0.482***	10.72	0.376***	8.42
Sichuan	−0.243***	−8.92	−0.358***	−5.95	−0.272***	−5.90	−0.242***	−4.73
Adverse Mill's ratio	−0.216***	−3.22	0.293***	3.23	−0.142***	−3.38	0.005	0.08
Constants	−0.352**	−2.07	−1.425***	−3.97	1.241***	3.20	2.164***	4.28
Observations	4670		1233		2619		1666	
Adj. R-squared	0.35		0.314		0.344		0.323	

Source: Calculated based on CHIPs 1995 and CHIPs 2007

Note: ***$p < 0.01$, **$p < 0.05$, *$p < 0.10$

Table 3.4 Results of wage function by sectors and wage percentiles for 1995 and 2007

	10%		*30%*		*60%*		*90%*	
	Public sector	*Private sector*	*Public sector*	*Private sector*	*Public sector*	*Private sector*	*Public sector*	*Private sector*
Panel A: 1995								
Years of schooling	0.0059	0.0113	0.0143***	0.0122	0.0112***	0.0171*	0.0139**	−0.0100
	0.86	0.67	4.17	0.94	3.10	1.84	2.20	−0.56
Tenure years	0.0041	0.0187	0.0099***	0.0092	0.0083**	0.0052	0.0095	−0.0029
	0.61	1.22	2.92	0.80	2.38	0.64	1.55	−0.20
Tenure years squared	−1.48E-05	−0.0002	−0.0002*	−0.0002	−0.0001	−0.0002	−0.0002	−0.0002
	−0.08	−0.53	−1.68	−0.63	−0.80	−0.70	−1.05	−0.44
Age	0.0775***	0.1195***	0.0475***	0.1249***	0.0321***	0.0479***	0.0258*	0.0335
	4.89	3.23	6.20	4.92	4.06	2.79	1.85	1.13
Age squared	−0.0008***	−0.0015***	−0.0004***	−0.0015***	−0.0003***	−0.0005**	−0.0002	−0.0004
	−3.98	−3.13	−4.47	−4.66	−2.89	−2.47	−1.16	−0.94
Adverse Mill's ratio	−0.4368***	0.5538***	−0.2622***	0.1913	−0.1734***	0.2423***	0.0366	0.4131***
	−3.36	3.34	−4.24	1.54	−2.74	2.86	0.32	2.71
Constant	−1.4561***	−2.6945***	−0.5840***	−2.0740***	0.1978	−0.6543**	0.4901*	0.3850
	−4.66	−3.89	−3.76	−4.28	1.23	−1.99	1.71	0.69
Observations	4,670	1,233	4,670	1,233	4,670	1,233	4,670	1,233
Adj. R-squared	0.2304	0.2032	0.2222	0.2125	0.2125	0.2171	0.2278	0.2215

(continued)

Table 3.4 (continued)

	10%		30%		60%		90%	
	Public sector	*Private sector*	*Public sector*	*Private sector*	*Public sector*	*Private sector*	*Public sector*	*Private sector*
Panel B: 2007								
Years of schooling	0.0273***	0.0170**	0.0330***	0.0253***	0.0235***	0.0249***	0.0155***	0.0312***
	5.22	2.41	6.28	4.06	6.41	4.48	3.09	3.51
Tenure	0.0078***	0.0280***	0.0148***	0.0315***	0.0128***	0.0290***	0.0112***	0.0060
	4.69	3.69	8.40	4.34	10.24	4.32	6.75	0.53
Tenure squared	−4.96E-06***	−0.0010***	−8.49E-06***	−0.0009***	−7.39E-06***	−0.0008***	−6.57E-06***	−0.0001
	−5.95	−4.10	−9.63	−4.06	−11.84	−3.79	−7.92	−0.35
Age	0.0177*	−0.0076	0.0028	−0.0066	0.0049	−0.0077	−0.0098	−0.0399*
	1.62	−0.54	0.24	−0.47	0.56	−0.60	−0.85	−1.94
Age squared	−0.0002*	4.64E-05	−0.0001	0.0001	−0.0001	0.0001	2.51E-05	0.0004*
	−1.76	0.27	−0.44	0.35	−0.98	0.59	0.18	1.69
Adverse Mill's ratio	−0.0707	−0.0876	−0.1059**	−0.0703	−0.2153***	0.0051	−0.0786	0.0803
	−1.37	−1.03	−1.99	−0.96	−5.55	0.08	−1.48	0.84
Constant	0.7448***	1.9028***	0.9555**	1.4628***	1.6555***	2.7101***	1.9268***	3.3074***
	2.69	5.97	2.11	3.48	6.26	6.44	6.95	6.57
Observations	2,619	1,666	2,619	1,666	2,619	1,666	2,619	1,666
Adj. R-squared	0.2261	0.2100	0.2178	0.2264	0.2261	0.2236	0.1942	0.1812

Source: Calculated based on CHIPs 1995 and CHIPs 2007

Note:

(1) $^{***}p < 0.01$, $^{**}p < 0.05$, $^{*}p < 0.10$

(2) Male, race, married, occupation, industry, and province are estimated, but these are not expressed in the table

First, from 1995 to 2007, the return to education increased in wage distributions among the 10th, 30th, 60th, and 90th percentiles in both sectors. The effect in the public sector is highest at the 30th percentile in 1995 and 2007. For the private sector, it is highest at the 60th percentile in 1995 and the 90th percentile in 2007. Rates of return to education are higher for middle- and high-wage groups in 1995 and 2007.

Second, compared with 1995, coefficients of tenure increase across the entire wage distribution in both sectors, and the statistical significance of tenure becomes notable in 2007. For example, tenure does not significantly influence private sector wages across all percentiles in 1995, whereas estimated results of tenure are significant at the 10th, 30th, and 60th wage percentiles in 2007. Firm-specific human capital became a more important wage determinant for low- and middle-wage groups in the private sector.

Third, the influence of age on wage declines from 1995 to 2007. In 1995, in both sectors, age significantly influences wage at the 10th, 30th, and 60th percentiles. However, 2007 coefficients of age are insignificant at the 10th, 30th, 60th, and 90th percentiles. Reform of China's seniority wage system had a greater relative effect on low- and middle-wage groups.

3.3.3 *What Determines the Wage Gaps Between the Public Sector and Private Sector?*

Decomposition results using the Blinder–Oaxaca decomposition model are summarized in Table 3.5. Characteristics effects increase from 35.2% in 1995 to 74.5% in 2007. In other words, the price effect declined from 64.8% in 1995 and 24.6% in 2007. These results denote the greater influence of market mechanisms as a factor in wage gaps, while the influence of institutional factors declined as economic reforms proceeded.

In addition, in 1995, occupation (16.7%), education (10.2%), and industry (9.8%) are the most robust factors in characteristics effects, and race (53.7%), marital status (38.1%), and tenure (16.9%) are the most robust contributors to price effects. In 2007, industries (52.6%), tenure (30.4%), and employment status (26.7%) are the greatest factors in characteristics effects, and occupations (145.9%), industries (115.5%), and tenure (20.5%) have the greatest price effects.

These results reveal that human capital such as education, tenure, occupation, and industry-specific knowledge became primary determinants of wage gaps.

Table 3.5 Blinder–Oaxaca decomposition results

	Characteristics effects		*Price effects*	
	Values	*Percentage (%)*	*Values*	*Percentage (%)*
1995				
Wage gaps:				
0.2852	***0.100***	*35.2*	***0.185***	*64.8*
Years of schooling	0.029	10.2	−0.186	−65.0
Tenure years	0.009	3.0	0.048	16.9
Age	0.012	4.3	−0.663	−232.3
Male	0.012	4.4	−0.009	−3.3
Race	0.000	0.0	0.153	53.7
Married	0.003	1.1	0.109	38.1
Occupation	0.048	16.7	−0.064	−22.5
Employment status	0.016	5.6	−0.003	−1.1
Industry	0.028	9.8	0.004	1.4
Province	−0.057	−19.9	−0.014	−4.9
Constant	0.000	0.0	0.810	283.8
2007				
Wage gaps:				
0.2872	***0.207***	*74.5*	***0.071***	*25.5*
Years of schooling	0.027	9.6	−0.001	−0.4
Tenure years	0.085	30.4	0.057	20.5
Age	−0.006	−2.0	−0.006	−2.0
Male	0.000	0.0	−0.013	−4.8
Race	0.000	0.0	−0.112	−40.3
Married	0.003	1.2	0.019	6.9
Occupation	−0.040	−14.5	0.406	145.9
Employment status	0.074	26.7	0.003	1.2
Industry	0.146	52.6	0.321	115.5
Province	−0.082	−29.4	0.025	9.0
Constant	0.000	0.0	−0.629	−226.0

Source: Calculated based on CHIPs 1995 and CHIPs 2007

Figure 3.5 displays the decomposition results of wage gaps between China's public and private sectors using the Machado–Mata decomposition model. The main findings are as follows.

First, to compare the influences of the coefficient effect (price effect), the characteristics effect, and the residual effect on wage gaps by wage percentiles, the price effect exhibits the greatest influence in 1995, and the characteristics effect is greatest in 2007. The results indicate that the differences in the wage determination system can primarily explain the wage gaps in 1995, whereas factor endowments can primarily explain the wage gaps in 2007.

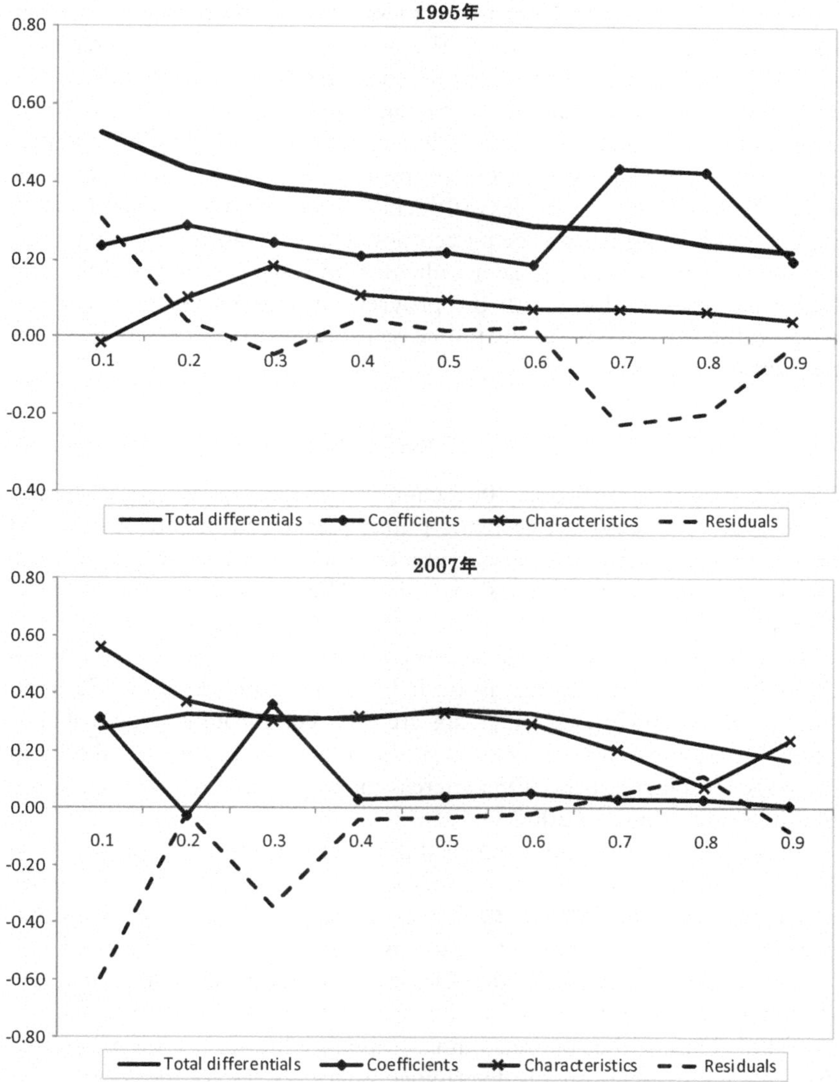

Fig. 3.5 Machado–Mata decomposition results of wage gaps between public and private sectors for 1995 and 2007. *Source*: Calculated based on CHIPs 1995 and CHIPs 2007

Second, characteristics effects exert less influence on the low-wage percentiles (10th percentile) than on the middle- and high-wage percentiles in 1995, whereas they exert more influence on low-wage percentiles (10th and 20th percentiles) than on middle- and high-wage percentiles in 2007. The coefficient effects exert less influence on low- and middle-wage percentiles than on high-wage percentiles in 1995, whereas in 2007 their effects on low-wage percentiles (10th and 30th percentiles) are larger than on the middle- and high-wage percentiles. These results indicate that market mechanisms attained greater influence on wages among middle- and high-wage groups along with the progress of economy system reforms, whereas the wage system in the public sector retained greater influence for the low-wage group.

3.4 Conclusions

Using the CHIPs 1995 and 2007 data, this chapter investigates whether there exist wage gaps between the public sector and private sector, and how the wage system (price effect) and endowment factors (characteristics effect) affected the wage gaps in China. The major conclusions are as follows.

First, holding human capital factors constant, wage gaps appear between the public and private sectors in both 1995 and 2002, but they declined from 1995 to 2007. The wage gaps are different through wage distributions. For example, it is observed that the wage gaps become smaller with the wage level increase in 1995, whereas the wage gaps are greatest among middle-wage groups in 2007.

Second, education and tenure exhibit growing influence on wages in both the public sector and private sector in 1995 and 2007. The influence of age declined from 1995 to 2007 in both sectors. These results show that market mechanisms began to function as economy reform progressed.

Finally, the results of Blinder–Oaxaca decomposition denote that the characteristics effect increased in influence from 35.23% for 1995 to 74.51% for 2007. During that period, human capital, education, tenure, occupations, and industries primarily determined wage gaps. Decomposition results based on the Machado–Mata model reveal that in 1995 the wage determination system can primarily explain the wage gaps between the public sector and private sector, whereas in 2007 the differences in factor endowments can primarily explain the wage gaps. The results also show that even though the market mechanisms gained importance as determinants among middle- and high-wage groups as economy reform progressed, the wage system in the public sector retained greater influence for low-wage groups.

Our estimation results pose several policy implications as follows. During economic transition, the government partially controlled wage determination systems. As a result, market mechanisms have been unable to function adequately in the public sector. It is necessary for government to promote further corporate governance reforms (such as privatization of SOEs) and the deregulation of monopolies in the future. Therefore, the influence of market mechanisms on wage determination may eventually become greater and the distortion of the labor pricing and labor force allocation should be corrected. In the interim, mitigating income inequality will require active labor policies, such as vocational training policy, the Minimum Wage Act, and unemployment insurance policy. More rigorous studies to estimate the influence of these wage policies on wage determination should be done (please refer to Chap. 7 in the book).

Finally, some research limitations should be pointed out. Although using the employee information from CHIPs (1995 and 2007), the determinants of wage gaps between the public and private sectors are estimated in this chapter, it is thought that other labor demand factors such as firm productivity, firm human resource management (HRM) systems, and unobservable variables of firms should affect the wage gaps. Using employer-employee matched data and firm panel data to estimate the wage gaps should form future research.

Notes

1. Because this chapter focuses on wage gaps between the two sectors, it is believed that sample selection bias appears in the worker's choice of public or private sector employment. Therefore, the unemployed are not sampled in this analysis and a probit regression model is used.
2. Job search routes and the married status variables are used as identification variables in this chapter for several reasons. First, the government is likely to exert greater influence on labor arrangements in the public sector; so if the worker gained the first job by government mediation, the possibility of working in the public sector is relatively higher in the research year. Second, according to statistical discrimination theory, in the private sector, if employers consider the average work willingness of single women higher than that of married women, it is thought that the possibility for the married women to be employed is lower than for single women. Because gender equality in employment was promoted in the public sector during the planned economy period,

it can be thought that the influence of marriage status on public sector employment is smaller.

3. It is debated that there exists an index number problem in the Blinder–Oaxaca model. Estimated results may vary with the kinds of comparison groups utilized. Given space constraints and because the two sets of decomposition results are almost identical, only estimated results using Eq. (3.3a) are presented in this chapter.

References

Blinder, A. S. (1973). Wage discrimination: Reduced form and structural estimation. *Journal of Human Resources, 8*(4), 436–455.

Chen, G., Demurger, S., & Fournier, M. (2005). Wage differentials and ownership structure of China's enterprises. *World Economic Paper, 6*, 11–31 (In Chinese).

Demurger, S., Fournier, M., Li, S., & Wei, Z. (2007). Economic liberation with rising segmentation in China's urban labor market. *Asian Economic Papers, 5*(3), 58–103.

Demurger, S., Li, S., & Yang, J. (2012). Earning differentials between the public and private sectors in China: Exploring changes for urban local residents in the 2002s. *China Economic Review, 23*, 138–153.

Dong, X., & Bowles, P. (2002). Segmentation and discrimination in China's emerging industrial labor market. *China Economic Review, 13*, 170–196.

Heckman, J. J. (1979). Sample selection bias as a specification error. *Econometrica, 47*(1), 153–161.

Koenker, R. W., & Bassett, G. J. (1978). Regression quantile. *Econometrica, 46*(1), 33–50.

Li, S., & Ma, X. (2015). Impact of minimum wage on gender wage gaps in urban China. *IZA Journal of Labor and Development, 4*, 20.

Lu, Z., Wang, X., & Zhang, P. (2012). Do Chinese state-owned enterprises pay high wage? *Economic Research, 3*, 28–39 (In Chinese).

Ma, X. (2007). A comparative study on occupational segregation and its impact on gender wage differentials: Based on micro-data from household survey in Japan and China. *Journal of Chinese Economic Studies, 4*(1/2), 14–33 (In Japanese).

Ma, X. (2009). The enterprise ownership reforms and the change of wage structure in China: Comparison of gender wage profiles differentials by ownership. *Journal of Chinese Economic Studies, 6*(1), 48–64 (In Japanese).

Ma, X. (2014). Wage policy: Economy transition and wage differentials of sectors. In K. Nakagane (Ed.), *How did Chinese economy changed? Evaluation of economic systems and policies in post-reform period*. Tokyo: Kokusai Shoin Co., Ltd (In Japanese).

Machado, J. A. F., & Mata, J. (2005). Counterfactual decomposition of changes in wage distributions using quantile regression. *Journal of Applied Econometrics, 20*(4), 445–465.

Oaxaca, R. (1973). Male-female wage differentials in urban labor markets. *International Economic Review, 14*(3), 693–709.

Ono, A. (1989). *Employment systems and labor market in Japan*. Tokyo: Nihon Keizai Shimbun Inc. (In Japanese).

Xing, C. (2006). Wage decision and returns to education by ownerships in China based on quantile regression. *World Economic Papers, 1*, 1–25.

Xing, C., & Li, S. (2012). Residual wage inequality in urban China, 1995–2007. *China Economic Review, 23*, 205–222.

Ye, L., Li, S., & Luo, C. (2011). Industrial monopoly, ownership and enterprises wage inequality: An empirical research based on the first national economic census of enterprises data. *Management World, 4*, 26–36 (In Chinese).

Yin, Z., & Gan, L. (2009). Wage differentials between public and nonpublic sector in China. *Economic Research, 4*, 129–140 (In Chinese).

Zhang, J., & Xue, X. (2008). State and non-state sector wage differentials and human capital contribution. *Economic Research, 4*, 15–25 (In Chinese).

Zhang, Y. (2012). The change of income differentials between public and non-public sector in China. *Economic Research, 4*, 77–88 (In Chinese).

CHAPTER 4

Monopoly Industrial Sector and Its Influence on the Wage Gaps Between Migrants and Local Urban Residents

4.1 Introduction

This chapter focuses on two phenomena during the economic transition period. First, the Chinese urban market is segmented by the "*Hukou*" system (the household registration system). The *Hukou* system influences the opportunity of entry to various sectors (e.g. public sector vs. private sector; and monopolistic industry vs. competitive industry), wage level, and the social security system, creating discrimination against migrants in employment and wages (Meng and Zhang 2001; Roberts 2001; Wang 2003, 2005; Zhang 2003; Song and Appleton 2006; Wang and Zhang 2014; Ma 2011, 2016a, b). Second, the wage gaps between the monopolistic industry sector (e.g. production and supply of electricity, heat, gas, and water industry; transport, storage, and post industry; financial intermediation industry; education; and the health service industry) and the competitive industry sector (e.g. manufacturing, construction, retail, and wholesale industries) has widened since the 1990s (Cai 1996; Luo and Li 2007; Demurger et al. 2007; Jin and Cui 2008; Ma 2012, 2014).

This chapter is a revised version of Ma, X. (2018). Labor Market Segmentation by Industry Sectors and Wage Gaps between Migrants and Local Urban Residents in Urban China. *China Economic Review*, 47, 96–115. Copyright ©: Elsevier.

X. Ma, *Economic Transition and Labor Market Reform in China*,
https://doi.org/10.1007/978-981-13-1987-7_4

In considering the determinants of wage gap between migrants and local urban residents, the labor market segmentation by industry sectors may be one of the main reasons for the wage gap. For example, if there is discrimination against migrants when they enter monopolistic industries, which means the opportunity of entry to the monopolistic industry sector differs for migrants and local urban residents, the proportion of workers in the various industry sectors may differ between these two groups. For the issue of the wage gap between the migrants and local urban residents, most previous studies focus on the influence of human capital differentials and discrimination; the previous studies which considered the influence of sector segmentation on wage gap only focus on the occupational segregation, and ownership types. Even though it is predicted that labor market segmentation by the monopolistic and competitive industries may affect the wage gap, there is no empirical study to investigate how the difference between the migrants and local urban residents in the opportunity to be employed in the monopolistic industry or the competitive industry affects the wage gap, and how the discrimination against migrant groups in the same industry sector affects the wage gap. This chapter of the book provides evidence to develop the discussion on this neglected area.

This chapter is structured as follows. Section 4.2 gives the background to the empirical study. It introduces the *Hukou* system deregulation and policy change for monopolistic and competitive industries during the economic transition period, particularly in the 2000s. Section 4.3 summarizes the theory and hypotheses about discrimination and empirical studies relating to China. Section 4.4 describes the analytic methods, including an introduction to data and models. Section 4.5 discusses the description analysis results, and Sect. 4.6 introduces the quantitative analysis results. The last section summarizes the main conclusions.

4.2 *Hukou* System Reform and Policy Change for Monopolistic Industries in China

In order to understand the background of this empirical study, the system and policy changes during the economic transition periods are reviewed. Two kinds of system transformation or reform relate to the issue: *Hukou* system deregulation and state-owned enterprises (SOEs) reform.

4.2.1 **Hukou** *System Deregulation in China*

In the planned economy period (from 1949 to 1977), in order to promote the development of the heavy manufacturing industry (e.g. iron and steel manufacturing industry), the Chinese government implemented policies during which the labor market segmented into the rural and urban regions. The *Hukou* system (Household Registration System) was one of these policies. The *Hukou* system was implemented in 1958. Although limitation of migration from rural regions to urban regions was not enacted directly in the *Hukou* system, the fourteen kinds of regulations[1] which relate to the *Hukou* system de facto inhibit migration from rural regions to the urban regions. The government strictly controlled rural-to-urban migration.

From 1984 to 1988, the *Hukou* system was deregulated, and migration from the rural regions to the urban regions was permitted. In the period, the "Household Production Contract" system ("*Jiating Liangchan Chengbao Zerenzhi*") was implemented in the rural regions so that a household unit in the rural regions could allocate the family members by itself. The "Household Production Contract" system enlarged the work effort in the agriculture industry and increased labor productivity in the rural regions. As the problem of food supply was addressed in the urban regions, the government permitted the rural residents to work in the urban regions when they were able to provide food for themselves. Because there was a lot of a surplus labor in the rural regions, with the deregulation of the *Hukou* system, rural migrants significantly increased in the short-term in the urban regions. This was called the "*Mingong Chao*". To address the problem, during the period 1989–1991, the government controlled internal migration.

The *Hukou* system was further deregulated from 1992 to 1994. From the end of the 1990s SOE reform was enforced by the government. As a result of the adjustment of employment in the SOEs the unemployment rate of local urban residents increased significantly and the migrant group became a competitor of local urban residents. Thus during the period from 1995 to 2000 migration to the urban regions was strictly controlled by the government, particularly, migrants could only be employed in jobs designated by the local governments (Song et al. 2006).

During the 2000s, with membership of the World Trade Organization (WTO) from 2001, the number of firms in competitive industries, such as privately owned enterprises (POEs) and foreign-owned enterprises (FOEs) in the manufacturing industry sector, increased greatly. Based on the market mechanism, POEs and FOEs in competitive industries strove to reduce labor costs to gain the maximum profit. Because migrants are surplus labor in the rural regions, the wage level of migrants may be set at a low level almost equal to the subsistence level (Lewis 1954). Thus in the competitive industries, the labor demand is greater for migrants than for local urban residents. As the number of migrant workers increased dramatically in the urban regions, the government promoted *Hukou* system reform during the 2000s. Examples of parts of reform are: a set of policies on migrant children's education; the public security policy for migrants during the 2000s; and the establishment of an Urban-Rural Integration Registration System (URIRS) in a section of regions (e.g. Chongqing, Guangzhou, Beijing) (Wei 2016; Song 2016). However, the housing system, children's education system, and social security system still differ for migrants and local urban residents, and it is predicted that the discrimination against migrants persists in the urban regions.[2]

4.2.2 Monopolistic Industries in China

During the planned economy period (1949–1977) in the urban regions all organizations/enterprises in various industries were SOEs or collectively owned enterprises (COEs), in which the employment and wage levels were managed by the government. With the implementation of the *Hukou* system in 1958, the migration from the rural regions to the urban regions was inhabited. Therefore, in the urban regions, workers in various industries were the urban residents. The *Hukou* system segmented the labor market, and there were no competitive industries during the period.

Since the 1980s, the Chinese government performed the economic system reform to permit the existence of POEs and FOEs.

At the end of the 1990s, the government promoted the SOEs reform, and a part of the middle-sized and small SOEs and most COEs transformed to become POEs ("*Zhua Da Fang Xiao*"), whereas the large SOEs are still controlled by the government.

Since the 2000s, in order to enlarge the economic and political influence in the world, the Chinese government implemented policies to encourage large SOEs to participate in global competition and to establish overseas enterprises ("*Zouchuqu*"); therefore the government influence on the monopolistic industries increased during the 2000s. For example, in 1999 at the Communist Party Conference the government made efforts to support those industries which affect the national safety, monopolistic industries, and public sectors which provide the public goods and services, and important industries such as the machinery industry, electronics industry, petrochemical industry, automotive industry, and construction and building materials industries. In 2006, the government promulgated the policy to emphasize that central government will focus on those sectors which influence the national safety and national economy greatly, and provide more public finance investment to these sectors. After the global financial crisis of 2007–2008, the Chinese government invested 400 million yuan to stimulate economic recovery. The main beneficiaries of the policy were the large SOEs, most of which are in the monopolistic industries. In 2012, at the 18th Communist Party Conference, the government declared that the central government will provide more public finance investment to important industries which affect national safety and the national economy. Moreover, the Xi Jinping government is enforcing the industry upgrading and promoting the "One Belt and One Road Initiative" ("*Yidaiyilu*")[3] policy; the implementation of these new policies might cause the influence of the Chinese government on the monopolies to increase. It is predicted that the problem of labor market segmentation by monopolies and competitive industries might become even more serious. Therefore, to investigate the influence of industrial factors on the wage gap is an important issue.

4.3 The Channels of the Influence of Industrial Factors on the Wage Gap: Inter-industry Differentials and Intra-industry Differentials

4.3.1 The Channels of the Influence of Industry Sector on the Wage Gap Between Migrants and Local Urban Residents

What determines the wage gap between migrants and local urban residents? The hypotheses and discrimination theories from the economic perspective are summarized as follows.

Based on the employer discrimination hypothesis (Becker 1957), discrimination against migrants might be shown by employers, customers, and colleagues: this discrimination causes the wage gap. As it is pointed out in Becker (1957), under a perfect competitive market, the discrimination should disappear in the long term because the discrimination should reduce the firm's profit. In China, compared with the monopolistic industry sector in which the proportion of the SOEs and public organizations is greater, the firms in the competitive industry sector in which the proportion of POEs and FOEs are greater face a competitive market in which they strive to maximize their profit. It is thought that market competition should reduce discrimination against migrants in the long term. Thus the wage gaps between migrants and local urban residents may be smaller in the competitive industry sector than in the monopolistic industry sector. In the monopoly industry sector, the government determines the employment plan; therefore, discrimination may exist when a migrant enters the monopolistic industry sector via the *Hukou* system. There may exist a difference of opportunity to enter the monopolistic industry sector.

In human capital theory (Becker 1964; Mincer 1974), it is pointed out that in the perfect competitive labor market, the individual wage level is determined by a worker's labor productivity; the labor productivity is in relation to a worker's human capital factor. Thus a worker with a higher level of human capital (higher education level, or more years of experience[4]) should gain a higher wage. For example, when the education level is lower for the migrant group than for the local urban resident group, a wage gap between these two groups may appear in the same industry sector. When highly skilled workers with higher education are needed in the monopolistic industry sector, because most the education/skill level is lower for the migrant group than that for the urban resident group, the differentials of the chance of entry to the monopolistic industry sector in which the wage level is higher may arise. This will affect the wage gap between migrants and local urban residents.

In addition, based on the crowded hypothesis (Bergmann 1974), the proportion in the migrant-dominated industry sectors (competitive industries-manufacturing, construction, retail/wholesale industries) is greater for the migrant group. When the wage level in the migrant-dominated industry sector is lower than in the local urban resident-dominated industry sector (monopolistic industries-financial industry, management of water conservancy and environment industry, transport, storage and post industry), the wage gap may be created.

Based on these theories and hypotheses, and the changes in government policies for the monopolistic industries during the 2000s, described in Sect. 4.2, the mechanism on the influences of industrial factors on wage gaps can be considered as follows.

First, because regular worker employment in the monopolistic industries is still managed by the government, and the influence of the government on large SOEs increased, the opportunity of entry to the monopolistic industries may differ between migrants and local urban residents. This may cause differences in industry sector distribution between these two groups. Because there remains an industrial wage gap between these two sectors,[5] if employment opportunities in the monopolistic industry sector are fewer for the migrants than for the local urban residents, the wage gap between migrants and local urban residents may appear. The wage gap caused by the differences in the opportunity of entry to various industry sectors is designated as an *inter-industry sector differential.*

Second, in a given industry sector, migrants may earn less than local urban residents. This is designated as an *intra-industry sector differential.*

Third, in both inter-industry sector differential and intra-industry sector differential, based on the ideas from Blinder (1973) and Oaxaca (1973), two factors may cause wage gaps. These are the explained differentials (differentials based on individual characteristics, including the human capital), and the unexplained differentials (discrimination against migrants). For example, in a given sector (a case of *intra-industry sector differential*), based on the employer discrimination hypothesis (Becker 1957), when an employer prefers the local urban residents, which may be caused by the influence of the employment system in the planned economy period, the discrimination against migrants may be created. Therefore, even though the human capital of the migrants is constant with the local urban residents, a wage gap may appear (a case of *unexplained component in the intra-industry sector differential*). On the other hand, when the labor productivity (e.g. education or skill level) is lower for migrants than for local urban residents, even though there is no discrimination against migrants, due to the market mechanism, the migrants may earn less than the local urban residents (a case of *explained component in the intra-industry sector differential*).

Thus, the influence of segmentation by industry sectors on wage gap can be divided into four factors: (i) the explained component in intra-industry sector differentials, (ii) the unexplained component in intra-industry sector differentials, (iii) the explained component in inter-industry sector differentials, and (iv) the unexplained component in inter-industry sector differentials. It is thought the four factors may affect the wage gap. Even though it can be thought when monopolies are strengthened by government policies during the 2000s, the discrimination against migrants might increase to cause an increase in the influence of the unexplained component from 2002 to 2013. We cannot predict the influence of these four industrial factors quantitatively: an empirical study is required to provide the evidence.

4.3.2 *Summary of Empirical Studies on the Wage Gap Between Migrants and Local Urban Residents*

In previous empirical studies there are three main perspective approaches to analyze the wage gap between migrants and local urban residents in China.

First, based on the Blinder–Oaxaca decomposition model (Blinder 1973; Oaxaca 1973), the decomposition of mean values is employed. Although previous studies pointed out that the explained differentials (e.g. education attainment differentials) between these two groups and the unexplained differentials (e.g. the discrimination against migrants) affect the wage gap, the estimated values of the unexplained differentials are not consistent in these studies. For example, some studies denoted that the unexplained differentials are greater than the explained differentials, and thus discrimination is the main factor causing the wage gaps. Concretely, the estimated values of the unexplained differentials are 24.88-94.11% in 1999–2000 (Maurer-Fazio and Dinh 2004), 60% in 2002 (Deng 2007), 55.2% in 2003–2004 (Xie and Yao 2006), and 54.25% in 2004–2011 (Chang and Zhao 2016). Whereas some studies showed the unexplained differentials are smaller than the explained differentials; it is pointed out that the estimated values of the unexplained differentials are 38.10% in 1993–2000 (Chang and Zhao 2016), 27% in 2002 (Guo and Zhang 2011), 36.9% in 2002 (Ma 2016a), 26.3% in 2002 and 42.3% in 2007 (Zhu 2016), 4% in 2005 (Xing and Luo 2009), 10% in 2005 (Xing 2008; Lee 2012), 27.11% in 2006 (Meng and Wu 2014), and 36% in 2007 (Zhang et al. 2014). Demurger et al. (2009) showed that the population effect (e.g. education) is 138% (education 113%), which is the greatest factor to contribute to the wage gap in 2002. Messinis (2013) pointed out the explained differentials, especially the education gaps between migrants and local urban residents, is the main factor causing the wage gap, and when the endogenous problem of education is addressed, the wage gap completely disappears. Ma (2016a) also points out that the explained differentials is 125.4–130% in 2013, and the results are similar to Demurger et al. (2009) and Messinis (2013). In summary, the explained differentials seem like the main factor causing the wage gap, and its influence increases during the economic transition period.

Second, based on the wage distribution decomposition method (e.g. Juhn et al. 1993; Fortin and Lemieux 1998; Machado and Mata 2005; Melly 2006) models, Deng (2007), Xing and Luo (2009), Yu and Chen

(2012), and Zhu (2016) analyzed the wage gap by wage percentiles. Deng (2007) showed that the influence of the unexplained differentials in 2002 is greater for the low- and middle-wage groups, whereas it is smaller for high-wage groups. Xing and Luo (2009) pointed out that the explained differentials are greater (94%) than the unexplained differentials, and the unexplained differentials (skill price effect) are higher for the low-wage group than for the high- and middle-wage group. Yu and Chen (2012) showed that the influence of the unexplained differentials is greater for middle-wage groups than for low- and high-wage groups in 1997, 2004, and 2009, but it is greater for the low-wage group than for middle- and high-wage groups in 1994; the effect is mostly similar between the low-, middle-, and high-wage groups in 2000. Zhu (2016) showed that the unexplained differentials are higher for the high-wage groups than for low- and middle-wage groups in both 2002 and 2007. In summary, these studies estimate the values of the unexplained and explained differentials by wage percentiles, and indicate that the influence of these factors differs by various percentile wages. But these estimated results are not consistent, which is caused by the difference of analyzed period, survey data, and variables utilized in models.

Third, some studies analyze the influence of labor market segmentation by various sectors on the wage gap based on the Brown et al. model (Brown et al. 1980). For example, Meng and Zhang (2001) analyzed occupational segregation (white collar, wholesale and retail trade, services, laborers) and the wage gap between migrants and local urban residents. They found that the value of discrimination in the same occupation (the unexplained component in the intra-occupation differential) is 105.74%, which is the main factor underlying the wage gap, and the total value of the unexplained differentials is 110.59%, which is significantly higher than that of explained differentials in 1995–1996. Wang (2005) analyzed sector segmentation (self-employed, workers in the public sector, workers in the private sector, manager, and technician in the private sector) on wage gaps, and found that the value of the explained components of inter-sector (31.80%) is greatest, and the total value of the explained differentials is 57.12%, which is higher than that of explained differentials in 2005. Wu and Zhang (2014) analyzed the influence of occupational segregation (38 kinds of occupation classification), and found the value of the explained differentials of inter-sector (130.66%) is greatest, and the total value of the explained differentials is 175.64%, which is higher than that of explained differentials in 2005. Zhang and Guo (2014) analyzed the influence of occupational segregation (low-, middle-, and high level occupations) on wage gap, and pointed out that the influences of the factors on wage gap differ by various industry sectors. For example, the total value of the unexplained differentials is greatest in the wholesale and retail trade industry (533.093%) and is smallest in the post industry (−1263.714%) in 2012. However, the previous studies did not sufficiently analyze how the wage gap is influenced by labor market segmentation in various industry sectors.

This chapter focuses on the influence of industrial factors on the wage gap between migrants and local urban residents. Using two period survey data and the Brown model, it investigates three questions. First, when migrants enter an industry sector how does discrimination affect the wage gap (entry opportunity discrimination)? When human capital factors are constant, how does the discrimination against a migrant worker in the same industry sector (workplace discrimination) affect the wage gap? Second, how do the overall explained differentials (e.g. the differentials of individual characteristics, including human capital) in the same industry sector (intra-industry sector) or between the various industry sectors (inter-industry sector) affect the wage gap? Third, does the influence of these discriminations change during the 2000s? It is believed this is the first study to utilize the Brown et al. decomposition model for the estimations required to answer these questions. It is to be hoped these results provide new evidence for the issue on the determinants of the wage gap between migrants and local urban residents from the industrial segmentation perspective; it enables us to better understand the influence of government and labor market segmentation on the wage gap.

4.4 Methodology and Data

4.4.1 Model

To estimate the consistency of other factors like human capital when examining how the segmentation by industry sectors affects the wage levels, the wage functions are calculated. The OLS model is utilized; it is expressed as Eq. (4.1a).[6]

$$\ln W_i = \alpha + \beta_X H_i + \beta_I \text{Ind}_i + u_i \tag{4.1a}$$

In Eq. (4.1a), i represents the individual (a migrant or a local urban resident), ln W is the logarithm of the average wage, H represents factors (e.g. education, experience years) which affect wage, Ind represents industry sector dummy variables, β is estimated coefficient, α is a constant item, and u is a random error item. When β is statistically significant, it indicates that when the other factors (e.g. human capital) are held constant, there are wage gaps between various industry sectors.

First to consider the sample selection bias problem (a worker can choose to enter an industry sector) left in the OLS model, the Maddala model (Maddala 1983) is used. Using the estimated results of the distribution function and the density function by the probit regression model (the dependent variable is Prob (y_i = 1) which indicates probability of the choice to enter an industry sector), selectivity items ($\lambda = \psi(\cdot)/\Phi(\cdot)$) for each industry sector are calculated. The probit regression model includes the identification variables.[7] The corrected wage function expressed by Eq. (4.1b) is estimated using these selectivity items.

$$\ln W_i = \alpha + \beta_X H_i + \beta_I \text{Ind}_i + \beta_\lambda \lambda_i + u_i \tag{4.1b}$$

Second, the wage functions by the industry categories are estimated. Wage functions by k kinds of industry categories are expressed by Eq. (4.2). X represents factors which affect wage. To solve the sample selection bias problem (a worker can choose to enter an industry sector), selectivity items ($\lambda = \psi(\cdot)/\Phi(\cdot)$) for each industry sectors are calculated based on the probit regression model. In addition, based on the estimated results by the multinomial logit regression model, the migrants' imputed industrial distributions (P^{*rm}) are calculated. P^{*rm} are calculated on an assumption condition that there do not exist discriminations when migrants enter these industry sectors.

$$\ln W_{ik} = \alpha_k + \beta_{ikX} X_{ik} + \beta_{ik\lambda} \lambda_{ik} + u_{ik} \tag{4.2}$$

Third, the estimated results based on industrial wage functions and the mean values of variables are used to decompose the influence of industry sector segmentation on the wage gap into four categories. The decompositions are shown in Eq. (4.3).

$$\begin{aligned} \ln W_u - \ln W_{rm} &= \sum P_k^{rm} \beta_k^u \left(X_k^u - X_k^{rm}\right) \quad \text{(A)} \\ &+ \sum P_k^{rm} \left(\alpha_k^u - \alpha_k^{rm}\right) + \sum P_k^{rm} X_k^{rm} \left(\beta_k^u - \beta_k^{rm}\right) \quad \text{(B)} \\ &+ \sum W_k^u \left(P_k^u - P_k^{*rm}\right) \quad \text{(C)} \\ &+ \sum W_k^u \left(P_k^{*rm} - P_k^{rm}\right) \quad \text{(D)} \end{aligned} \tag{4.3}$$

In Eq. (4.3), P_k^{rm}, P_k^u represent the actual industry distributions of migrants and local urban residents, P^{*rm} are the imputed industry distributions of migrants, X_k^u, X_k^{rm} represent mean values of variables, and β_k^u are the parameters estimated based on wage functions by industry categories.

To find the econometric meanings of decomposition results by Eq. (4.3) three steps are taken. First, $\sum P_k^{rm} \beta^u{}_k \left(X_k^u - X_k^{rm}\right)$ (A) represents the individual characteristics differentials in the intra-industry sector differentials (explained component in the intra-industry sector differentials), the total value of $\sum P_k^{rm}\left(\alpha_k^u - \alpha_k^{rm}\right) + \sum P_k^{rm} X_k^{rm}\left(\beta_k^u - \beta_k^{rm}\right)$ (B) represents the unexplained component (e.g. discrimination about the migrants in the same industry) in the intra-industry sector differentials, $\sum W_k^u\left(P_k^u - P_k^{*rm}\right)$ (C) represents the individual characteristics differentials in the inter-industry sector differentials (explained component in the inter-industry sector differentials), $\sum W_k^u\left(P_k^{*rm} - P_k^{rm}\right)$ (D) represents the unexplained component (e.g. the discriminations against the migrants when they enter an industry sector) in the inter-industry sector differentials.

Second, the total value of A and C represents the overall explained differentials caused by the differentials of individual characteristics when the migrants enter an industry sector, or when the migrants work together with local urban residents in the same industry. The total value of B and D represents the overall unexplained differential, both of these caused by the discrimination when the migrants enter an industry sector, or when the migrants work together with local urban residents in the same industry.

Third, the total value of A and B represents the overall intra-industry sector differentials caused by discrimination against migrants and the differentials of individual characteristics including human capital in the same industry sector; the total value of C and D represents the overall inter-industry sector differentials caused by the discrimination against migrants and the differentials of individual characteristics when migrants enter an industry sector.

4.4.2 *Data*

Two period survey data from the Chinese Household Income Project survey (CHIPs) conducted in 2003 and 2014 (CHIPs 2002, CHIPs 2013) are used for the analysis. These data are from the CHIPs conducted by Economic Institute of Chinese Academy of Social Sciences (CASS) and Beijing Normal University in 2003 and 2014, including information about the individual characteristic factors, industries, and wages of migrants[8] and local urban residents. Because there are design similarities of the data in the questionnaire, the same information for analysis for two periods can be utilized. To make comparisons in the two periods, the regions (provinces or metropolies) covered in both surveys, including Beijing, Shanxi, Liaoning, Jiangsu, Anhui, Guangdong, Henan, Hubei, Sichuan, Yunnan, and Gansu, are selected.

The analytic objects are workers, excluding the unemployed. In considering the retirement system implemented in the public sector (government organizations and SOEs), the analytic objects are limited to the age of 16 to 59. No answer samples, abnormal value samples,[9] and missing value samples are deleted.

To see the dependent variables setting, first, in the probability function of entry to industries, the dependent variable is a category variable. To maintain the analysis samples by each industry category and consider the feature of the industry distributions of migrants, the industrial categories in the CHIPs are reclassified.[10] Five kinds of industries, construction, manufacturing, retail and wholesale industries, service, and other industries, are used to construct the category variables.

Second, in the wage function, the dependent variable is the logarithm of wage rate. The wage rates are calculated based on total wage and work hours. The total wage is the total value of the basic wage, bonus, cash subsidy, and non-cash subsidy which is calculated based on the market price, excluding layoff living assistance, minimum income assistance, and living assistance by firms, income by asset and financials, and security transfer income. We use the consumption price index (CPI) in 2002 as the standard, and adjust the nominal wage in 2013. Because the questionnaire items on wage are different for migrants and local urban residents the information about yearly wage for local urban residents and monthly wage for migrants can be obtained. To unify the dependent variable, the wage rate (hourly wage) is calculated using yearly work hours for local urban residents and monthly work hours for migrants. Work hours yearly for local urban residents are calculated by "work hours daily × work days monthly × work month yearly", and work hours monthly for migrants are calculated by "work hours daily × work days weekly × 4". Wage rates are calculated by total wage divided by appropriate work hours.

The independent variables are the variables likely to affect the wage level and the probability of entry to industry; they are as follows. First, education (primary school or below, junior high school, senior high school/vocational school, college and above), experience years, age, and health status (very good, good, fair, bad) are used as the index of human capital. It is thought that these factors might affect the wage level and the probability of entry to industries.

Second, it is pointed out that there are wage gaps between public and private sectors.[11] The public sector dummy variable and the private sector dummy variable are employed to control the influence of ownership types on the wage gap. Concretely, the public sector includes SOEs and government organizations. The private sector is composed of COEs and foreign/privately owned enterprises (FOEs/POEs), self-employed workers, and other ownership sectors.

Third, it is pointed out that special political membership may affect the probability of entry to industry and the wage levels.[12] A party membership dummy variable is used in the analysis.

Fourth, in the previous studies, it is pointed out that there is a gender wage gap in the Chinese labor market.[13] To control the influence of gender disparity on wage, the gender dummy variable is constructed. Moreover, considering family status and race[14] may affect the probability of entry to industry or wage levels, married and Han majority dummy variables are also used.

Fifth, because of regional disparity for economic development levels, and because the labor markets differ between the regions, Eastern, Central, and Western regions dummy variables are used to control these influences.[15]

The descriptive statistics of variables for 2002 and 2013 are summarized in Table 4.1. These values are used in the Brown et al. decomposition model.

4.5 Econometric Analysis Results

4.5.1 Do Wage Gaps Between Various Industrial Sectors Exist?

Do wage gaps between various industrial sectors exist? To answer the question, wage functions including dummy variables for industry categories are estimated. The results are shown in Table 4.2.

First, the Maddala model (Maddala 1983) is used to adjust the sample selection bias caused by the choice of entry to an industry. Because a worker should decide to enter an industry sector based on the choice from five industry sector options (the manufacturing, construction, retail/

Table 4.1 Descriptive statistics for 2002 and 2013

	Migrant						*Urban*					
	Total	*Cons.*	*Manu.*	*Retails*	*Service*	*Others*	*Total*	*Cons.*	*Manu.*	*Retails*	*Service*	*Others*
Panel A: 2002												
ln wage rate	0.861	1.342	1.095	0.769	0.782	0.957	1.525	1.563	1.401	1.111	1.331	1.745
Age	34	34	33	34	34	36	40	42	41	39	40	41
Experience years	26	26	25	27	26	27	29	30	31	28	29	28
Education category												
Primary school	0.254	0.250	0.179	0.275	0.264	0.222	0.036	0.054	0.050	0.049	0.043	0.021
Junior high school	0.546	0.566	0.547	0.562	0.538	0.505	0.266	0.259	0.357	0.372	0.297	0.182
Senior high school	0.177	0.164	0.233	0.151	0.172	0.229	0.375	0.393	0.389	0.418	0.417	0.345
College	0.023	0.020	0.041	0.012	0.025	0.044	0.323	0.294	0.204	0.161	0.243	0.451
Health status category												
Very good	0.354	0.336	0.314	0.366	0.343	0.364	0.250	0.259	0.207	0.263	0.236	0.273
Good	0.559	0.592	0.585	0.557	0.561	0.536	0.431	0.415	0.438	0.417	0.413	0.435
General	0.071	0.066	0.091	0.059	0.080	0.083	0.284	0.297	0.315	0.287	0.302	0.261
Bad	0.016	0.007	0.009	0.019	0.017	0.017	0.035	0.029	0.039	0.033	0.049	0.030
Party	0.033	0.046	0.041	0.024	0.031	0.054	0.293	0.262	0.239	0.158	0.217	0.378
Female	0.567	0.868	0.594	0.509	0.536	0.675	0.559	0.700	0.591	0.454	0.431	0.592
Han race	0.916	0.901	0.906	0.924	0.920	0.896	0.959	0.971	0.970	0.956	0.965	0.951
Married	0.898	0.908	0.877	0.912	0.880	0.893	0.884	0.904	0.929	0.825	0.844	0.883
Ownership category												
Public sector	0.070	0.066	0.113	0.019	0.110	0.140	0.667	0.645	0.569	0.293	0.502	0.861
Private sector	0.116	0.270	0.226	0.067	0.122	0.140	0.138	0.192	0.231	0.212	0.177	0.054
Self-employment	0.730	0.559	0.585	0.891	0.671	0.475	0.091	0.070	0.034	0.363	0.180	0.030
Other	0.084	0.105	0.075	0.023	0.097	0.244	0.104	0.093	0.166	0.133	0.141	0.055
Region category												
East	0.368	0.388	0.447	0.342	0.368	0.390	0.391	0.422	0.368	0.453	0.527	0.350
Central	0.345	0.224	0.358	0.361	0.298	0.386	0.342	0.278	0.350	0.302	0.244	0.376
West	0.287	0.388	0.195	0.296	0.334	0.224	0.268	0.300	0.282	0.245	0.229	0.273
Observations	3,289	152	318	1,563	715	541	9,577	313	2,457	1,169	1,127	4,511

Table 4.1 (continued)

	Migrant						*Urban*					
	Total	*Cons.*	*Manu.*	*Retails*	*Service*	*Others*	*Total*	*Cons.*	*Manu.*	*Retails*	*Service*	*Others*
Panel B: 2013												
ln wage rate	2.143	2.411	2.179	2.031	2.162	2.175	2.310	2.481	2.302	2.040	2.153	2.466
Age	37	41	35	37	38	37	41	42	40	40	40	41
Experience years	28	32	26	28	29	27	29	31	29	30	29	29
Education category												
Primary school	0.142	0.191	0.105	0.170	0.130	0.110	0.047	0.100	0.044	0.070	0.062	0.027
Junior high school	0.515	0.564	0.545	0.539	0.502	0.437	0.261	0.351	0.322	0.367	0.300	0.173
Senior high school	0.224	0.182	0.244	0.223	0.223	0.228	0.304	0.287	0.368	0.366	0.308	0.258
College	0.120	0.064	0.105	0.068	0.144	0.224	0.388	0.262	0.266	0.196	0.329	0.542
Health status category												
Very good	0.397	0.382	0.493	0.380	0.326	0.413	0.340	0.334	0.327	0.318	0.318	0.364
Good	0.469	0.455	0.426	0.489	0.526	0.429	0.480	0.519	0.483	0.498	0.478	0.467
General	0.121	0.145	0.077	0.120	0.135	0.134	0.161	0.130	0.169	0.164	0.178	0.155
Bad	0.014	0.018	0.005	0.011	0.014	0.024	0.019	0.017	0.021	0.021	0.026	0.014
Party	0.043	0.000	0.053	0.030	0.051	0.071	0.208	0.123	0.135	0.050	0.148	0.328
Female	0.590	0.836	0.555	0.484	0.581	0.701	0.557	0.804	0.610	0.405	0.494	0.598
Han race	0.950	0.955	0.967	0.936	0.967	0.945	0.952	0.940	0.968	0.941	0.953	0.953
Married	0.844	0.918	0.799	0.864	0.847	0.811	0.866	0.909	0.865	0.856	0.831	0.879
Ownership category												
Public sector	0.088	0.036	0.086	0.016	0.047	0.272	0.407	0.185	0.272	0.078	0.211	0.685
Private sector	0.391	0.409	0.694	0.259	0.349	0.398	0.323	0.464	0.620	0.364	0.400	0.164
Self-employment	0.444	0.400	0.187	0.695	0.460	0.224	0.189	0.232	0.074	0.511	0.240	0.073
Other	0.077	0.155	0.033	0.030	0.144	0.106	0.081	0.119	0.034	0.046	0.149	0.078

(*continued*)

Table 4.1 (continued)

	Migrant						*Urban*					
	Total	*Cons.*	*Manu.*	*Retails*	*Service*	*Others*	*Total*	*Cons.*	*Manu.*	*Retails*	*Service*	*Others*
Region category												
East	0.432	0.345	0.660	0.411	0.363	0.374	0.419	0.362	0.544	0.389	0.431	0.392
Central	0.395	0.345	0.301	0.418	0.400	0.449	0.350	0.304	0.323	0.336	0.313	0.385
West	0.173	0.309	0.038	0.170	0.237	0.177	0.231	0.334	0.133	0.275	0.256	0.223
Observations	1,228	110	209	440	215	254	9,620	470	1,390	1,685	1,780	4,295

Source: Panel A is calculated based on CHIPs 2002; Panel B is calculated based on CHIPs 2013

Table 4.2 Results of wage function (total samples) for 2002 and 2013

	2002				*2013*			
	Migrant		*Urban*		*Migrant*		*Urban*	
	Coef.	*t-value*	*Coef.*	*t-value*	*Coef.*	*t-value*	*Coef.*	*t-value*
Industries (Manufacturing)								
Construction	0.223***	3.62	0.087**	2.42	0.233***	2.78	0.205***	5.32
Retail/Catering	−0.250***	−6.38	−0.092***	−4.04	−0.095	−1.54	−0.116***	−4.22
Service	−0.229***	−5.45	−0.050**	−2.25	0.025	0.36	−0.086***	−3.29
Other	−0.081*	−1.82	0.210***	13.13	−0.034	−0.51	0.044*	1.85
Correct item1	9.686	1.04	5.656	1.53	11.524	1.48	5.819***	2.62
Correct item2	−7.983	−0.89	−5.456**	−2.52	−6.901	−0.80	−3.024	−1.22
Correct item3	5.660	0.57	−2.214	−0.96	−10.614	−1.26	−6.374**	−2.42
Correct item4	7.860	0.93	−6.110***	−2.85	−10.678	−1.59	−3.019	−1.46
Correct item5	−8.165	−0.72	−3.630	−1.56	−14.149	−1.48	−9.200***	−3.94
Constants	−25.811	−0.81	16.901**	2.44	38.392	1.42	20.583***	2.71
Observations	3,289		9,577		1,228		9,620	
Adj R-squared	0.175		0.311		0.149		0.201	

Source: Calculated based on CHIPs 2002 and CHIPs 2013

Note:

(1) *, **, ***: statistically significant levels are 10%, 5%, and 1%

(2) Experience year, education, healthy, female, Han race, ownership sectors and regional dummy variables are estimated, these results are not expressed in the table

wholesale, service, and the other industries in the study) simultaneously, it is thought that a worker will compare the utilities of these choice options to select an industry sector where he/she can gain the maximum profit. Thus the five kinds of selection bias should be corrected. The five correct items (correct item1 to correct item5 in Table 4.2) calculated based on the probit regression model are used to adjust these selection biases. The marriage dummy variable and age are used as identification variables in the model. It is thought that marriage and age may affect the opportunity of entry to various industry sectors. For example, the opportunity of entry to competitive industries (e.g. the manufacturing, construction, retail/wholesale, service industries) may be higher for single and younger workers than married and older workers. If these correct items are statistically significant, they show the selection bias may exist without the correction. In both 2002 and 2013, the correct items are not statistically significant for migrants, and it is indicated that the influence of marital status and age on the decision to enter various industry sectors is smaller. This may be because there are not many job selection options for the migrants. Whereas in both 2002 and 2013, the correct items are statistically significant for the local urban residents' group and the coefficients of these correct items are negative values for the construction industry and the service industry in 2002, positive values for the manufacturing industry and the other industry in 2013. It is shown that for the local urban residents' group, the wage function results by the OLS model may be overestimated or underestimated when these selection biases are not adjusted. Because local urban resident workers may have more opportunities to choose an industry sector which they prefer to enter, these correct item results have more sensitivity for local urban residents than migrants.

Second, wage gaps between various industrial sectors do exist for both migrants and local urban residents. For example, holding the other factors constant, compared with the manufacturing industry, wage levels in construction are higher for both migrants (0.223 in 2002, 0.233 in 2013) and local urban residents (0.087 in 2002, 0.205 in 2013). Moreover, for the local urban residents group, compared with the manufacturing industry, wages levels are lower in the retail and wholesale industry as well as in the service industry in both 2002 and 2003. For migrants, wages levels are lower in 2003 in the retail and wholesale, service, and other industries, whereas the industrial wage gaps between manufacturing, retail and wholesale, service, and other industries are not statistically significant in 2013. The industrial wage disparities may be caused by individual characteristics differentials (e.g. education attainment) in various industry sectors, and it may be because the wage determination systems differ in the monopolies and competitive industry sectors. It is predicted that these factors may influence the wage gap between migrants and local urban residents.

4.5.2 *How Do Industrial Sectors Affect the Wage Gap Between Migrants and Local Urban Residents?*

To decompose the influences of industrial sectors on the wage gap based on the Brown et al. decomposition model, first, wage functions by industry category are estimated. The results are shown in Table 4.3. The estimations show in both 2002 and 2013 that human capital, gender, and ownership have the greatest effect on wage levels in various industry sectors; the influences of human capital on wage levels differ between migrants and local urban residents; they are greater for the local urban residents. These results are consistent with previous studies on the wage structures of migrants and local urban residents in urban China (Wang 2003; Zhang and Xue 2008; Zhang 2012; Ma 2014, 2016a, b). These results can be explained by the human capital theory, and the labor market segmentation hypotheses.

Then, the imputed industry sector distributions are summarized in Table 4.4. The main findings are as follows.

In 2002, if discrimination against migrants does not exist (based on the assumption that the migrants have the same opportunity to enter an industry sector), the proportions in the manufacturing and the other industries will increase, whereas the proportions in the construction, the retail/wholesale, and the service industries will decrease. For local urban residents, if the advantage for local urban residents does not exist (based on the assumption that the opportunity of entry to an industry sector for local urban residents is similar to migrants), the proportions in the manufacturing and other industries will decrease, whereas the proportions in the construction, the retail/wholesale, and the service industries will increase.

Moreover, in 2013, for migrants, if the discrimination against migrants does not exist, the proportions in the construction, the manufacturing, and the service industries will increase, whereas the proportions of migrants in the retail/wholesale and other industries will decrease. For local urban residents, if the advantage for local urban residents does not exist,

Table 4.3 Results of wage function by industry categories for 2002 and 2013

	Construction		*Manufacturing*		*Retail/Wholesale*		*Service*		*Other*	
	Migrants	*Urban*	*Migrants*	*Urban*	*Migrants*	*Urban*	*Migrants*	*Urban*	*Migrants*	*Urban*
Panel A: 2002										
Experience years	0.057*	0.036*	0.059***	0.025***	0.007	0.043***	0.022*	0.008	0.039***	0.033***
	(1.93)	(1.85)	(2.96)	(3.29)	(0.56)	(3.99)	(1.82)	(0.73)	(2.74)	(7.46)
Experience years squared	−0.001	−1.810E-04	−0.001***	−2.935E-04***	−2.463E-04	−0.001***	0.000**	4.700E-05	−0.001***	0.000***
	(−1.33)	(−0.53)	(−3.07)	(−2.32)	(−1.27)	(−4.51)	(−2.42)	(0.24)	(−3.21)	(−3.85)
Education (Junior high school)										
Primary school	−0.339**	−0.062	−0.076	−0.192***	−0.112***	0.074	−0.096*	−0.202*	−0.114	−0.154**
	(−2.13)	(−0.23)	(−0.63)	(−3.32)	(−2.75)	(0.72)	(−1.66)	(−1.83)	(−1.39)	(−2.02)
Senior high school	0.441**	0.171	0.262**	0.255***	0.180**	0.105	0.176***	0.218***	4.173E-04	0.180***
	(2.44)	(1.52)	(2.13)	(6.80)	(2.20)	(1.50)	(2.88)	(4.22)	(0.00)	(2.89)
College/ University	0.883**	0.536***	0.426*	0.556***	0.556*	0.065	0.523***	0.580***	−0.469	0.317**
	(2.25)	(4.32)	(1.69)	(7.89)	(1.92)	(0.41)	(3.74)	(7.26)	(−0.80)	(2.03)
Health	−0.142	0.044	−0.086	0.016	0.027	−0.002	0.013	−0.007	0.236	−0.049*
	(−0.69)	(0.56)	(−0.60)	(0.59)	(0.25)	(−0.05)	(0.18)	(−0.15)	(1.28)	(−1.76)
Party	0.025	−0.063	0.313	0.148***	0.070	0.077	−0.017	0.031	−0.138	0.034
	(0.09)	(−0.43)	(1.46)	(4.41)	(0.49)	(1.12)	(−0.14)	(0.50)	(−0.77)	(0.61)
Female	0.373	−0.305	−0.241***	−0.093***	−0.304**	−0.073	−0.191***	−0.234***	0.016	−0.035
	(0.88)	(−1.24)	(−3.12)	(−3.10)	(−2.46)	(−1.26)	(−3.41)	(−2.75)	(0.07)	(−1.39)
Ownership (Public)										
Private	−0.032	0.074	0.076	−0.120***	0.137	−0.143**	0.217**	−0.368***	0.360***	−0.199***
	(−0.15)	(0.75)	(0.57)	(−4.19)	(1.04)	(−2.50)	(2.44)	(−6.60)	(3.29)	(−5.24)

(*continued*)

Table 4.3 (continued)

	Construction		*Manufacturing*		*Retail/Wholesale*		*Service*		*Other*	
	Migrants	*Urban*	*Migrants*	*Urban*	*Migrants*	*Urban*	*Migrants*	*Urban*	*Migrants*	*Urban*
Self-employed	0.101	−0.128	0.006	−0.360***	−0.013	−0.477***	0.151**	−0.596***	0.170*	−0.445***
	(0.48)	(−0.87)	(0.05)	(−5.61)	(−0.11)	(−9.18)	(2.17)	(−10.28)	(1.86)	(−8.79)
Other	−0.136	0.007	−0.025	−0.053*	−0.136	0.025	0.004	−0.380***	−0.066	−0.145***
	(−0.54)	(0.06)	(−0.14)	(−1.67)	(−0.87)	(0.39)	(0.04)	(−6.34)	(−0.68)	(−3.87)
Han race	Yes	Yes	Yes	Yes	Yes	Yes	Yes	Yes	Yes	Yes
Regions	Yes	Yes	Yes	Yes	Yes	Yes	Yes	Yes	Yes	Yes
Correct item	−12.010	24.688	−3.269	−1.559**	−2.175	4.201***	4.138*	−0.754	−9.984*	−1.313
	(−1.37)	(1.41)	(−0.64)	(−2.23)	(−0.99)	(2.72)	(1.64)	(−0.39)	(−1.77)	(−1.39)
Constants	9.482	−18.451	3.052	2.018***	2.125	−1.727*	−2.220	2.066*	7.199*	1.877***
	(1.51)	(−1.35)	(0.89)	(4.04)	(1.41)	(−1.85)	(−1.39)	(1.64)	(1.93)	(3.24)
Observations	152	313	318	2452	1563	1169	715	1127	541	4511
Adj R-squared	0.165	0.2469	0.179	0.187	0.099	0.287	0.151	0.290	0.206	0.233

	Construction		*Manufacturing*		*Retail/Wholesale*		*Service*		*Other*	
	Migrants	*Urban*	*Migrants*	*Urban*	*Migrants*	*Urban*	*Migrants*	*Urban*	*Migrants*	*Urban*
Panel B: 2013										
Experience years	0.011	0.080***	0.074***	0.026***	0.041***	0.047***	0.021	0.024**	0.038*	0.025***
	(0.33)	(5.65)	(3.09)	(3.14)	(2.64)	(2.14)	(0.72)	(2.33)	(1.79)	(5.01)
Experience years squared	−4.071E-04	−0.001***	−0.001***	−4.117E-04***	−0.001**	−0.001***	−0.001	−3.772E-04**	−0.001**	−4.747E-04***
	(−0.86)	(−4.85)	(−3.46)	(−2.92)	(−2.19)	(−4.48)	(−1.51)	(−2.26)	(−2.23)	(−5.69)

(*continued*)

Table 4.3 (continued)

	Construction		*Manufacturing*		*Retail/Wholesale*		*Service*		*Other*	
	Migrants	*Urban*	*Migrants*	*Urban*	*Migrants*	*Urban*	*Migrants*	*Urban*	*Migrants*	*Urban*
Education (Junior high school)										
Primary school	0.041	−0.116	−0.085	−0.045	−0.029	−0.022	0.494**	−0.062	0.159	0.044
	(0.26)	(−0.75)	(−0.52)	(−0.44)	(−0.23)	(−0.26)	(2.22)	(−0.72)	(0.91)	(0.57)
Senior high school	0.224**	−0.005	0.073	0.190***	0.271***	0.249***	0.052	0.154***	0.030	0.005
	(1.40)	(−0.06)	(0.63)	(3.91)	(3.17)	(4.59)	(0.36)	(2.80)	(0.21)	(0.10)
College/University	0.129***	0.460***	0.547***	0.559***	0.742***	0.726***	−0.048	0.598***	−0.199	−0.182
	(0.46)	(3.87)	(2.99)	(8.90)	(2.76)	(4.38)	(−0.18)	(7.27)	(−0.43)	(−1.12)
Health	−0.003	0.016	−0.031	0.043	0.094	0.071	0.145	0.073	0.215	0.041
	(−0.02)	(0.16)	(−0.18)	(0.81)	(0.95)	(1.47)	(0.94)	(1.33)	(1.16)	(1.32)
Party	(omitted)	−0.141	−0.165	0.234***	0.170	0.175	0.183	−0.033	0.013	−0.359***
	(omitted)	(−1.26)	(−0.58)	(3.53)	(0.82)	(1.21)	(0.74)	(−0.49)	(0.05)	(−3.70)
Female	−0.084	−0.178	−0.260	−0.045	−0.434**	−0.402***	−0.440***	−0.156***	−0.259	−0.113***
	(−0.26)	(−1.28)	(−1.40)	(−0.54)	(−2.44)	(−3.54)	(−3.81)	(−2.79)	(−1.10)	(−3.88)
Ownership (Public)										
Private	−0.098	−0.143	0.250	−0.059	−0.129	0.021	−0.162	−0.025	−0.216*	−0.073**
	(−0.32)	(−1.57)	(1.43)	(−1.33)	(−0.49)	(0.29)	(−0.63)	(−0.50)	(−1.86)	(−2.44)
Self-employed	0.083	−0.045	0.335*	0.114	−0.247	−0.055	0.145	−0.052	−0.157	−0.119***
	(0.27)	(−0.42)	(1.73)	(1.48)	(−0.97)	(−0.77)	(0.57)	(−0.87)	(−1.18)	(−2.78)
Other	−0.036	−0.142	−0.588*	−0.373***	−0.439	−0.025	−0.450	−0.238***	−0.440***	−0.284***
	(−0.11)	(−1.11)	(−1.93)	(−3.56)	(−1.41)	(−0.23)	(−1.59)	(−3.68)	(−2.59)	(−6.79)

(*continued*)

Table 4.3 (continued)

	Construction		*Manufacturing*		*Retail/Wholesale*		*Service*		*Other*	
	Migrants	*Urban*	*Migrants*	*Urban*	*Migrants*	*Urban*	*Migrants*	*Urban*	*Migrants*	*Urban*
Han race	Yes	Yes	Yes	Yes	Yes	Yes	Yes	Yes	Yes	Yes
Regions	Yes	Yes	Yes	Yes	Yes	Yes	Yes	Yes	Yes	Yes
correct item	−2.033	0.997	−2.836	−4.141*	−1.417	−1.721	−5.921	2.974*	−3.290	−4.148***
	(−0.50)	(0.33)	(−0.83)	(−1.84)	(−0.68)	(−1.05)	(−1.30)	(1.66)	(−0.92)	(−4.33)
Constants	4.389	1.181	3.485	5.229***	2.458**	2.741***	7.014*	0.021	4.210*	5.070***
	(1.29)	(0.52)	(1.28)	(3.08)	(2.01)	(2.59)	(1.87)	(0.02)	(1.85)	(7.29)
Observations	110	470	209	1390	440	1685	215	1780	254	4295
Adj R-squared	0.1159	0.1345	0.168	0.142	0.127	0.128	0.151	0.208	0.130	0.169

Source: Panel A is calculated based on CHIPs 2002; Panel B is calculated based on CHIPs 2013

Note:

(1) *, **, ***: statistically significant levels are 10%, 5%, and 1%

(2) *z* values are shown in the parentheses

Table 4.4 Industry distributions by the actual values and the imputed values for 2002 and 2013

	Actual value (A) (%)		*Imputed value (I) (%)*		*Differentials (I–A) (%)*	
	Migrant	*Urban*	*Migrant*	*Urban*	*Migrant*	*Urban*
2002						
Construction	4.6	3.3	2.9	13.7	−1.7	10.4
Manufacturing	9.7	25.7	24.7	10.9	15.1	−14.8
Retail/Catering	47.5	12.2	28.0	19.1	−19.5	6.9
Service	21.7	11.8	12.2	20.7	−9.5	9.0
Other	16.3	47.0	32.1	35.6	15.8	−11.4
Total	100.0	100.0	100.0	100.0		
2013						
Construction	9.0	4.9	13.2	3.6	4.3	−1.3
Manufacturing	17.0	14.4	17.6	17.6	0.6	3.1
Retail/Catering	35.8	17.5	25.3	26.8	−10.5	9.3
Service	17.5	18.5	31.9	36.9	14.4	18.4
Other	20.7	44.7	11.9	15.1	−8.8	−29.6
Total	100.0	100.0	100.0	100		

Source: Calculated based on CHIPs 2002 and CHIPs 2013

the proportion in the manufacturing and other industries will decrease, whereas the proportions in the manufacturing, the retail/wholesale, and the service industries will increase.

It should be noted that in both 2002 and 2013, for local urban residents, if there is no discrimination against migrants, the proportion of workers in the other industry sector should decrease 11.4% in 2002 and 29.6% in 2013. Because the other industry sector includes the monopolistic industries, the results indicate discrimination against migrants when they enter the monopolistic industries during the 2000s.

The next question is: How does discrimination against migrants when they enter these sectors affect the wage gap? How does discrimination against migrants in the same sectors affect the wage gap? The decomposition results shown in Table 4.5 are used to discuss these issues. To be understood easily, percentage contribution values are used to introduce these findings as follows.

First, to compare the influences between intra-industry sector differentials and inter-industry sector differentials, the values of intra-industry sector differentials are 80.6% in 2002 and 145.7% in 2013, whereas the values of inter-industry sector differentials are 19.4% in 2002 and −45.7% in

Table 4.5 Decomposition results based on Brown et al. model

	Actual value	*Estimation1*	*Estimation2*
		Percentage (%)	*Percentage (%)*
		2002	
Total wage differentials	0.6571	100.0	
Inter-industry differential	0.1272	19.4	100.0
Explained	0.0780	11.9	61.4
Unexplained	0.0492	7.5	38.6
Intra-industry differential	0.5299	80.6	100.0
Explained	0.4022	61.2	75.9
Unexplained	0.1277	19.4	24.1
		100	
Total explained differentials	0.4802	73.1	
Total unexplained differentials	0.1769	26.9	
		2013	
Total wage differentials	0.1676	100	
Inter-industry differential	−0.0767	−45.70	100
Explained	−0.0944	−56.3	−123.1
Unexplained	0.0177	10.6	23.1
Intra-industry differential	0.2443	145.7	100
Explained	0.1303	77.7	53.3
Unexplained	0.1140	68.0	46.7
		100	
Total explained differentials	0.0359	21.4	
Total unexplained differentials	0.1317	78.6	

Source: Calculated based on CHIPs 2002 and CHIPs 2013

2013. The results reveal that the influence on the wage gap is greater for the intra-industry sector differentials. They are the main factor underlying the wage gap in both 2002 and 2013, and their influence increased from 2002 to 2013. Both the intra-industry sector and inter-industry sector differentials can be divided into two parts: the explained component and the unexplained component. The detailed decomposition results need to be scrutinized in order to understand the influence of the intra-industry sector differentials and inter-industry differentials as follows.

Second, for the decomposition results of the influence of the intra-industry sector differentials, (1) the value of explained component (61.2% in 2002, 77.7% in 2013) is greater than that of the unexplained components (19.4% in 2002, 68.0% in 2013) in both 2002 and 2013. The results indicate that the differentials of individual characteristics (e.g. human capital) in the same industry sector are the main reason for the wage gap during the

2000s. To consider the results, it is known that the number of new generation migrants who are the children of first-generation migrants is increasing in the recent period.[16] Because compared with the first-generation migrants, the education level is higher for the new generation migrants,[17] it is predicted that the education attainment gap between migrants and local urban residents may decrease, which may contribute to reducing the wage gap. However, the calculated results shown in Table 4.1 indicate that differentials of human capital between the two groups remain: the proportion of low-education workers is greater in the migrant group than in the local urban resident group in both 2002 and 2013. Although the Chinese government enforced compulsory education and increased public education investment in the rural regions, the education attainment gap continues into the 2000s. This may be because it takes time for these policies to reduce the education gap and it should be considered in the long term. It is thought that vocational education and training for migrants helps to reduce the education gap in the short term. However, vocational education and training for migrants by government and firms is scarce in China (Cai et al. 2011).

(2) Moreover, the values of the unexplained component of intra-industry sector differentials are positive values in both 2002 and 2013, and the value rises greatly from 2002 to 2013: 19.4% (2002) and 68.0% (2013). This result shows that if other factors are held constant, discrimination against migrants in the same industry sector is the main reason for the wage gap, and the problem of discrimination against migrants has become more serious in recent years.

The reasons for the positive value results in both 2002 and 2013 can be explained as follows. It may be because the wage determination systems differ by the migrants and local urban residents in the same industry sector. For example, in the monopolistic industries, the wage levels for the regular workers, most of whom are local urban residents, are controlled by the government. Firms in the monopolistic industries can let the local urban residents earn more than the market equilibrium wage because monopolies can gain monopoly rents, whereas because the migrants are surplus labor in the rural regions, the wage level of migrants can be set at a low level just above subsistence level (Lewis 1954). The difference of the wage determination system for the local urban residents and migrants may cause the wage gap in the same industry sector.

Why did the discrimination against migrants in the same industry sector increase during the 2000s? It can be explained as follows: first, the Chinese government implemented a set of policies such as the technology upgrading policy and the policies which promote the SOEs (most of which are in the monopolistic industries) to enlarge. Second, after the global financial crisis of 2007–2008, the Chinese government provided greater public financial support to the SOEs in the monopolistic industry sectors to stimulate economic recovery. Thus the problem of the discrimination against migrants in the monopolistic industries might become serious from 2002 to 2013.

Third, to consider the influence of the inter-industry sector differentials, the decomposition results show that the value of the unexplained component increased from 7.5% (2002) to 10.6% (2013), whereas the value of the explained component decreased from 11.9% (2002) to −56.3% (2013).

The results indicate that when a migrant worker enters an industry sector, discrimination increased from 2002 to 2013. These results can be explained as follows. As described in Sect. 4.2, monopolistic industries are strengthened by the government's protection policies, and local urban residents are given preferential treatment in employment by the monopolistic industry sectors in which the influence of the employment system established in the period of planned economy is even greater. During the 2000s, particularly after the global financial crisis in 2007, the influence of government on the public sector has become greater, and thus the problem of the administration against migrants to obtain job opportunities in the monopolistic industries may become serious from 2002 to 2013.

The results also show that influence of the evaluation differential of individual characteristics (e.g. human capital) on the opportunity gap decreased from 2002 to 2013. In particular, it contributes to reducing the wage gap in 2013. It can be explained that for the probability to enter the competitive industries, when the other unobserved factors (e.g. effort to work, willingness to work long hours) are evaluated more positively for migrants than for local urban residents, the opportunities to enter the competitive industries may be higher for migrants.

Fourth, to consider the influence of overall explained differentials and unexplained differentials, the explained differentials (73.1%) are greater than the unexplained differentials (26.9%) in 2002, whereas the explained differentials (21.4%) are smaller than the unexplained differentials (78.6%) in 2002. These results indicate that explained differentials are the main factor in 2002, whereas the unexplained differentials are the main factor in 2013 and caused the wage gaps.

Because the results for 2013 are the newest results for the issue, here we compare the result for 2002 with the previous studies. The results of unexplained differentials for 2002 (26.9%) in the study are consistent with Guo and Zhang (2011), Ma (2016a), Chang and Zhao (2016), and Zhu (2016). The values of the unexplained differentials are 27% in 2002 (Guo and Zhang

2011), 36.9% in 2002 (Ma 2016a), 26.3% in 2002 (Zhu 2016), and 38.10% in 1993–2000 (Chang and Zhao 2016) based on the Blinder–Oaxaca model.

The new finding is that the influence on wage gap is greater for the unexplained differentials than for the explained differentials in 2013. The result indicates that the influence of the unexplained differentials increased from 2002 to 2013. Based on the Brown et al. decomposition model, the unexplained differentials include wage discriminations against migrants when the migrants work together with local urban residents in the same industry sector, and when migrants try to enter an industry sector, particularly the monopolistic industries in which the wage level is higher. These results may be because during the 2000s, particularly after the global financial crisis in 2007, the monopolistic industries were strengthened by government protection policies; therefore, the problem of discrimination against migrants became more serious.

4.6 Conclusions

This chapter explores labor market segmentation by various industry sectors (e.g. the monopolistic industry sector and the competitive industry sector) and its impact on the wage gaps between rural-to-urban migrants and local urban residents in China. Using survey data from the CHIPs conducted in two periods, 2003 and 2014 (CHIPs 2002, CHIPs 2013), we analyzed the probabilities of entry to various industries for both migrant and local urban resident groups; using the Brown et al. decomposition model, we then undertook a decomposition analysis of the wage gaps. Several major conclusions emerge.

First, to consider the overall influence of intra-industry differentials and inter-industry differentials on wage gaps, the results reveal that the intra-industry differentials are the main factors underlying the wage gap in both 2002 and 2013, and their influence increased from 2002 to 2013.

Second, to see the influence of intra-industry differentials, the value of explained component (61.2% in 2002, 77.7% in 2013) is greater than that of the unexplained components (19.4% in 2002, 68.0% in 2013) in both 2002 and 2013. The results indicate that the existence of differentials in individual characteristics (including human capital) in the same industry sector is the main cause of the wage gaps. In addition, the value of the unexplained component of intra-industry differentials rises greatly from 19.4% (2002) to 68.0% (2013): this indicates that if other factors are held constant, the problem of discrimination against migrants in the same industry sector has become more serious in recent years.

Third, to see the influence of the inter-industry differentials: the value of the unexplained component increased from 7.5% (2002) to 10.6% (2013), whereas the value of the explained component decreased from 11.9% (2002) to −56.3% (2013). The results indicated the discrimination when a migrant worker enters an industry sector is increasing during 2002–2013, whereas the differentials of individual characteristics (e.g. human capital) between migrants and local urban residents groups decreased from 2002 to 2013: it contributes to reducing the wage gaps in 2013.

Fourth, to consider the influence of explained differentials and unexplained differentials: the explained differentials (73.1%) are greater than the unexplained differentials (26.9%) in 2002, whereas the explained differentials (21.4%) are smaller than the unexplained differentials (78.6%) in 2013. These results indicate that the explained differentials are the main factor in 2002, whereas in 2013 the unexplained differentials are the main factor which caused the wage gap.

These findings indicate that to reduce wage gaps between migrants and local urban residents, employment equality laws and an equal pay for equal work policy are immediate priorities. Policies that aim to reduce human capital differentials between these two groups, such as reducing the education gaps between the rural regions and urban regions, should be implemented in the long term, and vocational education and training systems for migrants should also be developed to increase the skill levels of migrants. Moreover, the monopoly industry sector is protected by the government. The implementation of new policies encouraged the monopoly industry sector to become strong in the 2000s, which increased discrimination against migrants from 2002 to 2013. To reduce the influence of the monopoly sector in the urban labor market, a set of ownership reforms, such as SOEs reform and deregulation of entry to the monopoly sector for POEs and FOEs, should be implemented by the Chinese government.

Notes

1. The regulations included food supply, house supply, education, employment, wage, public pension, and public health insurance systems, which are only available for local urban residents.
2. Cai and Bai (2006) and Li and Ding (2013) indicate that the housing system, education and health care service systems, the social security system, and the employment and wage systems are different for migrants and local urban residents.

3. The Chinese government promoted the "One Belt and One Road Initiative" policy since 2013. It includes many countries from Singapore to Syria, most of which are near the historic trade route known as the Silk Road. The Chinese government encourages active participation in overseas infrastructure investment and construction by exporting mechanical equipment.
4. Experience years = age-6-years of schooling.
5. For empirical studies on the industrial wage disparity, please refer to Cai (1996), Luo and Li (2007), Demurger et al. (2007), Jin and Cui (2008), and Ma (2012, 2014). They indicate that the wage level in the competitive industries is lower than that in the monopolistic industries when factors (e.g. education attainment, experience years) which can affect the wage are controlled.
6. In order to simplify the expression of equations all constant items are omitted.
7. Marital status, age, and age squared are used as identification variables in this study.
8. A sampling bias problem may exist in the migrant survey. In the survey of CHIPs 2002, and CHIPs 2013, only migrants officially registered and who were living in the urban area in the survey year can become the random selection sampling objectives; therefore most migrants who live in apartments near the workplace provided by firms may not be surveyed (Li et al. 2008).
9. Variable values are in the range of "mean value ± three times S.D." which is defined as abnormal value here.
10. The numbers of industry categories are sixteen in the survey for local urban residents and twenty-five in the survey for migrants in CHIPs.
11. For the empirical studies on the wage gap between public and private sectors in China, please refer to Chen et al. (2005), Zhang and Xue (2008), Ye et al. (2011), Demurger et al. (2012), Zhang (2012), and Ma (2014, 2015, 2016b).
12. Gustafsson and Li (2000), Wu and Xie (2003), Knight and Yueh (2008), and Appleton et al. (2009) found that there remains a Communist Party member wage premium in China.
13. Gustafsson and Li (2000), Liu et al. (2000), Maurer-Fazio and Hughes (2002), Demurger et al. (2007), Ma (2007, 2009), Guo and Zhang (2010), Li and Yang (2010), Li et al. (2011), and Ma et al. (2013) analyzed the gender wage gaps based on the decomposition methods and found that the discrimination against women is the main factor in China.
14. Gustafsson and Li (2003, 2014), Li and Ding (2013), and Campos et al. (2016) point out the wage gap between the Han majority and non-Han majority in China, and the minority/majority income gap has widened rapidly during the economic transition period. However, Gustafsson and

Li (2014) indicate there is no income gap between the Hui Muslim minority and Han majority in Ningxia rural region. These results show that the wage gap between the Hui Muslim minority and Han majority differs by region (e.g. minority region vs. national region, urban region vs. rural region).

15. Chen and Fleisher (1996), Chen and Groenewold (2010), Li and Haynes (2011), Song (2013), and Tian et al. (2016) indicate there remains regional income disparity in China and the wage level is higher for the Eastern region than for the Western and Central regions; they also point out that the regional income inequality expanded since the 1990s.
16. Based on the survey of new generation migrants conducted in 2010 by the National Bureau of Statistics (NBS), there are 84.87 million new generation migrants; the ratio of new generation migrants to total migrants was 58.4% in 2010 (Cai et al. 2011).
17. Based on the survey of new generation migrants conducted in 2010 by the NBS, the average years of schooling are longer for the new generation migrants (9.8 years) than for the first-generation migrants (8.8 years) (Cai et al. 2011).

References

Appleton, S., Knight, J., Song, L., & Xia, Q. (2009). The economics of communist party membership: The curious case of rising numbers and wage premium during China's transition. *Journal of Development Studies, 45*(2), 256–275.

Becker, G. S. (1957). *The economics of discrimination*. Chicago: University of Chicago Press.

Becker, G. S. (1964). *Human capital: A theoretical and empirical analysis, with special reference to education*. New York: Columbia University Press.

Bergmann, B. R. (1974). Occupational segregation, wages and profits when employers discriminate by race and sex. *Eastern Economic Journal, 1*, 103–110.

Brown, R. S., Moon, M., & Zoloth, B. S. (1980). Incorporating occupational attainment in studies of male-female earnings differentials. *Journal of Human Resources, 15*(1), 3–28.

Blinder, A. S. (1973). Wage discrimination: Reduced form and structural estimation. *Journal of Human Resources, 8*(4), 436–455.

Cai, F. (1996). Cause and change of the industrial wage gaps. *Financial and Trade Economic, 11*, 3–5 (In Chinese).

Cai, F., & Bai, N. (2006). *Labor migration in transition China*. Beijing: Social Science Academic Press (In Chinese).

Cai, F., Du, Y., & Zhang, Z. (2011). *Reports on China's population and labor No. 12: Challenge during the 12th five-year plan period: Population, employment, and income distribution*. Beijing: Social Science Academic Press (In Chinese).

Campos, B. C., Ren, Y., & Petrick, M. (2016). The impact of education on income inequality between ethnic minorities and Han in China. *China Economic Review, 41*, 253–267.

Chang, J., & Zhao, H. (2016). The impact of work unit's ownership on wage differentials between the Labor of urban and rural household registration. *Chinese Economic Quarterly, 15*(2), 627–646 (In Chinese).

Chen, A., & Groenewold, N. (2010). Reducing regional disparities in China: An evaluation of alternative policies. *Journal of Comparative Economics, 38*(2), 189–198.

Chen, G., Demurger, S., & Fournier, M. (2005). Wage differentials and ownership structure of China's enterprise. *World Economic Paper, 6*, 11–31 (In Chinese).

Chen, J., & Fleisher, B. M. (1996). Regional income inequality and economic growth in China. *Journal of Comparative Economics, 22*(2), 141–164.

Demurger, S., Fournier, M., Li, S., & Wei, Z. (2007). Economic liberation with rising segmentation in China's urban labor market. *Asian Economic Papers, 5*(3), 58–103.

Demurger, S., Gurgand, M., Li, S., & Yue, X. (2009). Migrants as second-class workers in urban China? A decomposition analysis. *Journal of Comparative Economics, 37*, 610–628.

Demurger, S., Li, S., & Yang, J. (2012). Earning differentials between the public and private sectors in China: Exploring changes for urban local residents in the 2000s. *China Economic Review, 23*, 138–153.

Deng, Q. (2007). Earning differential between urban residents and rural migrants: Evidence from Oaxaca Blinder and quantile regression decompositions. *Chinese Journal of Population Science, 2*, 8–16 (In Chinese).

Fortin, N., & Lemieux, T. (1998). Rank regressions, wage distributions, and the gender gap. *Journal of Human Resources, 33*(3), 610–643.

Guo, F., & Zhang, S. (2010). Gender wage gap in state and non-state sector. *The Journal of Quantitative & Technical Economics, 12*, 91–102 (In Chinese).

Guo, F., & Zhang, S. (2011). The effect of education discrimination and household discrimination on the wage differences between urban workers and migrant workers. *Issues in Agricultural Economy, 6*, 35–42 (In Chinese).

Gustafsson, B., & Li, S. (2000). Economic transformation and the gender earnings gap in urban China. *Journal of Population Economics, 13*(2), 305–329.

Gustafsson, B., & Li, S. (2003). The ethnic minority-majority income gap in rural China during transition. *Economic Development and Cultural Change, 51*(4), 805–822.

Gustafsson, B., & Li, S. (2014, December). Why is there no income gap between the Hui Muslim minority and the Han majority in rural Ningxia, China? *The China Quarterly, 220*, 968–987.

Jin, Y., & Cui, Y. (2008). Effect of industrial factors on marginal labor income and the detailed effects: An analysis based on quantile regression model. *Journal of Finance and Economics, 34*(7), 4–15 (In Chinese).

Juhn, C., Murphy, K., & Pierce, B. (1993). Wage inequality and the rise in returns to skill. *Journal of Political Economy, 101*(3), 410–442.
Knight, J., & Yueh, L. (2008). The role of social capital in the labour market in China. *Economics of Transition, 16*, 389–414.
Lee, L. (2012). Decomposing wage differentials between migrant workers and urban workers in urban China's labor markets. *Chinese Economic Review, 23*, 461–470.
Lewis, W. A. (1954). Economic development with unlimited supplies of labor. *Manchester School of Economic and Social Studies, 22*(2), 139–191.
Li, H., & Haynes, K. E. (2011). Economic structure and regional disparity in China: Beyond the Kuznets transition. *International Regional Science Review, 34*(2), 157–190.
Li, S., & Ding, S. (2013). An empirical analysis of income inequality between a minority and the majority in urban China: The case of Ningxia Hui autonomous region. *Review of Black Political Economy, 40*(3), 341–355.
Li, S., Sicular, T., & Gustafsson, B. (2008). *Income distribution in China III*. Beijing: Beijing Normal University Press (In Chinese).
Li, S., Song, J., & Liu, X. (2011). Evolution of the gender wage gap among China's urban employees. *Social Sciences in China, 32*(3), 161–180 (In Chinese).
Li, S., & Yang, X. (2010). The determinants of gender wage gaps in migrants. *Comparative Economic & Social Systems, 5*(151), 82–89 (In Chinese).
Liu, P., Meng, X., & Zhang, J. (2000). Sectoral gender wage differentials and discrimination in the transitional Chinese economy. *Journal of Population Economics, 13*(2), 331–352.
Luo, C., & Li, S. (2007). Human capital, industrial features and income inequality. *Management World, 10*, 20–30 (In Chinese).
Ma, C., Gu, H., & Li, J. (2013). Change of gender wage gaps in Chinese labor market: Evidence from quantile decomposition analysis of panel data. *World Economic Papers, 2*, 96–108 (In Chinese).
Ma, X. (2007). A comparative study on occupational segregation and its impact on gender wage differentials; based on micro-data from household survey in Japan and China. *Journal of Chinese Economic Studies, 4*(1–2), 14–33 (In Japanese).
Ma, X. (2009). The enterprise ownership reforms and the change of wage structure in China: Comparison of gender wage profiles differentials by ownership. *Journal of Chinese Economic Studies, 6*(1), 48–63 (In Japanese).
Ma, X. (2011). Immigration and labor market segmentation in urban China: An empirical analysis of income gaps between migrants and urban register workers. *Japanese Journal of Comparative Economics, 48*(1), 39–55 (In Japanese).
Ma, X. (2012). Industrial segregation in labor market: An empirical study on the wage gaps between the monopoly industry and competitive industry. *Chinese Labor Economics, 7*(*1*), 44–82 (In Japanese).

Ma, X. (2014). Wage policy: Economy transition and wage differentials of sectors. In K. Nakagane (Ed.), *How did the Chinese economy change? The evaluations of economic systems and policies in post-reform period*. Greater Taegu City: Kokusai Shoin Co., Ltd (In Japanese).

Ma, X. (2016a). Determinants of the wage gap between migrants and local urban residents in China: 2002–2013. *Modern Economy, 7*, 786–798.

Ma, X. (2016b). Changes of wage structures in Chinese public and private sectors: 1995–2007. *Management Studies, 4*(6), 1–13.

Machado, J., & Mata, J. (2005). Counterfactual decompositions of changes in wage distributions using quantile regression. *Journal of Applied Econometrics, 20*(4), 445–465.

Maddala, G. S. (1983). *Limited-dependent and qualitative variables in econometrics*. New York: Cambridge University Press.

Maurer-Fazio, M., & Dinh, N. (2004). Differential rewards to, and contributions of, education in urban China's segmented labor markets. *Pacific Economic Review, 9*(3), 173–189.

Maurer-Fazio, M., & Hughes, J. (2002). The effects of market liberalization on the relative earning of Chinese women. *Journal of Comparative Economics, 30*, 709–731.

Melly, B. (2006). Estimation of counterfactual distributions using quantile regression. *Review of Labor Economics, 68*(4), 543–572.

Meng, F., & Wu, J. (2014). The differences of registration discrimination and employer-employee relation between migrants and urban residents in Chinese labor market. *World Economic Papers, 2*, 62–71 (In Chinese).

Meng, X., & Zhang, J. (2001). Two-tier labor market in urban China: Occupational segregation and wage differentials between urban residents and rural migrants in Shanghai. *Journal of Comparative Economics, 29*(2), 485–504.

Messinis, G. (2013). Returns to education and urban-migrant wage differentials in China: IV quantile treatment effects. *China Economic Review, 26*, 39–55.

Mincer, J. (1974). *Schooling, experience and earning*. New York: Columbia University Press.

Oaxaca, R. (1973). Male-female wage differentials in urban labor markets. *International Economic Review, 14*(3), 693–709.

Roberts, K. D. (2001). The determinants of job choice by rural labor migrants in Shanghai. *Chinese Economics Review, 12*, 15–39.

Song, H. (2016). Accelerate the reform of rural household registration system to promote the integrated development of both urban and rural areas. *Research of Agricultural Modernization, 37*(6), 1011–1028 (In Chinese).

Song, H., Huang, H., & Liu, G. (2006). An analysis on the policy of the flow of rural labor force. In F. Cai & N. Bai (Eds.), *Labor migration in transition China*. Beijing: Social Science Academic Press (In Chinese).

Song, L., & Appleton, S. (2006). Urban laid-off workers versus rural migrants: Sectoral choice and job search. In F. Cai & N. Bai (Eds.), *Labor migration in transition China*. Beijing: Social Science Academic Press (In Chinese).

Song, Y. (2013). Rising Chinese regional income inequality: The role of fiscal decentralization. *China Economic Review, 27*, 294–309.

Tian, X., Zhang, X., Zhou, Y., & Yu, X. (2016). Regional income inequality in China revisited: A perspective from club convergence. *Economic Modelling, 56*, 50–58.

Wang, M. (2003). Wage differentials in the transition period: An econometric analysis on the discrimination. *The Journal of Quantitative & Technical Economics, 5*, 94–98 (In Chinese).

Wang, M. (2005). Work chance and wage differentials in the urban labor market: Work and wage of migrants. *Chinese Social Sciences, 5*, 36–46 (In Chinese).

Wang, X., & Zhang, Z. (2014). Household registration, occupational segregation and income inequality in urban China. *Chinese Social Sciences, 6*, 118–140.

Wei, H. (2016). Situations and promotions on the urban-rural registration system integration strategies under the new-normal economy. *Chinese Rural Economy, 1*, 2–16 (In Chinese).

Wu, X., & Xie, Y. (2003). Does the market pay off? Earnings returns education in urban China. *American Sociological Review, 68*(3), 425–442.

Wu, X., & Zhang, Z. (2014). Household registration, occupational segregation and income inequality in urban China. *Chinese Social Sciences, 6*, 118–140 (In Chinese).

Xie, S., & Yao, X. (2006). Econometric analysis on the wage discrimination against migrants. *Chinese Rural Economics, 4*, 39–55 (In Chinese).

Xing, C. (2008). Income inequality between migrants and urban residents. *Management World, 5*, 55–64 (In Chinese).

Xing, C., & Luo, C. (2009). Income inequality between migrants and urban residents: A semi-parameter analysis. *The Journal of Quantitative & Technical Economics, 10*, 74–86 (In Chinese).

Ye, L., Li, S., & Luo, C. (2011). Industrial monopoly, ownership and enterprises wage inequality: An empirical research based on the first national economic census of enterprises data. *Management World, 4*, 26–36 (In Chinese).

Yu, X., & Chen, X. (2012). Empirical research on the effect of the household registration system evolvement on labor market segmentation in China: From dual perspectives of employment opportunities and wage gap. *Economic Research, 12*, 97–110 (In Chinese).

Zhang, D., & Guo, Z. (2014). Industry segmentation, job segregation and wage gaps by registration system. *Agriculture Technical Economic, 5*, 30–41 (In Chinese).

Zhang, J., & Xue, X. (2008). State and non-state sector wage differentials and human capital contribution. *Economic Research, 4*, 15–25 (In Chinese).

Zhang, L., Li, S., Darity Jr., W. A., & Sharpe, R. V. (2014). Wage discrimination by registration in Chinese labor market. *Management World, 11*, 35–46 (In Chinese).

Zhang, Y. (2012). The change of income differentials between public and non-public sector in China. *Economic Research, 4*, 77–88 (In Chinese).

Zhang, Z. (2003). Labor market. *Chinese Journal of Population Science, 4*, 45–62 (In Chinese).

Zhu, R. (2016). Wage differentials between urban residents and rural migrants in urban China during 2002–2007: A distributional analysis. *Chinese Economic Review, 3*, 2–1.

CHAPTER 5

Labor Market Segmentation by Public-Private Sector and Its Influence on Gender Wage Gap

5.1 Introduction

The increase in income inequality has become a serious social problem during the economic transition period. There have been many studies on the issue, such as those of Zhao et al. (1996) and Li et al. (2008, 2013, 2017). The study of wage gaps is one of great significance to income inequality because wages are the largest share of the income. There exists a variety of wage gaps in China. For example, Chap. 3 analyzed the wage gaps between public sector and private sector, and Chap. 4 investigated the wage gaps between migrants and local urban residents. Currently, the gender wage gap has also become significant.

Why does the issue on gender wage gap attract concern now? There are two significant reasons. First, the widening gender wage gap contributes to greater income inequality. Second, from the 1980s the gender wage gap expanded with institutional reforms (Gustafsson and Li 2000; Ma 2009a; Li et al. 2011). Based on data from the third Chinese Female Social Status Survey (CFSSS) conducted by the National Female Federation (NFF), the gender wage gap (the ratio of female wage to male wage) in the urban region increased from 77.5% (1990) to 63.7% (2010). Thus it can be con-

This chapter is a revised version of Ma, X. (2018). Ownership Sector Segmentation and Gender Wage Gaps in Urban China during the 2000s. *Post-Communist Economies*, June 2008, 1–30. Copyright ©: Taylor & Francis Ltd.

X. Ma, *Economic Transition and Labor Market Reform in China*,
https://doi.org/10.1007/978-981-13-1987-7_5

sidered a quasi-natural experiment model for a study on the influences of policies or systems change on the gender wage gap. In addition, as it is analyzed in Chap. 2, the labor market in China is segmented by the public sector and the private sector (Chen et al. 2005; Demurger et al. 2007; Luo and Li 2007; Zhang and Xue 2008; Ye et al. 2011; Demurger et al. 2012; Ma 2009a, 2014, 2015, 2016). The expansion of the gender wage gaps in urban China can be explained in many ways; however, labor market segmentation by ownership types may be a significant factor which influences the gender wage gap. For example, it is thought the gender wage gap is smaller for the public sector than the private sector; when the proportion of workers in the public sector differs by gender, the gender wage gap may appear. However, there is no detailed empirical study about the influence of labor market segmentation by ownership sectors on gender wage gaps in the 2000s, a period in which the Chinese government enforced the transition to a market-based economy. This chapter focuses on the issue and provides the new evidence on gender wage gaps in China.

This chapter is structured as follows. Section 5.2 introduces the changing gender gap in urban China. Section 5.3 summarizes economic theory about the gender gap, and previous empirical studies on the issue. Section 5.4 describes the methods of analysis, including introduction to models and data. Section 5.5 states and interprets the econometric results. Section 5.6 presents the main conclusions.

5.2 Changes in Gender Equality Policy and the Gender Wage Gap in Urban China During the Economic Transition Period

To place this study in context there follows a review of the change of the gender equality policies and the gender wage gap in urban China. In the planned economy period, the government implemented the "socialism reconstruction" campaign. By the 1960s all privately owned enterprises (POEs) and foreign-owned enterprises (FOEs) were reformed into state-owned enterprises (SOEs) or collectively owned enterprises (COEs), comprising the "the public sector" ("*Gongyouzhi Bumen*"). In the public sector, the Chinese government controlled the number of workers and wage level and implemented a long-term employment system and seniority wage system. In order to enforce communist policy, the government implemented policies to promote female employment and gender equality. The government controlled employment and wage determination, and although wage level determination and promotion did not obey the market mechanism, wage distribution was relatively equal, and the gender gap in employment and wage in urban China was small (Gustafsson and Li 2000; Liu et al. 2000; Maurer-Fazio and Hughes 2002; Ma 2009b, 2011).

Conversely, from the 1980s, the Chinese government implemented reforms of the economic system, for example the SOEs reform. These reforms had an indirect effect on the expansion of the gender wage gap. How did reform of the economic system affect the gender wage gap? Three key reasons should be discussed. First, reform of SOEs may affect the gender wage gap. The reform allowed most SOEs to expand management authority: they could decide the wage level and individual bonus based on the firm's total wage account. The government determined the firm's total wage account based on the production plan which was set by agreement in the previous year; a firm could retain the excess above the production plan target as the firm's saving; the reserved firm's saving could be used to pay the worker's bonus. The reform motivated SOEs to increase their productivity, and therefore it promoted the SOEs to pay more to highly productive workers (a highly skilled or highly educated worker). Thus when labor productivity is higher for the male group than for the female group, the gender wage gap may increase as a result of the SOEs reform. In addition, in SOEs, the long-term employment system was replaced by the labor contract system from 1986 and employment system reform in SOEs was enforced from the end of the 1990s. Appleton et al. (2002), Knight and Li (2006), and Ma (2008) found that the risk of retrenchment was higher and reemployment rates lower for the female group; the average wage of reemployed workers was lower for the female group than for the male group in the SOEs. Moreover, a section of small and middle-sized SOEs and COEs changed their ownership types to the POEs from the 1980s.

Second, the government implemented the open economy policy from the 1980s. China joined the World Trade Organization (WTO) in 2001 and this led to a significant increase in FOEs in China. POEs and self-employment was permitted by the government from the 1990s. Firms in the private sector (FOEs, POEs, self-employed sector) face a competitive market and therefore determine the wage based on the market mechanism. As a result the wage level is determined by a worker's productivity. The competitive market may decrease discrimination against female workers. However, because the employer in the private sector can decide a worker's wage by himself, it is possible that discrimination against female workers can occur more easily in the private sector than in the public sector. Although some empirical studies show that the gender wage gap differs between the public sector and the private sector, the results are not consistent. For example, Ma (2009a) utilized CHIPs 1995 and CHIPs 2002 data to conduct an empirical study, and found that in all ownership sectors the gender wage gap increased from 1995 to 2002: the gender wage gap is greater for the private/foreign sector than that of the SOEs in 2002. In contrast, Guo and Zhang (2010) utilized Labor Survey data from 2006 for the Northeast region to analyze the gender wage gap in the public sector and the private sector; they argued that the gender wage gap is greater for the public sector than for the private sector. Thus a more detailed empirical study is needed.

Third, the Chinese government introduced a number of new policies and regulations from the 1980s in order to address the gender gap in labor markets. For example, the central government implemented a compulsory education policy, and increased public education subsidies to poorer rural regions. These policies may have decreased the gender education gap, which is considered to be "discrimination before entry to the labor market". For example, based on the third CWSSS data (Chinese Women's Social Status Survey), the gender gap of years of schooling decreased from 1.9 years in 1990 (male 6.6 years, female 4.7 years) to 0.3 years in 2010 (male 9.1 years, female 8.8 years). In addition, the Labor Law ("*Laodong Fa*") was published in 1995, and the Labor Contract Policy ("*Laodong Hetong Fa*") was promulgated in 2008; these labor policies protect the right of both male and female groups, and promote the equality of employment and wage for both male and female groups. Local government also promulgated a policy to promote the equality of employment and wages between these two groups. For example, Shenzhen city government (in Guangdong province) implemented a policy named "*Gender Equality Promotion Law in the Economy Special Zone*" in June 2012. This is the first law for gender equality introduced in China. These positive policies may influence the employment and wage gap between the male and female groups in China.

5.3 The Channel of the Influence of Ownership Sector on Gender Wage Gap and Empirical Study on the Issue

5.3.1 *General Economic Theories to Explain the Influence of Ownership Sector on Gender Wage Gap in Urban China*

What causes the gender wage gap in urban China? Some economic theories may explain it. First, based on the employer discrimination hypothesis (Becker, 1957), discrimination against female workers may be shown by employers, customers, and colleagues: this discrimination causes the gender wage gap. To consider the situation in China, compared with the public sector (government organizations, SOEs), in the private sector (COEs, POEs, FOEs), an employer's influence on employee wage determination is greater. As a result of gender discrimination by the employer, the gender wage gap may be higher in the private sector than the public sector.

Second, the statistics discrimination hypothesis (Arrow 1972, 1973; Phelps 1972) suggests that because the employer cannot have perfect information about the employees, he has to make the decision on employment and wage for a male or female worker based on the average values of some factors which are not observed in the present (work effort, possibility of turnover). When the employer predicts that the probability to do more housework (child care, family care, home cleaning, cooking) is greater for the female group than for the male group, he may set a lower wage level for the female group.

Third, based on human capital theory (Becker 1964; Mincer 1974), in the perfectly competitive labor market, the individual wage level is determined by a worker's labor productivity. Labor productivity is in relation to a worker's human capital (e.g., education, experience, health status). With economic development, workers moved from the rural regions to the urban regions, and they are employed in the manufacturing industry, in which both physical strength and skill are needed (Lewis 1954; Minami and Ma 2010, 2014). Men may be stronger and have a better education than women. In addition, because of gender role segregation (e.g. men for work, women for child and family) in households, the labor supply (e.g. labor force participation and working hours) is less for women. Thus, the men can obtain higher wages than women. Because the POEs and FOEs operate in a competitive market, they may determine the wage based on the market mechanism, which means the wage is determined by a worker's productivity. Thus, with the human capital factor being constant, the gender wage gap may be lower in the private sector than in the public sector.

Lastly, the labor market segmentation hypotheses may explain the existence of gender wage gaps. For example, Piore (1970) suggests that the labor market is not a perfect competitive market; it is segmented by the primary market in which the wage level is higher and secondary market in which the wage level is lower. Thus when the male group concentrates in the primary market (the public sector), and the female group concentrates in the secondary market (the private sector), the gender wage gap may appear.

5.3.2 *How Do the Ownership Sectors Affect the Gender Wage Gap in Urban China?*

How does labor market segmentation by various ownership sectors affect the gender wage gap? Based on the ideas of Brown et al. (1980),[1] the influences of segmentation by ownership types on gender wage gap can be divided into four parts as follows.

First, in a given sector (e.g. public sector or private sector), the wage may differ between the male and female groups. This is designated as an intra-sector differential.

Second, the opportunity of entry to various ownership sectors may differ between male and female groups, which can cause proportion differentials by ownership types between male and female groups. If the proportion of workers in the private sector, in which the average wage level is lower than that in the public sector, is greater for the female group than for the male group, a wage gap will thus be created. The wage gap caused by the gender differences in the opportunity for entry to various ownership sectors is designated as an inter-sector differential.

Third, in both inter-sector differential and intra-sector differential, based on Blinder (1973) and Oaxaca (1973), two causes of the wage gap are pointed out: first the explained components (differentials based on individual characteristics such as human capital), and second the unexplained components (the discrimination against female workers).[2] For example, in the intra-sector differential, in a given sector (e.g. POEs), the employer held greater authority to determine the wage level than the employer in the public sector. Based on the employer discrimination hypothesis (Becker 1957), when an employer discriminates against the female group, even though the human capital of the female group is constant with the male group, the gender wage gap may appear (a case of unexplained components in the intra-sector differential). When the education level is lower for female workers than for male workers, even though there is no discrimination against female workers, due to the market mechanism, female workers may earn less than male workers (a case of explained components in the intra-sector differential). In the inter-sector differential, when discrimination against female workers (a case of unexplained components) and gender differentials of human capital (a case of explained components) occur together, the chances of entry to various ownership sectors will be different for male and female groups, which also causes a gender wage gap.

Thus, the effect of labor market segmentation by various ownership sectors can be divided into four parts: (i) the explained component in intra-sector differential; (ii) the unexplained component in intra-sector differential; (iii) the explained component in inter-sector differential; and (iv) the unexplained component in inter-sector differential.

5.3.3 *Empirical Studies on the Gender Wage Gap in Urban China*

The empirical studies on the gender wage gap in urban China, Gustafsson and Li (2000), Liu et al. (2000), Ma (2007a, b, 2009b, 2011), Li and Yang (2010), Li et al. (2011), Yang (2012); Ma et al. (2013), and Zhao (2014), use the Blinder–Oaxaca model (Blinder 1973; Oaxaca 1973), the Oaxaca and Ransom (1994) model, or the Melly (2006) model to employ the decomposition analysis. They point out that both the explained differentials and the unexplained differentials affect the gender wage gap. Comparison of the influences between these two parts, in most of the studies, shows the influence of the unexplained differentials is greater than that for the explained differentials. Thus it is indicated that discrimination against female workers is the main reason that causes the gender wage gaps in China. The influence of unexplained differentials for the local urban residents group is 52.49% in 1988, 63.20% in 1995 (Gustafsson and Li 2000); 44.2–49.3% in 1995, 51.0–58.0% in 2002 (Ma 2009b); and 52.0% in 1995, 69.0% in 2002, and 77.7% in 2007 (Li et al. 2011). The value for migrants is 74.32–84.38% in 2008 (Li and Yang 2010), and the value for the local urban residents and migrants is 49.18% in 1996 (Meng and Zhang 2001). In addition, the values are 86.08–101.80% in 2006 and 45.31–91.73% in 2009 by wage percentiles (Ma et al. 2013).

There are many empirical studies on the effect of labor market segmentation by sectors on gender wage gaps in China.[3] Wang (2005), Li and Ma (2006), Ma (2007a, b), and Yao and Huang (2008) analyze the influence of occupational segregation on gender wage gaps. Wang (2005), Ge (2007), and Wang and Cai (2008) analyze the influences of segmentation by industry sector on gender wage gap. All these studies use the Brown et al. (1980) decomposition model (which may be abbreviated as "Brown et al. model"). It indicates that the unexplained component in the intra-sector differentials is the main reason for the gender wage gap.

However, previous studies on the effect of labor market segmentation by various ownership sectors on gender wage gaps are inconclusive. Even though Liu et al. (2000), Maurer-Fazio and Hughes (2002), Demurger et al. (2007), and Guo and Zhang (2010) use the Blinder–Oaxaca model to decompose the factors affecting the gender wage gaps in the public and private sectors separately, it is not clear how the intra-sector differentials and the inter-sector differentials affect gender wage gap. Moreover, we do not know how the influence of these factors changes with institutional reform as described in Sect. 5.2.

This chapter investigates the following four questions using two period repeated cross-section survey data (CHIPs 2002 and CHIPs 2013). First, how do intra-sector differentials and inter-sector differentials affect the wage gap? Second, how is the wage gap affected by discrimination against women that arises when a female worker wants to enter the public sector or private sector, as well as by discrimination against women that exists within the same ownership sector? Third, to consider the intra-sector differentials and inter-sector differentials, how do unexplained components and explained components affect the gender wage gap? Finally, do these factors change from 2002 to 2013? This is believed to be the first study to investigate the effect of labor market segmentation by ownership types on the gender wage gap and compare the influence change of these factors during the 2000s in urban China. These results are an original contribution to knowledge.

5.4 Methodology and Data

5.4.1 Model

The OLS model is used when other factors, for example years of schooling, are consistent, to estimate how labor market segmentation by ownership types affects the male and female wage levels. It is expressed as Eq. (5.1a).[4]

$$\ln W_i = \alpha + \beta_X X_i + \beta_O \mathrm{OWN} + u_i \tag{5.1a}$$

The Heckman two-step model (Heckman 1979) is used to address the sample selection bias problem (a worker can choose to work or not) found in the OLS model. On the basis of the estimated results of the distribution function and the density function by the probit regression model (the dependent variable is $Pr(\Upsilon_i = 1)$ which indicates probability of the choice to work), selectivity items ($\lambda = \psi(\cdot)/\Phi(\cdot)$) are calculated. The probit regression model includes the identification variables. The corrected wage functions expressed by Eqs. (5.1b and 5.1c) are estimated using these selectivity items.

$$\ln W_i = \alpha + \beta_M \text{Male}_i + \beta_O \text{OWN}_i + \beta_X X_i + \beta_\lambda \lambda_i + u_i \quad (5.1b)$$

$$\ln W_{ij} = \alpha_j + \beta_{oj} \text{OWN}_{ij} + \beta_{Xj} X_{ij} + \beta_{\lambda j} \lambda_{ij} + u_{ij} \quad \left(j : \text{male, female}\right) \quad (5.1c)$$

In Eqs. (5.1a–5.1c), i represents the individual and j represents the male or female worker. ln W is the logarithm of the average wage, X represents factors (e.g. years of schooling, experience years, industry and occupation dummy variables) which affect wage, OWN is ownership sector dummy, α is a constant item and u is a random error item. The results from Eq. (5.1b) indicate the overall influences of segmentation by ownership sectors on wage for the total sample, and the results from Eq. (5.1c) show the influence for male and female groups separately.

Next, the Brown et al. model is used to decompose the influence factors of segmentation by ownership type on gender wage gaps.[5] The model is expressed as follows.

First the imputed probabilities of entry to ownership sectors are estimated based on a multinomial logit regression model, and then the wage functions by the sector categories are estimated. Considering the sample selection bias problem in Eq. (5.1a), the sample selection bias corrected wage function model is proposed (Maddala 1983), which is expressed by Eq. (5.2).

$$\ln W_{iK} = \alpha_K + \beta_{KX} X_{iK} + \beta_{K\delta} \delta_{iK} + u_{iK} \quad (5.2)$$

In Eq. (5.2), the estimated results of the distribution function and the density function by the probit regression model are used (in which P_{iK} = Prob(y_{ik} = Sector$_{ik}$)) indicates the probability of entry to a sector). The selectivity items ($\delta = \psi(\cdot)/\Phi(\cdot)$) for various ownership types are calculated. Third, the estimated results based on the imputed probabilities of entry to various sectors, wage functions by ownership types, and the mean values of variables are used to decompose the influences of segmentation by ownership types on gender wage gap into four types of cause. The decomposition contents are shown in Eq. (5.3).

$$
\begin{aligned}
\ln W_m - \ln W_f = & \sum P_k^f \beta_k^m \left(X_k^m - X_k^f \right) \quad (\mathrm{A}) \\
& + \sum P_k^f \left(\alpha_k^m - \alpha_k^f \right) + \sum P_k^f X_k^f \left(\beta_k^m - \beta_k^f \right) \quad (\mathrm{B}) \\
& + \sum W_k^m \left(P_k^m - P_k^{*f} \right) \quad (\mathrm{C}) \\
& + \sum W_k^u \left(P_k^{*f} - P_k^m \right) \quad (\mathrm{D})
\end{aligned}
\tag{5.3}
$$

In Eq. (5.3), P_k^m, P_k^f represent the actual proportions of female and male groups, $\hat{P}_k^f$ are the imputed proportions of female group, X_k^m, X_k^f represent mean values of variables, and β_k^m, β_k^f are the parameters estimated based on wage functions by sector categories.

Then, first, in order to see the econometric meanings of decomposition results by Eq. (5.3), the following were applied. First, $\sum P_k^f \beta_k^m \left(X_k^m - X_k^f \right)$ (A) represents the individual characteristic differentials between male and female groups in a given sector (the explained component in intra-sector differentials); $\sum P_k^f \left(\alpha_k^m - \alpha_k^f \right) + \sum P_k^f X_k^f \left(\beta_k^m - \beta_k^f \right)$ (B) represents the unexplained component (the discriminations against female workers in the same sector) in a given sector (the explained component in intra-sector differentials); $\sum W_k^m \left(P_k^m - P_k^{*f} \right)$ (C) represents the individual characteristic differentials between male and female workers which determine the chance (probability) of entry to various ownership sectors (the explained component in inter-sector differentials); $\sum W_k^u \left(P_k^{*f} - P_k^m \right)$ (D) represents the unexplained component (the discrimination against female workers) when they enter a sector (the unexplained components in inter-sector differentials).

Second, the total value of (A) and (B) represents the total intra-sector differential, and the total value of (C) and (D) represents the total inter-sector differential.

Third, the total value of (B) and (C) represents the total unexplained differential caused by discrimination when female workers enter a sector, or when the female workers work together with the male workers in the same sector. The total value of (A) and (D) represents the total explained differential.

5.4.2 *Data*

The survey data of CHIPs 2002 and CHIPs 2013 is used for the analysis. The data was compiled by Economic Institute of Chinese Academy of Social Science (CASS) and Beijing Normal University in 2003 and 2014, which is similar to that in Chap. 4 of this book.

The analytic objects of this chapter are workers, and the sample selection bias for the choice of work or non-work is considered in the study, and the working and non-working individual samples are analyzed. In considering the retirement system implemented in the public sector, the analytic objects are limited to groups aged 16 to 60. All the no answer samples, abnormal value samples,[6] and missing value samples are deleted.

In order to reveal the dependent variables setting, the following steps were taken (see Table 5.1). First, in the probability function of entry to sectors, the dependent variable is a category variable. To maintain the analysis samples by each ownership sector and consider the feature of each sector, based on the CHIPs 2013 questionnaire, the sectors are divided into seven categories: (i) the group in the public organization, which includes the government organizations and the public organizations, which is defined as the work units relation with the government named as *Shiye Danwei* (Government organizations); (ii) the group in the SOEs; (iii) the group in the collectively owned enterprises (COEs); (iv) the group in the privately owned enterprises and foreign-owned enterprises, (POEs/FOEs);[7] (v) the group in the self-employed sector (Self-employed); (vi) the group in other ownerships sector which is not included in (i)–(v) (Others); and (vii) the non-working group.

Next, in the wage function, the dependent variable is the logarithm of wage rate. Wage rates are calculated by total annual wage divided by annual work hours. Consumption price index (CPI) in 2002 is used as the standard to adjust the nominal wage in every year. The wage is defined as the total earnings from work (called "the total wage"). Here, it comprises the basic wage, bonus, and subsidy, which is calculated based on market prices. Annual work hours are calculated by "work hours daily × work day monthly × work months yearly".

The independent variables are the variables likely to affect the wage level and the probability of entry to sectors as follows. First, age, years of schooling, experience years,[8] and health status (if the answer is "very

Table 5.1 Statistics description for 2002 and 2013

	Male						*Female*					
	Pub.	*SOE*	*COE*	*Pri.*	*Self.*	*Others*	*Pub.*	*SOE*	*COE*	*Pri.*	*Self.*	*Others*
Panel A: 2002												
ln wage rate	1.894	1.633	1.252	1.547	1.050	1.314	1.758	1.460	1.144	1.371	0.758	1.217
Age	42	42	43	39	39	39	39	39	40	36	37	41
Experience years	29	31	32	28	29	28	27	28	30	25	28	30
Years of schooling	13	11	10	11	10	11	13	11	10	11	10	11
Health	72.8%	69.4%	65.4%	66.1%	72.7%	78.9%	67.4%	64.9%	67.5%	63.9%	67.4%	63.0%
Han race	95.1%	96.5%	96.9%	97.0%	93.8%	93.3%	95.0%	96.7%	93.4%	96.6%	94.8%	97.9%
Married	91.5%	89.9%	90.9%	83.4%	87.6%	83.3%	87.4%	90.1%	91.1%	77.5%	85.5%	80.8%
Occupation category												
Manager	26.5%	14.2%	15.4%	9.2%	41.3%	7.8%	9.2%	4.3%	5.0%	4.2%	41.0%	4.1%
Technician	29.3%	14.2%	14.0%	14.1%	3.9%	11.1%	34.8%	23.0%	15.2%	17.9%	3.2%	25.3%
Manufacturing worker	30.3%	17.8%	14.7%	19.4%	4.8%	13.3%	39.5%	19.3%	15.7%	17.5%	2.6%	4.8%
Clerical staff	11.3%	48.4%	43.7%	42.5%	23.2%	16.7%	9.1%	36.8%	40.2%	32.3%	8.1%	6.2%
Others	2.6%	5.4%	12.2%	14.8%	26.8%	51.1%	7.4%	16.6%	23.9%	28.1%	45.1%	59.6%
Industry category												
Cons. & Manu.	1.2%	48.1%	54.5%	52.9%	16.3%	11.1%	1.0%	44.3%	47.0%	46.8%	6.7%	9.6%
Retail	0.9%	6.7%	13.6%	14.8%	41.7%	18.9%	0.9%	13.4%	15.2%	24.6%	57.3%	10.3%
Service	8.2%	4.9%	11.5%	11.6%	18.8%	28.9%	15.1%	8.5%	18.4%	10.0%	27.3%	50.7%
Others	89.7%	40.3%	20.4%	20.7%	23.2%	41.1%	83.0%	33.8%	19.4%	18.6%	8.7%	29.4%
Region category												
East	31.6%	39.4%	47.9%	45.5%	45.0%	41.1%	32.0%	37.0%	48.6%	44.9%	42.4%	63.7%
Central	38.4%	36.8%	28.3%	31.0%	31.0%	32.2%	38.1%	36.7%	27.6%	28.5%	29.4%	18.5%
West	30.0%	23.8%	23.8%	23.5%	24.0%	26.7%	29.1%	26.3%	23.8%	26.6%	28.2%	17.7%
Observations	1,652	2,207	286	758	436	90	1,371	1,292	381	613	344	146

(*continued*)

Table 5.1 (continued)

	Male						*Female*					
	Pub.	*SOE*	*COE*	*Pri.*	*Self.*	*Others*	*Pub.*	*SOE*	*COE*	*Pri.*	*Self.*	*Others*
Panel B: 2013												
ln wage rate	2.618	2.559	2.372	2.384	2.243	2.131	2.415	2.381	2.103	2.146	1.869	1.889
Age	43	42	43	39	42	44	40	40	40	38	41	43
Experience years	24	24	25	22	26	28	20	21	23	20	25	27
Years of schooling	14	12	11	12	10	10	14	13	11	12	10	10
Health	83.4%	80.7%	80.4%	83.0%	82.2%	77.7%	82.1%	82.3%	78.6%	85.9%	79.0%	75.1%
Han race	94.6%	96.9%	96.2%	95.9%	94.4%	93.0%	94.9%	97.3%	96.0%	95.3%	94.0%	93.0%
Married	92.6%	85.1%	89.8%	81.1%	88.6%	87.3%	88.2%	84.2%	88.6%	82.7%	89.0%	88.9%
Occupation category												
Manager	10.4%	5.0%	3.8%	6.1%	4.3%	2.6%	6.6%	4.2%	3.0%	4.0%	3.8%	1.8%
Technician	38.9%	11.4%	9.8%	9.1%	1.6%	7.8%	31.7%	16.4%	13.9%	13.8%	2.2%	13.7%
Manufacturing worker	9.2%	14.2%	8.1%	8.0%	2.3%	2.6%	11.0%	18.6%	9.5%	7.4%	1.8%	3.6%
Clerical staff	3.0%	43.9%	32.8%	33.6%	19.6%	16.9%	1.4%	22.6%	19.4%	21.7%	8.7%	6.5%
Others	38.5%	25.1%	45.5%	43.2%	72.2%	70.1%	49.3%	38.2%	54.2%	53.1%	83.5%	74.4%
Industry category												
Cons. & Manu.	1.5%	30.1%	30.2%	40.7%	16.5%	19.0%	0.2%	23.7%	24.9%	30.0%	6.5%	7.5%
Retail.	1.1%	4.0%	9.8%	14.1%	38.1%	9.4%	1.9%	10.6%	15.9%	29.3%	57.8%	11.1%
Service	7.2%	9.2%	23.0%	21.6%	21.9%	29.4%	10.0%	14.7%	28.4%	23.4%	24.9%	37.6%
Others	90.2%	56.7%	37.0%	23.6%	23.5%	42.2%	87.9%	51.0%	30.8%	17.3%	10.8%	43.8%
Region category												
East	37.7%	34.6%	52.8%	50.3%	35.8%	44.7%	38.8%	37.5%	53.7%	49.8%	35.0%	44.3%
Central	39.4%	46.7%	26.4%	28.6%	40.3%	28.1%	38.3%	42.8%	28.9%	28.0%	35.9%	27.5%
West	22.9%	18.7%	20.8%	21.2%	23.9%	27.2%	22.9%	19.7%	17.4%	22.2%	29.1%	28.2%
Observations	1,269	1,022	235	1,404	957	385	1,012	549	201	1,203	846	386

Source (Panel A): Calculated based on CHIPs 2002

Source (Panel B): Calculated based on CHIPs 2013

good" or "good", it is equal to 1, otherwise it is equal to 0) are used as the indices of human capital. It is thought that these factors may affect the wage or the probability of entry to various ownership sectors. Second, considering marital status (married is equal to 1, otherwise 0), and race (Han race is equal to 1, minority is equal to 0) might affect the probability of entry to sector or wage levels, these dummy variables are used. Third, it is thought occupation influences the wage for male and female workers. Occupation dummy variables (manager, professional worker and technician, production worker, clerical staff, others) are constructed. Fourth, because wage gaps occur by industries, industry dummy variables are used. To maintain the analysis samples by each industry category, the industrial categories[9] are reclassified. Five kinds of industries, construction, manufacturing, retail and wholesale industries, service, and other industries, are used to construct the industry dummy variables. Fifth, because the regional disparity for economic development levels and the labor markets are different by region, East, Central, and West regions dummy variables are used to control these influences.

5.5 Econometric Analysis Results

5.5.1 *How Do the Ownership Sectors Affect Wage Levels?*

When other factors including ownership types are constant, does a gender wage gap exist? Does the gender wage gap differ by ownership types? To answer these questions wage functions are estimated by using the total sample and subsample of various ownership sectors; the results are shown in Tables 5.2 and 5.3. The Heckman two-step model is used to correct the sample selection bias caused by the choice of work or non-work in these analyses.

The main findings are as follows. First, when other factors are constant, the logarithm of wage rate of male group is 5.9% (2002), and 18.5% (2013) higher than for the female group (Table 5.2). The results show that the gender wage gap existed in both 2002 and 2013, and the gender wage gap expanded from 2002 to 2013.

Next, the gender wage gap differs by various sectors, and the wage gap changed from 2002 to 2013 in all sectors (Table 5.3). In Table 5.3, the coefficient of the male dummy variable in wage function is utilized as an index of the gender wage gap. When the coefficient is a positive value and

Table 5.2 Results of wage function for 2002 and 2013

	2002		*2013*	
	Coef.	*t-value*	*Coef.*	*t-value*
Male	0.059***	3.67	0.185***	9.76
Ownership types (government organization)				
SOEs	−0.082***	−4.65	0.086***	3.41
COEs	−0.385***	−13.76	−0.051	−1.33
POEs	−0.094***	−4.11	0.011	0.44
Self-employed	−0.564***	−19.81	−0.012	−0.43
Others	−0.324***	−7.79	−0.143***	−4.47
Inverse Mill's ratio	−0.146***	−3.59	−0.141***	−2.98
Constant	0.817***	6.79	1.165***	11.42
Total observations	14,607		13,549	
Censored observations	5,211		4,080	
Uncensored observations	9,396		9,469	
Wald chi2(19)	3928.230		1850.200	
Prob > chi2	0.000		0.000	

Source: Calculated based on CHIPs 2002 and CHIPs 2013

Note:

(1) *, **, ***: statistically significant levels are 10%, 5%, and 1%

(2) Calculated by Heckman two-step model

(3) Calculated by Heckman two-step model. Years of schooling, experience year, health, race, occupation, industry, and region dummy variables are calculated; these results are not expressed in Table 5.2

it is statistically significant at the 5% or 1% statistical level, it denotes that the gender wage gap is higher than that for the reference group. It is indicated that the gender wage gap in SOEs, POEs/FOEs, self-employed sector, and others sector is higher than that in public organizations in 2002. The gender wage gap in SOEs, COEs, POEs/FOEs, the self-employed sector, and others sector is higher than that in government organizations in 2013. The results show that the gender wage gap is higher in the private sector than that in the public sector in both 2002 and 2013, and the disparity of gender wage gaps between the public and private sector rose from 2002 to 2013. It is predicted that the difference of the proportions in various sectors between male and female groups contributes to the gender wage gap because the gender wage gap differs by types even though other factors are controlled.

Table 5.3 Estimated gender wage gap by ownership sectors for 2002 and 2013

	2002		*2013*	
	Coef.	*t-value*	*Coef.*	*t-value*
Results of male dummy variables				
Public sector	0.051***	2.59	0.145***	5.59
SOE	0.110***	5.05	0.188***	5.20
COE	0.044	0.85	0.294***	4.18
Private sector	0.091**	2.55	0.214***	7.58
Self-employed sector	0.196***	3.53	0.304***	7.64
Others	0.238**	2.19	0.219***	3.81

Sources: Calculated based on CHIPs 2002 and CHIPs 2013

Note:

(1) *, **, ***: statistically significant levels are 10%, 5%, and 1%

(2) Calculated by Heckman two-step model

(3) Calculated by Heckman two-step model. years of schooling, experience year, health, race, occupation, industry, region dummy variables, and selectivity items are calculated; these results are not shown in Table 5.3

5.5.2 *How Does the Segmentations by Ownership Type Affect Gender Wage Gap?*

Wage functions by ownership type are estimated using the Brown et al. decomposition model. The results are shown in Tables 5.4A and 5.4B. These results are used to make the decomposition analysis.

The imputed values are summarized in Table 5.5. These results for 2002 show that if there is no discrimination against female groups then the proportion of female workers in government organizations, COEs, POEs/FOEs, and self-employed sectors will increase, whereas the proportion in SOEs and others sector will decrease. In 2013 the proportion of female workers in SOEs, COEs, and POEs/FOEs will increase, whereas the proportion in government organizations, self-employed sector, and the others sector will decrease. The proportion of female workers is greater in the public sector (government organizations or SOEs). This indicates that a female worker is appreciated when she enters the public sector, whereas discrimination against the female group exists in the private sector. The results reveal that there may be an irrational allocation of male and female workers in all sectors. These results may be explained as follows. In the public sector, employment is controlled by the government, particularly in public organizations. Governmental employment equality

Table 5.4A Results of wage function by ownership types (2002)

	Government		*SOEs*		*COEs*		*POEs*		*Self-employed*	
	Coeff.	t-*value*	*Coeff.*	t-*value*	*Coeff.*	t-*value*	*Coeff.*	t-*value*	*Coeff.*	t-*value*
2002: Male										
Years of schooling	−0.025	−1.35	0.050***	7.52	0.046	1.07	0.073	5.5	0.077**	2.51
Experience years	0.004	0.34	0.027**	2.34	0.031	0.86	0.005	0.3	0.015	0.62
Experience years squared	0.000	0.75	0.000*	−1.67	0.000	−0.57	0.000	0.84	0.000	−0.32
Health	−0.057*	−1.81	−0.036	−1.28	0.076	0.89	−0.016	−0.32	0.052	0.64
Han race	0.096*	1.62	−0.079	−1.13	0.058	0.24	−0.080	−0.59	0.173	1.16
Occupation (Clerical staff)										
Manager	0.144***	4.19	0.112**	2.35	0.015	0.10	0.235**	2.42	0.094	0.50
Technician	0.142***	4.37	0.093**	2.08	0.032	0.22	0.224***	2.76	0.296	1.24
Manufacturing worker	−0.054	−1.20	−0.078**	−1.98	−0.069	−0.55	0.008	0.11	−0.088	−0.47
Others	−0.300***	−3.67	−0.278***	−4.19	−0.337**	−2.02	−0.034	−0.38	−0.092	−0.48
Industries (Cons. & Manu.)										
Retail/catering	−0.309*	−1.93	−0.168***	−6.23	−0.255***	−2.68	−0.106*	−1.81	−0.068	−0.56
Service	−0.291**	−2.19	−0.177***	−3.21	−0.310**	−2.16	−0.127	−1.56	−0.273***	−2.99
Other	−0.002	−0.04	−0.080	−1.32	−0.198	−1.35	−0.202**	−2.47	−0.224**	−2.08
Region (East)										
Central	−0.508***	−13.21	−0.368***	−12.61	−0.363**	−1.99	−0.459***	−8.1	−0.330***	−3.59
West	−0.471***	−9.46	−0.250***	−7.20	−0.302**	−2.08	−0.466***	−7.9	−0.429***	−4.37
Correction item	−2.439***	−4.13	−1.093*	−1.79	−3.561	−0.40	−2.013	−1.31	−2.222	−1.09
Constant	3.636***	4.92	1.630***	3.19	3.186	0.47	2.103	1.57	1.785	1.32
Observations	1652		2027		286		758		436	
Adj R-squared	0.251		0.195		0.129		0.258		0.130	
2002: Female										
Years of schooling	0.036**	1.98	0.056***	6.31	0.043*	1.63	0.068***	3.93	−0.012	−0.22

(*continued*)

Table 5.4A (continued)

	Government		*SOEs*		*COEs*		*POEs*		*Self-employed*	
	Coeff.	*t-value*	*Coeff.*	*t-value*	*Coeff.*	*t-value*	*Coeff.*	*t-value*	*Coeff.*	*t-value*
Experience years	0.041***	3.46	0.033	1.52	0.015	0.40	0.005	0.26	0.075**	2.49
Experience years squared	0.000**	−2.25	0.000	−0.95	0.000	−0.05	0.000	0.62	−0.001**	−2.08
Health	−0.025	−0.77	−0.063*	−1.80	−0.016	−0.20	0.028	0.50	0.109	1.17
Han race	−0.002	−0.03	−0.159*	−1.62	−0.247	−1.35	−0.097	−0.67	0.001	0.01
Occupation (Clerical staff)										
Manager	0.101*	1.88	0.354***	4.04	0.063	0.38	0.130	0.91	−0.660***	−2.61
Technician	0.182***	5.38	0.001	0.02	0.243**	2.02	0.150*	1.70	−0.311	−0.91
Manufacturing worker	−0.081	−1.48	−0.092*	−1.94	−0.113	−1.06	−0.271***	−3.25	−0.640**	−2.20
Others	−0.240***	−3.91	−0.208***	−3.47	−0.213*	−1.94	−0.290***	−3.30	−0.674***	−2.71
Industries (Cons. & Manu.)										
Retail/catering	−0.197	−1.11	−0.145***	−3.69	−0.177**	−2.03	−0.062	−0.83	−0.357	−1.43
Service	−0.236	−1.59	−0.218***	−3.71	−0.159	−1.38	−0.054	−0.65	−0.429***	−2.85
Other	−0.157***	−3.69	−0.165**	−2.52	−0.232**	−2.08	−0.225**	−2.19	−0.348**	−2.16
Region (East)										
Central	−0.511***	−12.28	−0.429***	−10.90	−0.347***	−2.65	−0.461***	−6.93	−0.436***	−3.24
West	−0.373***	−7.83	−0.280***	−6.51	−0.144	−1.24	−0.426***	−6.62	−0.334***	−3.07
Correction item	−0.927	−1.56	−0.609	−0.66	1.308	0.35	−1.774	−1.02	5.832	1.15
Constant	1.446**	1.97	1.224	1.36	−0.109	−0.04	2.086	1.39	−3.217	−0.96
Observations	1371		1292		381		613		344	
Adj R-squared	0.290		0.203		0.126		0.264		0.098	

Source: Calculated based on CHIPs 2002

Note:

(1) *, **, ***: statistically significant levels are 10%, 5%, and 1%

(2) Wage function of Others group is also calculated, but the results are not shown in the table

Table 5.4B Results of wage function by ownership types (2013)

	Government		*SOEs*		*COEs*		*POEs*		*Self-employed*	
	Coeff.	t-*value*	*Coeff.*	t-*value*	*Coeff.*	t-*value*	*Coeff.*	t-*value*	*Coeff.*	t-*value*
2013: Male										
Years of schooling	0.139***	5.23	0.076***	5.50	0.069***	2.67	0.089***	10.67	0.102***	3.76
Experience years	0.057***	5.41	0.029***	2.83	0.017	0.74	0.032***	3.25	0.012	0.85
Experience years squared	−0.001***	−4.18	0.000**	−1.99	0.000	−0.78	0.000*	−1.84	0.000	−0.11
Health	0.035	0.76	0.168***	3.19	0.019	0.16	0.080	1.49	0.071	0.92
Han race	0.095	1.33	0.145	1.14	−0.266	−1.07	0.048	0.49	0.002	0.01
Occupation (Clerical staff)										
Manager	0.108*	1.93	0.068	0.62	0.140	0.50	0.222**	2.19	0.777***	3.25
Technician	0.027	0.46	0.280***	3.50	0.222	1.01	0.013	0.14	0.663**	2.51
Manufacturing worker	0.052	0.53	−0.083	−1.17	−0.163	−0.94	−0.282***	−3.73	0.436**	2.06
Others	−0.035	−0.95	−0.115	−1.60	−0.330**	−1.98	−0.251***	−3.50	0.390*	1.87
Industries (Cons. & Manu.)										
Retail/catering	−0.234	−1.16	−0.205*	−1.85	0.242	1.36	−0.090	−1.32	−0.294***	−3.31
Service	−0.168	−1.16	0.009	0.11	0.049	0.34	−0.094*	−1.64	−0.287***	−3.09
Other	−0.059	−0.44	0.096**	2.02	0.234**	1.99	0.002	0.04	−0.158*	−1.77
Region (East)										
Central	−0.274***	−5.41	−0.129	−1.59	0.069	0.33	−0.189***	−2.61	−0.095	−1.54
West	−0.154***	−2.77	−0.277***	−4.68	0.088	0.51	−0.148**	−2.52	−0.172*	−2.51
Correction item	1.180	1.59	0.572	0.44	−11.446	−1.10	−1.076	−0.79	−1.993*	−1.69
Constant	−0.761	−0.79	0.646	0.55	10.500	1.32	1.803*	1.89	2.086***	2.90
Observations	1269		1022		235		1404		957	
Adj R-squared	0.252		0.182		0.111		0.190		0.082	
2013: Female										
Years of schooling	0.018	0.68	0.067***	2.81	0.058**	2.37	0.086	9.62	0.001	0.03

(*continued*)

Table 5.4B (continued)

	Government		*SOEs*		*COEs*		*POEs*		*Self-employed*	
	Coeff.	*t-value*	*Coeff.*	*t-value*	*Coeff.*	*t-value*	*Coeff.*	*t-value*	*Coeff.*	*t-value*
Experience years	0.006	0.52	0.002	0.10	0.042	1.19	0.013	1.17	0.029	1.57
Experience years squared	0.000	0.09	0.000	0.51	−0.001	−0.98	0.000	−0.37	−0.001*	−1.78
Health	0.096*	1.82	−0.046	−0.59	−0.032	−0.24	0.206***	3.26	0.136*	1.82
Han race	0.113	1.24	−0.571***	−2.89	−0.097	−0.32	−0.079	−0.87	0.073	0.59
Occupation (Clerical staff)										
Manager	0.118	1.39	−0.052	−0.32	0.315	0.95	0.173	1.59	−0.099	−0.41
Technician	0.040	0.58	0.073	0.74	0.607***	2.68	−0.040	−0.46	−0.023	−0.08
Manufacturing worker	0.013	0.07	−0.113	−1.09	−0.048	−0.22	−0.112	−1.52	−0.413*	−1.84
Others	−0.066	−1.46	−0.152*	−1.73	−0.074	−0.48	−0.139**	−2.27	−0.239	−1.23
Industries (Cons. & Manu.)										
Retail/catering	−0.278	−0.59	−0.200*	−1.69	−0.032	−0.17	−0.135**	−2.14	−0.507***	−3.41
Service	−0.407	−0.90	0.081	0.76	0.216	1.25	−0.077	−1.23	−0.529***	−3.50
Other	−0.088	−0.20	0.085	1.04	−0.195	−1.23	0.041	0.62	−0.334**	−1.99
Region (east)										
Central	−0.296***	−5.19	−0.439***	−4.63	0.020	0.10	−0.229***	−3.61	−0.142**	−2.02
West	−0.293***	−4.89	−0.224***	−2.72	0.230	1.06	−0.170***	−3.01	0.018	0.23
Correction item	−2.211***	−3.12	−3.149	−1.28	−2.659	−0.21	−1.513	−1.24	1.554	0.97
Constant	3.551***	3.47	4.515*	1.95	3.089***	0.30	2.086**	2.28	1.197	1.19
Observations	1012		549		201		1203		846	
Adj R-squared	0.195		0.211		0.089		0.223		0.053	

Source: Calculated based on CHIPs 2013

Note:

(1) *, **, ***: statistically significant levels are 10%, 5%, and 1%

(2) Wage function of Others group is also calculated, but the results are not shown in the table

Table 5.5 Proportions of ownership types: actual values and imputed values

	Actual value		*Imputed value*	*Gaps*
	M (%)	*F (%)*	*F(I) (%)*	*(F(I) − F) (%)*
2002				
Government	31.4	33.0	40.8	7.8
SOEs	38.6	31.1	0.0	−31.1
COEs	5.5	9.1	10.8	1.7
POEs	14.3	14.8	28.9	14.1
Self-employed	8.5	8.5	16.1	7.6
Others	1.7	3.5	3.3	−0.2
2013				
Government	23.8	23.8	15.8	−8.0
SOEs	19.2	13.0	19.3	6.3
COEs	4.5	4.8	4.9	0.1
POEs	27.0	28.8	32.5	3.7
Self-employed	18.1	20.3	19.5	−0.8
Others	7.4	9.3	8.0	−1.3

Source: Calculated based on CHIPs 2002 and CHIPs 2013

policy was enforced in both the planned economy period and the economic transition period. Thus the proportion of female workers is greater in the public sector than the private sector. However, in the private sector, where the employer has authority to make discriminatory choices, according to the employer discrimination hypothesis or the statistic discrimination hypothesis, discrimination against the female worker may easily occur.

Does the discrimination against a female worker who tries to enter a sector affect gender wage gap? How does the discrimination against a female worker in the same sector affect gender wage gap? The following estimated results based on the Brown et al. model may provide an answer. These results are shown in Table 5.6. The main results are as follows.

First, how do intra-sector differentials and inter-sector differentials affect the wage gap? The influence of intra-sector differentials is greater than the influence of inter-sector differentials in both 2002 and 2013. The results reveal that the intra-sector differential is the main factor underlying

Table 5.6 Decomposition results based on the Brown et al. model

	Actual value	*Percentage (%)*
2002		
Total wage differentials	0.179	100
Inter-sector differential	0.016	8.9
Explained differential	0.061	34.0
Unexplained differential	−0.045	−25.1
Intra-sector differential	0.163	91.1
Explained differential	0.070	39.1
Unexplained differential	0.093	52.0
		100
Total explained differentials	0.131	73.1
Total unexplained differentials	0.048	26.9
2013		
Total wage differentials	0.270	100
Inter-sector differential	0.018	6.7
Explained differential	0.020	7.4
Unexplained differential	−0.002	−0.7
Intra-sector differential	0.252	93.3
Explained differential	0.036	13.3
Unexplained differential	0.216	80.0
		100
Total explained differentials	0.056	20.7
Total unexplained differentials	0.214	79.3

Source: Calculated based on CHIPs 2002 and CHIPs 2013

the gender wage gap in both 2002 and 2013, and its influence increased from 2002 to 2013.

Second, to evaluate the total influences of both explained and unexplained differentials, in 2002, the influence of the explained differentials is greater than that of the unexplained differentials. Whereas in 2013, the influence of the unexplained differentials is greater than that of the explained differentials. They indicate that discrimination against the female group increased from 2002 to 2013. The progress of economic reform in the 2000s is accompanied by discrimination against female groups.

Third, which factor has the greatest influence on gender wage gap? Based on the overall decomposition results of [estimation1], the highest value obtained is the unexplained component of the intra-sector differential. The results indicate that discrimination between male and female workers in the same sector is the main cause of the gender wage gap in both 2002 and 2013, and the influence of this factor increased from 2002 to 2013. Moreover, the value of explained component of the intra-sector differential implies that the gender gaps of individual characteristics including human capital in a given sector or the differentials between various sectors also have an influence on the gender wage gap.

Fourth, to consider the influence of explained and unexplained components in the inter-sector and intra-sector differentials separately, in the inter-sector differentials, the influences of the explained component are greater than that of the unexplained component for both 2002 and 2013. The influences decrease from 2002 to 2013; in the intra-sector differentials, the unexplained component is greater than that of the explained component, and the influences increase from 2002 to 2013. These results indicate that in both 2002 and 2013, the explained component is the main factor in the inter-sector differential, and the unexplained differential is the main factor in the intra-sector differentials which caused the gender wage gap. The influence of the unexplained component increased from 2002 to 2013.

5.6 Conclusions

This chapter explores the labor market segmentation by various ownership types and its impact on gender wage gaps in China in the 2000s. Using the Chinese Household Income Project survey (CHIPs) data from 2003 and 2014 (CHIPs 2002 and CHIPs 2013), the probabilities of entry to various sectors for both male and female groups are analyzed; a decomposition analysis of the gender wage gaps based on the Brown et al. model is employed. Several major conclusions emerge. First, it is shown that the gender wage gap existed in both 2002 and 2013, and the wage gap expanded from 2002 to 2013. Second, in general, the influence of endowment effects (e.g. human capital differentials by gender) decreased from 2002 to 2013, whereas the influence of unexplained differentials including discrimination increased from 2002 to 2013. Third, the discrimination against female workers in the same sector is the main cause of the gender wage gap, and its influence increased from 2002 to

2013, which shows that the discrimination against female workers in the same sector became severe from 2002 to 2013. Fourth the influence of endowment effects decreased from 2002 to 2013, whereas the influence of unexplained differentials including discrimination increased from 2002 to 2013.

The policy implications are as follows. It is indicated that along with SOEs reform, the influence of the gender equality regulation became smaller, which caused the discrimination against female workers to become severe, and the gender wage gap to expand in the 2000s. In order to reduce the gender wage gap, the Chinese government needs to enforce employment equality laws and an equal pay for equal work policy again. There may exist a compliance problem in the private sector. Therefore, even more effective monitoring of the implementation of the employment equality policy for both the private and public sector is needed. The results also show that gender wage gaps are caused by human capital differentials (e.g. education gaps). Therefore, policies that reduce human capital differentials by gender groups, such as the gender gaps in education and experience year, need to be implemented in the long term.

Notes

1. Brown et al. (1980) analyzed the effect of occupational segregation on gender wage gaps, and divided the causes of gender wage gaps into two parts: inter-occupation differentials and intra-occupation differentials.
2. Although Reimers (1983), Cotton (1988), Neumark (1988), Oaxaca and Ransom (1994), and Fortin (2008) argue the "index number" problem in the basic Blinder–Oaxaca model, the classifications of the unexplained differentials and the unexplained differentials are similar to Blinder (1973) and Oaxaca (1973) in these studies.
3. For the issue of sector segmentation and gender wage gaps in the TVPs (township, village, and privately-owned enterprises), which are in the rural regions, please refer to Meng and Miller (1995), Meng (1998a, b), Meng and Zhang (2001), Rozelle et al. (2002), and Dong et al. (2003).
4. In order to simplify the expression of equations as follows, all constant items are omitted.
5. Appleton et al. (1999) tried to utilize a non-discrimination wage function in the Brown et al. (1980) model to address the index number problem based on the idea which is similar to Reimers (1983), Cotton (1988), Neumark (1988), Oaxaca and Ransom (1994), and Fortin (2008), but there is a lot

of argument about the Appleton et al. (1999) model. Thus this study only employs the basic model, the Brown et al. model, to do the analysis, which is similar to the most of the previous studies.

6. That variable values are not in the range of "mean value ± three times S.D." that is defined as an abnormal value here.
7. In CHIPs 2002, the sample of workers working in foreign-owned enterprises is relatively small and cannot be analyzed in the decomposition analysis; consequently the workers who are working in POEs or FOEs are combined into one group.
8. Experience years = age-6-years of schooling.
9. There are sixteen industry categories in CHIPs 2002, and fifty in CHIPs 2013.

References

Appleton, S., Hoddinott, J., & Krishnan, P. (1999). The gender wage gap in three African countries. *Economic Development and Cultural Change, 47*(2), 289–312.

Appleton, S., Knight, J., Song, L., & Xia, Q. (2002). Labor retrenchment in China: Determinants and consequences. *China Economic Review, 13*(2–3), 252–275.

Arrow, K. J. (1972). Some mathematical models of race discrimination in the labor market. In A. Pascal (Ed.), *Racial discrimination in economic life*. Lexington, MA: DC Heath.

Arrow, K. J. (1973). The theory of discrimination. In O. Asehenfelter & A. Rees (Eds.), *Discrimination in labor markets*. Princeton, NJ: Princeton University Press.

Becker, G. S. (1957). *The economics of discrimination*. Chicago: University of Chicago Press.

Becker, G. S. (1964). *Human capital: A theoretical and empirical analysis, with special reference to education*. New York: Columbia University Press.

Blinder, A. S. (1973). Wage discrimination: Reduced form and structural estimation. *Journal of Human Resources, 8*, 436–455.

Brown, R. S., Moon, M., & Zoloth, B. S. (1980). Incorporating occupational attainment in studies of male-female earnings differentials. *Journal of Human Resources, 15*(1), 3–28.

Chen, G., Demurger, S., & Fournier, M. (2005). Wage differentials and ownership structure of China's enterprises. *World Economic Paper, 6*, 11–31 (In Chinese).

Cotton, J. (1988). On the decomposition of wage differentials. *Review of Economics and Statistics., 70*(2), 236–243.

Demurger, S., Fournier, M., Li, S., & Wei, Z. (2007). Economic liberation with rising segmentation in China's urban labor market. *Asian Economic Papers, 5*(3), 58–103.

Demurger, S., Li, S., & Yang, J. (2012). Earning differentials between the public and private sectors in China: Exploring changes for urban local residents in the 2002s. *China Economic Review, 23*, 138–153.

Dong, X., Macphail, F., Bowles, P., & Ho, S. P. S. (2003). Gender segmentation at work in China's privatized rural industry: Some evidence from Shandong and Jiangsu. *World Development, 32*(6), 979–998.

Fortin, N. M. (2008). The gender wage gap among young adults in the United States: The importance of money versus people. *Journal of Human Resources, 43*(3), 884–918.

Ge, Y. (2007). Sectoral choice and the gender wage gap: 1988–2001. *China Economic Quarterly, 6*(2), 607–628.

Guo, F., & Zhang, S. (2010). Gender wage gap in state and non-state sector. *The Journal of Quantitative & Technical Economics, 12*, 91–102.

Gustafsson, B., & Li, S. (2000). Economic transformation and the gender earnings gap in urban China. *Journal of Population Economics, 13*(2), 305–329.

Heckman, J. J. (1979). Sample selection bias as a specification error. *Econometrica, 47*(1), 153–161.

Knight, J., & Li, S. (2006). Unemployment duration and earnings of re-employed workers in urban China. *Chinese Economic Review, 17*(2), 103–119.

Lewis, W. A. (1954). Economic development with unlimited supplies of labor. *Manchester School of Economic and Social Studies, 28*(2), 139–151.

Li, S., & Ma, X. (2006). Occupational segregation and gender wage differentials in urban China. *Chinese Journal of Population Science, 5*, 1–14.

Li, S., Sato, H., & Sicular, T. (2013). *The analysis of the changes of income distribution in China*. The People's Press (In Chinese).

Li, S., Sicular, T., & Gustafsson, B. (2008). *Income distribution in China III*. Beijing: Beijing Normal University Press (In Chinese).

Li, S., Song, J., & Liu, X. (2011). Evolution of the gender wage gap among China's urban employees. *Social Sciences in China, 32*(3), 161–180 (In Chinese).

Li, S., & Yang, X. (2010). The determinants of gender wage gaps in migrants. *Comparative Economic & Social Systems, 5*(151), 82–89 (In Chinese).

Li, S., Yue, X., Sicular, T., & Sato, H. (2017). *Latest change of income distribution situations in China: The research on Chinese income distribution V*. Beijing: China Financial and Economic Press (In Chinese).

Liu, P., Meng, X., & Zhang, J. (2000). Sectoral gender wage differentials and discrimination in the transitional Chinese economy. *Journal of Population Economics, 13*(2), 331–352.

Luo, C., & Li, S. (2007). Human capital, industrial features and income inequality. *Management World, 10*, 20–30 (In Chinese).

Ma, C., Gu, H., & Li, J. (2013). Change of gender wage gaps in Chinese labor market: Evidence from quantile decomposition analysis of panel data. *World Economic Papers, 2*, 96–108 (In Chinese).

Ma, X. (2007a). A comparative study on occupational segregation and its impact on gender wage differentials: Based on micro-data from Household Survey in Japan and China. *Journal of Chinese Economic Studies, 4*(1–2), 14–33 (In Japanese).

Ma, X. (2007b). An empirical analysis of factor decomposition of differences between Japan and China of male-female wage differentials. *The Japanese Journal of Labor Studies, 49*(560), 96–107 (In Japanese).

Ma, X. (2008). The gender differentials of employment adjustment and reemployment wages in urban China: An empirical analysis using Chinese Household Income Survey 2002. *The Japanese Journal of Labor Studies, 50*, 104–119 (In Japanese).

Ma, X. (2009a). The enterprise ownership reforms and the change of wage structure in China: Comparison of gender wage profiles differentials by ownership. *Journal of Chinese Economic Studies, 6*(1), 48–63 (In Japanese).

Ma, X. (2009b). The Cause about the change of gender wage differentials in urban China: Empirical analysis using 1995 and 2002 Chinese Household Income Project Survey. *Asian Economic (AJIA KEIZAI), 50*(7), 2–25 (In Japanese).

Ma, X. (2011). *Female labour participation in China: Transformation of the urban labour market in the marketization process.* Tokyo: Keio University Press (In Japanese).

Ma, X. (2014). Wage policy: Economy transition and wage differentials of sectors. In K. Nakagane (Ed.), *How did Chinese economy changed? Evaluation of economic systems and policies in post-reform period.* Tokyo: Kokusai Shoin Co., Ltd (In Japanese).

Ma, X. (2015). Economic transition and wage differentials between public and private sectors in China. *China-USA Business Review, 14*(10), 477–494.

Ma, X. (2016). Changes of wage structures in Chinese public and private sectors: 1995–2007. *Management Studies, 4*(6), 1–13.

Maddala, G. S. (1983). *Limited-dependent and qualitative variables in econometrics.* New York: Cambridge University Press.

Maurer-Fazio, M., & Hughes, J. (2002). The effects of market liberalization on the relative earning of Chinese women. *Journal of Comparative Economics, 30*, 709–731.

Melly, B. (2006). Estimation of counterfactual distributions using quantile regression. *Review of Labor Economics, 68*(4), 543–572.

Meng, X. (1998a). Gender occupational segregation and its impact on the wage differential among rural-urban migrant: A Chinese case study. *Applied Economics, 30*(6), 741–752.

Meng, X. (1998b). Male-female wage determination and gender wage discrimination in China's rural industrial sector. *Labor Economics, 5*, 67–89.

Meng, X., & Miller, P. (1995). Occupational segregation and its impact on gender wage discrimination in China's rural industrial sector. *Oxford Economic Papers, 47*(1), 136–155 (New Series).
Meng, X., & Zhang, J. (2001). Two-tier labor market in urban China: Occupational segregation and wage differentials between urban residents and rural migrants in Shanghai. *Journal of Comparative Economics, 29*(3), 485–504.
Minami, R., & Ma, X. (2010). The Lewisian turning point of Chinese economy: Comparison with Japanese experience. *China Economic Journal, 3*(2), 165–181.
Minami, R., & Ma, X. (2014). Labor market and Lewisian turning point in China. In R. Minami, F. Makino, & K. Kim (Eds.), *Lewisian turning point in the Chinese economy.* London: Palgrave Macmillan.
Mincer, J. (1974). *Schooling, experience and earning.* New York: Columbia University Press.
Neumark, D. (1988). Employer's discriminatory behavior and the estimation of wage discrimination. *Journal of Human Resources, 23*(3), 279–295.
Oaxaca, R. L. (1973). Male-female wage differentials in urban labor markets. *International Economic Review, 14*(3), 693–709.
Oaxaca, R. L., & Ransom, M. (1994). On discrimination and the decomposition of wage differentials. *Journal of Econometrics, 61*(1), 5–21.
Phelps, E. S. (1972). The statistical theory of racism and sexism. *American Economic Review, 62*(4), 659–661.
Piore, M. J. (1970). Job and training. In S. H. Beer & R. Barringer (Eds.), *The state and the poor* (pp. 53–83). Cambridge, MA: Winthrop.
Reimers, C. W. (1983). Labor market discrimination against Hispanic and black men. *Review of Economics and Statistics, 65*(4), 570–579.
Rozelle, S., Dong, X., Zhang, L., & Mason, A. (2002). Gender wage gaps in post-reform rural China. *Pacific Economic Review, 7*(1), 157–179.
Wang, M. (2005). Gender wage differentials in China's urban labor market. *Economic Research, 12,* 35–44 (In Chinese).
Wang, M., & Cai, F. (2008). Gender earning differential in urban China. *Review of Development Economics, 12*(2), 442–454.
Yang, P. (2012). Education, industry segregation and gender wage gap: Evidence from college graduates surveys in China. *Peking University Education Review, 10*(3), 95–113 (In Chinese).
Yao, X., & Huang, Z. (2008). Occupational segregation and its effect on estimates of the gender wage differential: Evidence from 2002 UHS Data. *Journal of Chongqing University (Social Science Edition), 14*(2), 53–57 (In Chinese).
Ye, L., Li, S., & Luo, C. (2011). Industrial monopoly, ownership and enterprises wage inequality: An empirical research based on the first national economic census of enterprises data. *Management World, 4,* 26–36 (In Chinese).

Zhang, J., & Xue, X. (2008). State and non-state sector wage differentials and human capital contribution. *Economic Research, 4*, 15–25 (In Chinese).

Zhao, R., Li, S., & Riskin, K. (1996). *Restudies on income distribution in China*. Beijing: Chinese Financial and Economic Press.

Zhao, X. (2014). Measurement and decomposition of gender discrimination in China's urban labor market. *Management Review, 7*, 62–71 (In Chinese).

CHAPTER 6

The Determinants of Labor Supply of Informal Sector: Two Hypotheses on Self-Employment

6.1 Introduction

This chapter discusses the labor market segmentation by the informal sector[1] and formal sector in China. The self-employed sector is a representative informal sector of the employment market, and it has an influence on income inequality as noted in previous studies.[2] Transition economists believe the rise of self- employment to be a sign of the growing importance of markets (Hanley 2000; Catherine et al. 2005; Dimova and Gang 2007; Jackson and Mach 2009). Along with the economic transition and economic development in China, the number of self-employed workers ("*Geti Gongshang Hu*")[3] in urban China increased from 0.15 million in 1978 to 21.36 million in 2000, before further increasing to 70.09 million in 2014 (National Bureau of Statistics: NBS 2015). Why was there a large change in the size of the self-employed sector in urban China during the economic transition period?

Two hypotheses about self-employment have been discussed in previous studies: the "disguised unemployment hypothesis", which posits that although the individual wants to work in the formal sector to gain

This chapter is a revised version of: Ma, X. (2016). Economic Transition and the Determinants of Self-employment in Urban China: 2007–2013. *Journal of Chinese Economic and Business Studies*, 14(3), 279–307.

X. Ma, *Economic Transition and Labor Market Reform in China*,
https://doi.org/10.1007/978-981-13-1987-7_6

more income, he has to work in the self-employed sector involuntarily; and the "business creation hypothesis", which means that the self-employed workers may be successful business owners who create new jobs for others, new business opportunities, and many innovative new products for society to produce new employment and economic growth (Earle and Sakova 2000; Hanley 2000; Dimova and Gang 2007).

Based on these two hypotheses, there are two views on self-employment in China. First, migrants in the self-employed sector can be explained by this hypothesis, based on Lewis' dualism theory (Lewis 1954; Todarro 1969; Harris and Todarro 1970). As has been pointed out, a section of migrants are working long hours for low wages in the self-employed sector (Wang 2003; Xie and Yao 2006; Song and Appleton 2006; Deng 2007; Xing and Luo 2009; Ma 2011, 2016; Ma and Deng 2016). Second, along with the transition from a planned economy to a market economy, the government enforced ownership reform of state-owned enterprises (SOEs) since the 1990s, a section of employees with local urban residents in the SOEs became laid-off workers, and some of them became self-employed workers in order to make a living (Knight and Song 1999; Cai et al. 2005; Haggard and Huang 2008). Thus, workers in SOEs who lost their jobs because of SOEs' reconstruction entrance to the self-employed sector is also evidence in support of the disguised unemployment hypothesis. Considering these two cases, self-employment may result from forced recourse to the informal sector, in which the individual's activities and wage differ slightly from what they would be if the individual were unemployed. It is thought that self-employed workers barely make a living from working, receiving lower wages and working longer hours than those in the formal sector.

Conversely, along with SOEs reform progress, part of the Chinese communist party members or cadres with local urban registration left SOEs to become owners of privately owned enterprises (POEs) and establish a new firm (or company) to start new businesses, and it has been pointed out that such social capital (Chinese communist party membership, cadres of SOEs before entry to the self-employed) positively affects the probability to enter the self-employed sector and gain a higher income (Wu 2006; Yueh 2009a, b).[4]

As a result, a high percentage of self-employed workers may reflect an environment that encourages risk-taking, business creation, and market development ("business creation hypothesis"), or it may be a result of the lack of jobs in the formal sector ("disguised unemployment hypothesis").

Which hypothesis can explain self-employment in urban China? In this chapter, we provide some evidence to answer this question.

This chapter is structured as follows. Section 6.2 summarizes the background of self-employment in China, Sect. 6.3 summarizes the empirical studies on the self-employed, and Sect. 6.4 describes estimate methods, including introduction to the survey data and models. Section 6.5 states estimated results, and Sect. 6.6 presents the main conclusions.

6.2 Economic Transition and Changes of Self-Employment in China

Before 1949, the year of establishment of the People's Republic of China, the prevalent ownership type in China was the private sector, including self-employment. Since 1949, the "socialism reconstruction" campaign was enforced by the government. Through this, by the 1960s all POEs and foreign-owned enterprises (FOEs) were reformed into SOEs and collective-owned enterprises (COEs). There were few self-employed units for the retail and social service industries in the planned economy period (from 1949 to 1977). Based on the data published in the *China Statistical Yearbook* by the National Bureau of Statistics (NBS), self-employed workers decreased from 5.359 million in 1952 to 0.479 million in 1965, and to an all-time low of 0.178 million in 1978.

Under the economic transition period (post 1978), self-employment underwent dramatic changes. During the economic transition process, the changes were divided mainly into three periods—the 1978–1986 period, the 1987–1998 period, and the period since 1999.

In the 1978–1986 period, with the implementation of the "Household Production Contract System" ("*Jiating Lianchan Chengbao Zerenzhi*"), self-employed workers who provided essential services and goods were concentrated in rural regions. In urban areas, unemployment among the young was a serious problem, because the young groups who were in the senior high schools or colleges with local urban registrations had been to rural regions ("*Zhishi Qingnian*") and they returned to their local urban regions, where there were not enough jobs. To overcome this problem, the Chinese government helped these young workers to become self-employed and take up service, repair, and manual jobs in the urban region. In 1980, the government published "The Notice on the National Labor Employment Meeting Document" and clearly stated that self-employment should be supported. As a result, the total number of self-employed workers increased to 20 million by 1986. Based on the perspective of a planned economy, the government favored large SOEs, particularly those in the heavy industrial sectors. However, as with the ideology and mission of communism and socialism, economic progress and the growth of self-employment were disputed. Some economists suggested that no more than seven workers should be hired for firms (or units) in the self-employed sector based on the estimation given in the book *Capital* (Marx 1867). Thus, in 1981, the Chinese government published "The Guide on Non-agriculture Self-employment Policy"; it also declared that an employer in the self-employed sector can work jointly with one or two family members and hire less than five workers (i.e., the total number of workers excepting the owner should be less than seven) in the manual, retail, catering, transportation, and repair service industries.

In the 1987–1998 period, along with the progress of the economic transition from the planned economy to the marketization economy, self-employment increased significantly. The number of self-employed workers increased from 20.93 million in 1990 to 24.14 million in 1998 (NBS 1999). This change can be attributed to two reasons. First, as the *Hukou* system was deregulated, the surplus labors in the rural regions moved to urban regions (Minami and Ma 2010, 2014). As most of these migrants were not highly educated or skilled, they did not qualify for entry to the public sector. Thus, a share of these migrants had to work in the self-employed sector, where manual, retail, catering, transportation, and repair service jobs were in high demand and the SOEs did not provide these services. Second, since the 1980s, particularly at the end of the 1990s, SOEs' restructure reform was enforced by the government. Most of the workers who were laid off did not prefer to return to SOEs, and they chose to work in the self-employed sector for their living. The remaining share of party members began to establish new businesses and became the owners of small firms.

In 1987, to manage and monitor the self-employed sector, the government published the "Provisional Regulations on the Self-employment for the Urban and Rural Regions" and "Provisional Regulations on the Private Sector". In 1988, it also amended the constitution to add content such as "the private sector is a complementary part of socialist public economy, government protects the rights and interests in the private sector, and government leads, supervises, and manages the private economy". Moreover, in 1992, the "Enterprises Law" was established, which was implemented in 1993; the self-employed sector and small-sized enterprise are defined in the "Enterprises Law".

Post 1998, as the GDP grew significantly and the tertiary industry saw development, particularly the enforcement of SOEs reforms by the government, some part of the middle-level and small SOEs and most COEs moved from the public sector to the private sector. In addition, the government implemented the *Hukou* system reform, and therefore the rural to urban migrants increased to 150–170 million in the 2000s. Moreover, in 1999, the government amended the constitution again and added content such as "the self-employment, the private sector economy is an important part of socialist marketization economy". Under this political and economic environment, which is favorable for self-employment, the number of workers in the private sector, including the self-employed, is increasing. For example, the number of self-employed workers increased from 31.60 million in 1999 to 54.96 million in 2007 and to 93.36 million in 2013, and the proportion of self-employed workers to the total workers decreased from 4.48% in 1999 to 7.14% in 2007 and then increased to 12.13% in 2013 (NBS 2000, 2008, 2014).

6.3 Theories and Empirical Studies on the Labor Supply of Self-employment

First, for self-employment in a developing country, according to Lewis' dualism theory in development economics, in the prior period of economic development, there exists surplus labor in the traditional sector (agriculture industry sector), and when the modern sector (manufacture industry sector) offers a wage close to or a little more than subsistence level, migration from the rural region to the urban region will occur until the economy passes Lewis' turning point (Lewis 1954). Todarro (1969) and Harris and Todarro (1970) developed the Lewis model and pointed out that the migrant expects the high wages of the modern sector in the urban market, so when he does not find a job in the formal sector immediately, he always works in the informal sector (the self-employed sector) to wait (or do a job search) for a formal sector job.

Second, for the determinants of self-employment, based on the empirical studies for the developed countries and developing countries, it is indicated that individual attributes affect the choice to become a self-employed worker. For example, gender, human capital, and family background are often used as control variables in previous studies (e.g. Borjas 1986; Amit et al. 1990; Evans and Leighton 1989; Yamada 1996; Bruce 1999; Le 1999; Hamilton 2000; Dunn and Holtz-Eakin 2000; Zhang and Pan 2012). In addition, Evans and Jovanovic (1989), Lentz and Laband (1990), Holtz-Eakin et al. (1994), and Dunn and Holtz-Eakin (2000) indicated that financial constraints also affect entry to self-employment. Reviewing empirical studies on the determinants of self-employment in China beyond the factors of human capital, family background, and liquidity constraints, the effects of party membership and social capital are also pointed out (Wu 2006; Yueh 2009a, b; Zhang and Zhao 2015).

Third, regarding the determinants of the self-employment in economic transition countries, Earle and Sakova (2000), Hanley (2000) and Dimova and Gang (2007) pointed out the two previous hypotheses ("disguised unemployment hypothesis" and "business creation hypothesis") and tested them for Central and Eastern European transition countries. Earle and Sakova (2000) distinguished the workers in the self-employed sector into two categories: self-employed employers who create jobs for others and own-account workers who work on their own or with the support of unpaid family helpers. They showed that for both own-account workers and self-employed employers in almost every country (Bulgaria, the Czech Republic, Hungary, Poland, Russia, and Slovakia), the probabilities are estimated to be negatively affected by wage premiums-wage gaps between own-account workers and employees and positively affected by wage gaps between the self-employed employer and employees. This corroborates the disguised unemployment hypothesis. Hanley (2000) also tested these hypotheses to estimate wage gaps between self-employed employers, own-account workers, and employees, pointing out that the disguised unemployment hypothesis is supported by the observations for the Czech Republic, Poland, and Slovakia. Ma and Deng (2016) conducted an empirical study and indicated that the disguised unemployment hypothesis is also supported for migrant groups in China.

To compare with the previous studies, the main features of this study are as follows. First, in this study, the model proposed by Earle and Sakova (2000) to verify the business creation and disguised unemployment hypotheses for the entire workforce in urban China (either local urban residents or migrant) is used to compare determinants of entry to self-employment between these two groups.

Second, Ma and Deng (2016) only conducted tests using CHIPs 2007, which was carried out before the global financial crisis of 2008 (economic downturn precipitated by the Lehman Brothers' bankruptcy in 2008). Named the Roman shock, this study analyzes these two hypotheses using CHIPs 2007 and CHIPs 2013 to consider the change of determinants of self-employment before and after the global financial crisis.

Third, the labor market is segmented into the public and private sectors, and the wage gap between these two sectors in China has grown since the 1990s.[5] It is believed that the wage level in the self-employed sector might be on a par with the employee wages in POEs, but not that of the public sector. This study used two kinds of employee wage indices to test the hypotheses.

Fourth, the subsamples of groups comprising individuals aged less than 50 years and those comprising individuals aged 50 years and over were also utilized to estimate the age effect; the difference of cohort effects for these two groups is also discussed in the study.

Fifth, as has been pointed out, huge regional disparities exist in China, and the level of economic development and labor demand and supply differs by regions. For example, along with regional development policies such as "Let a share of the population become richer first", which was enforced in the prior period of economy reform, most private firms were established in the Eastern region, and most foreign-owned enterprises (FOEs) entered that region. Thus, the probability of entry into the self-employed sector might be higher in the Eastern region than in the Western and the Central regions. Considering this regional disparity, estimations by regional groups were also employed in the study.

6.4 Methodology and Data

6.4.1 Models

First, to explicate the determinants for self-employment in urban China, the work status probability function is estimated using a multinomial logit model, which is represented in Eq. (6.1). The explained variable takes on one value for four categories of work status (self-employed employer, own-account worker, employee, and the unemployed). The reference category is the employee group.

$$
\begin{aligned}
&Y^*_{mi} = \alpha_m + \beta_{Hm} H_{mi} + \varepsilon_{mi} \quad (i = 1,2,\ldots,N)\\
&Y^* = n \quad \text{if } \beta_n H_n - \beta_{Hm} H_m > (\alpha_m - \alpha_n) + (\varepsilon_m - \varepsilon_n) \quad (m \neq n)\\
&\text{Prob}(Y^*_i = n) = \exp(\alpha_n + \beta_{Hn} H_{ni}) / \Sigma \exp(\alpha_m + \beta_{Hm} H_{mi}) \quad (m = 1,\ldots n,\ldots M)
\end{aligned}
\tag{6.1}
$$

Here, referring to the definitions in Earle and Sakova (2000) and Hanley (2000) and considering the features for the Chinese urban labor market, the four groups are defined as follows: (i) own-account workers are those who work in the self-employed sector (small firm or unit) on their own or jointly with unpaid family helpers; this concept is similar to the "individual self-employed worker"; (ii) self-employed employers are those who work in the self-employed sector with less than seven workers; they are the owners of these small firms (or units); employers who are the owners of firms with more than eight workers are not included in the group; (iii) employees are all those who work in the firms (with either less than seven or more than eight workers) and they are not owners of firms; and (v) the unemployed are those who are not working. The generic term including own-account worker (individual self-employed worker), self-employed employer (owner of small firm or unit in the self-employed sector), and a section of employees who work in the firms with less than seven workers is "*Geti gongshang hu*" as mentioned in the *China Statistical Yearbook* by the NBS.

In Eq. (6.1), i denotes workers and (m = 1, … n, … M) denotes work status as the above. Prob($Y_i = n$) indicates probability of one kind of work status, H are factors affecting the work status probability, β are the estimated coefficients, and α is a constant. For example, the probability to become a self-employed employer is expressed as Prob($Y^* = 1$), and the other probability (such as employee, own-account worker, the unemployed) is expressed as Prob($Y^* \neq 1$).

Then the Earle and Sakova (2000) model is utilized to test the "disguised unemployment hypothesis" and "business creation hypothesis". In order to gain the imputed wage, wage functions by different employment status groups are estimated. Here, the Maddala (1983) model is used to deal with the sample selection bias problem, which has been shown in Eqs. (6.2a–6.2b).

Wage function estimated by the OLS model is expressed as Eq. (6.2a).

$$\ln W_i = b + \gamma_X X_i + u_i \tag{6.2a}$$

In Eq. (6.2a), *i* denotes workers, and ln W_i indicates the dependent variable (as the logarithm of wage rate). *X* are factors affecting wages. γ_X are the estimated coefficients, *b* is a constant, and *u* is the error term.

Considering the sample selection bias problem in Eq. (6.2a), the selection bias corrected wage function model is proposed (Maddala 1983). Using the estimated results of the distribution function and the density function by the probit regression model (Prob(Y^* = 1)) indicates probability of one kind of work status), selectivity items ($\lambda = \psi(\cdot)/\Phi(\cdot)$) are calculated. The corrected wage functions expressed by Eq. (6.2b) can be estimated using these selectivity items. The variables utilized in the probit regression model are similar to those in Eq. (6.1), which includes the identification variables.[6]

$$\ln W_i = b + \gamma_X X_i + \gamma_\lambda \lambda_i + u_i \tag{6.2b}$$

Based on Eq. (6.2b), wage premiums (WP)-wage gaps between work status groups on the probability of work status are calculated.

A multinomial logit model shown in Eq. (6.3) is utilized to test two hypotheses. In Eq. (6.3), WP are added as new variables; the other variables are similar to Eq. (6.1).

$$E\left(\text{Prob}\left(Y_i^* = 1\right)\right) = \exp\left(\alpha_n + \beta_{WP} WP_{ni} + \beta_{Hn} H_{ni}\right) / \\ \Sigma \exp\left(\alpha_m + \beta_{WP} WP_{mi} + \beta_{Hm} H_{mi}\right) \quad \left(m = 1, \ldots n, \ldots M\right) \tag{6.3}$$

In Eq. (6.3), the *WP* is a general term. It is composed of a set of the imputed wage gaps between work status groups. Concretely, "Woa" is the wage for the own-account workers group and "Wer" is the wage for the self-employed employers' group. It is believed that the wage level for the own-account workers group might be close to the employee wages in the POEs. This study used two kinds of employee wage indexes to test the hypotheses: (i) the imputed wage of employees who are working in either the public sector (e.g. government organizations, SOEs) or the private sector (e.g. POEs, FOEs), represented as "Wee", and (ii) the imputed wage of employees who are working in the private sector, represented as "Weepri". The imputed wage premiums are calculated as follows: (i) the wage ratio of an own-account worker to an employee who works in either the public sector or the private sector (Woa/Wee); (ii) the wage ratio of a self-employed employer to an employee who works in either the public sector or the private sector (Wer/Wee); (iii) the wage ratio of an own-account worker to an employee who works in the private sector (Woa/Weepri); and (iv) the wage ratio of a self-employed employer to an employee who works in the private sector (Wer/Weepri). As the distribution of wage variables is skewed, the natural logarithmic forms are used. The first two indices are used to employ the main hypotheses testing as used in the previous studies, and the last two indices are used to employ the new analysis.

It is thought that the higher the wage premium, the higher the probability to choose the work status. For example, when the estimated results of wage premium ("Wer/Wee") are positive significantly on the probability to become a self-employed employer, it is shown that the self-employed sector is a new business to gain more income and create more values (such as create new jobs for others, and new goods), so the "business creation hypothesis" is supported. Whereas when the estimated results of wage premium ("Wer/Wee") are negative significantly (or insignificantly) on the probability to become a self-employed employer, it is shown that although becoming an employer in a small firm cannot gain more, he (she) has to choose to become an employer in a small firm, and it indicates that the entry to the self-employed sector may be an involuntary behavior, and the "disguised unemployment hypothesis" is supported.

6.4.2 *Data*

The 2007 and 2013 Chinese Household Income Project Surveys data (CHIPs 2007 and CHIPs 2013) are used for the analysis. These surveys were conducted by National Bureau of Statistics and Beijing Normal University in December 2008 and 2014, including respective information about employment status and wages of the urban registration residents and migrants. Particularly, based on CHIPs 2007 and CHIPs 2013, we can distinguish self-employment status between two groups—own-account workers and self-employed employers—to test the hypotheses. In both CHIPs 2007 and CHIPs 2013 data, most of the survey items are similar. However, we can utilize both data to compare the change of determinants of entry to self-employment before and after the financial crisis. CHIPs 2007 and CHIPs 2013 covered the represented districts in

China, including Beijing, Shanxi, Liaoning, Jiangsu, Anhui, Guangdong, Henan, Hubei, Sichuan, Yunnan, and Gansu. We utilize the samples in districts that are surveyed in both 2008 and 2014 to adjust the district selection bias.

The sample comprises workers and non-workers. The four groups, namely self-employed employers, own-account workers, employees, and the unemployed, are analyzed in the study. Based on three questionnaire items, "job status", "work status", and "How many workers do you employ except family helpers?" the four groups are distinguished. For example, when the individual's work status is "self-employment" and the number of employed workers except family helpers is "0" (no family helper), it means he/she works in the self-employed sector by himself (herself) or just works together with family helpers; thus he/she is an own-account worker (individual self-employed worker); when the individual's work status is "self-employment" and the number of employed workers except family helpers in his/her firm or unit is more than "1", it means he/she works as an owner in the self-employed sector and creates new jobs for others; thus he/she is a self-employed employer; when the individual's work status is "non-employer, or non-owner" who gains the wage, he/she is an employee; when the individual's work status is "no job (no work)", he/she is unemployed.

Based on the above, the main dependent variable is a work status category variable including the four groups in the work status probability function. The dependent variable in the wage function by work status groups is the logarithm of wage rate.[7]

The independent variables are as follows (Table 6.1 shows sample descriptive statistics by work status groups, local urban residents and migrants groups, and by survey years 2007 and 2013).

We used independent variables as follows. First, we utilized some variables used in previous studies.[8] These include individual variables likely to affect employment status choice, such as years of schooling, tenure years, health status (very good, good, fair, poor) dummy variables, which are the index of human capital, female (female is a binary variable coded 1 if the respondent is a female and 0 otherwise), and Han race (Han race is a binary variable coded 1 if the respondent is Han race, and 0 minority). In addition, it is thought the risk aversion preferences vary with these individual attributes, and the risk aversion preference becomes more likely with increasing age.

Table 6.1 Descriptive statistics by local urban residents and migrants for 2007 and 2013

	Urban registration residents						*Migrants*					
	Employee		*Employer*		*Own-account*		*Employee*		*Employer*		*Own-account*	
	Mean	*S.D.*	*Mean*	*S.D.*	*Mean*	*S.D.*	*Mean*	*S.D.*	*Mean*	*S.D.*	*Mean*	*S.D.*
Panel A: 2007												
Age	38	11	35	11	38	12	30	9	34	8	36	9
Years of schooling	12	3	11	3	11	3	9	2	9	2	8	2
Health status												
Very good	0.184	0.387	0.232	0.424	0.177	0.383	0.447	0.497	0.394	0.490	0.406	0.491
Good	0.567	0.496	0.625	0.486	0.569	0.496	0.405	0.491	0.489	0.502	0.397	0.490
Fair	0.231	0.421	0.125	0.332	0.234	0.425	0.136	0.343	0.102	0.304	0.176	0.381
Poor	0.019	0.135	0.018	0.133	0.019	0.137	0.012	0.108	0.015	0.120	0.022	0.146
Female	0.536	0.499	0.536	0.501	0.550	0.499	0.648	0.478	0.613	0.489	0.634	0.482
Ethnicity (Han)	0.990	0.097	0.991	0.094	0.981	0.137	0.979	0.142	0.985	0.120	0.987	0.112
Married	0.765	0.424	0.741	0.440	0.766	0.425	0.008	0.090	0.007	0.085	0.011	0.104
Household income	10.895	0.642	11.141	0.550	10.734	0.730	9.935	0.600	9.872	0.606	9.955	0.606
Father: senior high school and over	0.215	0.411	0.152	0.360	0.163	0.370	0.126	0.332	0.066	0.249	0.094	0.292
Father: manager	0.070	0.255	0.071	0.259	0.038	0.192	0.041	0.197	0.044	0.205	0.049	0.216
Hukou change by house purchase	0.060	0.237	0.170	0.377	0.129	0.336	0.001	0.024	0.000	0.024	0.002	0.043
Number of relations	38	44	36	32	32	29	34	54	36	59	33	130
The frequency of contact relations												
Once every week	0.599	0.490	0.545	0.500	0.474	0.501	0.590	0.492	0.606	0.490	0.558	0.497
Once every month	0.337	0.473	0.384	0.489	0.469	0.500	0.342	0.475	0.321	0.469	0.353	0.478
Once every year	0.064	0.245	0.071	0.259	0.057	0.233	0.068	0.251	0.073	0.261	0.089	0.285

(*continued*)

Table 6.1 (continued)

	Urban registration residents						*Migrants*					
	Employee		*Employer*		*Own-account*		*Employee*		*Employer*		*Own-account*	
	Mean	*S.D.*	*Mean*	*S.D.*	*Mean*	*S.D.*	*Mean*	*S.D.*	*Mean*	*S.D.*	*Mean*	*S.D.*
Regions												
East	0.536	0.499	0.571	0.497	0.368	0.484	0.605	0.489	0.358	0.481	0.250	0.433
West	0.173	0.378	0.161	0.369	0.191	0.394	0.154	0.361	0.073	0.261	0.136	0.343
Central	0.291	0.454	0.268	0.445	0.440	0.498	0.241	0.428	0.569	0.497	0.614	0.487
Observations	5,247		112		209		1,702		137		552	

	Urban registration residents						*Migrants*					
	Employee		*Employer*		*Own-account*		*Employee*		*Employer*		*Own-account*	
	Mean	*S.D.*	*Mean*	*S.D.*	*Mean*	*S.D.*	*Mean*	*S.D.*	*Mean*	*S.D.*	*Mean*	*S.D.*
Panel B: 2013												
Age	40	10	42	8	42	9	36	10	40	7	40	8
Years of schooling	12	3	11	3	10	3	10	3	9	2	9	3
Health status												
Very good	0.341	0.474	0.432	0.497	0.327	0.470	0.406	0.491	0.486	0.507	0.330	0.471
Good	0.480	0.500	0.456	0.500	0.498	0.501	0.455	0.498	0.432	0.502	0.511	0.501
Fair	0.162	0.369	0.095	0.294	0.146	0.353	0.123	0.329	0.081	0.277	0.144	0.352
Poor	0.017	0.128	0.018	0.132	0.029	0.168	0.016	0.124	0.000	0.000	0.016	0.126
Female	0.442	0.497	0.320	0.468	0.452	0.498	0.585	0.493	0.757	0.435	0.612	0.489
Ethnicity (Han)	0.956	0.204	0.935	0.247	0.923	0.267	0.959	0.197	1.000	0.000	0.941	0.235
Married	0.859	0.348	0.929	0.258	0.938	0.242	0.795	0.404	0.973	0.164	0.952	0.214

(continued)

Table 6.1 (continued)

	Urban registration residents						*Migrants*					
	Employee		*Employer*		*Own-account*		*Employee*		*Employer*		*Own-account*	
	Mean	*S.D.*	*Mean*	*S.D.*	*Mean*	*S.D.*	*Mean*	*S.D.*	*Mean*	*S.D.*	*Mean*	*S.D.*
Household income	10.891	0.586	11.226	0.669	10.780	0.691	10.643	0.561	11.055	0.471	10.884	0.588
Father: senior high school and over	0.174	0.379	0.130	0.337	0.092	0.289	0.089	0.285	0.108	0.315	0.048	0.214
Father: manager	0.066	0.248	0.047	0.213	0.048	0.214	0.013	0.114	0.027	0.164	0.005	0.073
Hukou change by house purchase	0.101	0.302	0.077	0.267	0.117	0.321	0.003	0.051	0.054	0.229	0.011	0.103
Being trustworthy to friends	0.685	0.465	0.698	0.460	0.698	0.460	0.648	0.478	0.730	0.450	0.649	0.479
Being trustworthy to others	0.685	0.465	0.698	0.460	0.698	0.460	0.648	0.478	0.730	0.450	0.649	0.479
Regions												
East	0.430	0.495	0.438	0.498	0.404	0.491	0.495	0.500	0.297	0.463	0.372	0.485
West	0.220	0.414	0.201	0.402	0.188	0.391	0.170	0.376	0.189	0.397	0.096	0.295
Central	0.350	0.477	0.361	0.482	0.408	0.492	0.335	0.472	0.514	0.507	0.532	0.500
Observations	7,511		169		480		764		37		188	

Source (Panel A): Calculated based on CHIPs 2007
Source (Panel B): Calculated based on CHIPs 2013

Some previous studies indicate that family factors, such as child, marital status, father's education, and father's occupations, can affect the choice to become a self-employed worker, particularly for female workers. We used a marriage dummy, number of children, father's education level (a senior high school and over dummy), and father's occupation dummy (manager dummy) variables to control the influence of these factors.

As indicated in the liquidity constraint hypothesis, financial factors may affect the choice to become self-employed, and here, living with parents and household income are used as the liquidity constraint indices.

It is pointed out that social capital also affects self-employment. It is thought that with higher social capital, there is a greater possibility for settling financial constraint problems and thus a greater chance for success with self-employment. Two variables are used, the number of relations and the frequency of contact relations, as the index of social capital for 2007, using the following questionnaire items: "How many persons do you contact?" and "How frequently do you contact your relations?" In addition, "Being trustworthy to friends" and "Being trustworthy to others" are used as the index of social capital for 2013. Please note that the indices of social capital are different for 2007 and 2013, because the survey items on social capital are different in CHIPs 2007 and CHIPs 2013.

The influences of some special factors in the Chinese labor market are also considered. For example, in urban China, the change from rural registration to urban registration is very difficult except under special conditions, such as workers with higher levels of schooling or with higher skill levels, enlistment in the army, and the purchase of a commercial house (investment in housing) in the urban area. It is thought that the method of registration change may influence the choice to become a self-employed worker, so we add a registration change dummy (a binary variable coded 1 if the worker experienced a registration change by the purchase of a commercial house and 0 otherwise) for the urban residents' group with urban registration in survey year. In addition, because there are regional disparities in China, it is thought that labor demands vary by region, so we add three regional dummies (Western, Eastern, and Central regions).

In order to test the hypotheses, as it is defined in Part III, each wage premium ($\overline{WP}$) is calculated: Wer/Wee, Woa/Wee, Wer/Weepri, and Woa/Weepri.

Employee wages are distinguished by private and public sector and robustness checks are performed to test the hypotheses. Reduced earning function estimation results are utilized to calculate these imputed wages and wage gaps (Woa/Weepri, Wer/Weepri).

Finally, to consider that the retirement system is structured within the public sector, in order to diminish the effect of that system on analysis results, the analytic objects are limited to groups between the ages of 16 and 60. The samples utilized in the following empirical studies comprise 10,806 local urban residents and 6267 migrants.

6.5 Econometric Analysis Results

6.5.1 What Determines the Choice to Enter the Self-employed Sector?

Table 6.2 shows the estimated results of the determinants of work status by both the local urban resident and migrant groups.

First, the demographic variables affect the choice of self-employment (to become a self-employed employer or an own-account worker) for both the local urban resident and migrant groups would be more appropriate. For example, while there exists an inverse "U" shape relation between age and self-employment for the migrant group in 2007, the same relation exists for both the migrant and the local urban resident groups in 2013.

Second, in both the local urban resident and migrant groups, work status choices are affected by the level of education. That is, the probability to become a self-employed employer decreases with an increase in the level of education and vice versa in 2007 and 2013.

Third, there exists a change in the effects of household income on the self-employed employer for the migrant group. For example, the estimated results show that the probability to become a self-employed employer decreases with the household income rise in 2007, while this probability increases in 2013. However, for the local urban resident group, the probability to become a self-employed employer increases with the household income rise in both 2007 and 2013. This can be explained by the existence of liquidity constraints for self-employed employers, and the problem became serious for the migrant group in 2013. These estimated results reveal that the influence of liquidity constraints increased from 2007 to 2013, and provide evidence that for successful job and business creation, policies (such as financial support policies for small-sized enterprises) to resolve liquidity constraint problems are important in a transition economy (and elsewhere), particularly since after the global financial crisis of 2008, liquidity constraint problems have become severe.

Table 6.2 Determinants of entry to the self-employed sector by local urban residents and migrants for 2007 and 2013

	Urban registration residents						*Migrants*					
	Employer		*Own-Account*		*Unemployed*		*Employer*		*Own-Account*		*Unemployed*	
	Coeff.	*z-value*	*Coeff.*	*z-value*	*Coeff.*	*z-value*	*Coeff.*	*z-value*	*Coeff.*	*z-value*	*Coeff.*	*z-value*
Panel A: 2007												
Age	0.027	0.35	−0.047	−0.90	−0.240***	−11.08	0.331***	4.58	0.312***	8.14	−0.032	−0.76
Age squared/100	−0.088	−0.92	0.038	0.59	0.400***	15.44	−0.411***	−3.99	−0.363***	−6.83	0.070	1.18
Years of schooling	−0.150***	−4.65	−0.108***	−4.58	−0.023**	−2.51	−0.010	−0.26	−0.158***	−6.57	−0.186***	−6.03
Health status (Poor)												
Very good	−0.216	−0.29	−0.044	−0.08	−1.110***	−6.44	0.172	0.22	0.134	0.32	−0.816*	−1.93
Good	−0.199	−0.27	0.075	0.14	−1.055***	−6.79	0.309	0.40	−0.110	−0.27	−0.648	−1.55
Fair	−0.805	−1.05	0.140	0.26	−0.785***	−4.97	−0.250	−0.31	0.011	0.03	−1.132***	−2.53
Female	0.095	0.48	0.090	0.62	−1.493***	−21.97	−0.196	−1.04	−0.051	−0.45	−1.899***	−12.24
Ethnicity (Han)	−0.260	−0.25	−0.808	−1.51	−0.148	−0.46	0.245	0.33	0.420	0.92	−0.155	−0.31
Married	0.554	1.43	0.462*	1.63	−0.008	−0.07	−0.364	−0.34	−0.213	−0.39	−0.090	−0.14
Household income	0.830***	5.24	−0.070	−0.56	−0.567***	−10.36	−0.349**	−2.22	−0.163*	−1.79	−0.121	−1.10
Father: senior high school and over	−0.376	−1.37	−0.170	−0.86	−0.222***	−2.59	−0.702*	−1.95	−0.327*	−1.81	−0.122	−0.58
Father: manager	0.179	0.47	−0.608*	−1.64	−0.112	−0.86	−0.018	−0.04	0.042	0.16	0.035	0.11

(*continued*)

Table 6.2 (continued)

	Urban registration residents						*Migrants*					
	Employer		*Own-Account*		*Unemployed*		*Employer*		*Own-Account*		*Unemployed*	
	Coeff.	*z-value*	*Coeff.*	*z-value*	*Coeff.*	*z-value*	*Coeff.*	*z-value*	*Coeff.*	*z-value*	*Coeff.*	*z-value*
Hukou change by house purchase	0.796***	2.91	0.776***	3.47	0.458***	3.67	−11.518	−0.01	0.538	0.35	−10.460	−0.01
Number of relations	−0.003	−1.03	−0.002	−1.06	−0.004***	−4.14	0.000	0.44	0.000	0.06	−0.002	−1.19
The frequency of contact relations (Once every week)												
Once every month	0.249	1.22	0.571***	3.88	0.109*	1.68	−0.053	−0.27	0.152	1.30	−0.187	−1.23
Once every year	0.291	0.75	0.171	0.55	−0.083	−0.63	−0.126	−0.35	0.134	0.66	−0.270	−0.97
Region (West + Central regions)												
East region	−0.210	−1.00	−0.650***	−4.07	−0.169**	−2.55	−0.870***	−4.18	−1.296***	−9.97	−1.102***	−6.59
Constant	−11.843***	−4.86	0.250	0.14	9.579***	11.89	−4.679**	−2.08	−3.934***	−3.06	3.813***	2.61
Observations			7,744						2,691			
Log likelihood			−4718.812						−2295.241			
Pseudo R^2			0.218						0.156			
Chi-squared			2630.710						850.010			

(*continued*)

Table 6.2 (continued)

	Urban registration residents						*Migrants*					
	Employer		*Own-Account*		*Unemployed*		*Employer*		*Own-Account*		*Unemployed*	
	Coeff.	*z-value*	*Coeff.*	*z-value*	*Coeff.*	*z-value*	*Coeff.*	*z-value*	*Coeff.*	*z-value*	*Coeff.*	*z-value*
Panel B: 2013												
Age	0.237***	2.83	0.106**	2.20	−0.523***	−23.15	0.544**	2.48	0.216**	2.49	−0.333***	−4.74
Age squared/100	−0.287***	−2.88	−0.143**	−2.50	0.697***	26.05	−0.652**	−2.40	−0.238**	−2.22	0.449***	5.13
Years of schooling	−0.175***	−6.25	−0.234***	−13.15	−0.130***	−12.46	−0.049	−0.67	−0.077**	−2.26	−0.141***	−4.16
Health status (Poor)												
Very good	0.088	0.15	−0.129	−0.43	−1.312***	−8.80	12.954	0.02	0.181	0.26	−1.357***	−2.87
Good	−0.184	−0.30	−0.112	−0.37	−1.219***	−8.47	12.503	0.02	0.257	0.37	−1.530***	−3.27
Fair	−0.685	−1.07	−0.393	−1.25	−0.983***	−6.61	11.964	0.02	0.275	0.39	−1.274***	−2.57
Female	0.636***	3.73	0.053	0.54	−1.668***	−26.25	1.012**	2.39	0.230	1.29	−2.119***	−9.90
Ethnicity (Han)	−0.609*	−1.85	−0.594***	−3.18	−0.237*	−1.88	11.925	0.03	−0.486	−1.24	0.028	0.07
Married	0.192	0.55	0.652***	2.99	−0.052	−0.52	0.930	0.83	0.756*	1.82	0.613*	1.90
Household income	1.289***	9.03	0.035	0.40	−0.493***	−9.80	1.455***	4.51	0.889***	5.45	−0.451***	−2.84
Father: senior high school and over	−0.304	−1.25	−0.414**	−2.46	−0.102	−1.10	0.413	0.67	−0.480	−1.22	−0.468	−1.16
Father: manager	−0.345	−0.92	−0.107	−0.47	−0.041	−0.34	−0.299	−0.25	−1.333	−1.22	0.649	0.95

(*continued*)

Table 6.2 (continued)

	Urban registration residents						*Migrants*					
	Employer		*Own-Account*		*Unemployed*		*Employer*		*Own-Account*		*Unemployed*	
	Coeff.	*z-value*	*Coeff.*	*z-value*	*Coeff.*	*z-value*	*Coeff.*	*z-value*	*Coeff.*	*z-value*	*Coeff.*	*z-value*
Hukou change by house purchase	−0.645**	−2.14	−0.337**	−2.20	−0.085	−0.96	4.533***	3.68	1.961*	1.77	0.146	0.11
Being trustworthy to friends	−0.013	−0.07	0.214*	1.94	−0.062	−1.00	0.173	0.41	0.002	0.01	0.411**	2.05
Being trustworthy to others	0.165	0.90	−0.175	−1.48	−0.063	−0.89	0.571	1.37	−0.195	−0.83	−0.012	−0.06
Region (West + Central regions)												
East region	−0.261	−1.55	0.031	0.31	−0.082	−1.36	−1.157***	−2.84	−0.552***	−3.06	−0.390**	−2.17
Constant	−20.296***	−8.51	−2.295*	−1.69	16.474***	23.05	−55.149	−0.08	−15.115***	−5.96	11.971***	5.57
Observations			10,582						1,204			
Log likelihood			−6513.081						−996.234			
Pseudo R^2			0.216						0.170			
LR chi2			3585.870						409.280			

Source: Panel A is calculated based on CHIPs 2007; Panel B is calculated based on CHIPs 2013

Note:

(1) *, **, ***: statistically significant at 10%, 5%, and 1% level

(2) Reference category = employee group

Fourth, the *Hukou* system influences entry into the self-employed sector. For example, in 2007, the probability to become a self-employed employer increases when a worker changes his registration by purchase of a house as residential property for the local urban resident group, whereas its effect is small for the migrant group. However, in 2013, the probability to become a self-employed employer or an own-account worker decreases when a worker changes his registration by purchase of a house for the local urban resident group, whereas this probability increases for the migrant group.

The influence of house purchase on the choice to become a self-employed worker increases from 2007 to 2013 for the migrant group, particularly for the probability of becoming a self-employed employer. These results also indicate there exists a liquidity constraint problem: housing might become a trust condition for a self-employed employer when he receives a loan from the formal or informal financial market. It is thought that because the liquidity constraint problem is serious for the migrant group in 2013, the influence of house purchase on the choice to become a self-employed worker increases from 2007 to 2013 for the migrant group. The estimation results of housing purchase effect for the migrants' group are consistent with the results of the household income.

Considering social capital, compared with the workers who contact relations once every week, those who contact relations once every month are more likely to become own-account workers for the local urban resident group in 2007, whereas the influence of social capital on self-employment is not statistically significant for the migrant group in 2007. Moreover, these results are statistically insignificant for both the local urban resident and migrant groups in 2013.

Finally, in the migrant group, compared with workers in the Western and Central regions, the probability of becoming a self-employed employer and own-account worker is lower for those in the Eastern region in both 2007 and 2013. In addition, in the local urban resident group, the probability of becoming an own-account worker is lower for those in the Eastern region in both 2007 and 2013. This may be because compared with the Western and the Central regions, the level of economic development is higher in the Eastern region, so labor demands for the employees results from the modern industrial sector are also relatively higher in that region.

6.5.2 *Hypothesis Testing: Business Start-ups or Disguised Unemployment?*

The analysis of the hypotheses test results uses the imputed wages calculated on the basis of the results shown in Table 6.3. The reduced multinomial logit analysis is estimated and the results are represented in Table 6.4.

First, for the local urban resident group, the results show that the wage premium (log Wer/Wee −0.361 and log Woa/Wee 0.433 in 2007, log Wer/Wee −0.183 and log Woa/Wee −0.077 in 2013) does not statistically affect the probability of the choices to become a self-employed employer or an own-account worker in both 2007 and 2013.

Based on the individual utility maximum rule (to gain the highest income), workers possibly choose to become a self-employed employer or an own-account worker when their associated wage levels are higher than those for employees. However, estimated results indicated that the choice to enter the self-employed sector (as either self-employed employers or own-account workers) does not result from perceived economic gains and benefits. These results support the disguised unemployment hypothesis in both 2007 and 2013.

Second, for the migrant group, the probability of becoming a self-employed employer is estimated to be negatively affected by the wage premium (log Wer/Wee −0.767) in 2007, and the probability of becoming an own-account worker is estimated to be negatively affected by the wage premium (log Woa/Wee −2.204) in 2013. It is revealed that although a worker may recognize that there is an economic loss associated with becoming a self-employed employer in 2007 or an own-account worker in 2013, there may be no chance to become an employee, so the worker has no choice but to enter the informal sector and become a self-employed worker in both 2007 and 2013. In that case, the disguised unemployment hypothesis is supported.

In addition, the influence of the wage premium (log Woa/Wee) on the probability of becoming an own-account worker is statistically insignificant in 2007, and the influence of the wage premium (log Wer/Wee) on the probability of becoming a self-employed employer is statistically insignificant in 2013—the disguised unemployment hypothesis is supported again.

Table 6.3 Wage function by local urban residents and migrants for 2007 and 2013

	Urban registration residents						*Migrants*					
	Employee		*Employer*		*Own-account*		*Employee*		*Employer*		*Own-account*	
	Coeff.	*t-value*	*Coeff.*	*t-value*	*Coeff.*	*t-value*	*Coeff.*	*z-value*	*Coeff.*	*z-value*	*Coeff.*	*z-value*
Panel A: 2007												
Age	−0.060***	−8.10	0.046	0.57	0.096*	1.96	0.039***	4.25	−0.053	−0.71	−0.055	−1.52
Age squared/100	0.092***	8.99	−0.096	−0.87	−0.179***	−2.90	−0.061***	−4.94	0.056	0.58	0.064	1.43
Tenure years	0.035***	11.48	−0.087**	−2.52	0.018	0.65	0.047***	7.85	0.095**	2.07	0.021	1.58
Tenure years squared/100	−0.065***	−7.33	0.309**	2.49	−0.002	−0.02	−0.133***	−4.40	−0.637**	−2.51	−0.076	−1.24
Years of schooling	0.019***	6.02	0.062*	1.64	0.038	1.51	0.045***	6.95	0.022	0.31	0.051***	2.76
Learning achievement	0.097***	5.04	0.254	1.55	−0.291**	−2.06	0.027	1.07	0.046	0.27	−0.145**	−2.09
Health status (Poor)												
Very good	−0.251***	−3.42	−1.056*	−1.85	−0.445	−0.82	0.051	0.50	0.419	0.70	0.014	0.07
Good	−0.200***	−2.81	−0.232	−0.41	−0.308	−0.59	0.058	0.57	0.201	0.33	0.026	0.13
Fair	−0.171**	−2.42	−0.657	−1.13	−0.836	−1.58	0.041	0.39	0.294	0.47	−0.131	−0.64
Female	−0.262***	−10.02	0.002	0.01	0.148	1.07	−0.130***	−4.37	−0.150	−0.58	−0.120*	−1.73
Ethnicity (Han)	−0.038	−0.42	−0.750	−0.91	−0.448	−0.91	0.020	0.26	0.459	0.81	0.305	1.24
Married	0.103***	3.18	0.831*	2.51	0.695***	2.59	−0.030	−0.25	0.114	0.13	0.343	1.28
Training	0.055***	2.96	−0.334*	−1.89	−0.263*	−1.88	0.088***	2.58	−0.352	−1.54	−0.127*	−1.71
Industrials (No-Manufacture)												
Manufacture	−0.171***	−8.85	−0.217	−1.35	−0.148	−1.09	−0.056**	−2.23	0.514	1.19	−0.080	−0.44
Region (West + Central regions)												
East region	0.353***	18.10	0.638***	3.05	0.160	1.10	0.321***	6.73	0.301	0.64	0.585***	4.33
lambda(employees)	−3.764***	−15.15	–	–	–	–	−0.017	−0.05	–	–	–	–
lambda(employers)	–	–	−0.427	−0.14	–	–	–	–	0.131	0.03	–	–

(*continued*)

Table 6.3 (continued)

	Urban registration residents						*Migrants*					
	Employee		*Employer*		*Own-account*		*Employee*		*Employer*		*Own-account*	
	Coeff.	*t-value*	*Coeff.*	*t-value*	*Coeff.*	*t-value*	*Coeff.*	*z-value*	*Coeff.*	*z-value*	*Coeff.*	*z-value*
lambda(own-account)	–	–	–	–	6.136	1.14	–	–	–	–	−1.495	−1.44
Constant	4.304***	17.19	2.681	0.86	−3.727	−0.93	0.210	0.94	1.963	0.54	2.732**	2.17
Observations	5,054		110		203		1,687		135		547	
Adj R-squared	0.254		0.332		0.229		0.245		0.046		0.107	

	Urban registration residents						*Migrants*					
	Employee		*Employer*		*Own-account*		*Employee*		*Employer*		*Own-account*	
	Coeff.	*t-value*	*Coeff.*	*t-value*	*Coeff.*	*t-value*	*Coeff.*	*z-value*	*Coeff.*	*z-value*	*Coeff.*	*z-value*
Panel B: 2013												
Age	−0.015	−1.44	0.019	0.30	−0.049	−0.94	0.106***	3.33	−0.457**	−2.32	0.117*	1.69
Age squared/100	0.028**	2.08	−0.019	−0.25	0.064	1.00	−0.153***	−3.62	0.543**	2.23	−0.119	−1.36
Tenure years	0.022***	7.29	0.061**	2.11	0.031**	1.99	0.022**	2.16	0.062	1.12	0.066**	2.56
Tenure years squared/100	−0.029***	−3.23	−0.207**	−2.11	−0.095*	−1.92	−0.011	−0.31	−0.204	−0.98	−0.245***	−2.99
Years of schooling	0.053***	13.24	0.097***	3.55	0.152***	4.71	0.039***	2.85	0.094	1.55	0.131***	2.84
Learning achievement	0.086***	4.44	−0.096	−0.55	0.036	0.27	0.152*	1.68	−0.065	−0.18	0.011	0.04
Health status (Poor)												
Very good	0.046	0.70	0.667	1.43	0.223	0.89	0.248	1.21	−0.767	−1.66	0.400	0.97
Good	−0.002	−0.03	0.598	1.29	0.251	1.03	0.263	1.30	−0.527	−1.12	0.390	0.97
Fair	−0.042	−0.64	0.700	1.42	0.340	1.31	0.331	1.59	−0.638	−0.09	0.225	0.53

(*continued*)

Table 6.3 (continued)

	Urban registration residents						*Migrants*					
	Employee		*Employer*		*Own-account*		*Employee*		*Employer*		*Own-account*	
	Coeff.	*t-value*	*Coeff.*	*t-value*	*Coeff.*	*t-value*	*Coeff.*	*z-value*	*Coeff.*	*z-value*	*Coeff.*	*z-value*
Female	−0.101***	−4.48	−0.133	−0.92	−0.292***	−3.13	−0.428***	−5.41	−0.446	−1.49	−0.147	−1.22
Ethnicity (Han)	0.026	0.70	0.703***	2.65	0.529***	2.85	0.129	1.04	−0.001	−0.22	0.724***	2.93
Married	0.034	1.27	−0.090	−0.36	0.071	0.39	−0.038	−0.53	−0.104	−0.15	−0.751**	−2.56
Industrials (No-Manufacture)												
Manufacture	−0.021	−0.98	0.245	1.27	0.233	0.64	0.026	0.45	0.222	0.58	0.520*	1.95
Region (West + Central regions)												
East region	0.197***	12.46	0.174	1.37	0.051	0.59	0.098**	1.98	0.219	0.84	0.011	0.10
lambda(employees)	−1.944***	−7.81	–		–		1.277	1.58	–	–	–	–
lambda(employers)	–	–	−10.410***	−4.25	–		–	–	−9.722	−1.61	–	–
lambda(own-account)	–	–	–		−9.698***	−2.83	–	–	–	–	−7.125**	−1.76
Constant	2.241***	6.82	7.702***	3.27	7.947***	2.78	−0.702	−0.70	19.017***	2.92	3.008	0.87
Observations	7,399		164		478		749		37		183	
Adj R-squared	0.242		0.263		0.128		0.128		0.105		0.197	

Source: Panel A is calculated based on CHIPs 2007; Panel B is calculated based on CHIPs 2013

Note: *, **, ***: statistically significant at 10%, 5%, and 1% level

Table 6.4 Results of hypothesis testing by local urban residents and migrants for 2007 and 2013

	Employer		*Own-account*	
	coeff.	*z-value*	*coeff.*	*z-value*
Panel A: 2007				
Urban registration residents				
log(Woa/Wee)	0.062	0.16	0.434	1.50
log(Wer/Wee)	−0.361	−1.36	−0.084	−0.45
Migrants				
log(Woa/Wee)	−0.770	−0.99	0.044	0.09
log(Wer/Wee)	−0.767***	−3.26	−0.756***	−4.46
Panel B: 2013				
Urban registration residents				
log(Woa/Wee)	−2.644***	−5.70	−0.077	−0.20
log(Wer/Wee)	−0.183	−0.44	3.828***	9.37
Migrants				
log(Woa/Wee)	−1.351	−1.27	−2.204***	−3.81
log(Wer/Wee)	−0.048	−0.03	1.843**	2.21

Source: Calculated based on CHIPs 2007 and CHIPs 2013

Note:

(1) *, **, ***: statistically significant at 10%, 5%, and 1% level

(2) The specification of structural multinomial logit regression model is similar to that shown in Table 6.2, but dependent variable has only three categories (omitting unemployment group) and the predicted earning differentials log(Woa/Wee) and log(Wer/Wee) are added to the regressors. All other independent variables shown in Table 6.2 are also included here, but not shown in Table 6.4

6.5.3 *Robustness Checks of Hypotheses Testing*

We also perform three robustness checks of the hypotheses testing, and these results are shown in Tables 6.5–6.7.

First, considering that the labor market in urban China is segmented by the public sector and private sector, and the wage level in the self-employed sector is close to that in the POEs but not that in the public sector, the wage premiums based on the wage of the employee in the POEs are utilized to test the two hypotheses again (see Table 6.5).

In 2007, the influences of wage premiums (log Wer/Weepri) on the probability of becoming a self-employed employer are negatively significant for both the local urban resident and the migrant groups (−0.464 for the local urban resident group and −0.695 for the migrant group). In addition, the influence of the wage premium (log Woa/Weepri) on the

Table 6.5 Hypotheses test by the wage premiums based on the wage of the employee in the POEs

	2007				*2013*			
	Employer		*Own-account*		*Employer*		*Own-account*	
	Coeff.	*z-value*	*Coeff.*	*z-value*	*Coeff.*	*z-value*	*Coeff.*	*z-value*
Urban registration residents								
log(Woa/Weepri)	−0.588*	−1.71	−0.258	−1.02	−0.698	−1.31	−3.417***	−8.89
log(Wer/Weepri)	−0.464**	−2.14	0.026	0.17	1.464***	3.70	2.327***	7.98
log(Woa/Weepub)	−0.276	−0.68	0.309	1.03	−0.453***	−0.97	−2.762***	−8.55
log(Wer/Weepub)	−0.424*	−1.96	0.101	0.67	1.717	4.23	2.494***	8.29
Migrants								
log(Woa/Weepri)	−0.847	−1.05	−0.056	−0.11	−2.290***	−1.57	−3.534***	−4.85
log(Wer/Weepri)	−0.695***	−2.94	−0.737***	−4.34	0.043***	0.04	1.688***	2.56
log(Woa/Weepub)	1.173*	1.76	1.809***	4.42	1.312	0.171	−3.388***	−5.01
log(Wer/Weepub)	−0.668***	−2.76	−0.630***	−3.70	−0.218	−0.18	1.378**	2.10

Source: Calculated using CHIPs 2007 and CHIPs 2013

Note:

(1) *, **, ***: statistically significant at 10%, 5%, and 1% level

(2) The specification of structural multinomial logit regression model is similar to that shown in Table 6.2, but dependent variable has only three categories (omitting unemployment group) and the predicted earning differentials log(Woa/Wee) and log(Wer/Wee) are added to the regressors. All other independent variables shown in Table 6.2 are also included here, but not shown in Table 6.5

Table 6.6 Hypotheses test by age groups

	2007				2013			
	Employer		*Own-account*		*Employer*		*Own-account*	
	Coeff.	*z-value*	*Coeff.*	*z-value*	*Coeff.*	*z-value*	*Coeff.*	*z-value*
Urban registration residents								
log(Woa/Wee)	0.004	0.01	0.311	1.07	−1.899***	−3.95	0.009	0.02
log(Wer/Wee)	−0.390	−1.38	0.161	0.80	−2.670***	−4.70	3.980***	9.28
log(Woa/Wee)*aged50 and over	0.986	1.59	0.714*	1.88	−1.488***	−2.62	−0.175	−0.33
log(Wer/Wee)*aged50 and over	0.287	0.46	−1.210***	−2.83	4.198***	5.90	−0.595	−1.25
Migrants								
log(Woa/Wee)	−0.733	−0.94	0.047	0.10	−1.286	−1.12	−2.590***	−4.17
log(Wer/Wee)	−0.686***	−2.83	−0.671***	−3.83	−0.110	−0.07	1.506*	1.78
log(Woa/Wee)*aged50 and over	−3.072	−0.85	−1.248	−0.78	−0.846	−0.55	1.036*	1.90
log(Wer/Wee)*aged50 and over	−1.048	−1.00	−0.956	−1.35	1.298	1.17	0.081	0.18

Source: Calculated using CHIPs 2007 and CHIPs 2013

Note:

(1) *, **, ***: statistically significant at 10%, 5%, and 1% level

(2) The specification of structural multinomial logit regression model is similar to that shown in Table 6.2, but dependent variable has only three categories (omitting unemployment group) and the predicted earning differentials log(Woa/Wee) and log(Wer/Wee) are added to the regressors. All other independent variables shown in Table 6.2 are also included here, but not shown in Table 6.6

Table 6.7 Hypotheses test by regional groups

	2007				*2013*			
	Employer		*Own-account*		*Employer*		*Own-account*	
	Coeff.	*z-value*	*Coeff.*	*z-value*	*Coeff.*	*z-value*	*Coeff.*	*z-value*
Urban registration residents								
East region								
log(Woa/Wee)	−0.266	−0.51	0.415	0.84	−1.460**	−2.50	−1.158**	−2.15
log(Wer/Wee)	−0.859**	−2.26	0.113	0.38	−0.437	−0.73	3.147***	5.33
Central/West region								
log(Woa/Wee)	0.548	0.91	0.424	1.15	−4.038***	−6.17	0.791	1.49
log(Wer/Wee)	0.145	0.38	−0.181	−0.76	0.043	0.07	4.700***	8.29
Migrants								
East region								
log(Woa/Wee)	−1.744	−1.27	0.023	0.02	−1.732	−0.74	−3.442***	−3.23
log(Wer/Wee)	−1.729***	−3.92	−2.302***	−6.83	1.427	0.35	2.979*	1.77
Central/West region								
log(Woa/Wee)	−0.898	−0.90	−0.565	−0.97	−1.174	−0.91	−1.832**	−2.53
log(Wer/Wee)	−0.184	−0.60	0.055	0.29	−0.623	−0.37	1.350	1.38

Source: Calculated using CHIPs 2007 and CHIPs 2013

Note:

(1) *, **, ***: statistically significant at 10%, 5%, and 1% level

(2) The specification of structural multinomial logit regression model is similar to that shown in Table 6.2, but dependent variable has only three categories (omitting unemployment group) and the predicted earning differentials log(Woa/Wee) and log(Wer/Wee) are added to the regressors. All other independent variables shown in Table 6.2 are also included here, but not shown in Table 6.7

probability of becoming an own-account worker is insignificant for both the local urban resident and migrant groups. These results are consistent with the above, and the disguised unemployment hypothesis is supported, whereas the business creation hypothesis is rejected again in 2007.

However, in 2013, the influences of wage premiums (logWer/Weepri) on the probability of becoming a self-employed employer are positively significant for both the local urban resident and migrant groups (1.474 for the local urban resident group and 0.043 for the migrant group). Thus, the business creation hypothesis is supported when a worker opts to become a self-employed employer for both the local urban resident and migrant groups; these are the new findings in the robustness checks analysis. The influences of wage premiums (logWoa/Weepri) on the probability of becoming an own-account worker are negatively significant for both the local urban resident and migrant groups (−3.418 for the local urban residents group and −3.534 for the migrant group); thus, the business creation hypothesis is rejected and the disguised unemployment hypothesis is supported again in the case of entry to the informal sector as an own-account worker in 2013.

In 2007, the robustness check results are consistent with the results, using the wage premiums based on the imputed employee wages which were used in the previous studies (Earle and Sakova 2000; Hanley 2000) for both the local urban resident and migrant groups. However, in 2013, when the new wage premiums index was utilized, the test results for the self-employed employer, which are shown in Tables 6.4 and 6.5, are different. The robustness check results indicated that compared with 2007, in 2013, becoming a self-employed employer seems like a suitable choice for both the local urban resident and migrant groups, since a worker can gain more benefit if he chooses to become a self-employed employer than to become an employee in a POE.

Why is there a difference in the hypotheses testing results for 2007 and 2013? There is an explanation for the difference. First, the global financial crisis occurred in 2008. It is believed that the global financial crisis of 2008 affected foreign trade in China. Thus, it might have influenced the labor demand for low-skilled workers and caused more employees to enter into the self-employed sector.

Second, it might be caused by the private sector development policy enforced by the government. For example, the financial support for the innovation firms and small firms by the Chinese government increased after the global financial crisis. As a result, more workers entered the self-employed sector to establish a new business in 2013 than in 2007.

Third, the work conditions in the private sector became more serious, and this can explain the results. Concretely, since the 2000s, although the surplus labor decreased in the rural regions (Cai et al. 2005; Minami and Ma 2010, 2014), the wage level in private firms increased, and the wage gaps between the public and private sectors also increased since the 1990s. Because employment in the public sector is still controlled by the government, only a small fraction of workers can enter this sector. Unlike workers in private firms with a lower pay and relatively longer work hours, self-employed workers might earn more and control the work hours themselves. Thus, when the wage premiums based on the imputed private firm wage are used, the business creation hypothesis is supported in 2013.

However, although the new indices are used, the hypotheses test results for the own-account worker group are consistent with those shown in Table 6.4—the business creation hypothesis is rejected and the disguised unemployment hypothesis is supported again for both the migrant and local urban resident groups in 2007 and 2013. These results indicate that when the individual is a less educated or a low-skilled worker, or when the recruitment information of the private firms is not known by the individual, which is addressed by the information asymmetry hypothesis, even though the individual may recognize that there is an economic loss associated with becoming an own-account worker, there may be no chance of becoming an employee of POEs. Thus, the worker has no choice but to enter the informal sector and become an own-account worker. This result suggests that becoming an own-account worker is still not a suitable choice from the perspective of monetary gain, and it may be an involuntary choice for a low-level living (subsistence level pointed out by Lewis' dualism theory in development economics) in both 2007 and 2013.

Second, Table 6.6 shows the results by age groups. In 2013, the influence of wage premiums (log Wer/Weep) on the probability of becoming a self-employed employer is positively significant for the group aged more than 50 years old (4.198), while it is negatively significant for the group aged less than 50 years old (−2.670) in the local urban resident group. Therefore, the business creation hypothesis is supported for the older generation group in 2013, while it is rejected for the younger generation group in the case of choice to become a self-employed employer for local urban residents. In contrast, for the migrant group, the differences between the younger generation group and the older generation group are small. These results might be explained by the SOEs' reconstruction reform. As described above, at the end of the 1980s, along with ownership reform progress, a part of communist party members or cadres with local urban registration who are the group aged more than 50 years old in the two survey years (CHIPs 2007 in 2008, CHIPs 2013 in 2014) left SOEs or government organizations to become owners of small POEs.

Then, considering the influence of wage premiums (logWoa/Weep) on the probability of becoming an own-account worker, when the statistical significance level is set at 10%, the influences of wage premiums on the probability of becoming an own-account worker are positively significant for the group aged more than 50 years old in local urban residents in 2007 (0.714) and in migrants in 2013 (1.036).

The results reveal that entry to the informal sector (the choice to become a self-employed employer and an own-account worker for the local urban resident group; the choice to become an own-account worker for the migrant group) in the initial labor market reform period can provide more benefit for both the migrant and local urban resident groups. Thus, the business creation hypothesis is supported for the older generation group, whereas this hypothesis is rejected for the younger generation group. The results also indicate that the monetary motivation has been decreasing for the younger generation recently.

Third, we also estimated the results on a regional basis. The results in Table 6.7 suggest that the business creation hypothesis is rejected and the disguised unemployment hypothesis is supported in the Central, Western, and Eastern regions for both local urban resident and migrant groups in 2007 and 2013. However, the regional disparities in these hypothesis test results are small.

These small regional disparities can be explained as follows. As the number of enterprises is more in the Eastern region than the Western and Central regions, since the 2000s, the Chinese government has adjusted the regional development policy to promote the Western and Central regions in order to address the inequality. For example, the government has enforced the "Great Development in the West Regions" ("*Xibu Dakaifa*") policy since 1999. Moreover, the government has promoted the "Development in the Central Regions" ("*Zhongbu Jueqi*") policy since 2003 and "Promote the Industrial Zones in the East-North Regions" policy since 2004. In the 2000s, the government provided more public financial investment for the Western and Central regions, and promoted the private sector and self-employment development in these regions. Because the internal environment difference for the self-employment and private sector between regions decreased, more migrants chose to come back to their hometown from the Eastern regions as their hometown provided more work opportunities than before. As a result, the hypotheses testing results are similar in the Eastern, Western, and Central regions for 2007 and 2013. Along with the economic transitions and marketization economy reforms, it is thought that the labor mobility and capital (money) transfer by the regions is freer in the 2000s, so the labor market segmentation by regions has become reduced in the 2000s.

6.6 Conclusions

This chapter provides evidence about the determinants of self-employment for local urban residents and migrants in urban China. The employment status is divided into four categories using CHIPs 2007 and CHIPs 2013: self-employed employers, own-account workers, employees, and the unemployed. The main findings are as follows.

First, generally, utilizing the imputed wage premiums (the wage ratio of own-account worker or self-employed employer to employee who works in either the public sector or the private sector), which were used in previous studies, the business creation hypothesis is rejected; the disguised unemployment hypothesis is supported for both the local urban resident and the migrant groups in 2007 and 2013. These conclusions are consistent with previous studies (Earle and Sakova 2000; Hanley 2000; Dimova and Gang 2007; Ma and Deng 2016).

Second, as the labor market in urban China is segmented into public and private sectors, the results utilized the new wage premiums (the wage ratio of own-account worker or self-employed employer to employee who works in the private sector) and showed that the business creation hypothesis was supported when a worker chose to become an employer for both the migrant and local urban resident groups in 2013.

Third, when the sample is divided into two subsamples, the group aged 50 and above (the older generation) and the group aged less than 50 years old (the younger generation), the business creation hypothesis is relevant for the older generation group of local urban residents in 2013, whereas this hypothesis is rejected for the younger generation group, for both the local urban resident and migrant groups in 2007 and 2013.

Fourth, the business creation hypothesis is rejected in the Central, Western, and Eastern regions, as the regional disparity in the hypotheses test results is small in both 2007 and 2013.

These estimated results reveal that excepting the case in which a worker chose to become a self-employed employer in 2013 and the case in which a member of the older generation group chose to become an employer in 2013, compared with employees, a worker in the self-employed sector does not gain more, and there is seemingly no better choice in urban China. Some policy implications based on these empirical study results are discussed here.

One implication is that a self-employed employer has to face business risks and liquidity constraints problems. If the self-employed employer (the owner of a small private firm) cannot settle the liquidity constraint problem through the formal financial market (by getting a loan from a government bank), business continuity will become difficult. Liquidity constraint problems already exist (Haggard and Huang 2008). It is known that the public banks do not like to lend to small private firms, so most small firms gain financial support through informal financial markets (inter-household risk sharing and illegal loans). The estimated results in this chapter (see Table 6.4) showed that the effect of household income on the self-employed employer group is greater than that for the other groups. In order to promote more new business for greater economic growth in the future, the Chinese government should establish and implement financial support policies for small firms.

These results reflect the possibility of a job-rationing problem in the Chinese urban labor market, so a second implication is the relation with labor market segmentation by the formal and informal sectors. It is thought that this segmentation results from human capital endowment differentials and some system discriminations. For example, there is employment discrimination in the public sector by the *Hukou* system, so most migrants cannot be recruited as regular workers in the public sector. In addition, it is known that in urban China, social security systems differ between the formal and informal sectors. For example, in the public sector, firms charge a portion of the social security fee to their employees, whereas most workers in the self-employed sector have to pay the social security fee themselves, and the compensation (firm welfare) is more for employees who worked in the public sector or for large firms than that for those who worked in other sectors. An important challenge for the Chinese government is to diminish the segmentation of the informal sector and the formal sector in urban China, and integrate the social security system.

Finally, although we conducted an empirical study to reveal the determinants of self-employment and used the hypothesis tests discussed in this chapter, there are two points worthy of attention. First, because we utilized one period of cross-sectional data, there might be heterogeneity and endogenous problems, and a study using longitudinal survey data should be conducted in the future. Second, this chapter is a static analysis for self-employment. It is thought that empirical studies on dynamic change in self-employment (the transition into and exit from self-employment) are also important (Le 1999),[9] and dynamic analysis using longitudinal analysis methods is our research topic for another paper.

Notes

1. For the definition of informal sector, please refer to International Labor Organization (ILO) (1972).
2. For detailed surveys of empirical studies on the self-employed, please see Yamada (1996) and Le (1999).
3. There is no unified definition of self-employed workers in previous studies in China. Here, self-employed workers are close to "*Geti gongshang hu*", and the total number of workers of "*Geti gongshang hu*" is published in the *Chinese Statistical Yearbook* by the National Bureau of Statistics (NBS). "*Geti gongshang hu*" includes the self-employed employer (the owner of small firm or unit with less than seven employees), the own-account worker (individual self-employment worker with or without family helpers), and a section of employees who work in firms with less than seven workers.
4. The phenomenon of communist party members and cadres leaving the public sector to become business owners in the private sector in the 1980s is called "*Xia Hai*" in Chinese.
5. For empirical studies on labor market segmentation by public and private sector in urban China, please see Chap. 3 of the book, Dong and Bowles (2002), Yin and Gan (2009), Chen et al. (2005), Zhang and Xue (2008), Ye et al. (2011), Demurger et al. (2012), Lu et al. (2012), and Ma (2009, 2014, 2015, 2016)
6. Number of children, household income, family background (father's education, father's occupation), and social capital (the number of relations and the frequency of contact with relations in CHIPs 2007, and being trustworthy to friends and being trustworthy to others in CHIPs 2013) are used as identification variables in this study.
7. Wage survey items in CHIPs 2007 for urban registration residents comprises the basic wage, bonus, cash subsidy, and non-cash subsidy, whereas the wage survey for migrants comprises the basic wage, so the logarithm of the monthly wage based on the basic wage is utilized in the study.

8. For example, Blau (1985), Borjas (1986), Evans and Leighton (1989), Amit et al. (1990), Bruce (1999), Hamilton (2000), Dunn and Holtz-Eakin (2000), and Zhang and Pan (2012) pointed out that individual attributes (such as gender, human capital, and family background) should affect the choice to become a self-employed worker. In addition, Evans and Jovanovic (1989), Lentz and Laband 1990), Holtz-Eakin et al. (1994), and Dunn and Holtz-Eakin (2000) indicated that financial constraints also affect the entry to the self-employed sector.
9. For longitudinal analysis using panel data, please see Blau (1987), Evans and Jovanovic (1989), Blanchflower and Meyer (1992), and Xie (2012) for the transition into self-employment, and Evans and Leighton (1989) and Bates (1990) for the exit from self-employment.

References

Amit, R., Glosten, L., & Muller, E. (1990). Entrepreneurial ability, venture investments, and risk sharing. *Management Science, 36*(10), 1232–1245.

Bates, T. (1990). Entrepreneur human capital inputs and small business longevity. *The Review of Economics and Statistics, 72*(4), 551–559.

Blanchflower, D. G., & Meyer, B. (1992). A longitudinal analysis of young entrepreneurs in Australia and the United States. In R. G. Gregory & T. Karmel (Eds.), *Youth in the eighties, papers from the Australian longitudinal survey research project*. Canberra: DEET and Centre for Economic Policy Research, Australian National University.

Blau, D. M. (1985). Self-employment and self-selection in developing country labor markets. *Southern Economic Journal, 52*(2), 351–363.

Blau, D. M. (1987). A time-series analysis of self-employment in the United States. *Journal of Political Economy, 95*(3), 445–467.

Borjas, J. (1986). The self-employment experience of immigrants. *The Journal of Human Resources, 21*(4), 485–506.

Bruce, D. (1999). Do husbands matter? Married women entering self-employment. *Small Business Economics, 13*(4), 317–329.

Cai, F., Du, Y., & Wang, M. (2005). *Transition and development of the labor market China*. Beijing: Commercial Press (In Chinese).

Catherine, Y. C., Gang, I. N., & Yun, M. (2005). Self-employment and wage earning in Hungary. *Review of Development Economics, 9*(2), 150–165.

Chen, G., Demurger, S., & Fournier, M. (2005). Wage differentials and ownership structure of China's enterprises. *Economic Development and Cultural Change, 53*(4), 933–958.

Demurger, S., Li, S., & Yang, J. (2012). Earning differentials between the public and private sectors in China: Exploring changes for urban local residents in the 2002s. *China Economic Review, 23*(1), 138–153.

Deng, Q. (2007). Earning differentials between urban residents and rural migrants: Evidence from Oaxaca Blinder and quantile regression decompositions. *Chinese Journal of Population Sciences, 2*, 8–16 (In Chinese).

Dimova, R., & Gang, I. N. (2007). Self-selection and wages during volatile transition. *Journal of Comparative Economics, 35*(3), 612–629.

Dong, X., & Bowles, P. (2002). Segmentation and discrimination in China's emerging industrial labor market. *China Economic Review, 13*(2–3), 170–196.

Dunn, T. A., & Holtz-Eakin, D. (2000). Financial capital, human capital, and transition to self-employment: Evidence from intergenerational links. *Journal of Labor Economics, 18*(2), 282–305.

Earle, J. S., & Sakova, Z. (2000). Business star-ups or disguised unemployment? Evidence on the character of self-employment from transition economics. *Labor Economics, 7*, 575–601.

Evans, D. S., & Jovanovic, B. (1989). An estimated model of entrepreneurial choice under liquidity constraints. *Journal of Political Economy, 97*(4), 808–827.

Evans, D. S., & Leighton, L. (1989). Some empirical aspects of entrepreneurship. *American Economic Review, 79*(3), 519–535.

Haggard, S., & Huang, Y. (2008). The political economics of private sector development in China. In L. Brandt & T. G. Rawski (Eds.), *China's great economic transformation*. Cambridge: Cambridge University Press.

Hamilton, B. H. (2000). Does entrepreneurship pay? *The Journal of Political Economy, 108*(3), 604–631.

Hanley, E. (2000). Self-employment in post-communist Eastern Europe: A refuge from poverty or road to riches. *Communist and Post-Communist Studies, 33*(3), 379–402.

Harris, J. R., & Todarro, M. P. (1970). Migration, unemployment and development: A two sector analysis. *American Economic Review, 60*(1), 126–142.

Holtz-Eakin, D., Joulfaian, D., & Rosen, H. S. (1994). Sticking it out: Entrepreneurial survival and liquidity constraints. *Journal of Political Economy, 102*(1), 53–75.

International Labor Organization (ILO). (1972). *Employment, incomes and equality: A strategy for increasing productive employment in Kenya*. Geneva: ILO.

Jackson, J., & Mach, B. (2009). Job creation, job destruction, labour mobility and wages in Poland, 1988–1998. *Economics of Transition, 17*(3), 503–530.

Knight, J., & Song, L. (1999). *The rural-urban divide: Economic disparities and interactions in China*. Oxford: Oxford University Press.

Le, A. T. (1999). Empirical studies of self-employment. *Journal of Economic Surveys, 13*(4), 381–461.

Lentz, B. F., & Laband, D. N. (1990). Entrepreneurial success and occupational inheritance among proprietors. *Canadian Journal of Economics, 23*(3), 563–579.

Lewis, W. A. (1954). Economic development with unlimited supplies of labor. *Manchester School of Economic and Social Studies, 28*(2), 139–151.

Lu, Z., Wang, X., & Zhang, P. (2012). Do Chinese state-owned enterprises pay high wage? *Economic Research, 3*, 28–39 (In Chinese).

Ma, X. (2009). The enterprise ownership reforms and the change of wage structure in China: Comparison of gender wage profiles differentials by ownership. *Journal of Chinese Economic Studies, 6*(1), 48–64 (In Japanese).

Ma, X. (2011). Immigration and labor market segmentation in urban China: An empirical analysis of income gaps between migrants and urban register workers. *Japanese Journal of Comparative Economics, 48*(1), 39–55 (In Japanese).

Ma, X. (2014). Wage policy: Economy transition and wage differentials by sectors. In K. Nakagane (Ed.), *How did Chinese economy change? Evaluation on economy systems and policies after the economy reform period*. Tokyo: Kokuseisioyin (In Japanese).

Ma, X. (2015). Economic transition and wage differentials between public and private sectors in urban China. *Chinese-USA Business Review, 14*(10), 477–494.

Ma, X. (2016). Determinants of the wage gap between migrants and local urban residents in China: 2002–2013. *Modern Economy, 7*, 786–798.

Ma, X., & Deng, Q. (2016). Economic transition and self-employment of migrants in urban China. *Journal of Chinese Economic Studies, 13*(1), 78–92.

Maddala, G. S. (1983). *Limited-dependent and qualitative variables in econometrics*. New York: Cambridge University Press.

Marx, K. (1867). *Capital* (Vol. 1). London: Harmondsworth, Penguin.

Minami, R., & Ma, X. (2010). The Lewisian turning point of Chinese economy: Comparison with Japanese experience. *China Economic Journal, 3*(2), 165–181.

Minami, R., & Ma, X. (2014). Labor market and Lewisian turning point in China. In R. Minami, F. Makino, & K. Kim (Eds.), *Lewisian turning point in the Chinese economy*. London: Palgrave Macmillan.

National Bureau of Statistics (NBS) of China. (1999). *China statistical yearbook*. Beijing: Chinese Statistics Press.

National Bureau of Statistics (NBS). (2000). *China statistical yearbook 1999*. Beijing: Chinese Statistics Press (In Chinese).

National Bureau of Statistics (NBS). (2008). *China statistical yearbook 2007*. Beijing: Chinese Statistics Press (In Chinese).

National Bureau of Statistics (NBS). (2014). *China statistical yearbook 2013*. Beijing: Chinese Statistics Press (In Chinese).

National Bureau of Statistics (NBS) of China. (2015). *China statistical yearbook*. Beijing: Chinese Statistics Press.

Song, L., & Appleton, S. (2006). The fight between gaining interests group and non-gaining interests group in Chinese labor market: Searching for job and government intervention. In F. Cai & N. Bai (Eds.), *Transition and migrants in China*. Beijing: Social Sciences Academic Press (In Chinese).

Todarro, M. P. (1969). A model of labor migration and urban unemployment in less developed countries. *American Economic Review, 69*(1), 486–499.

Wang, M. (2003). Wage differentials in the transition period: An econometric analysis on the discrimination. *Quantitative & Technical Economics, 5*, 94–98 (In Chinese).

Wu, X. (2006). Communist cadres and market opportunities: Entry into self-employment in China, 1978–1996. *Social Forces, 85*(1), 389–411.

Xie, E. (2012). Transitions to non-farm self-employment in China. *Economic Research, 2*, 54–66 (In Chinese).

Xie, S., & Yao, X. (2006). An analysis on the discrimination on migrants. *Chinese Agriculture Economics, 4*, 39–55 (In Chinese).

Xing, C., & Luo, C. (2009). Income inequality between migrants and local urban residents: A semiparametric approach. *Quantitative & Technical Economics, 10*, 74–86 (In Chinese).

Yamada, G. (1996). Urban informal employment and self-employment in developing countries: Theory and evidence. *Economic Development and Culture Change, 44*(2), 289–314.

Ye, L., Li, S., & Luo, C. (2011). Industrial monopoly, ownership and enterprises wage inequality: An empirical research based on the first national economic census of enterprises data. *Management World, 4*, 26–36 (In Chinese).

Yin, Z., & Gan, L. (2009). Wage differentials between public and nonpublic sector in China. *Economic Research, 4*, 129–140 (In Chinese).

Yueh, L. (2009a). Self-employment in urban China: Networking in a transition economy. *China Economic Review, 20*(3), 471–484.

Yueh, L. (2009b). China's entrepreneurs. *World Development, 37*(4), 778–786.

Zhang, J., & Xue, X. (2008). State and non-state sector wage differentials and human capital contribution. *Economic Research, 4*, 15–25 (In Chinese).

Zhang, J., & Zhao, Z. (2015). Social-family network and self-employment: Evidence from temporary rural-urban migrants in China. *IZA Journal of Labor & Development, 4*(1), 4.

Zhang, Q. F., & Pan, Z. (2012). Women's entry into self-employment in urban China: The role of family in creating gendered mobility patterns. *World Development, 40*(6), 1201–1212.

PART II

Policy Reform and Its Impact on Labor Market Performance

CHAPTER 7

Impact of Minimum Wage on Wage Distribution and Wage Gap Between Rural and Urban Registration Groups

7.1 Introduction

The rationale behind minimum wage policy is to increase the wage level for the low-wage group, and reduce the poverty and narrow income inequality between the high-wage group and low-wage group. Thus, the minimum wage implementation is an important labor policy in both developing and developed countries.

In China, income inequality increased during the economic transition period (Li et al. 2008, 2013, 2017). Along with market-oriented reform progress, the Chinese government also implemented the minimum wage. Minimum wage was first promulgated as a law, Enterprise's Minimum Wage Regulations, in 1993. The minimum wage level is designed to be determined by the local governments (provincial government or city government), consulting with the union, and the representatives of companies. However, in reality, the provincial and city governments can determine primarily the minimum wage levels. Hence, minimum wage implementation situations are different across the regions. In 2004, the central government published a new minimum wage policy to promote the implementation of minimum wage in the whole of China; moreover, after the global financial crisis in 2008, the central government enforced the minimum wage policy. Therefore, there was a large increase in minimum wage level after 2004 and 2008. Based on the 2004 minimum wage policy, the minimum wage level is adjusted once every one or two years. There are many factors to be considered in setting minimum wage levels such as

X. Ma, *Economic Transition and Labor Market Reform in China*,
https://doi.org/10.1007/978-981-13-1987-7_7

the local living cost, consumer price index, social insurance (e.g. the public pension, health care insurance) contributions and housing provident fund that individual workers should pay for, average wage level, economic development level, and employment situation in the local labor market. The local government adjusts the minimum wage level; as a result, there are regional disparities in minimum wage levels (Xing and Xu 2016). For example, the minimum wage level is higher in the Eastern regions as compared to Western and Central regions, and the rise within these bands of the minimum wage levels is different across regions. These regional disparities allow us to utilize a quasi-natural experiment model to estimate the effects of minimum wage policy on wage distribution.

There are some empirical studies on the effects of minimum wage on employment, wage gaps, and income inequality for developed countries, but there are few empirical studies on the effects of minimum wage on wage distribution and wage gap in China. This chapter utilizes the longitudinal data of the Chinese Health and Nutrition Survey (CHNS)[1] from 1991 to 2011 to provide empirical evidence on this issue.

Concretely, this study attempts to answer the following questions. First, does the minimum wage affect average wage level? Does the effect of minimum wage on wage differ by various percentile wage groups? Second, does the minimum wage effect differ by the rural and urban groups?[2] Third, does the minimum wage reduce the wage gap between the rural and urban groups? This chapter analyzes the effect of the minimum wage policy on wage distribution and wage gap for the whole of China. It also compares the minimum wage effect for the rural group and urban group. Considering that the policy effect might differ by the enforcement behavior of the government, the period from 1991 to 2011 is divided into three periods: the minimum wage promulgate period, the minimum wage implementation period, and the minimum wage enforcement period. Moreover, considering that the minimum wage primarily affects low-income groups, the effects of the minimum wage throughout the wage distribution are also analyzed.

This chapter of the book is structured as follows. Section 7.2 reviews the literature on the effects of minimum wage on wage distribution and points out the main contribution of this chapter. Section 7.3 describes analysis methods, including introduction to models (e.g. OLS model, quantile regression model, and difference in difference method), survey data and national minimum wage database utilization, and variables setting—particularly the definition of wage and treatment group. Section 7.4 presents and interprets the results, compares these results based on different empirical analysis methods, and gives the explanation on these results. The last section presents the main conclusions and points out some policy implications.

7.2 Hypotheses and Empirical Studies on the Effects of Minimum Wage on Wage Distribution

There are some empirical studies[3] on the effects of minimum wage on employment[4], wage gaps and income inequality[5] for the developed counties, but the empirical studies on the effects of minimum wage on wage distribution in China are scarce.[6] To study the effect of minimum wage on wage distributions, three types of analyses were conducted on individual survey data.

The first analysis involved OLS (ordinary least squares) and QR (quantile regression) models to investigate the effects of minimum wage (MW) on average wage and various percentile wage groups (Card 1992a, b; Katz and Krueger 1992; Card and Krueger 1995a, b; Neumark 2001; Gindling and Terrell 2005; Neumark et al. 2006; Hohberg and Lay 2015).

The second analysis is similar to the one conducted by Neumark et al. (2004) in 2004, who analyzed the effect of minimum wage change on wage level change throughout wage distribution by using a special model.[7]

The third analysis used the difference-in-differences (DID) method to evaluate the minimum wage policy effect to address the heterogeneity problem. It is caused by unobservable factors, which perhaps affect whether or not the minimum wage policy performs or increases largely in different regions (Neumark et al. 2006; Dinkelman and Ranchhod 2012; Bhorat et al. 2014).

How does the minimum wage affect wage distributions? Earlier studies highlight the spike and spillover effects. First, the spike effect appears when the MW affects a group with wages below the MW or the group with wages slightly above the minimum wage (called the group with a wage around the minimum wage). If there are no compliance problems, the spike effect should be visible when a minimum wage policy is implemented. Neumark and Wascher (1992), Card and Krueger (1995a, b), Baker et al. (1999), and Lee (1999) pointed out that the spike effect of minimum wage was visible in the U.S. and U.K.

Second, the minimum wage might also affect groups with wages above the minimum wage, which is defined as "spillover effect of minimum wage" (Grossman 1983; Card and Krueger 1995a; Lee 1999; Neumark et al. 2004). Although previous studies using these models focused on the estimation of the minimum wage effect on wage distribution, particularly on the spillover effect of minimum wage, the empirical study results were not consistent. For example, Lee (1999) found that the spillover effect existed, whereas Autor et al. (2010) pointed out that the spillover effect was not noticeable.

There are some hypotheses to explain the spillover effect of minimum wage. For example, based on neoclassical economic theory, the skill substitution hypothesis proposes that implementing a minimum wage policy increases labor costs for low-skilled workers, so firms might employ high-skilled workers rather than low-skilled workers. This causes the increase of high-skilled worker wage resulting from the increase of the demand for high-skilled workers. The substitution effect is particularly greater for workers closer to the low-skilled group (e.g., the middle-wage group) (Pettengill 1981). In addition, the monopoly hypothesis explains that when a firm increases the wage level for the low-wage group, the wage gaps between the low-wage group and middle- or high-wage group should decrease, which could cause the decrease of work effort for the groups whose wages are not affected by the minimum wage. In order to keep the wage gap consistent, a firm might also increase the wage levels for groups not affected by the minimum wage to provide motivation. The efficient wage hypothesis can also explain why firms increase wage levels for groups who are not covered by the minimum wage regulations. However, the labor cost constraint hypothesis proposes that when the labor cost is constant, when the minimum wage is implemented, the increase in labor costs for the low-wage group might decrease the firm's profit in the short term, so the firm should not increase wage levels for groups not covered by the minimum wage. When the effect of the labor cost constraint hypothesis outweighs the effects of the skill substitution hypothesis, the motivation hypothesis, and the efficient wage hypothesis, the spillover effect does not appear. This issue requires empirical examination because predicting the spillover effect based on economic theories is complex.

Then, considering empirical studies on the issue for China, Jia and Zhang (2013) analyze the spillover effects of minimum wage in China using 1997–2009 data from the CHNS. They found that the spillover effect of the minimum wage increase can reach to 1.00–1.25 times the minimum wage level on the male and female wage distributions. Di and Han (2015) analyzed the effect of minimum wage on Chinese urban residents' income using 1996–2010 data from CHNS, and revealed that when the minimum wage level increases by 1%, the average wage will increase by 0.281–0.899%, and the affect mainly concentrates in the low-income group. Moreover, they pointed out that the minimum wage especially provides protection for the elderly and low-skilled workers. Wang and Tang (2014) utilized the 2003–2006 Migrant Household Survey conducted by the Research Center of Rural Economy (RCRE) to analyze the effect of minimum wage on the wage distribution, and found minimum wage increase has a positive lagged effect on wage level increase for the group with lowest income, but this effect is not significant for workers whose wage is near the minimum wage level. In addition, Ma et al. (2012) utilized Chinese manufacturing firm-level data and city-level minimum wage from 1997 to 2007 to analyze the effect of minimum wage, and found that if the minimum wage increases by 10%, the average wages in firms pick up by 0.4–0.5%.

To compare the previous studies for China, the main contributions of this study are as follows. First, the previous studies only analyze the minimum wage effect for the whole of China or migrant group; it is not clear whether the minimum wage effect differs by the rural and urban groups. Because the average wage level is lower for the rural group than for the urban group, the minimum wage effect might be greater for the rural group than for the counterpart. Whereas, because most rural workers work in the small-sized firms of the private sector in which the minimum wage might not be implemented well, the effect of the minimum wage might be smaller for the rural group. Thus, the difference of the minimum wage effect on wage distribution between the rural and urban groups is not clear. This chapter of the book will compare the minimum wage effect for the rural and urban groups.

Second, the previous studies only focus on the intra-group wage gap based on the QR model, whereas the empirical studies on the wage gaps between various groups are scarce.[8] This study will investigate its effect on the wage gap between the rural and urban groups, and the results will provide new evidence to evaluate the minimum wage policy effects.

Third, to consider the changes of minimum wage policy by period, this study analyzes the effects of minimum wage policy for the three periods: the minimum wage promulgate period (1997–2000), the minimum wage implementation period (2004–2006), and the minimum wage enforcement period (2009–2011). This shows the disparities of minimum wage effects on wage distribution, which is perhaps caused by the government's enforcement behaviors.

7.3 Methodology and Data

7.3.1 Model

First, the OLS (ordinary least squares) model is used to investigate the effects of minimum wage on average wage, which is expressed as Eq. (7.1).

$$\ln W_{ijt} = \alpha_t + \beta_1 \ln \mathrm{MW}_{jt} + \beta_2 X_{ijt} + \varepsilon_{ijt} \tag{7.1}$$

In Eq. (7.1), *i* represents individual workers, *t* represents periods, and *j* represents regions. ln *W* is the logarithmic value of wage, ln MW is the logarithmic value of minimum wage, *X* is other variables affecting wages (such as education and work experience as a proxy for human capital, male, occupation, and public sector dummies), α is a constant, ε is an error term, and β_1, β_2 represent the estimated coefficients of variables. The coefficients of ln MW (β_1) show the effects of minimum wage level on average wage.

Second, to see the effects of the minimum wage on wage by different percentile wage groups, I adopt the Quantile Regression Model (Koenker and Baset 1978), which can be expressed as:

$$\min\left[\sum_{h_1:\ln W_{ijt} \geq \beta_{ijt} H_{ijt}} \theta \left|\ln W_{ijt} - \beta H_{ijt}\right| + \sum_{h_0:\ln W_{ijt} < \beta_{ijt} H_{ijt}\ \ \rho(\theta)\in(0\sim1)} (1-\theta)\left|\ln W_{ijt} - \beta H_{ijt}\right|\right] \tag{7.2}$$

In Eq. (7.2), *i* represents individual workers, and θ represents percentile of wages (1 percentile is expressed as 1th). The equation's other variables are the same as those of Eq. (7.1). $\rho(\theta)$ is a selection function for the different wage percentiles. *H* indicates ln MW and *X* presented in Eq. (7.1). The QR model is designed for estimation using the optimal method, which minimizes the two error terms in Eq. (7.2). The coefficients of ln MW show the effect of minimum wage on wage levels by different percentile wage groups.

Finally, to prove the influence of minimum wage on wage is difficult because the direction of causality goes both ways. For example, the policy is that each locality's minimum wage should be set with reference to the local average wage level; in other words, the local minimum wage is a function of local average wage. Although the effects of minimum wage on wage can be estimated by the OLS and QR models, these analyses show that the two variables are correlated, but they don't control for the fact that there is causality in both ways and so cannot tell us if the minimum wage in fact affects wages. To consider this problem and identify the "real" effect of minimum wage policy on wages and wage gaps, here, the DID (Difference in Difference) method, which is frequently used for policy evaluation, is applied, and can be represented as follows:

$$\ln W_{ijt} = \alpha + \gamma_1 \text{Year}_{ij} + \gamma_2 \text{Treat}_{ij} + \gamma_3 \text{DID}_{ij} + \gamma_4 X_{ij} + u_{ij} \quad (7.3)$$

$$\ln W_{ijt} = \alpha + \gamma_1 \text{Year}_{ij} + \gamma_2 \text{Treat}_{ij} + \gamma_3 \text{DID}_{ij} + \gamma_4 \text{Rur}_{ij} + \gamma_5 \text{Mig} * \text{DID}_{ij} + \gamma_6 X_{ij} + \varepsilon_{ij} \quad (7.4)$$

In Eqs. (7.3 and 7.4), i stands for the individual, j represents categories of regions, *Year* is the minimum wage level adjustment year dummy variable, *Treat* is the treatment group dummy variable, *DID* is interaction of *Year* and *Treat*, and *Mig* is the dummy variable of the worker with the rural registration and gaining the wage from non-agriculture work. *Mig*DID* are interaction items. X represents other variables affecting wage. α is the constant term, and v is the error term. γ represents the estimated coefficient for each variable. In Eq. (7.3), if γ_3 is a positive value and it is statistically significant, it indicates that if the minimum wage level increases, the wage level will increase, and vice versa. In Eq. (7.4), if γ_5 is a positive value and it is statistically significant, it indicates that when the other factors are constant, the effect of the minimum wage policy on wage is greater for the rural group than for the urban group, and therefore the minimum wage policy might contribute to reducing the wage gap between the rural and urban registration groups, and vice versa.

7.3.2 Data

The longitudinal survey data of the Chinese Health and Nutrition Survey (CHNS) from 1991 to 2011 are utilized for the analysis. For detailed information on the CHNS, please refer to Section 2.3 in Chap. 2 of this book. Because there are design similarities in the questionnaire, this study can use the same information for analysis for three periods and every survey year. The CHNS covers the representative regions in China, including Beijing, Liaoning, Heilongjiang, Shanghai, Jiangsu, Shandong,

Henan, Hubei, Hunan, Guangxi, and Guizhou Chongqi in 2011.[9] Utilizing the information of the whole regions (e.g. province, municipality), I merge the regional (province-level) minimum wage levels based on the Chinese National Minimum Wage Databases (CNMWD) with the CHNS survey data to construct a new dataset—including the individual-level data and the regional-level MW data for the analysis.

The wage is the basic wage excluding the bonus.[10] The unit of analysis object in the study is the monthly wage.[11] The consumption price index (CPI) is utilized as the standard to adjust the wage in every survey year.

The analytic objects are non-agriculture workers, excluding the unemployed and the workers on the family farm. Considering the retirement system in the public sector, the analytic objects are limited to those aged 16–60 (male workers aged from 16 to 60, female workers aged from 16 to 55).

In the wage function, the explained variable is the logarithm of the monthly wage, and the explaining variables are the variables likely to affect the wage, such as years of schooling, experience years,[12] health status, monthly working hours, sectors by ownership type,[13] occupation,[14] employment status,[15] district (the Eastern, Central, and Western Regions), and the survey year dummy variables which are usually used in the previous studies.

The analysis based on the DID method requires the construction of the appropriate DID items (see Eqs. (7.3 and 7.4)). As described above, I gain the regional maximum wage levels based on the Chinese National Minimum Wage Databases (CNMWD). CPI is utilized as the standard to adjust the nominal monthly minimum wage in every year. I utilized the information about the maximum wage levels in the prior survey year and the survey year to conduct the control and treatment groups. Concretely, the treatment group is the group in which the minimum wage level has increased largely from the prior survey year to the survey year; the control group is the group in which the minimum wage level has not changed in both the prior survey year and the survey year or has just increased a little from the prior survey year to the survey year, and is closest to the target group's region. I construct the DID items based on the information for the regions shown in Table 7.1. Moreover, based on the implementation and enforcement year of the minimum wage policy, the pre-policy and post-policy year dummy variables are also constructed (see Table 7.1).

Table 7.1 DID items and policy years setting

Policy	*Pre-policy*	*Post-policy*	*Treatment*	*Control*
1993 policy	1991–1993	1997	Jiangsu	Others
2004 policy	1997–2000	2004–2006	Jiangsu Shanghai	Others
2008 policy	2006	2009–2011	Hernan Hubei	Others

Source: Based on the questionnaires of CHNS 1989–2011
Note: Regions include Beijing, Liaoning, Herlongjiang, Shanggai, Jiangsu, Shanodng, Hernan, Hubei, Hunanm Guangxi, Guizhou, Chongqing

Descriptive statistics of variables are summarized in Table 7.2. (1) The mean value of wage is higher for the rural workers than for the urban workers. (2) The average education level is higher for the urban workers than for the counterpart. (3) The proportion of technicians and managers is higher for the urban workers than for the counterpart. (4) The proportion of regular workers is higher for the urban workers than for the counterpart. (5) The proportion of workers in the government organizations, public organizations (*Shiye Danwei*), and SOEs is higher for the urban workers than for the counterpart. (6) The proportion of workers in the eastern region is higher for the rural workers than for the counterpart. It is observed that the individual characteristics differ by these two groups, and the labor market is segmented by various sectors (e.g. the formal sector and informal sector, the public sector and private sector).

7.4 Econometric Analysis Results

7.4.1 Estimated Results of Minimum Wage Effects on Wage Distribution Using OLS and QR Models

First, Table 7.3 shows the results of wage function using the OLS model. We observe the effect of minimum wage on wage through the estimated coefficient of the minimum wage logarithmic value. The estimated coefficients of minimum wage logarithmic values is 0.142, 0.059 for the total sample (the total of the rural and urban workers) and the rural worker, which are statistically significant at the 10% level during the period from 1997 to 2011. Whereas the effect of the minimum wage policy is not statistically significant for the urban group. These results indicate that the

Table 7.2 Descriptive statistics by total, rural, and urban groups

	(1) Total		*(2) Rural*		*(3) Urban*	
	Means	*S.D.*	*Means*	*S.D.*	*Means*	*S.D.*
ln monthly wage	6.344	1.187	6.275	1.163	6.439	1.212
Monthly work hours	180	62	182	68	178	52
Years of schooling	9	4	9	4	10	4
Experience years	14	12	14	12	14	12
Male	0.555	0.497	0.541	0.498	0.573	0.495
Health	6.202	2.534	5.910	2.188	6.609	2.900
Occupation						
Technician	0.133	0.339	0.108	0.311	0.166	0.372
Manager	0.072	0.258	0.054	0.227	0.096	0.295
Clerk	0.087	0.282	0.068	0.251	0.114	0.317
Agriculture worker	0.140	0.347	0.191	0.393	0.070	0.255
Manufacturing worker (H)	0.132	0.339	0.123	0.329	0.144	0.351
Manufacturing worker (L)	0.182	0.386	0.196	0.397	0.162	0.368
Service worker	0.127	0.333	0.121	0.326	0.135	0.342
Others	0.127	0.333	0.138	0.345	0.112	0.316
Employment status						
Regular worker	0.525	0.499	0.457	0.498	0.620	0.485
Irregular worker I	0.113	0.316	0.101	0.301	0.129	0.336
Irregular worker II	0.137	0.344	0.159	0.365	0.107	0.309
Self-employees I	0.031	0.173	0.030	0.172	0.031	0.174
Self-employees II	0.187	0.390	0.247	0.431	0.105	0.307
Others	0.007	0.083	0.007	0.082	0.007	0.084
Ownership						
Government	0.223	0.416	0.171	0.377	0.294	0.456
Public organization	0.164	0.370	0.161	0.367	0.168	0.374
SOE	0.114	0.318	0.084	0.278	0.155	0.362
COE	0.300	0.458	0.389	0.487	0.178	0.382
Private/foreign	0.200	0.400	0.196	0.397	0.205	0.404
Regions						
East	0.414	0.493	0.433	0.495	0.388	0.487
Central	0.358	0.480	0.324	0.468	0.406	0.491
West	0.228	0.419	0.243	0.429	0.206	0.405
Survey year						
y1991	0.103	0.304	0.102	0.302	0.104	0.306
y1993	0.101	0.302	0.105	0.307	0.096	0.295
y1997	0.109	0.312	0.111	0.314	0.107	0.309
y2000	0.119	0.324	0.120	0.325	0.118	0.323
y2004	0.110	0.313	0.108	0.310	0.114	0.317
y2006	0.125	0.331	0.126	0.332	0.124	0.330

(*continued*)

Table 7.2 (continued)

	(1) Total		*(2) Rural*		*(3) Urban*	
	Means	*S.D.*	*Means*	*S.D.*	*Means*	*S.D.*
y2009	0.127	0.333	0.133	0.340	0.119	0.323
y2011	0.205	0.404	0.196	0.397	0.218	0.413
Urban	0.419	0.493	0	0	1	0
Observations	23,992		13,940		10,431	

Source: Calculated based on CHNS 1989–2011

Note: w is monthly wage in the prior survey year ($t - 1$), MW is highest minimum wage level in survey year (t)

Table 7.3 Results of effects of minimum wage policy on average wage by the OLS

	(1) Total		*(2) Rural*		*(3) Urban*	
	Coeff.	*SE*	*Coeff.*	*SE*	*Coeff.*	*SE*
MW	0.142*	0.076	0.059*	0.101	0.251	0.114
Working hours	0.000***	0.000	0.001***	0.000	0.000***	0.000
Registration (Rural)						
Urban	0.184**	0.015				
Years of schooling	0.020***	0.003	0.021***	0.003	0.016***	0.004
Experience years	−0.022***	0.002	−0.021***	0.002	−0.020***	0.003
Experience years squared	0.000***	0.000	0.000***	0.000	0.000***	0.000
Male	0.051**	0.014	0.041**	0.019	0.055**	0.021
Health	−0.005*	0.003	0.011***	0.004	−0.013***	0.004
Occupation (Clerk)						
Technician	0.177***	0.030	0.152**	0.045	0.161**	0.040
Manager	0.122***	0.035	0.034	0.054	0.183**	0.045
Agriculture worker	−0.295***	0.044	−0.462***	0.058	−0.041*	0.072
Manufacturing worker (H)	−0.243***	0.031	−0.279***	0.046	−0.232**	0.042
Manufacturing worker (L)	−0.426***	0.030	−0.550***	0.044	−0.287**	0.043
Service worker	−0.445***	0.032	−0.604***	0.047	−0.266**	0.044
Others	−0.151***	0.033	−0.317***	0.048	0.025**	0.046
Employment status (Regular worker)						
Irregular worker I	0.159***	0.024	0.225***	0.034	0.092**	0.033
Irregular worker II	0.002	0.026	0.056*	0.034	−0.082**	0.041
Self-employees I	0.063	0.043	0.067	0.058	0.064*	0.062
Self-employees II	0.070**	0.033	0.094**	0.043	0.007*	0.054

(*continued*)

Table 7.3 (continued)

	(1) Total		(2) Rural		(3) Urban	
	Coeff.	SE	Coeff.	SE	Coeff.	SE
Others	−0.153*	0.084	−0.168	0.113	−0.117	0.124
Sector (Government)						
Public organization	0.380***	0.024	0.225***	0.034	0.534**	0.034
SOE	0.385***	0.027	0.365***	0.042	0.369**	0.035
COE	0.368***	0.028	0.398***	0.038	0.309**	0.042
Private/Foreign	0.824***	0.027	0.888***	0.038	0.704**	0.037
Regions (East)						
Central	−0.164***	0.022	−0.203***	0.030	−0.113**	0.034
West	−0.167***	0.030	−0.182***	0.040	−0.140**	0.046
Year (1997)						
y2000	0.145***	0.033	0.158***	0.044	0.116**	0.050
y2004	0.309***	0.034	0.299***	0.045	0.319*	0.051
y2006	0.175**	0.069	0.171*	0.093	0.187*	0.104
y2009	0.335***	0.078	0.320***	0.104	0.363	0.116
y2011	0.597***	0.097	0.512***	0.130	0.703	0.145
Constants	5.061***	0.446	5.564***	0.594	4.607	0.673
Observations	19,093		11,055		8038	
Adj R-squared	0.232		0.189		0.294	

Source: Calculated based on CHNS 1997–2011
Note:
(1) *, **, ***: statistically significant at 10%, 5%, and 1% levels
(2) OLS models are utilized in these calculations

minimum wage could positively affect the average wage level for the rural group, but it might not influence the wage level for the urban group. When the minimum wage level increases by 1%, the average wage will increase by 0.142% and 0.059% for the total group and the rural group.

Second, Table 7.4 summarizes the results based on the Heckman two-step model. The coefficients of reverse Mill's rate are positive values, and they are statistically significant for the total, the rural, and the urban groups. It indicates that when the sample selection bias problem is not addressed, the results of wage function might be underestimated. Therefore, the Heckman two-step model should be utilized in the analysis. The coefficients of the minimum wage is 0.165, 0.259 for the total and the urban workers. They are statistically significant at the 5% level, and it is shown that when the minimum wage level increases by 1%, the average wage will increase by 0.165%, 0.259% for the total and the urban groups, but it does not influence the wage level for the rural workers.

Table 7.4 Results of effects of minimum wage policy on average wage by the Heckman two-step model

	(1) Total		*(2) Rural*		*Urban*	
	Coeff.	*SE*	*Coeff.*	*SE*	*Coeff.*	*SE*
MW	0.165**	0.076	0.090	0.101	0.259**	0.114
Working hours	0.000***	0.000	0.001***	0.000	0.000	0.000
Registration (Rural)						
Urban	0.263***	0.021				
Years of schooling	0.043***	0.005	0.061***	0.009	0.026***	0.006
Experience years	−0.016***	0.002	−0.012***	0.003	−0.016***	0.003
Experience years squared	0.000***	0.000	0.000***	0.000	0.000	0.000
Male	0.051***	0.014	0.043**	0.020	0.055***	0.021
Health	0.000	0.003	0.022***	0.005	−0.010***	0.004
Occupation (Clerk)						
Technician	0.171***	0.030	0.148***	0.045	0.157***	0.040
Manager	0.113***	0.035	0.021	0.054	0.179***	0.045
Agriculture worker	−0.286***	0.044	−0.449***	0.058	−0.037	0.072
Manufacturing worker (H)	−0.239***	0.031	−0.273***	0.046	−0.229***	0.042
Manufacturing worker (L)	−0.415***	0.030	−0.537***	0.044	−0.280***	0.043
Service worker	−0.439***	0.032	−0.597***	0.048	−0.262***	0.044
Others	−0.150***	0.033	−0.313***	0.048	0.023	0.046
Employment status (Regular worker)						
Irregular worker I	0.156***	0.024	0.224***	0.034	0.087***	0.033
Irregular worker II	−0.007	0.026	0.049	0.034	−0.091**	0.041
Self-employees I	0.066	0.043	0.069	0.058	0.068	0.062
Self-employees II	0.076**	0.033	0.101**	0.043	0.010	0.054
Others	−0.152*	0.084	−0.169	0.112	−0.115	0.124
Sector (Government)						
Public organization	0.384***	0.024	0.230***	0.034	0.537***	0.034
SOE	0.384***	0.027	0.361***	0.042	0.370***	0.035
COE	0.362***	0.028	0.389***	0.038	0.307***	0.042
Private/foreign	0.821***	0.027	0.882***	0.038	0.703***	0.037
Regions (East)						
Central	−0.238***	0.026	−0.345***	0.042	−0.138***	0.035
West	−0.238***	0.033	−0.272***	0.045	−0.191***	0.050
Year (1997)						
y2000	0.263***	0.039	0.355***	0.060	0.171***	0.054
y2004	0.416***	0.039	0.478***	0.058	0.367***	0.054
y2006	0.259***	0.071	0.308***	0.097	0.232**	0.105
y2009	0.417***	0.079	0.458***	0.108	0.406***	0.117

(*continued*)

Table 7.4 (continued)

	(1) Total		*(2) Rural*		*Urban*	
	Coeff.	*SE*	*Coeff.*	*SE*	*Coeff.*	*SE*
y2011	0.676***	0.098	0.660***	0.134	0.739***	0.146
Mill's ratio	0.336***	0.060	0.521***	0.106	0.172***	0.066
Constants	4.209***	0.471	4.217***	0.652	4.260***	0.686
Total observations	67,992		48,096		19,896	
Censored observations	48,913		37,045		11,868	
Uncensored observations	19,079		11,051		8,028	
Wald chi2(27)	4434.380		2052.150		3642.880	
Prob > chi	0.000		0.000		2903.100	

Source: Calculated based on CHNS 1997–2011

Note:

(1) *, **, ***: statistically significant at 10%, 5%, and 1% levels

(2) Heckman two step models are utilized in these calculations

(3) Age, age squared, years of schooling, male, health, family number, household non-labor earning income region, year variables are used in the first step estimation of Heckman Two Step models, these results are not shown in the table

Third, to consider the effect of the minimum wage policy on wage throughout the wage distribution, I employed the estimations based on the QR model. These results are summarized in Table 7.5. In order to observe the minimum wage effect by the periods, I took the analyses by four periods: the 1997–2000, 2004–2006, and 2009–2011 periods and the period from 1997 to 2011. To compare the minimum wage effect between rural and urban groups, I also took the estimation by these two groups. The main findings are as follows.

(1) Generally, in the minimum wage promulgate period (1997–2000), the minimum wage positively affects the wage from the 5th to 80th wage percentiles, whereas the coefficients of the minimum wage for the lowest wage (1th wage) group and the highest wage (90th) group are not statistically significant; and to compare the coefficient values between various wage percentile groups, it indicates that the effect of the minimum wage is greater for the low-wage group (from 5th to 30th) than for the middle- and high-wage groups (from 40th to 80th). In the minimum wage implementation period (2004–2006), even though the minimum wage positively affects the wage for the low-, middle-, and high-wage groups, the effect is greater for the middle- and high-wage group than that for the low-wage group. In the minimum wage enforcement period

Table 7.5 Results of effects of minimum wage policy on wage distribution by the QR model

	(1) 1997–2000		*(2) 2004–2006*		*(3) 2009–2011*		*(4) 1997–2011*	
	Coeff.	*SE*	*Coeff.*	*SE*	*Coeff.*	*SE*	*Coeff.*	*SE*
Total								
1th	−0.009	0.529	−0.639	0.416	0.221	0.855	−0.450	0.318
5th	0.663***	0.240	0.406*	0.250	−0.376	0.398	−0.186	0.167
10th	0.795***	0.219	0.481**	0.218	0.119	0.325	−0.080	0.162
20th	0.922***	0.256	0.462**	0.215	0.288	0.306	0.003	0.127
30th	0.730***	0.226	0.676***	0.180	0.203	0.241	0.186*	0.112
40th	0.533***	0.206	0.679***	0.146	0.343*	0.201	0.225**	0.094
50th	0.478***	0.175	0.697***	0.138	0.305*	0.180	0.293***	0.086
60th	0.328*	0.175	0.756***	0.142	0.182	0.172	0.213	0.083
70th	0.410**	0.169	0.731***	0.135	0.093	0.167	0.153*	0.085
80th	0.448**	0.194	0.744***	0.171	0.113	0.160	0.206**	0.092
90th	0.244	0.205	0.756***	0.146	0.398**	0.189	0.268***	0.095
Rural								
1th	−0.017	0.792	−1.422***	0.496	−0.427	0.888	−0.427	0.888
5th	0.119	0.275	0.282	0.369	−0.663	0.527	−0.663	0.527
10th	0.519	0.373	0.391	0.327	−0.318	0.504	−0.318	0.504
20th	0.316	0.343	0.687**	0.284	−0.043	0.404	−0.043	0.404
30th	0.420	0.296	0.517**	0.256	0.374	0.338	0.374	0.338
40th	0.261	0.286	0.553***	0.209	0.375	0.274	0.375	0.274
50th	0.239	0.235	0.618***	0.186	0.332	0.257	0.332	0.257
60th	0.082	0.216	0.617***	0.192	0.597***	0.228	0.597***	0.228
70th	0.181	0.232	0.588***	0.181	0.367	0.237	0.367	0.237
80th	0.125	0.248	0.848***	0.230	0.597**	0.233	0.597***	0.233
90th	−0.081	0.278	0.728***	0.207	0.531**	0.242	0.531**	0.242
Urban								
1th	1.170*	0.722	−0.252	0.766	0.800	1.087	0.800	1.087
5th	1.149***	0.377	0.111	0.348	0.675	0.648	0.675	0.648
10th	1.100***	0.281	0.372	0.330	0.472	0.550	0.472	0.550
20th	0.963***	0.323	0.625**	0.302	0.389	0.405	0.389	0.405
30th	1.083***	0.349	1.021***	0.284	0.225	0.397	0.225	0.397
40th	1.000***	0.345	1.031***	0.243	0.133	0.283	0.133	0.283
50th	0.703**	0.314	0.944***	0.203	−0.336	0.248	−0.336	0.248
60th	0.648**	0.301	0.924***	0.222	−0.363	0.232	−0.363	0.232
70th	0.469*	0.285	0.817***	0.217	−0.432*	0.250	−0.432*	0.250
80th	0.738**	0.316	0.937***	0.254	−0.515**	0.255	−0.515*	0.255
90th	1.001***	0.387	0.687***	0.257	0.059	0.312	0.059	0.312

Source: Calculated based on CHNS 1997–2011

Note:

(1) *, **, ***: statistically significant at 10%, 5%, and 1% levels

(2) The results by 1%–90% (1th–90th) wage percentiles are estimated using quantile regression model

(3) The coefficients of logarithm value of MW are shown in the table

(4) Years of schooling, experience year, male, health, occupations, employment status, sectors by ownership type, urban region (Central, West), year variables are also included in these estimations

(2009–2011), the minimum wage positively affects the middle-wage (40th, 50th) group and the high-wage (90th) group, but the effect of the minimum wage on the low-wage group is not statistically significant. For the long-term (from 1997–2011), the minimum wage positively affects the middle-wage (30th, 40th, 50th) group and the high-wage (70th, 80th, 90th) group, but the effect of the minimum wage on the low-wage group is not statistically significant.

(2) The effect of the minimum wage on wage distribution is different by the rural and urban groups. For example, in the minimum wage promulgate period (1997–2000), the effects of the minimum wage on wage distribution are not statistically significant throughout the wage distribution for the rural group, whereas the minimum wage positively affects the low-, middle-, and high-wage groups for the urban group. It might be because in the 1997–2000 period, the minimum wage was mainly implemented in the public sector, and most firms in the private sector did not carry out the minimum wage system. It is thought that most urban residents work in the public sector, whereas most rural residents work in the private sector, because the implementation situation of the minimum wage was different by the public sector and private sector, and the effect of the minimum wage on wage distribution might be different by the rural and urban groups. In the minimum wage implementation period (2004–2006), the minimum wage positively affects the low-, middle-, and high-wage groups for both the rural and urban groups. It might be because, based on the minimum wage policy published in 2004, the minimum wage was enforced to be implemented in both the public sector and private sector. In the minimum wage enforcement period (2009–2011), the minimum wage positively affects the high-wage group for the rural group, whereas it negatively affects the high-wage group for the urban group.

7.4.2 *Estimated Results of Minimum Wage Effects on Wage Distribution Using the DID Method*

Even though the results based on the OLS, Heckman two-step model, and QR models indicated that the minimum wage might affect the average wage and wage distribution which are consistent with the results in the previous studies, these cannot investigate the causal relation between the minimum wage policy and wage distribution. The results based on the DID method can provide the evidence on the "real" effect of minimum wage policy on wage distributions. The estimated coefficients of the DID variables are summarized in Tables 7.6A–7.6C.

Table 7.6A Results of the effects of the minimum wage policy on wage distribution by the DID method (1991–1997)

	(1) Total		*(2) Rural*		*(3) Urban*	
	Coeff.	*SE*	*Coeff.*	*SE*	*Coeff.*	*SE*
Panel A: 1991–1997						
DID variables						
Mean	0.294***	0.071	0.314***	0.090	0.236**	0.115
1th	0.108	0.193	−0.168	0.333	0.016	0.143
5th	0.098	0.100	0.077	0.150	0.343***	0.133
10th	0.218**	0.104	0.060	0.117	0.394***	0.102
20th	0.314***	0.078	0.196*	0.113	0.420***	0.135
30th	0.355***	0.080	0.310***	0.114	0.473***	0.118
40th	0.491***	0.101	0.432***	0.126	0.627***	0.135
50th	0.484***	0.100	0.447***	0.125	0.480***	0.168
60th	0.333***	0.107	0.379***	0.122	0.245	0.181
70th	0.299***	0.104	0.388***	0.124	0.137	0.178
80th	0.286***	0.111	0.332***	0.121	0.094	0.177
90th	0.236**	0.115	0.343**	0.139	0.092	0.215

Source: Calculated based on CHNS 1991–1997

Note:

(1) The results by 1%–90% percentiles wage distributions are estimated using quantile regression (QR) model; the results using mean value of wage are estimated by OLS

(2) The results of DID item are summarized in the table

(3) The other variables including post-policy period, treatment group dummy, years of schooling, experience year, male, health, occupation, employment status, sectors by ownership type, rural dummy variables are also estimated, these results are not shown in the table

(4) The treatment group is the group in which the MW level has increased largely from pre-policy period (1991, 1993) to post-policy period (1997); the control group is the group in which the MW level has just increased a little from pre-policy period to post-policy period

(5) DID items are intersection items of year and the treatment group dummy variables

(6) *, **, ***: statistically significant at 10%, 5%, and 1% levels

First, (1) generally, using the information for three years (1991, 1993, and 1997), the results show that the coefficients on the DID variables are statistically significant for average wage, and most percentile wage groups (from 10th to 90th), when the minimum wage increases 10%, the average wage will increase 2.94%, 3.14%, and 2.36% for the total, the rural, and the urban groups, respectively. However, the values for the lowest-wage groups (1st and 5th percentile) are not statistically significant.

(2) To compare the rural group and urban group, first, considering the effect on average wage, even though the minimum wage positively affects the average wage for both the rural and urban groups, the effect is greater for the rural group than for the urban group. Then, to see the

Table 7.6B Results of the effects of the minimum wage policy on wage distribution by the DID method (1997–2006)

	(1) Total		*(2) Rural*		*(3) Urban*	
	Coeff.	*SE*	*Coeff.*	*SE*	*Coeff.*	*SE*
Panel B: 1997–2006						
DID variables						
Mean	−0.110*	0.060	−0.018	0.084	−0.191**	0.086
1th	−0.173	0.285	−0.152	0.320	−0.199	0.289
5th	−0.104	0.122	0.075	0.188	−0.289	0.237
10th	−0.165	0.110	0.038	0.166	−0.194	0.131
20th	−0.179*	0.108	−0.148	0.168	−0.224*	0.139
30th	−0.170*	0.095	−0.082	0.114	−0.207*	0.121
40th	−0.110	0.075	−0.007	0.119	−0.238**	0.110
50th	−0.144*	0.069	0.036	0.094	−0.187*	0.106
60th	−0.089	0.068	0.078	0.084	−0.248**	0.110
70th	−0.082	0.071	0.065	0.100	−0.194*	0.107
80th	−0.114	0.079	−0.012	0.104	−0.164	0.107
90th	−0.057	0.088	0.089	0.113	0.059	0.150

Source: Calculated based on CHNS 1997–2006

Note:

(1) The results by 1%–90% percentiles wage distributions are estimated using quantile regression (QR) model; the results using mean value of wage are estimated by OLS

(2) The results of DID item are summarized in the table

(3) The other variables including post-policy period, treatment group dummy, years of schooling, experience year, male, health, occupation, employment status, sectors by ownership type, rural dummy variables are also estimated, these results are not shown in the table

(4) The treatment group is the group in which the MW level has increased largely from pre-policy period (1997, 2000) to post-policy period (2004, 2006); the control group is the group in which the MW level has just increased a little from pre-policy period to post-policy period

(5) DID items are intersection items of year and the treatment group dummy variables

(6) *, **, ***: statistically significant at 10%, 5%, and 1% levels

effect on different wage percentile groups, in the rural group, the coefficients on the DID variables are statistically significant for middle- and high-wage groups (from 30th to 90th), whereas in the urban group, the minimum wage positively affects the low- and middle-wage groups (from 5th to 50th). The results might be because in the period the minimum wage was mainly implemented in the public sector; most rural workers with low-wage jobs were in the private sector, in which the minimum wage policy was not carried out. For the high-wage urban worker group, because their wage level is higher than the minimum wage, which is mainly determined by the managed wage by the government

Table 7.6C Results of the effects of the minimum wage policy on wage distribution by the DID method (2006–2011)

	(1) Total		*(2) Rural*		*(3) Urban*	
	Coeff.	*SE*	*Coeff.*	*SE*	*Coeff.*	*SE*
Panel C: 2006–2011						
DID variables						
Mean	0.148*	0.089	0.055	0.127	0.176	0.123
1th	0.164	0.217	0.101	0.306	−0.454**	0.219
5th	−0.039	0.162	0.124	0.207	−0.166	0.238
10th	0.012	0.149	−0.032	0.183	−0.038	0.243
20th	0.154	0.154	−0.022	0.235	0.110	0.195
30th	0.176	0.135	0.032	0.178	0.222	0.204
40th	0.129	0.116	0.056	0.165	0.047	0.167
50th	0.136	0.107	−0.051	0.144	0.236*	0.145
60th	0.070	0.110	−0.050	0.168	0.306**	0.144
70th	0.060*	0.098	0.017	0.162	0.200	0.135
80th	0.159*	0.098	0.251*	0.148	0.046	0.126
90th	0.154	0.102	0.117	0.141	0.186	0.171

Source: Calculated based on CHNS 2006–2011

Note:

(1) The results by 1%–90% percentiles wage distributions are estimated using quantile regression (QR) model; the results using mean value of wage are estimated by OLS

(2) The results of DID item are summarized in the table

(3) The other variables including post-policy period, treatment group dummy, years of schooling, experience year, male, health, occupation, employment status, sectors by ownership type, rural dummy variables are also estimated, these results are not shown in the table

(4) The treatment group is the group in which the MW level has increased largely from pre-policy period (2006) to post-policy period (2009, 2011); the control group is the group in which the MW level has just increased a little from pre-policy period to post-policy period

(5) DID items are intersection items of year and the treatment group dummy variables

(6) *, **, ***: statistically significant at 10%, 5%, and 1% levels

or market mechanism, the minimum wage level does not affect their wage. Moreover, the minimum wage does not affect the wage level for the lowest-wage group (1 th) for both the rural and the urban groups. It might be because most of the workers with the lowest wage work in the informal sector and the minimum wage policy was not implemented in the sector. These results indicate that generally the 1997 minimum wage system did affect most of the low-, middle-, and high-wage groups, and the 1997 minimum wage system did have the spike effect and spillover effect. For the low-wage group, the spike effect is greater for the urban worker; for the middle-wage group, even though the spillover effect exists for both the rural and urban groups, the effects are greater for the urban group; for the high-wage group, the spillover effect exists only for the rural group. These results indicate that the firm might increase the wage level of middle- and high-wage rural workers to substitute the low-wage workers to respond to the implementation of minimum wage.

Second, Table 7.6B summarizes the results of the effect of the 2004 minimum wage policy using four years' (1997, 2000, 2004, 2006) survey data. (1) Generally, the results show that the coefficients on the DID variables are significant for average wage, and the low-wage (20th, 30th) and middle-wage (50th) groups at the 10% level, and these have a negative value. (2) In the rural group, the coefficients on the DID variables are not statistically significant for average wage, and all of the wage percentile groups. Whereas in the urban group, the minimum wage negatively affects average wage, and the middle-wage (40th, 60th) group, which might contribute to reducing the intra-group wage gap for the urban group. Based on the regulations of the 2004 minimum wage policy, the minimum wage implementation range expands from the public sector to the private sector. The results indicate that the compliance problem might exist for the private sector in the period.

Third, after 2008, the government enforced the implementation of the minimum wage. To investigate the enforcement effect of the minimum wage, the estimations based on three years' (2006, 2009, 2011) survey data are employed; the results are shown in Table 7.6C. (1) Generally, the minimum wage positively affects the average wage, high-wage group (70th, 80th) at 10% statistical level. The spike effect is not observed, whereas a small spillover effect might exist for the high-wage group. (2) To compare the rural and urban groups, the minimum wage negatively affects the low-wage group (1st) for the urban group, whereas it does not affect the low-wage group for the rural group. The minimum wage positively affects the high-wage (80th) group for the rural worker, and middle-wage (50th, 60th) group for the urban worker. The results indicate that the minimum wage enforcement by the government might not have the spike effect, whereas the spillover effect might remain for both the rural and the urban groups.

Fourth, to compare the spillover effect of minimum wage by the three periods, the results show that the spillover effect is greatest for the minimum wage promulgate period. Several reasons can explain the results. As described above, when the effect of the labor cost constraint hypothesis is less than that of the skill substitution hypothesis, the monopoly hypothesis, and the efficient wage hypothesis, the spillover effect will be visible. Around the 1997 minimum wage implementation period, the government did not enforce ownership reform in the public sector (e.g. SOEs); therefore, the public sector contributed a greater proportion to the economy and thus had a relatively higher influence on the wage determination system. It is thought that the public sector is a monopoly sector in China; since the monopoly hypothesis had a greater effect than the labor cost constraint hypothesis during the period, the spillover effect was greater in this period. However, the government enforced SOE reform since the end of the 1990s, and thus the influence of the market mechanism became greater, which might cause the influence of the labor cost constraint hypothesis to become greater than the other hypotheses, and therefore the spillover effect became small in the other periods. Moreover, the results indicate that for 1997–2006, most firms decreased urban worker wage levels for the middle-wage groups to respond to increases in labor costs from the minimum wage level increase in the higher ranges since 2004.

7.4.3 Estimated Results of Minimum Wage Effects on Wage Gap Between Rural and Urban Registration Groups Using the DID Method

The results shown in Tables 7.6A–7.6C indicate that the minimum wage effects on average wage and different wage percentile groups differ by the rural group and urban group. Because the wage level is lower for the rural group than for the urban group, it is expected that the positive effect of the minimum wage on wage might be greater for the rural group than for the urban group; therefore it is thought that the minimum wage might reduce the wage gap between these two groups. Whereas, because most of the rural workers work in the informal sector, when the policy compliance problem remains, the minimum wage policy might not contribute to reducing the wage gap. Did the minimum wage affect the wage gap between the rural and urban groups? The causal relation between the policy and wage gap is estimated directly based on the DID method, and the results are summarized in Table 7.7. When the coefficients of interaction of rural worker and DID variable dummy variables are positive and they are statistically significant, it indicates that when the other factors are constant, the positive effect of the minimum wage on wage is greater for the rural group than for the urban group, which could reduce the wage gap

Table 7.7 Results of the effects of the minimum wage policy on wage gap between the rural and urban groups by the DID method

	(1) 1991–1997		*(2) 1997–2006*		*(3) 2006–2011*	
	Coeff.	*SE*	*Coeff.*	*SE*	*Coeff.*	*SE*
DID variables						
Mean	0.456***	0.096	−0.106	0.074	0.194*	0.100
1th	0.331	0.272	0.022	0.353	0.089	0.241
5th	0.312**	0.128	−0.110	0.146	−0.018	0.191
10th	0.362***	0.132	−0.260*	0.135	−0.066	0.169
20th	0.373***	0.106	−0.217*	0.130	0.187	0.172
30th	0.432***	0.108	−0.191*	0.117	0.148	0.151
40th	0.695***	0.137	−0.112	0.093	0.147	0.129
50th	0.700***	0.132	−0.131	0.086	0.184	0.123
60th	0.578***	0.142	−0.128	0.084	0.184	0.120
70th	0.494***	0.139	−0.100	0.088	0.080	0.111
80th	0.504***	0.148	−0.082	0.097	0.220**	0.107
90th	0.444***	0.155	0.072	0.104	0.235**	0.113
Interaction of rural and DID dummy variables						
Mean	−0.254**	0.101	−0.007	0.074	−0.083	0.082
1th	−0.488*	0.287	−0.187	0.350	−0.100	0.198
5th	−0.328**	0.135	−0.043	0.145	−0.045	0.157
10th	−0.283**	0.139	0.199	0.134	0.080	0.139
20th	−0.090	0.112	0.082	0.130	−0.075	0.142
30th	−0.096	0.113	0.081	0.116	0.041	0.124
40th	−0.235*	0.144	0.012	0.092	−0.035	0.106
50th	−0.308**	0.139	−0.016	0.085	−0.099	0.101
60th	−0.318**	0.149	0.063	0.083	−0.150	0.098
70th	−0.336**	0.147	0.027	0.087	−0.039	0.092
80th	−0.359**	0.156	−0.057	0.097	−0.093	0.088
90th	−0.298*	0.163	−0.167	0.103	−0.143	0.093

Source: Calculated based on CHNS 1991–2011

Note:

(1) The results by 1%–90% percentiles wage distributions are estimated using quantile regression (QR) model; the results using mean value of wage are estimated by OLS

(2) The results of DID item are summarized in the table

(3) The other variables including post-policy period, treatment group dummy, years of schooling, experience year, male, health, occupation, employment status, sectors by ownership type, rural dummy variables are also estimated, these results are not shown in the table

(4) The treatment group is the group in which the MW level has increased largely from pre-policy period to post-policy period; the control group is the group in which the MW level has just increased a little from pre-policy period to post-policy period

(5) DID items are intersection items of year dummy and the treatment group dummy variables

(6) *, **, ***: statistically significant at 10%, 5%, and 1% levels

between these two groups. The results show that around the 1997 minimum wage system implementation period, the coefficients of the interaction variables are negative for the average wage and low-wage (1th, 5th, 10th wage percentiles) group, middle-wage (40th, 50th, 60th) group, and high-wage (70th, 80th, 90th) group, and the results are statistically significant at 10%–5% levels. It indicates that the 1997 minimum wage system implementation expanded the wage gap between the rural and urban groups. In addition, in the other periods (the 1997–2000 period, the 2006–2011 period), the minimum wage might not affect the wage gaps for the average wage group and wage distributions throughout different wage percentile groups. The reason may be that the policy compliance problem might remain in China (Ye et al. 2015).

7.5 Conclusions

The Chinese government has been officially implementing the minimum wage policy in the public sector since 1993 and enforced minimum wage policy in the whole of China since 2004. Since 2008, the government enforced the implementation of the minimum wage. The implementation of the minimum wage policy is expected to contribute to increasing incomes of low-wage groups and reducing poverty. In China, has the implementation of the minimum wage policy affected average wage and wage distribution? Particularly, has the minimum wage affected the wages for low-wage groups? Does the effect of the minimum wage differ by the rural and urban registration groups? Does the minimum wage reduce the wage gap between the rural and urban registration groups?

To answer these questions, this study employs empirical studies using the longitudinal survey data of the Chinese Health and Nutrition Survey (CHNS) from 1991 to 2011. I employed estimations by OLS, the Heckman two-step model, and the Quantile Regression (QR) model. I also utilize the DID method to investigate the "real" effect of the minimum wage on wage level and wage gap. Several major conclusions based on the DID method emerge.

First, considering the effect of the minimum wage on average wages, the 1997 minimum wage implementation positively affects the average wage for the total, rural, and urban groups. When the minimum wage increases 10%, the average wage will increase 2.94%, 3.14%, and 2.36% for the total, the rural, and the urban groups, respectively. Whereas the implementation of

2004 minimum wage policy decreases the average wage for the total and the urban group. The enforcement of the minimum wage policy since 2008 seems like it does not affect the average wage for both the rural and urban groups.

Second, considering the effect of the minimum wage on low-wage groups, the results indicate that the effect of minimum wage on wage level for the low-wage group is greater for the urban group than for the rural group around the 1997 minimum wage policy implementation period.

Third, the results for the spillover effects of minimum wage are as follows: the minimum wage affects the middle- and high-wage groups during the 1991–1997 and 2006–2011 periods for both rural and urban groups; the spillover effect is greater for the minimum wage implementation period (1991–1997) than the present period.

Fourth, the minimum wage might expand the wage gap between the rural and urban groups around the 1997 minimum wage implementation period, whereas the minimum wage policy might not affect the wage gap in the following periods.

According to these empirical analyses, there are three points worthy of attention. First, the results showed that the 1997 minimum wage implementation positively affects the average wage, and different wage percentile groups for both rural and urban groups. Since the minimum wage levels rose greatly in the policy promulgate period, which increased from zero, the increasing range of minimum wage level can be used as a method to reduce the problems of poverty or working poor in China. Of course, the effect of minimum wage on unemployment should be considered simultaneously when assessing the total effect of the minimum wage.

Second, the spillover effect was visible clearly only in the minimum wage promulgated period for both rural and urban groups, and the minimum wage might reduce the wage level for the middle- and high-wage groups for the urban group in this period. These results show that the effect of the minimum wage policy on reducing income inequality is complex. Detailed empirical studies on the effect of minimum wage on the intra-group income inequality and inter-group income inequality should be undertaken to gain greater insights in the future.

Third, the minimum wage compliance institution should affect how the minimum wage influences the wage distribution. Because the minimum wage compliance problem in the public sector differs from that in the private sector, and the labor market is segmented into these two sectors, future studies should conduct an analysis with sector segmentation.

Fourth, the results indicate that the effect of reducing the wage gap between the rural and urban groups is small by the minimum wage policy. Enforcing the policy implementation in the informal sector might contribute to reducing the income inequality in China.

Finally, though some hypotheses from neoclassical economics can explain the spillover effect of the minimum wage, this study does not analyze the influence of these hypotheses, which could be addressed in future research.

Notes

1. For details on the CHNS, please refer to Chap. 2 of the book.
2. In this chapter, based on the CHNS questionnaire for *Hukou* (rural and urban registrations), the rural group is defined as the workers with the rural registration, and the urban group is defined as the workers with the urban registration most of whom are local urban residents. The rural group includes the migrants who move from the rural region to urban region, and the workers who work in the rural regions with rural registration or without the permanent urban registration. Because the migrant sample from 1991 to 2011 is not enough for econometric analysis based on the DID (Difference in Difference) method, this chapter only focuses on the wage gap between the rural and the urban registration groups.
3. For the summary of the literature surveys on the effect of the minimum wage on employment and wage, please see Brown (1999), Card and Krueger (1995a, b), Machin and Manning (1997), Neumark and Wascher (2008), and Boeri and Ours (2013).
4. Regarding the debate on the minimum wage employment effect in the 1980s, it is indicated that there is a negative significant but modest −1% to −3% employment effect (Brown et al. 1982). After the 1990s, using cross-section data, Deere et al. (1995), Currie and Fallick (1996), Burkhauser et al. (2000), and Neumark and Wascher (1992, 2000, 2004) also found results consistent with the standard model prediction of a negative employment effect. On the other hand, using panel data to conduct quasi-natural experiment studies, Card (1992a, b), Katz and Krueger (1992), and Card and Krueger (1995a, b) pointed out that there are no unemployment effects. Similarly, there is no consensus on the effect of MW on employment.
5. For empirical studies on the effects of minimum wage on the wage gaps and income inequality, please see Card and Krueger (1995a, b), and DiNardo et al. (1996) for the U. S., and Robinson (2002, 2005) for the U.K.
6. For an empirical study on the effects of MW on gender wage gap in urban China, please see Li and Ma (2015).

7. They compared minimum wage and the wage change rates from the prior year to the survey year, in addition to the ratios of the wage level to the minimum wage level in the prior year, and these variables and their interactions were utilized to employ the analysis.
8. Li and Ma (2015) analyzed the effect of minimum wage on gender wage gap in China; they indicated that the minimum wage might reduce the gender wage gap in the long term.
9. The survey regions are different from 1991 to 2011. For example, Liaoning is added in the 1997 survey; Beijing, Shanghai, and Chongqi are added in the 2011 survey. The observations in the common regions are utilized in the analyses based on the DID model.
10. According to the Minimum Wage Article published in 1993, the main content of the MW consists of total earnings from work (except the overtime subsidy), any risk job allowance, and social security subsidy. I cannot obtain the detailed allowance and subsidy information from the CHNS survey data.
11. Even though the minimum wage level includes the monthly minimum wage and hourly minimum wage, the former is for the regular worker, and the latter is for the irregular worker. Because the monthly minimum wages can be gained from 1993 to 2011 in these survey regions, whereas the hourly minimum wage information is lacking in some regions, the monthly minimum wage data are used. Thus the monthly wage is used in the analysis.
12. Experience years = age – 6-years of schooling.
13. Ownership types are composed of the government organizations, public organizations (*Shiye Danwei*), state-owned enterprises (SOE), collectively owned enterprises (COEs), private-owned enterprises/foreign owned enterprises, and others.
14. Occupation is composed of technician, manager, clerk, agriculture worker, manufacturing worker (H), manufacturing worker (L), service worker, and others dummy variables. Based on the questionnaire of CHNS, manufacturing worker (H) is high-skilled manufacturing worker and manufacturing worker (L) is low-skilled manufacturing worker.
15. Employment status is composed of worker, irregular worker I, irregular worker II, self-employed I, self-employed II, and others dummy variables Regular worker is the individual who works for another person or enterprise as permanent employee; irregular worker(I) is the contractor with other people or enterprise; irregular worker(II) is temporary worker; the self-employed (I) is self-employed, owner-manager with employees; the self-employed (II) is self-employed, independent operator with no employee; others is the paid family worker, unpaid family worker, and others.

References

Autor, D., Manning, A., & Smith, C. (2010). The contribution of the minimum wage to U.S. wage inequality over three decades: A reassessment. *NBER Working Paper*, No. 16533.

Baker, M., Benjamin, D., & Stanger, S. (1999). The highs and lows of the minimum wage effect: A time-series cross-section study of the Canadian law. *Journal of Labor Economics, 17*(2), 318–350.

Bhorat, H., Kanbur, R., & Stanwix, B. (2014). Estimating the impact of minimum wages on employment, wage, and non-wage benefits: The case of agriculture in South Africa. *American Journal of Agriculture Economics, 96*(5), 1402–1419.

Boeri, T. B., & Ours, J. (2013). *The economics of imperfect labor markets*. Princeton, NJ: Princeton University Press.

Brown, C. (1999). Minimum wages, employment, and the distribution of income. In *Handbook of labor economics* (Vol. 3). Cambridge, MA: Elsevier (Chapter 32).

Brown, C., Curtis, G., & Andrew, K. (1982). The effect of the minimum wage on employment and unemployment. *Journal of Economic Literature, 20*(2), 487–528.

Burkhauser, R. V., Kenneth, A., & Wittenburg, D. C. (2000). A reassessment of the new economics of the minimum wage. *Journal of Labor Economics, 18*(4), 653–681.

Card, D. (1992a). Using regional variation in wages to measure the effects of the federal minimum wage. *Industrial and Labor Relations Review, 46*(1), 22–37.

Card, D. (1992b). Do minimum wages reduce employment? A case study of California, 1987–89. *Industrial and Labor Relations Review, 46*(1), 38–54.

Card, D., & Krueger, A. (1995a). *Myth and measurement: The new economics of the minimum wage*. Princeton, NJ: Princeton University Press.

Card, D., & Krueger, A. (1995b). Time-series minimum wage studies: A meta-analysis. *American Economic Review Papers and Proceedings, 85*(2), 238–243.

Currie, J., & Fallick, B. (1996). The minimum wage and the employment of youth: Evidence from the NLSY. *Journal of Human Resources, 31*(2), 404–428.

Deere, D., Murph, K., & Welch, F. (1995). Employment and minimum wage hike. *America Economic Review. Papers and Proceedings, 85*, 232–237.

Di, J., & Han, Q. (2015). The income effects of minimum wage increase. *Econometric and Technological Economic Research, 7*, 90–103 (In Chinese).

DiNardo, J., Fortin, N. M., & Lemieux, T. (1996). Labor market institutions and the distribution of wages, 1973–1992: A semiparametric approach. *Econometrica, 64*(5), 1001–1044.

Dinkelman, T., & Ranchhod, V. (2012). Evidence on the impact of minimum wage laws in an informal sector: Domestic workers in South Africa. *Journal of Development Economics, 99*(1), 27–45.

Gindling, T. H., & Terrell, K. (2005). The effect of minimum wages on actual wages in formal and informal sectors in Costa Rica. *World Development, 33*(11), 1905–1921.
Grossman, J. B. (1983). The impact of the minimum wage on other wages. *Journal of Human Resources, 18*(3), 3–8.
Hohberg, M., & Lay, J. (2015). The impact of minimum wages on informal and formal labor market outcomes: Evidence from Indonesia. *IZA Journal of Labor & Development, 4*, 14.
Jia, P., & Zhang, S. (2013). Spillover effects of minimum wage increase. *Statistical Research, 30*(4), 37–41 (In Chinese).
Katz, L. F., & Krueger, A. B. (1992). The effect of the minimum wage on the fast food industry. *Industrial and Labor Relations Review, 46*(1), 6–21.
Koenker, R. W., & Bassett, G. J. (1978). Regression quantile. *Econometrica, 46*(1), 33–50.
Lee, D. (1999). Wage inequality in the United States during the 1980s: Rising dispersion or falling minimum wage? *Quarterly Journal of Economics, 114*(3), 977–1023.
Li, S., & Ma, X. (2015). Impact of minimum wage on gender wage gaps in urban China. *IZA Journal of Labor and Development, 4*, 20.
Li, S., Sato, H., & Sicular, T. (2013). *The analysis of the changes of income distribution in China*. The People's Press (In Chinese).
Li, S., Sicular, T., & Gustafsson, B. (2008). *Income distribution in China III*. Beijing: Normal University Press (In Chinese).
Li, S., Yue, X., Sicular, T., & Sato, H. (2017). *Latest change of income distribution situations in China: The research on Chinese income distribution V*. Beijing: China Financial and Economic Press (In Chinese).
Ma, S., Zhang, J., & Zhu, X. (2012). The effect of minimum wage on average wage and employment. *Economic Research, 5*, 132–146 (In Chinese).
Machin, S., & Manning, A. (1997). Minimum wages and economic outcomes in Europe. *European Economic Review, 41*(3–5), 733–742.
Neumark, D. (2001). The employment effects of minimum wages: Evidence from a prespecified research design the employment effects of minimum wages. *Industry Relation, 40*(1), 121–144.
Neumark, D., Cunningham, W., & Siga, L. (2006). The Effects of the minimum wage in Brazil on the distribution of family incomes: 1996–2001. *Journal of Development Economics, 80*, 136–159.
Neumark, D., Schweitzer, M., & Wascher, W. (2004). Minimum wage effects throughout the wage distribution. *The Journal of Human Resources, 39*(2), 425–450.
Neumark, D., & Wascher, W. (1992). Employment effects of minimum and subminimum wages: Panel data on state minimum wage laws. *Industrial and Labor Relations Review, 46*(1), 55–81.

Neumark, D., & Wascher, W. (2000). The effect of New Jersey minimum wage increase on fast-food employment: A reevaluation using payroll records. *The America Economic Review, 90*(5), 1362–1396.

Neumark, D., & Wascher, W. (2004). Minimum wages, labor market institutions, and youth employment: A cross-national analysis. *Industrial and Labor Relations Review, 57*(2), 223–248.

Neumark, D., & Wascher, W. (2008). *Minimum wages.* Cambridge, MA: MIT Press.

Pettengill, J. S. (1981). The Long-run impact of a minimum wage on employment and the wage structure. In *Report of the minimum wage study commission 6.* Washington, DC: Government Printing Office.

Robinson, H. (2002). Wrong side of the track? The impact of the minimum wage on gender pay gaps in Britain. *Oxford Bulletin of Economics and Statistics, 64*(5), 417–448.

Robinson, H. (2005). Regional evidence on the effect of the national minimum wage on the gender pay gap. *Regional Studies, 39*(7), 855–875.

Wang, X., & Tang, X. (2014). *Minimum wage impact on wages, work time, and income distribution of migrant workers.* Presentation on the workshop of "Reforming Minimum Wage and Labor Regulation Policy in Developing and Transition Economies", organized by China Institute for Income Distribution (CIID) BNU Business School (BS), October 18–19, 2014, Beijing, China.

Xing, C., & Xu, J. (2016). Regional variation of the minimum wages in China. *IZA Journal of Labor & Development, 5*, 8.

Ye, L., Gindling, T. H., & Li, S. (2015). Compliance with legal minimum wages and overtime pay regulation in China. *IZA Journal of Labor & Development, 4*, 16.

CHAPTER 8

Impact of China's Higher Education Expansion Policy on Youth Employment

8.1 Introduction

Since 1978, the China economy system changed from the planned economy to marketization economy. Along with the great economic transition, a set of new policies were implemented by Chinese government, and China did experience great economic growth which achieved an average GDP growth rate of around 10% from the 1990s to 2000s. In 1999, the higher education expansion policy was implemented by the government. Along with the policy implementation, the number of college[1] graduates increased from 108 million in 1998 to 638.1 million in 2013 (NBS 2016). It is thought the increase of college graduate labor supply in the short term may affect college graduate employment. For example, based on the 2000 and 2010 Chinese Population Census, although the higher-educated proportion of employed worker in China is still low (they are 4.7% in 2000 and 10% in 2010), the unemployment rate of college graduates increased since 2000s, and among employed college graduates, many had to work in low-skilled job positions with low wages. They were called the "Ant tribe" (Lian 2011). The "Ant tribe" phenomenon emerged in 2003 when the first group of students graduated after the implementation of higher education expansion policy. Thus it is an important issue to investigate whether the higher education expansion policy impacts the labor market for young college graduates in China.

Although previous studies estimated the impact of higher education expansion policy on wage, labor force participation, and unemployment for

X. Ma, *Economic Transition and Labor Market Reform in China*,
https://doi.org/10.1007/978-981-13-1987-7_8

college graduates, there remain some issues which should be considered. Using the longitudinal survey data of the Chinese Health and Nutrition Survey (CHNS) conducted from 1997 to 2011, this chapter takes a quasi-natural experiment study to estimate the impact of higher education expansion policy on youth employment (to be at work or not) and employment status selection (to be regular worker, irregular worker, self-employed, or non-work) behavior. In addition, the regional disparity and the *Hukou* system are also considered in the study. These analyses can contribute to the empirical study on the issue.

This chapter is structured as follows. Sect. 8.2 introduces the implementation of higher education expansion policy. Sect. 8.3 introduces the ways in which the higher education expansion policy influences college graduate employment and previous empirical studies on the issue. Section 8.4 gives the framework of the empirical analysis, including models and datasets. Section 8.5 introduces the description results between the implementation policy and labor force participation rate of college graduate and senior high school graduate. Section 8.6 presents estimated results and explains these results, and Sect. 8.7 summarizes the conclusions.

8.2 Higher Education Expansion Policy in China During the Economic Transition Period

In the planned economy period, the Chinese government promoted the enrollment of compulsory education and higher education since the 1950s. This study focuses on the higher education expansion policy during the economic transition period.

Concretely, in 1999, the State Council approved the "Plan of Revitalizing Education in the Twenty-First Century" proposed by the Ministry of Education to expand higher education enrollment. This was done as part of the eleventh five-year plan that stressed the importance of prosperity for all and the need to create a harmonious society. The plan included various strategies to encourage colleges to set up multiple campuses as well as instituting a private college system; in addition, the plan called for an increase in public education expenditures, especially in tertiary education. The proposal also aimed at an increase in the gross enrolment ratio in tertiary education, a rise in the student-teacher ratio, and an increase in state educational fund. A target was set in the plan for China to reach, by 2010, a tertiary enrollment ratio of 15%, defined as "mass higher education" by Trow (1972, 1973). In addition, in 2004, A Plan of

Education Revitalization 2003–2007 was passed by the Chinese State Council. This plan focused on the improvement of teaching, mainly for universities on the "985" and "211" lists. It emphasized the design of subjects, the reform in the teaching and evaluation system, and the implementation of the Improvement of New Graduates Employment Program policy; it required the higher education system to prepare new graduates for seeking jobs. In 2010, the National Outline for Medium- and Long-term Reform and Development (2010–2020) was published. This plan sought to improve teaching, scientific research, and the social relevance of education. The goals of higher education development are stated explicitly. In 2020, the total number of enrolled college students is planned to reach 33 million; it implies that the higher education expansion will continue for the last 10 years at least.

As a social and economic background, the reasons for the government to promote higher education expansion policy can be considered as follows (Wang and Liu 2011; Yeung 2012). First, along with Chinese economic growth, the labor demand for high-skilled workers increased. The higher education expansion policy was necessary in order to increase the labor supply of high-education, high-skilled workers. The policy is expected to have a profound effect on improving people's educational quality and the nation's competitiveness. Second, it addresses the youth unemployment problem. In 1998, the Asian financial crisis broke out and China suffered. At the same time, the government promoted ownership reform of SOEs in the late 1990s. The number of laid-off workers increased with the progress of SOEs reform, which caused the rise in the unemployment rate since the 1990s.[2] To address the youth unemployment problem, the government promoted the enrollment in college. Third, the policy is expected to increase household education expenditure, and it is pointed out that the higher education expansion could increase household consumption by 100 billion RMB, which would contribute 0.5% to China's GDP growth rate per year. Fourth, it is expected to facilitate other industrial development (e.g. construction industry, education industry).

With the implementation of these policies, China's higher education developed rapidly (see Fig. 8.1). The number of enrollments of regular college[3] students expanded from 5.56 million to 26.25 million, and yearly college graduates increased from 0.95 million to 6.81 million during 2000–2015. In addition, the number of enrollments of senior high school students expanded from 12.01 million to 23.74 million, and yearly college graduates increased from 30.15 million to 79.77 million during

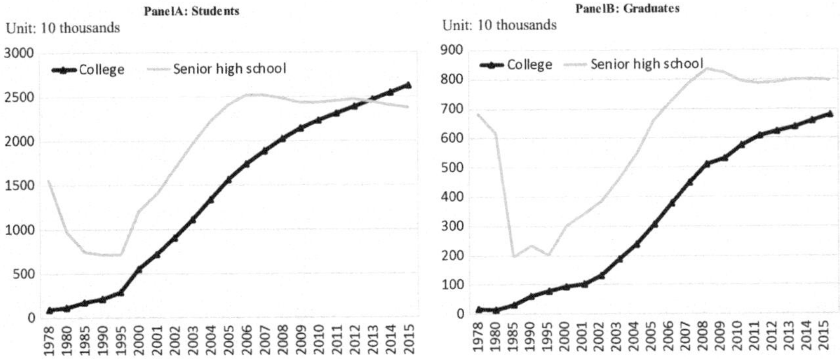

Fig. 8.1 Numbers of college students and graduates from 1990 to 2014. *Source*: Based on data from National Bureau of Statistics *China Statistical Yearbook 2016*

2000–2015. The change tendency of enrollment of college and senior high school is similar during 2000–2011, which is the analysis period in the study. It is observed that with the implementation of higher education expansion policy, both the students and graduates of college and senior high school increase greatly. It is thought that the labor supply change should affect the employment of young graduates.

8.3 The Channel of the Impact of Higher Education Expansion Policy on College Graduate Employment and Empirical Studies

8.3.1 The Channel of the Impact of Higher Education Expansion Policy on College Graduate Employment

Does the higher education expansion policy that has been enforced since 1999 affect labor force participation of young college graduates in China? Some channels can be considered as follows. First, in a perfect competitive market, based on the general equilibrium model, when labor demand is consistent, it is thought that the increase of the higher education labor supply may cause the decrease of employment probability for young college graduates in the short term. Second, when there are substitution effects between higher education graduate and lower education graduate (e.g. senior high school graduates), the college graduate can occupy the relatively lower-skill jobs which is usually done by the senior high school graduate—which is called "underemployment" or "over education". To consider the underemployment, the college graduate employment may be not down after the policy implementation. Third, in the long term, the increase of college graduates may promote the technology upgrading and the industry structure change which may increase the labor demand for college graduates, which may absorb the increasing college graduates labor supply. In addition, in a perfect competitive market, in the long term, the labor supply and demand of college graduates should be at an equilibrium by the market mechanism. Based on these economic theories, it could not be known whether the policy negatively affects the college graduate employment; it should take an empirical study to investigate it from both short-term and long-term perspectives.

8.3.2 *Empirical Studies on the Issue*

There are some empirical studies of the effects of the higher education expansion policy on youth labor force participation or unemployment for college graduates.[4] Wu and Zhao (2010) conducted studies on the impact of higher education expansion policy on college graduate labor force participation and unemployment. In particular, they used 2000 population census and 2005 1% population survey data and DID/DDD methods to investigate the policy effect. They indicated that higher education policy has reduced the labor force participation rate of college graduates, and increased their unemployment rate. Xing and Li (2011) and Li et al. (2014) also used 2000 population census and 2005 1% population survey data and DID methods to investigate the policy effect, and also found the policy increased the unemployment rate among young college graduates, and that the unemployment rate for college graduates increases more in non-coastal (especially Central) regions than in coastal regions. Yao et al. (2013) used 1998–2009 China Urban Household Survey (CUHS) data to construct city-level panel data, and the results based on a fixed effect model and random effect show that the increase of labor supply of higher education graduates positively affects the employment for both college graduates and lower education graduates. Knight et al. (2017) used 2002 and 2007 Chinese Household Income Project survey data (CHIPs) and 2002–2008 National Bureau of Statistics (NBS) survey data to investigate the effect of higher education expansion policy on labor market; they found that the policy raised the unemployment rate and reduced the proportion in good jobs (managerial and professional occupation).

8.3.3 Features of This Study

Although the previous studies investigate the impact of higher education expansion on college graduate employment, some issues should be considered as follows.

First, the impact of policy should change by the period. For example, in a perfect competitive market, in the short term, the shock of college graduate labor supply increase may affect the employment status of new college graduates. Whereas in the long term, the negative influence of the policy on college graduate employment may become smaller because the supply and demand of college graduates could be a general equilibrium by the market mechanism. Currently, there is no empirical study to consider the short-term and long-term effects. This study may address this lack to a certain extent.

Second, because there exists large regional disparity in China, it is thought that the labor market situations differ by region. This study also analyzes the policy effect by the Eastern, Central, and Western regions. In addition, because there remains discrimination against migrants based on the *Hukou* system in China (Meng and Zhang 2001; Wang 2005; Song and Appleton 2006; Ma 2011, 2016), this study also uses subsamples of rural and urban registration groups to estimate the policy effects.

8.4 Methodology and Data

8.4.1 Model

DID and DDD (Difference in Difference in Difference) methods can be represented as follows:

$$Y_{it} = \alpha + \beta_1 \text{year}_t + \beta_2 \text{age}_{(21-25)it} + \beta_3 \text{age}_{(21-25)it} \times \text{year}_t + \beta_4 X_{it} + \varepsilon_{it} \quad (8.1a)$$

$$Y_{it} = \alpha + \beta_1 \text{year}_t + \beta_2 \text{age}_{(21-25)it} + \beta_3 \text{Colle}_{it} + \beta_4 \text{age}_{(21-25)it} \times \text{year}_t \times \text{Colle}_{it} + \beta_5 X_{it} + \varepsilon_{it} \quad (8.1b)$$

Equation (8.1a) represents the DID method which is used for the college graduate sample, and Eq. (8.1b) represents the DDD method which is utilized for the samples including both college and senior high school graduates. In Eqs. (8.1a and 8.1b), Y is the labor force participation, i stands for the individual, t for years, year for policy implementation years

(2004, 2006, 2009, and 2011 in this study), age (21–25) for the treatment group, X for the individual characteristics variables (e.g. family numbers, health status, gender), registration system, the regional characteristics variables (region block dummy and province-level region dummy variables) and other variables.[5] α is the constant term, and ε is the error term. β represents the estimated coefficient for each variable.

The years before the implementation of the higher education expansion policy (1997 and 2000) are used as the initial years and the years 2004, 2006, 2009, and 2011 as the policy implantation years. The treatment group is defined as college graduates aged from 21 to 25 and control group as two types: college graduates aged from 31 to 40 years old and senior high school graduates aged from 21 to 25 years old.

β_3 in Eq.(8.1a), β_4 in Eq.(8.1b) is the estimated coefficient of DID item and DDD item. When β_3 or β_4 is a negative value, and it is statistically significant, it indicates that the implementation of the higher education expansion policy decreases the young college graduate employment, and vice versa.

8.4.2 Data

This study employs six waves (1997, 2000, 2004, 2006, 2009, and 2011) of longitudinal survey data of CHNS conducted from 1997 to 2011. For detailed information on the CHNS, please refer to Section 2.3 in Chap. 2 of this book.

The independent variables of employment are two types. One is a binary variable (equal to 1 if the individual is working, and equal to 0 if not). The other one is a category variable which includes regular worker, irregular worker, self-employment, and non-work.

Year is a set of year dummy variables, such as 1997, 2000, 2004, 2006, 2009, and 2011 dummy variables. 1997, 2000 is the initial years, and 2004, 2006, 2009, and 2011 is the policy implementation year.

DID item in Eq. (8.1a) is the interaction term of the two variables used: the policy implementation year dummy and treatment group dummy ($\text{year} \times \text{age}_{(21-25)}$).The DDD item in Eq. (8.1b) is the interaction term of the three variables used: the policy implementation year dummy, group aged from 21 to 25 years old dummy, and college graduate dummy ($\text{year} \times \text{age}_{(21-25)} \times \text{Colle}$).

To consider that individual characteristics should affect labor force participation, family number, health status, and gender dummy variables are used.

It is expected that the probability of labor force participation is greater for more family number group, better health status group, and male group.

Wu and Zhao (2010) showed that regional variables also affect individual labor force participation behavior. We used per capita GDP, the ratio of trade to GDP, the ratio of tertiary industry to GDP, and the ratio of fixed asset investment to GDP as regional level variables.[6]

To observe the impact of the higher education expansion policy on employment of young university graduates by age groups, the DID item by age groups is estimated as the following function:

$$Y_{it} = \alpha + \beta_1 \text{year}_t + \beta_2 \text{age}_{it} + \beta_{3a} \sum age_{it} \times \text{year}_t + \beta_4 X_{it} + \varepsilon_{it} \quad (\text{aged from 21 to 30}) \tag{8.2a}$$

$$Y_{it} = \alpha + \beta_1 \text{year}_t + \beta_2 \text{age}_{it} + \beta_3 \text{Colle}_{it} + \beta_{3a} \sum \text{age}_{it} \times \text{year}_t \times \text{Colle}_{it} + \beta_4 X_{it} + \varepsilon_{it} \quad (\text{aged from 21 to 30}) \tag{8.2b}$$

In Eqs. (8.2a and 8.2b), Υ represents the probability of labor force participation, i stands for the individual, t for years, year for policy implementation years (here, 2004, 2006, 2009, and 2011), age for the age dummy from 21 to 30 years old, and X for the individual characteristics variables (e.g. family numbers, health status, gender), the regional characteristics variables and other variables. α is the constant term, and ε is the error term. β represents the estimated coefficient for each variable. The results of β_{3a} are summarized in Table 8.1.

The results of estimation 1 based on the DID model and DDD model indicated that although not all the coefficients are statistically significant, the higher education expansion policy negatively influences the employment of college graduates aged from 21 to 25 years old, whereas it almost positively affects the employment of the university graduates aged from 26 to 30 years old. It is observed that the influences of the policy are different between the group aged 21 to 25 years old and the group aged 26 to 30 years old. The results of estimation 2 showed a similar tendency: the influence of the policy is negative for the treatment group (group aged from 21 to 25 years old), whereas it is almost positive for the other group. It is confirmed that to define the treatment group as college graduates aged from 21 to 25 years old may be adequate. However, the impacts of the policy on the college graduates group aged from 26 to 30 years old are various; it indicates that the estimated results may differ by the treatment group setting. We also do a robustness check and discuss it in Sect. 8.6.

Table 8.1 Test results for treatment group setting

	Model1:DD		*Model2:DDD*	
	Coeff.	*S.D.*	*Coeff.*	*S.D.*
Estimation1				
age21	−0.112	0.448	−0.264	1.723
age22	−0.298	0.349	−0.554	0.457
age23	0.000	0.370	−0.570	0.598
age24	0.292	0.356	−0.107	0.501
age25	−0.545***	0.185	−0.182	0.429
age26	−0.642***	0.193	0.591	0.484
age27	0.190	0.234	−0.027	0.511
age28	0.252	0.183	0.559	0.488
age29	0.280	0.186	0.558	0.530
age30	0.119	0.216	−0.044	0.556
Estimation2				
age21–25	−0.451	0.459	−0.284	0.309
age26–30	−0.147	0.117	0.224	0.290
age36–40	0.214	0.141	0.026	0.314

Source: Calculated based on CHNS 1997–2011
Note:
(1) *, **, ***: statistically significant levels are 10%, 5%, and 1%
(2) The treatment group, age, year, region dummy variables are estimated, these results are not expressed in the table. The DD item and DDD item coefficients are only summarized in the table

8.5 Descriptive Statistics Results

First, labor force participation rate (LFPR) of college graduate by age groups (groups aged from 20 to older than 70 years old) is shown in Fig. 8.2. To compare the LFPR of the young group who are aged from 21 to 25 years old between the pre-period (1997, 2000) and the post-period (2004, 2006, 2009, 2011), it is observed that the LFPR of young college graduates is greater (from 80 to 90 percentages) for the pre-period than that for the post-period (50 to 80 percentages). In addition, the decrease width of labor force participation rate among young college graduates is greater in 2009 and 2011.

Second, LFPR for senior high school graduates by age groups is shown in Fig. 8.3. We also compare the LFPR of the young group who are aged from 21 to 25 years old between the pre- and post-period; it is observed that the LFPR of young senior high school graduates is greater (from 60 to 80 percentages) for the pre-period than that for the post-period (from 50 to 70

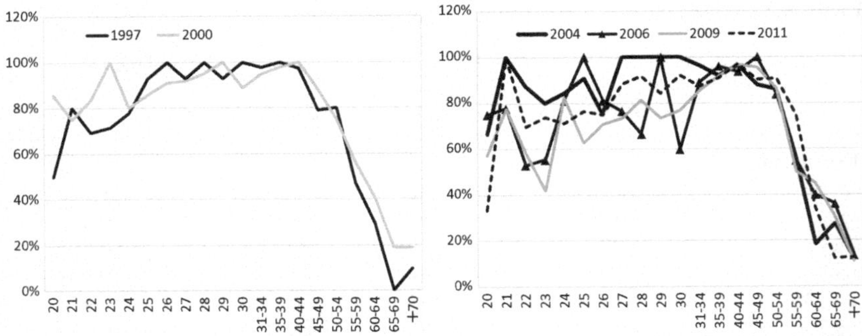

Fig. 8.2 Labor force participation rate of college graduates (1997–2011). *Source*: Calculated based on CHNS from 1997 to 2011

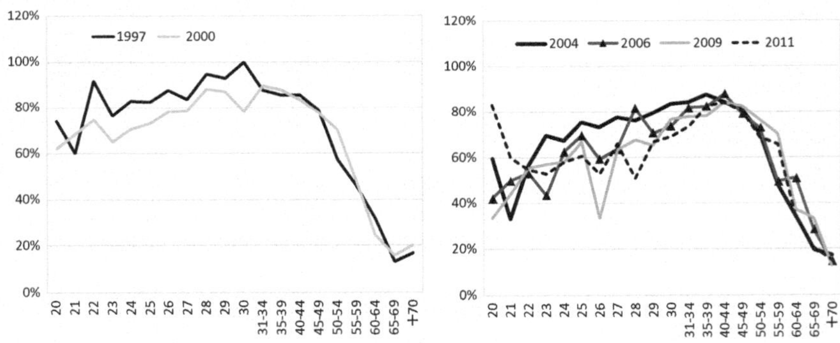

Fig. 8.3 Labor force participation rate of senior high school graduates (1997–2011). *Source*: Calculated based on CHNS from 1997 to 2011

percentages). Particularly, compared with the change in the short term (2000), the LFPR decrease is greater in the long term (2006, 2009, and 2011).

Third, the change tendency of LFPR from the pre-period to the post-period for the college graduate group and senior high school graduate group seems similar. To compare the difference between these two groups, the LFPR gaps between these two groups are calculated and they are shown in Fig. 8.4. It is observed that the LFPR gap between these two groups among youth who are aged from 22 to 25 is greater for the post-period than that for the pre-period.

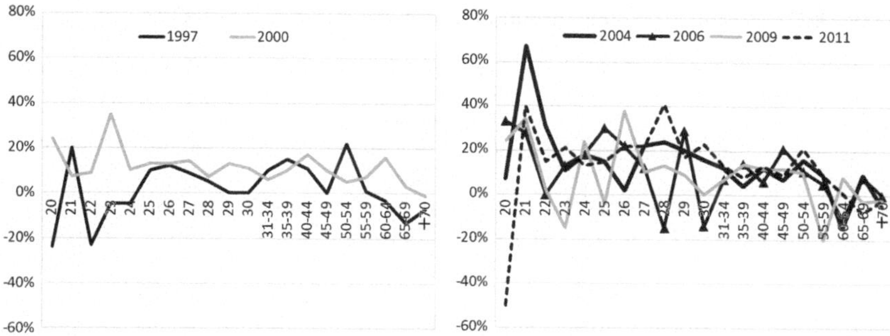

Fig. 8.4 Labor force participation rate gaps between higher education group and senior high school group (1997–2011). *Source*: Calculated based on CHNS from 1997 to 2011

These descriptions of LFPR in the pre- and post-periods for college and senior high school graduates indicated that the LFPR decreased after the policy implementation, but the change of LFPR gaps between college and senior high school graduates in the pre- and post-periods is small. However, these calculations do not control the other factors which should affect the individual employment, and do not consider the difference between college graduates and senior high school graduates, and the difference between the pre-period and post-period simultaneously. A more rigorous econometric analysis is needed to investigate the impact of the higher education expansion policy on college graduate employment.

8.6 Econometric Analysis Results

8.6.1 *Impact of Higher Education Expansion Policy on College Graduate Employment*

The calculated results of probability of labor force participation based on the DID model are shown in Table 8.2. The treatment group is college graduates aged from 21 to 25 years old, and the control group is college graduates aged from 31 to 40 years old. The year 2000 is the pre-period of policy implementation, and 2004, 2006, 2009, and 2011 are the post-periods. The values of DID items (D(T-C)) are from −1.7% to −22.0%, and it is indicated that the higher education expansion policy decreases the young college graduate employment.

Table 8.2 Result for college graduate group based on DID model

	2000	*2004*	*D(A–B)*		*2000*	*2006*	*D(A–B)*
Panel A				**Panel B**			
Treatment group	0.978	0.977	−0.001	Treatment group	0.978	0.959	−0.019
	(0.147)	(0.152)			(0.147)	(0.200)	
Control group	0.957	0.973	0.016	Control group	0.957	0.981	0.024
	(0.203)	(0.164)			(0.203)	(0.138)	
D(T–C)	0.021	0.004	−0.017	D(T–C)	0.021	−0.022	−0.043
	2000	**2009**	**D(A–B)**		**2000**	**2011**	**D(A–B)**
Panel C				**Panel D**			
Treatment group	0.978	0.766	−0.212	Treatment group	0.978	0.886	−0.092
	(0.147)	(0.427)			(0.147)	(0.319)	
Control group	0.957	0.965	0.008	Control group	0.957	0.948	−0.009
	(0.203)	(0.184)			(0.203)	(0.062)	
D(T–C)	0.021	−0.199	−0.220	D(T–C)	0.021	−0.062	−0.083

Source: Calculated based on CHNS from 1997 to 2011
Note: Values in parentheses are standard deviation

To compare with 2004 (−1.7%), the negative effect of the policy on the employment is greater for 2006 (−4.3%), 2006 (−22.0%), and 2009 (−8.3%).

The calculated results of probability of labor force participation based on the DID model shown in Table 8.2 did not control the factors which should affect individual labor force participation. When the other factors are considered, does the higher education expansion policy affect the college graduate employment? The econometric analysis results are summarized in Table 8.3. Panel A is the results based on the DID model, and Panel B is the results based on the DDD model. The results based on model2 and model3 in Panel A indicate that the higher education expansion policy might reduce the employment probability. However, the coefficients of DDD item are not statistically significant.

To consider the influence of the policy on employment by various periods (e.g. short term or long term of the policy implementation), the results in Table 8.4 showed that in 2006 and 2009, the coefficients

Table 8.3 Results of impact of higher education expansion policy on college graduate employment

	Model1		*Model2*		*Model3*	
	Coeff.	*S.D.*	*Coeff.*	*S.D.*	*Coeff.*	*S.D.*
Panel A: DD model						
Treatment	−0.106	0.354	−0.096	0.356	0.225	0.454
Year	−0.299	0.186	−0.297	0.186	0.545*	0.299
DD	−0.365	0.376	−0.363*	0.379	−0.670*	0.474
Family number			−0.053	0.042	−0.028	0.047
Health status			0.011	0.019	0.028	0.021
Male			0.024	0.111	0.050	0.116
Region (East)						
Central					0.019	0.187
West					−0.140	0.208
Urban					0.041	0.123
Ratio of fixed asset investment					−2.416***	0.674
Ratio of tertiary industry					−0.948	0.854
Ratio of trade					−0.698***	0.270
GDP per capita					0.000	0.000
Constants	1.962***	0.172	2.073***	0.273	2.877***	0.545
Observations	1,389		1,389		1,389	
Log likelihood	−303.781		−300.448		−277.891	
Pseudo R^2	0.0324		0.0339		0.0749	
Panel B: DDD model						
Treatment	−0.156**	0.077	0.134	0.089	0.128	0.092
Year	0.040	0.048	−0.233***	0.048	0.089	0.074
College	0.389***	0.075	0.696***	0.156	0.681***	0.159
Year × College	0.114	0.123	−0.397**	0.166	−0.321*	0.171
Year × Aged21–25	−0.515***	0.110	−0.519***	0.082	−0.484***	0.086
College × Aged21–25	−0.100	0.176	−0.206	0.342	0.102	0.428
DDD	−0.187	−0.260	−0.450	0.369	−0.089	−0.451
Region (East)						
Central			−0.223***	0.044	−0.242***	0.059
West			0.030	0.055	0.017	0.075
Urban			0.097	0.082	0.081	0.086
Family number			−0.026**	0.013	−0.032**	0.014
Health status			−0.008	0.007	−0.012*	0.007
Male			−0.027	0.039	−0.038	0.040
Ratio of fixed asset investment					−1.172***	0.217

(*continued*)

Table 8.3 (continued)

	Model1		*Model2*		*Model3*	
	Coeff.	*S.D.*	*Coeff.*	*S.D.*	*Coeff.*	*S.D.*
Ratio of tertiary industry					−1.700***	0.301
Ratio of trade					−0.012	0.134
GDP per capita					2.670E-06	2.300E-06
Constants	1.349***	0.046	1.447***	0.189	2.371***	0.243
Observations	7,844		7,844		7,844	
Log likelihood	−2506.256		−2645.065		−2480.912	
Pseudo R^2	0.037		0.049		0.058	

Source: Calculated based on CHNS from 1997 to 2011
Note: *, **, ***: statistically significant levels are 10%, 5%, and 1%

Table 8.4 Results of period effect of the impact of higher education expansion policy on college graduate employment

	Model1		*Model2*		*Model3*	
	Coeff.	*S.D.*	*Coeff.*	*S.D.*	*Coeff.*	*S.D.*
Panel A: DD model						
Treatment	−0.106	0.354	−0.104	0.356	0.227	0.460
y2004	−0.039	0.301	−0.051	0.301	0.165	0.350
y2006	0.108	0.291	0.100	0.290	0.584	0.471
y2009	−0.149	0.263	−0.152	0.264	0.176	0.651
y2011	−0.446**	0.192	−0.440**	0.193	−0.282	0.784
DDy2004	0.073	0.612	0.075	0.615	−0.180	0.691
DD*y2006	−0.331	0.542	−0.327	0.544	−0.882	0.641
DD*y2009	−0.934**	0.452	−0.946**	0.454	−1.181**	0.547
DD*y2011	−0.233	0.394	−0.205	0.398	−0.477	0.496
Family number			−0.034	0.044	−0.025	0.048
Health status			0.011	0.020	0.029	0.021
Male			0.065	0.113	0.063	0.118
Region (East)						
Central					0.224	0.287
West					0.138	0.306
Urban					0.012	0.126
Ratio of fixed asset investment					−1.699*	1.067
Ratio of tertiary industry					−1.255	0.913

(*continued*)

Table 8.4 (continued)

	Model1		*Model2*		*Model3*	
	Coeff.	*S.D.*	*Coeff.*	*S.D.*	*Coeff.*	*S.D.*
Ratio of trade					−0.738***	0.281
GDP per capita					0.000	0.000
Constants	1.962***	0.172	1.980***	0.278	2.545***	0.680
Observations	1,389		1,389		1,389	
Log likelihood	−294.748		−291.784		−273.924	
Pseudo R^2	0.061		0.062		0.088	
Panel B: DDD model						
Treatment	−0.128*	0.079	0.141	0.090	0.119	0.093
College	0.571***	0.079	0.639***	0.142	0.684***	0.151
y2004	0.014	0.073	−0.041	0.072	−0.078	0.090
y2006	−0.154**	0.066	−0.179***	0.066	−0.296**	0.118
y2009	−0.301***	0.067	−0.280***	0.066	−0.560***	0.201
y2011	−0.544***	0.057	−0.378***	0.060	−0.895***	0.238
Year × College	−0.051	0.126	−0.306	0.214	−0.432*	0.225
College × Aged21–25	0.001	0.326	0.160	0.134	0.182	0.140
Year × Aged21–25	−0.551***	0.112	−0.505***	0.081	−0.497***	0.085
DDDy2004	0.605	0.555	0.253	0.203	0.317	0.211
DDDy2006	−0.554	0.487	−0.312*	0.185	−0.484*	0.214
DDDy2009	−0.267	0.402	−0.007*	0.141	−0.025*	0.145
DDDy2011	−0.200	0.354	−0.028	0.118	−0.019	0.122
Region (East)						
Central			−0.269***	0.045	0.014	0.081
West			0.013	0.056	0.317***	0.096
Urban			0.095	0.083	0.062	0.086
Family number			−0.021	0.014	−0.032**	0.014
Health status			−0.011	0.007	−0.013*	0.008
Male			−0.029	0.039	−0.040	0.040
Ratio of fixed asset investment					−0.101	0.378
Ratio of tertiary industry					−1.927***	0.316
Ratio of trade					−0.034	0.137
GDP per capita					2.060E-05***	4.400E-06
Constants	1.595***	0.054	1.462***	0.190	1.859	0.283
Observations	7,844		7,844		7,844	
Log likelihood	−2443.299		−2620.378		−2463.415	
Pseudo R^2	0.062		0.058		0.065	

Source: Calculated based on CHNS from 1997 to 2011

Note: *, **, ***: statistically significant levels are 10%, 5%, and 1%

of DD item are statistically significant and they are negative values. In addition, even though the coefficients of DD item in 2004 and 2011 are negative values, they are not statistically significant. These results indicate that the influence of higher education expansion policy is greater for 2006 and 2009 than for 2004 and 2011. In other words, the influence of the policy on the labor force participation of college graduates is different by period since the policy was implementation. The reason for these results can be considered as follows. First, based on the NBS data (NBS 2016), in the short term (here, 2004 in which the new college graduates begin to enter the labor market after two years since the policy influence occurs), the increase of college graduates is less (23.91 million in 2004) than that in 2006 and 2009 (37.75 million in 2006, 53.11 million in 2009); therefore with the cumulative effect of college graduate unemployment, the negative effect of the policy may occur in 2006 and 2009. In addition, after the global financial crisis occurred in 2007, the trade decreased by the economic recession in the world; thus the labor demand of college graduates might decrease largely in 2009. Second, in the long term (2011), with the economic growth and technology progress, the labor supply and demand could be adjusted by the general equilibrium mechanism, and the negative effect of the policy become not significant.

8.6.2 *Results of Impact of Higher Education Expansion Policy on College Graduate Employment Status*

It is thought the labor demand may differ by work sector (e.g. regular work, irregular work, self-employment). The results of the impact of higher education expansion policy on the probability of entrance into various work sectors are summarized in Table 8.5.

The results in Panel A indicate that the higher education expansion policy decreases the probability to become both regular workers and irregular workers for young college graduates. However, the difference between the regular work and self-employment is not statistically significant. It may be that the new college graduates do not like to enter the self-employed sector in which the wage is lower, the social security is worse, and the unemployment risk is higher (Ma 2016; Ma and Deng 2016). It is shown that the policy implementation reduces the proportion in "good job" for young college graduates.

Table 8.5 Results of impact of higher education expansion policy on college graduate work status

	Regular/non-work		*Irregular/non-work*		*Self-employment/ non-work*	
	Coeff.	*S.D.*	*Coeff.*	*S.D.*	*Coeff.*	*S.D.*
Panel A: DD model						
Treatment	−0.298	0.828	1.934**	0.900	−0.607	1.338
Year	0.735	0.558	1.309*	0.670	0.517	0.809
DD	−1.546*	0.859	−2.324**	0.933	−0.427	1.389
Family number	−0.092	0.079	−0.072	0.091	0.120	0.109
Health status	0.040	0.035	0.032	0.040	0.208***	0.067
Male	0.271	0.197	0.056	0.220	0.314	0.307
Region (East)						
Central	−0.724**	0.315	−0.407	0.364	−0.705	0.524
West	−0.400	0.360	0.128	0.425	0.510	0.536
Urban	0.090	0.206	0.336	0.234	−0.917***	0.318
Ratio of fixed asset investment	−5.581	1.117	−4.669***	1.287	−4.533**	1.833
Ratio of tertiary industry	−2.223	1.449	−2.601*	1.610	−0.517	2.330
Ratio of trade	−0.957	0.475	−0.932*	0.518	−2.772***	0.964
GDP per capita	−6.800E-06***	1.070E-05	1.520E-05	1.220E-05	1.460E-05	1.750E-05
Constants	6.071	0.952	2.509**	1.095	0.614	1.497
Observations			1,370			
Log likelihood			−1169.100			
Pseudo R^2			0.114			
Panel B: DDD model						
Treatment	−0.731***	0.194	0.691***	0.202	−0.835***	0.232
Year	−0.238*	0.135	0.536***	0.153	−0.188	0.158
College	1.764***	0.318	0.610*	0.378	−0.386	0.415
Year × College	−0.515	0.336	−0.520	0.397	0.013	0.446
Year × Aged21–25	0.311	0.814	0.775	0.857	0.053	1.312
College × Aged21–25	−0.656***	0.237	−1.347***	0.234	−0.295	0.279
DDD	−0.442	0.849	−0.581	0.889	0.383	1.363
Family number	−0.153***	0.025	−0.058**	0.027	0.030	0.029
Health status	0.021	0.013	0.001	0.014	−0.016	0.016
Male	0.011	0.071	−0.122*	0.076	0.015	0.085
Region (East)						
Central	−0.331***	0.107	−0.436***	0.115	−0.294	0.152
West	−0.324**	0.134	0.125	0.138	0.207	0.168
Urban	0.095	0.072	0.059	0.077	−0.793***	0.091

(continued)

Table 8.5 (continued)

	Regular/non-work		*Irregular/non-work*		*Self-employment/ non-work*	
	Coeff.	*S.D.*	*Coeff.*	*S.D.*	*Coeff.*	*S.D.*
Ratio of fixed asset investment	−2.598***	0.383	−1.770***	0.402	−2.607***	0.477
Ratio of tertiary industry	−2.951***	0.525	−2.135***	0.551	−2.423***	0.660
Ratio of trade	0.567**	0.254	0.426*	0.259	−1.747***	0.478
GDP per capita	−2.790E-06	4.020E-06	9.000E-06**	4.170E-06	1.240E-05**	5.310E-06
Constants	3.807***	0.313	1.684***	0.336	2.757***	0.389
Observations			7,676			
Log likelihood			−8841.174			
Pseudo R^2			0.099			

Source: Calculated based on CHNS from 1997 to 2011
Note: *, **, ***: statistically significant levels are 10%, 5%, and 1%

8.6.3 Robustness Checks

1. *Results of impact of higher education expansion policy on employment by region*

It is pointed out that there exists large regional disparity in China. It is thought that the labor market situation differs by region. We investigate the impact of higher education expansion policy by three regions: Eastern, Central, and Western regions. The results are summarized in Table 8.6.

The results in Panel A and Panel B show that the regional disparity of policy influence on labor force participation of college graduates is small. The results are not consistent with Li et al. (2014), which found the policy increases the probability of unemployment for the non-coastal region (Central and Western region). The reason can be considered as follows. The estimated period is different. Li et al. (2014) estimate the impact of policy from 2000 to 2005, whereas the estimated period in this study is from 1997 to 2011. After 2005, the Chinese government promotes the economic growth in the Western and Central regions to reduce the regional disparity. As a result, the GDP growth rate becomes greater for the Western and Central regions than the Eastern region at present. For example, the

Table 8.6 Results of impact of higher education expansion policy on employment by regions

	East		*Central*		*West*	
	Coeff.	*S.D.*	*Coeff.*	*S.D.*	*Coeff.*	*S.D.*
Panel A: DD model						
Treatment	0.454	0.114	0.864	20.035	−1.218	0.744
Year	0.630	0.463	0.856	0.548	0.323	0.515
DD	−0.441	1.114	−0.722	1.035	−0.064	1.048
Family number	0.007	0.074	−0.100	0.123	−0.306**	0.154
Health status	0.038	0.030	0.062	0.043	−0.056	0.118
Male	0.063	0.156	0.205	0.270	0.105	0.170
Urban	−0.001	0.171	0.489*	0.298	−0.695	0.547
Ratio of fixed asset investment	−2.479***	0.866	0.440	2.659	−2.172	2.500
Ratio of tertiary industry	−0.834	0.968	−0.623	2.992	0.886	1.687
Ratio of trade	−0.730**	0.290	−2.064	6.200	0.334	5.611
GDP per capita	1.820E-06	7.480E-06	−4.190E-05	4.040E-05	2.420E-04	0.030
Constants	2.530***	0.757	1.962	1.465	2.037	2.632
Observations	709		432		248	
Log likelihood	−157.850		−50.989		−223.781	
Pseudo R^2	0.043		0.175		0.074	
Panel B: DDD model						
Treatment	0.122	0.200	0.145	0.135	−0.044	0.241
Year	0.052	0.177	−0.048	0.097	0.944**	0.464
College	0.267	0.276	0.807***	0.235	0.448	1.518
Year × College	−0.036	0.292	−0.319	0.259	−0.590	1.185
Year × Aged21–25	1.283	1.457	1.296	1.385	−0.274	0.413
College × Aged21–25	−0.468***	0.183	−0.505***	0.122	−0.791***	0.216
Urban	0.150	0.186	0.088	0.125	−0.202	0.224
Family number	0.024	0.033	−0.036*	0.021	−0.049	0.033
Health status	−0.026	0.017	−0.016	0.010	−0.010	0.026
Male	−0.030	0.076	−0.060	0.059	0.031	0.110
DDD	−0.809	1.457	−0.999	1.385	−0.107	0.413
Ratio of fixed asset investment	−1.131***	0.393	−0.109	0.521	−4.274***	1.185
Ratio of tertiary industry	−2.234***	0.439	−0.627	0.540	−2.188	6.668
Ratio of trade	−0.165	0.156	2.645*	1.421	−8.899	6.154
GDP per capita	6.260E-06**	3.120E-06	−1.900E-05**	8.500E-06	6.010E-05***	2.120E-05
Constants	2.485***	0.497	1.505***	0.366	4.249	3.033

(*continued*)

Table 8.6 (continued)

	East		*Central*		*West*	
	Coeff.	*S.D.*	*Coeff.*	*S.D.*	*Coeff.*	*S.D.*
Observations	2,643		3,344		1,048	
Log likelihood	−669.923		−1173.032		−327.755	
Pseudo R^2	0.051		0.070		0.111	

Source: Calculated based on CHNS from 1997 to 2011
Note: *, **, ***: statistically significant levels are 10%, 5%, and 1%

GDP growth rate is 7.8% for the Western region, 10.5% for the Central region, and 7.2% for the Eastern region in 2009 (NBS 2010). It can be thought that currently, the economic growth in the Western and Central regions may increase the college graduate labor demand in these regions.

2. *Results of impact of higher education expansion policy on employment by the urban and rural groups*

It is known that there remains discrimination by the *Hukou* system in China, and the employment and wage determination are different between the urban group who are workers with the local urban registration and the rural group who are the workers with the rural registration. Therefore, the employment situations may differ by the rural and urban groups. We also estimate the impact of higher education expansion policy to consider the labor market segmentation by the *Hukou* system. The results are shown in Table 8.7.

The results in Panel A indicate that the impact of higher education expansion policy on college graduate employment is greater for the urban group than for the rural group. Concretely, it is clear that the policy reduces the probability of employment for the urban group, whereas the impact of the policy for the rural group is not statistically significant. The reasons of the results can be considered as follows. The reservation wage is lower for the migrants than the local urban residents. When the migrant is not at work and without non-earning income (e.g. savings or other family member income), he (she) cannot live in the urban region, and therefore even though the migrant cannot access a good job, he (she) has to work at a bad job. Whereas the local urban resident may select to live with parents when he (she) cannot find a good job which he (she) wants to do. Thus, the probability to enter voluntary unemployment or non-work may be greater for local urban residents than for migrants.

Table 8.7 Results of impact of higher education expansion policy on employment by urban and rural groups

	Urban		*Rural*	
	Coeff.	*S.D.*	*Coeff.*	*S.D.*
Panel A: DD model				
Treatment	0.620	1.167	−0.235	0.624
Year	0.258	0.352	1.271*	0.673
DD	−0.646*	1.167	0.862	0.669
Family number	0.066	0.075	−0.095	0.070
Health status	−0.009	0.028	0.092**	0.041
Male	−0.063	0.152	0.234	0.205
Region (East)				
Central	0.325	0.250	−0.637*	0.349
West	−0.243	0.278	−0.116	0.363
Ratio of fixed asset investment	−1.832**	0.807	−3.725**	1.466
Ratio of tertiary industry	−0.435	0.986	−3.364*	2.028
Ratio of trade	−0.433	0.333	−1.608***	0.581
GDP per capita	0.000	0.000	0.000	0.000
Constants	2.324***	0.659	4.235***	1.151
Observations	909		480	
Log likelihood	−166.219		−94.183	
Pseudo R^2	0.0720		0.2164	
Panel B: DDD model				
Treatment	0.426**	0.191	0.255	0.179
Year	0.200*	0.108	0.087	0.104
University	0.859***	0.207	0.504**	0.251
Year × University	−0.561**	0.223	−0.059	0.273
Year × Aged21–25	2.941	0.111	−0.562	0.568
University × Aged21–25	−0.873***	0.217	−0.906***	0.198
DDD	−0.456	1.111	0.472	0.601
Family number	−0.029	0.023	−0.028	0.019
Health status	−0.024**	0.010	0.018	0.012
Male	−0.033	0.058	−0.044	0.055
Region (East)				
Central	−0.253***	0.085	−0.225***	0.085
West	0.023	0.110	0.053	0.106
Ratio of fixed asset investment	−1.554***	0.309	−0.803***	0.311
Ratio of tertiary industry	−1.457***	0.424	−2.166***	0.440
Ratio of trade	−0.336*	0.187	0.317	0.201
GDP per capita	0.000**	0.000	0.000	0.000
Constants	2.584***	0.248	2.444***	0.253
Observations	3,847		3,997	

(*continued*)

Table 8.7 (continued)

	Urban		*Rural*	
	Coeff.	*S.D.*	*Coeff.*	*S.D.*
Log likelihood	−1163.981		−1292.43	
Pseudo R^2	0.060		0.073	

Source: Calculated based on CHNS from 1997 to 2011
Note: *, **, ***: statistically significant levels are 10%, 5%, and 1%

3. *Test results using various treatment groups*

To consider that the estimated results may vary by the treatment group constructing, we also used two other types of treatment groups to investigate the policy effect. The results are summarized in Table 8.8. The main findings are as follows.

Estimation1 is the analysis using the college graduates aged from 21 to 27 years old as the treatment group; Estimation 2 is the analysis using the college graduate aged from 21 to 30 years old as the treatment group. Even though we utilized these two various treatment groups, the results are similar in these two estimations: the results indicate that the policy effects are statistically significant. To compare the results of Panel A in Table 8.3 which uses the same model, it is shown that the policy does reduce the employment probability of young college graduates aged from 21 to 30 years old, and there may be a spillover effect for the policy. Why does the policy affect not only the new college but also the other young group? The results can be explained as follows. First, the unemployment experience may have a negative effect for a new college graduate when he searches for a job. Therefore, the unemployment period may become longer. Second, when the group aged from 21 to 25 years old can be substituted by the group aged from 26 to 30 years old, the employment status of the group aged from 21 to 25 years old should affect that for the group aged from 26 to 30 years old.

4. *Results of the Placebo test*

To test the propriety of the DID/DDD models used in the study, we take a Placebo test. Concretely, because it is thought that the higher education expansion policy only affects the college graduate labor supply

Table 8.8 Test results using various treatment groups

	Model1		*Model2*		*Model3*	
	Coeff.	*S.D.*	*Coeff.*	*S.D.*	*Coeff.*	*S.D.*
Estimation1						
Treatment	0.163	0.331	0.1767	0.3321	0.471	0.426
Year	−0.299*	0.186	−0.2997*	0.1867	0.572***	0.289
DD	−0.642*	0.347	−0.6509*	0.3490	−0.936***	0.441
Family number			−0.0890**	0.0373	−0.070***	0.043
Health status			0.0203	0.0175	0.027***	0.019
Male			0.0148	0.1008	0.054***	0.105
Region (East)						
Central					−0.012***	0.173
West					0.011***	0.194
Urban					0.122***	0.110
Ratio of fixed asset investment					−2.346***	0.632
Ratio of tertiary industry					−1.214***	0.786
Ratio of trade					−0.464***	0.247
GDP per capita					0.000***	0.000
Constants	1.962***	0.172	2.1619***	0.2611	3.048***	0.510
Observations	1,617		1,617		1,617	
Log likelihood	−388.242		−366.007		−341.799	
Pseudo R^2	0.028		0.053		0.089	
	Model1		*Model2*		*Model3*	
	Coeff.	*S.D.*	*Coeff.*	*S.D.*	*Coeff.*	*S.D.*
Estimation2						
Treatment	0.216	0.284	0.225	0.285	0.422	0.323
Year	−0.299*	0.186	−0.301*	0.186	0.539**	0.267
DD	−0.588**	0.299	−0.577*	0.300	−0.752**	0.337
Family number			−0.091	0.033	−0.100***	0.038
Health status			0.012	0.016	0.013	0.017
Male			−0.001	0.090	0.031	0.093
Region (East)						
Central					−0.083	0.149
West					0.243	0.180
Urban					0.031	0.099
Ratio of fixed asset investment					−2.671***	0.552
Ratio of tertiary industry					−1.662**	0.709

(*continued*)

Table 8.8 (continued)

	Model1		*Model2*		*Model3*	
	Coeff.	*S.D.*	*Coeff.*	*S.D.*	*Coeff.*	*S.D.*
Ratio of trade					−0.358*	0.221
GDP per capita					1.680E-06	5.230E-06
Constants	1.962***	0.172	2.226***	0.247	3.524***	0.466
Observations	2,034		2,034		2,034	
Log likelihood	−472.411		−465.083		−437.061	
Pseudo R^2	0.037		0.046		0.080	

Source: Calculated based on CHNS from 1997 to 2011

Note:

(1) *, **, ***: statistically significant levels are 10%, 5%, and 1%

(2) For Estimation1, Treatment group: university graduation aged 21–27; Control group: university graduation aged 31–40

(3) For Estimation2, Treatment group: university graduation aged 21–30; Control group: university graduation aged 31–40

greatly. In other words, the influence of the policy on senior high school graduates is smaller. Therefore, when we use the senior high school graduate sample to take a similar analysis based on the DID model, the results should be different from that shown in Panel A of Table 8.3. In the placebo-controlled test, the treatment group is the senior high school graduates aged from 21 to 25 years old; the treatment group is the senior high school graduates aged from 31 to 40 years old. The results are summarized in Table 8.9.

It is found that the coefficient of DD items are positive values in these estimations based on model1, model2, and model3, and all of the values are statistically significant at the 1% level. In addition, these values in Table 8.9 are small (from 0.004 to 0.010). It indicates that even though the higher education expansion policy may increase the employment of young senior high school graduates, the impact of higher education expansion policy on young senior high school students is small. It is clear that these results are different from that for the college graduates shown in Table 8.3. Thus it is indicated that the DID and DDD models are valid.

Table 8.9 Results of the Placebo test

	Model1		*Model2*		*Model3*	
	Coeff.	*S.D.*	*Coeff.*	*S.D.*	*Coeff.*	*S.D.*
Treatment	0.001	0.001	−0.005***	0.002	−0.005**	0.002
Year	−0.165***	0.046	−0.696***	0.057	−0.202**	0.081
DD	0.004***	0.001	0.010***	0.002	0.010***	0.002
Central			−0.235***	0.044	−0.132*	0.071
West			0.038	0.054	0.175**	0.080
Urban			0.066*	0.040	0.062	0.042
Family number			−0.014	0.013	−0.009	0.014
Health status			−0.002	0.007	−0.004	0.008
Male			−0.040	0.038	−0.048	0.041
Ratio of fixed asset investment					−1.658***	0.218
Ratio of tertiary industry					−1.673***	0.309
Ratio of trade					0.566***	0.218
GDP per capita					0.000	0.000
Constants	1.110***	0.045	1.658***	0.100	2.510***	0.184
Observations	6,203		6,203		6,203	
Log likelihood	−2743.266		−2740.164		−2460.905	
Pseudo R^2	0.012		0.042		0.062	

Source: Calculated based on CHNS from 1997 to 2011

Note:

(1) *, **, ***: statistically significant levels are 10%, 5%, and 1%

(2) Treatment group: Senior high school graduation aged 21–25; Control group: Senior high school graduation aged 31–40

8.7 Conclusions

In 1999, the Chinese government implemented the higher education expansion policy. Along with the implementation of the policy, yearly college graduates increased from 0.8 million to 6.1 million from 1999 to 2011. It is thought that large increase of college graduate labor supply should affect the employment situation of young college graduates. Based on the natural experiment models (DID model and DDD model), this study takes an empirical study to provide evidence on the issue, using six waves (1997, 2000, 2004, 2006, 2009, and 2011) of longitudinal survey data of CHNS conducted from 1997 to 2011.

Several major conclusions emerge. First, generally, the higher education expansion policy reduces young college graduate employment. To compare with the policy effect in 2004 and 2011, the negative effect of the policy on the employment is greater in 2006 and 2009. Second, the higher education expansion policy decreases the probability to become both regular workers and irregular workers for young college graduates. However, the differences of the employment probability between the non-work and the self-employed by the policy implementation are small. It is shown that the policy implementation reduces the proportion in "good job/good sector" for new college graduates. Third, the difference of the employment probability between the Eastern, Central, and Western regions is small. Fourth, the policy reduces the employment probability for the group with the urban registration, whereas the impact of the policy for the group with the rural registration is not statistically significant. Finally, using various treatment groups shows that the higher education expansion policy affects the employment for the groups aged from 21 to 30 years old. In addition, the Placebo test indicated the results based on DID/DDD models are valid.

Based on these empirical study results, some policy implications could be considered as follows. First, the results indicate that with the implementation of higher education expansion policy, the over-education problem or underemployment problem among young college graduates may occur at present for college graduates (Li et al. 2008). To consider the over-education problem for the tertiary education, it is pointed out that only primary and junior high schools (low- and middle-level education) have strong positive effects on growth (Liu and Armer 1993). However, with the implementation of higher education expansion policy, the public investment in higher education increased greatly. Moreover, Wolf (2002), De Meulemeester, and Rochat (1995) argued that higher education can contribute to economic growth through training intellectuals and scientific and technological innovation, or if its content is shaped toward an objective. Chinese government should consider the balance of low-, middle-, and high-education development, and promote the industry structure upgraded through the technological innovation with the higher education expansion policy implementation in the future.

Second, even though the increase of college graduate labor supply causes the decrease of employment probability, to compare the developed countries, the proportion of higher education workers in the total population is smaller for China.[7] Based on the need of economic growth and technological innovation progress, to increase public education investment in higher education is still necessary in the future.

Third, it is thought the negative influence of the policy may be caused by the education quality decrease along with the university expansion in

China. In the study, we cannot gain information about the higher education quality among various college/university; it should be considered in the future research.

Fourth, based on information asymmetry hypothesis, the job search information scarce may cause the increase of college graduates' unemployment. To provide the education which is needed by the society and to provide the job search service by the government should be considered.

Notes

1. In China, college can be distinguished by two types—they are college with three school years, and university with four or five school years. In the study, we call these two types as "college" briefly.
2. Based on NBS data (NBS 2016), the urban registered unemployment rate increased from 3.0% in 1996 to 4.3% in 2001. It should be noted that the actual unemployment rate was higher than the unemployment rate published by government.
3. In China, college includes regular college and irregular college (such as the college which provides the education course at night, the college which provides the education course by television communication).
4. For the impact of higher education expansion policy on wage, please refer to He (2009), Chang and Xiang (2013), Wang (2014), Yao et al. (2014), Gao and Smyth (2015), and Xia et al. (2016). In Eq. (8.1b). X also includes the interaction item of age dummy and year dummy, the interaction item of higher education graduation dummy and year dummy, and the interaction item of higher education graduation dummy and age dummy.
5. In Eq. (8.1b), X also includes the interaction item of age dummy and year dummy variables, the interaction item of higher education graduation dummy and year dummy variables, and the interaction item of higher education graduation dummy and age dummy variables.
6. Regional level variables are obtained from *Chinese Statistics Yearbook* in survey year.
7. The proportion of higher education workers in the total population for China is 4.7% in 2000 and 10% in 2010 for China based on 2000 and 2010 Chinese Population Census.

References

Chang, J., & Xiang, J. (2013). Higher education expansion and return to college education. *Chinese Journal of Population Science, 3*, 104–111 (In Chinese).

De Meulemeester, J., & Rochat, D. (1995). A causality of the link between higher education and economic development. *Economics of Education Review, 14*(4), 351–361.

Gao, W., & Smyth, R. (2015). Education expansion and returns to schooling in urban China, 2001–2010: Evidence from three waves of the China urban labor survey. *Journal of the Asia Pacific Economy, 20*(2), 178–201.
He, Y. (2009). The changes of the rate of return to education: An empirical study based on the data of CHNS. *Chinese Journal of Population Science, 2*, 44–54 (In Chinese).
Knight, J., Deng, Q., & Li, S. (2017). China's expansion of higher education: The labor market consequences of a supply shock. *China Economic Review, 43*, 127–141.
Li, F., Morgan, W. J., & Ding, X. (2008). The expansion of higher education, employment and over-education in China. *International Journal of Educational Development, 28*(6), 687–697.
Li, S., Whalle, J., & Xing, C. (2014). China's higher education expansion and unemployment of college graduates. *China Economic Review, 30*, 567–582.
Lian, S. (2011). Ant tribe' study: Problem, reference and policy. In C. Pan (Ed.), *Annual report on the development of Chinese talents 2010*. Beijing: Social Sciences.
Liu, C., & Armer, M. J. (1993). Education's effect on economic growth in Taiwan. *Comparative Education Review, 37*(3), 304–321.
Ma, X. (2011). Immigration and labor market segmentation in urban China: An empirical analysis of income gaps between migrants and urban register workers. *Japanese Journal of Comparative Economics, 48*(1), 39–55 (In Japanese).
Ma, X. (2016). Economic transition and the determinants of self-employment in urban China: 2007–2013. *Journal of Chinese Economic and Business Studies, 14*(3), 279–307.
Ma, X., & Deng, Q. (2016). Economic transition and self-employment of migrants in urban China. *Journal of Chinese Economic Studies, 13*(1), 78–92.
Meng, X., & Zhang, J. (2001). Two-tier labor market in urban China: Occupational segregation and wage differentials between urban residents and rural migrants in Shanghai. *Journal of Comparative Economics, 29*(3), 485–504.
National Bureau of Statistics (NBS) of China. (2010). *China statistical yearbook*. Beijing: China Statistics Press.
National Bureau of Statistics (NBS) of China. (2016). *China statistical yearbook*. Beijing: China Statistics Press.
Song, L., & Appleton, S. (2006). Urban laid-off workers versus rural migrants: Sectoral choice and job-search. In F. Cai & N. Bai (Eds.), *Labor migration in transition China*. Beijing: Social Science Academic Press (In Chinese).
Trow, M. (1972). The expansion and transformation of higher education. *International Review of Education, 18*(1), 61–84.
Trow, M. (1973). *Problems in the transition from elite to mass higher education*. Carnegie Commission on Higher Education.

Wang, G. (2014). The effects of increased supply of graduates on college wage premium. *Studies in Labor Economic, 2*(1), 152–165 (In Chinese).

Wang, M. (2005). Work chance and wage differentials in the urban labor market: Work and wage of migrants. *Chinese Social Sciences, 5*, 36–46 (In Chinese).

Wang, X., & Liu, J. (2011). China's higher education expansion and the task of economic revitalization. *Higher Education, 62*, 213–229.

Wolf, A. (2002). *Does education matter? Myths about education and economic growth*. New York: Penguin Books.

Wu, Y., & Zhao, Q. (2010). Higher education expansion and employment of university graduates. *Economic Research, 9*, 93–108 (In Chinese).

Xia, Q., Wang, X., Li, S., & Zhou, H. (2016). The effects of China's higher education expansion on income distribution. *Social Science Front, 7*, 54–65 (In Chinese).

Xing, C., & Li, S. (2011). Higher education expansion, education opportunity, and unemployment of college graduates. *China Economic Quarterly, 10*(4), 1187–1208 (In Chinese).

Yao, X., Fang, X., & Qian, X. (2014). The effects of higher education expansion on wage of college graduates. *Population & Economics, 202*(1), 67–79 (In Chinese).

Yao, X., Fang, X., & Zhang, H. (2013). Changes in economic return to schooling and employment rate with the expansion of higher education. *Economic Issues in China, 277*(2), 3–11 (In Chinese).

Yeung, W. J. (2012). Higher education expansion and social stratification in China. *Chinese Sociological Review, 45*, 54–80.

CHAPTER 9

Impact of the New Rural Pension Scheme on Labor Supply

9.1 Introduction

China is experiencing rapid aging of its population and economic growth. The 2000 and 2010 population censuses show the proportion of population aged over 60 increased from 10.33% in 2000 to 13.26% in 2010, and the proportion of population aged over 65 increased from 6.96% in 2000 to 8.87% in 2010. The principal reasons for the population aging in China may be the decrease in total fertility rate associated with the one-child policy and the increase in the life expectancy. The social security systems were segmented by the *Hukou* system implemented from 1958. Since the 1980s many young workers with rural registration moved from the rural region to the urban region after the *Hukou* system was deregulated. The rate of aging is higher for the rural region than the urban region (Cai et al. 2012; Cai & Wang 2008; Cai and Cheng 2014). According to the 2000 and 2010 population censuses, in 2000 the proportion of population aged over 60 was 10.91% for the rural region and 9.68% for the urban region; in 2010 it was 14.98% for the rural region and 11.68% for the urban region.

To address the social and economic problems caused by the aging population, many governments around the world sought to establish a set of social security systems (a universal public pension scheme) to provide security for the elderly. Unlike the systems in other countries, the Chinese social security systems were segmented by the *Hukou* system. Most residents with rural registration were not covered by the public pension

X. Ma, *Economic Transition and Labor Market Reform in China*,
https://doi.org/10.1007/978-981-13-1987-7_9

scheme. Security for the elderly in rural regions was the family, a tradition associated with Confucianism. Since the late 1980s, the government began to implement public pension schemes in some provinces, but there was no universal public pension scheme for the whole rural elderly. The great change occurred in 2009. In September 2009, the State Council implemented the National Rural Pension Scheme (NRPS) for the whole residents with rural registrations. It is expected that the NRPS will provide minimum living standards for the rural elderly, and it is the first step to establish a universal public pension scheme.

Judging by the experience of developed countries, the public pension may reduce the labor supply, and therefore a public pension scheme may negatively affect economic growth in the long term (Krueger and Pischke 1992; Samwick 1998; Borsch-Supan 2000; Maloney 2000; Oshi et al. 2009; Blau and Goodstein 2010; Martin and Marcos 2010; Vere 2011; Kudrna and Woodland 2011; Shimizutani and Oshio 2013; Hernaes et al. 2016). The evaluation of the economic effects of public pension and whether the public pension affects labor supply is an important research issue. Because participation in the NRPS is voluntary and it was implemented in 2009, it becomes a quasi-natural experiment which can be used to investigate the causal relation of the public pension scheme and elderly labor supply in China.

Even though some previous studies estimate the impact of the NRPS on the elderly labor supply, most of them used the China Health and Retirement Longitudinal Survey (CHARLS), or only survey data for one province or a few provinces, and therefore the results are not consistent (Cheng 2014; Zhang et al. 2014; Zhang 2015; Xie 2015; Liu et al. 2016; Ning et al. 2016; Liu and Zeng 2016; Liu 2017). This study uses the new Chinese Health and Nutrition Survey (CHNS) longitudinal survey data to perform an empirical study using the quasi-natural experiment model to investigate the impact of the NRPS on labor force participation and employment status (regular worker, irregular worker, self-employed, or non-work) behavior. Regional disparity and gender disparity are also considered in this study. These analyses provide relevant new evidence.

This study is structured as follows. Section 9.2 introduces rural public pension scheme reform in China, and Section 9.3 introduces the channels in which the NRPS may influence the labor supply, and previous empirical studies for the developed and developing countries on the issue. Section 9.4 gives the framework for the empirical analysis, including models and datasets. Section 9.5 introduces the description results of labor force participation rate by the middle-aged group and the elderly group, and by the pensioner group and non-pensioner group in the rural region. Section 9.6 presents estimated results and explains these results. Section 9.7 summarizes the conclusions.

9.2 The Rural Public Pension Scheme in China During the Economic Transition Period

9.2.1 The Rural Public Pension Scheme in China Before 2009

In 1951, during the planned economy period (1949–1977), the People's Republic of China (PRC) enacted its first social security law, entitled *LaoDong BaoXian TiaoLi*, to provide social security including public pensions based on their wages for retired employees of state-owned enterprises (SOEs) and collective-owned enterprises (COEs). The public pension system for staff in the government organizations, public organizations (*Shiye Danwei*), and the cadre in the SOEs was implemented in 1955. It could be said that in the urban regions all workers and most of their families were covered by the public pension system. However, the public social security law did not include residents with rural registration. In the rural regions, the elderly were cared for and supported by their family and the people's commune (*Renmin Gongsher*).

During the economic transition period (1978 to the present), with the implementation of the Household Production Contract Responsibility System (*Jianting Lianchan Chengbao Zerrenzhi*), the people's commune collapsed. The one-child policy implemented in 1979 and the increased migration of younger people from rural areas associated with the deregulation of the *Hukou* system since the 1980s meant that family care for the elderly became problematic. The social security systems including the pension system became obsolete and this obstructed China's economic development and urbanization process.

As a part of the reform of the overall social security system beginning in 1986, the Chinese government initiated a voluntary social pension system in the rural regions. In 1991, the Ministry of Civil Affairs carried out a pilot reform in Shandong, Hubei, and Jiangsu provinces. In 1992, the government implemented the establishment of the rural pension scheme at county level, calling for the diffusion of reforms to many rural regions based on local socioeconomic development. After the Old Rural Pension

Scheme (ORPS) was implemented between 1992 and 1997, pension coverage expanded significantly. However, the Asian financial crisis in 1998 had a significant negative influence on Chinese economic growth. In 1999, the State Council declared that China did not have the infrastructure necessary to establish a universal rural pension system, and therefore the expansion of rural pensions stagnated.

In 2002, the Ministry of Labor and Social Security (MoLSS) conducted a survey of the state of the rural pension scheme. It found that the total number of rural residents covered by the rural pension scheme had decreased from 82 million in 1997 to 54 million in 2002. In 2003 to continue to support rural pension scheme reform, the "decision on some major issues concerning to improve the rural social security system" was taken at the plenary meeting of the 16th China Communist Party Central Committee Congress. In 2004, the MoLSS chose two models: the Daxing (Beijing) model and the Qingdao (Shandong) model as the experimental points for the reform of the ORPS. In 2007, at the plenary meeting of the 17th China Communist Party Central Committee Congress, the government committed to provide a universal social insurance scheme by 2020. In September 2009, the State Council implemented the NRPS for rural residents.

9.2.2 *The NRPS*

The basic design of the NRPS is as follows. First, residents aged 16 and over, not in education and not covered by an urban public pension scheme (e.g. UEPP: Urban Employee Pension Program; CSPP: Civil Servants Pension Program; or URPP: Urban Residents Pension Program), with rural registration can choose to participate in the NRPS. Participation in the NRPS is voluntary. When they decide to participate in the NRPS, they must register with their village administration, which is the lowest level of the hierarchy of government in China.

Second, the NRPS funds come from three sources: individual contributions, the collective and local government, and the central government. The individual contributions range from 100 RMB to 500 RMB a year. The contributions to the scheme are not calculated on the basis of earnings. Each county can decide the exact contribution range applying in its jurisdiction. In some regions, the collectives contribute to the fund. The local governments provide a partial matched contribution of at least 30 RMB a year for every insured person. If the insured person contributes more they will receive a greater matched contribution from the government. The country government or the municipal government generally administers the NRPS fund.[1]

Third, rural elderly residents are entitled to receive a pension if they are 60 or more at the time the scheme started. Those who are younger than 60 must contribute to it for at least 15 years in order to receive pension benefits.

Fourth, the insured person is entitled to receive benefits in two parts: (1) basic pension benefits of at least 55 RMB a month and (2) individual account funds. The insured person's contributions plus interest divided by the number of actuarial months (139 in 2012) is paid. Because there is no earnings test, the participants do not need to stop work when they receive the pension. Individual accounts can be inherited by the insured person's family if the insured dies early. The central government will assume the total basic guaranteed benefit (at least 55 RMB a month per insured person) in the Central and Western regions, and 50% of the basic guaranteed benefit in the Eastern region for a basic guarantee of the pension benefit. In addition, the benefit will be adjusted for inflation, but the adjustment mechanism is not yet determined (Cai et al. 2012).

Fifth, the local bureau of social security administers the scheme, and administrative costs come from general taxes.

After 2009, the Chinese government enforced the implementation of the NRPS. Based on data from the Ministry of Human Resources and Social Security, the total number of participants increased from 103.0 million in 2010 to 483.7 million in 2012, the contributions increased from 74.1 million in 2010 to 349.9 million in 2012, and the beneficiaries increased from 28.9 million in 2010 to 133.8 million in 2012. After August 2012, the NRPS and Urban Resident Pension Scheme were integrated into the "Urban and Rural Residents Social Pension Scheme".

9.3 Literature Review

9.3.1 *The Channels for the Impact of Public Pensions on Labor Force Participation*

Does the NRPS, implemented since 2009, affect labor force participation in China? First, according to neoclassical economic theory, in a perfect competitive market the budget constraint and preference of leisure (or work) can affect the individual labor supply. The pension can increase non-labor income and change the budget constraint situation, which causes a decrease of labor supply. Based on NRPS, when the rural elderly person reaches 60 years, if he contributed to the NRPS, the pension benefits are awarded. When the pension benefit is enough for living, the leisure preference should increase whereas the probability of working may become less. Second, the pension can be thought of as a kind of asset for an individual; the pension can be used to start a new business (e.g. to become a self-employed worker, to become the owner of small-sized firm), and therefore labor force participation may increase as the result of the implementation of the NRPS. It is not certain how the NRPS affects the rural elderly labor force participation, and therefore an empirical study is necessary.

9.3.2 Empirical Studies on the Impact of Public Pension on Labor Force Participation

There are a number of empirical studies on the impacts of the public pension on the labor market. Rural China can be thought as a developing region, and therefore this literature review surveys empirical studies of developing countries.[2]

For developing countries except China, most empirical studies indicate that pensions may reduce the labor supply of both the recipient and other household members. First, for South Africa, Bertrand et al. (2003) estimate the effect of pension uptake and pension eligibility on the labor supply of household members (primary-age individuals) based on the OLS model. They find a sharp drop in the working hours of prime-age individuals in households when women turn 60 years old or men turn 65 years old, the ages at which they become eligible for pensions, and the oldest son in the household reduces his working hours more than any other prime-age household member. Posel et al. (2006) examine the effect of the South African social pension on the labor supply of working age adults and use OLS and instrument variable (IV) methods. They find that rural African women are significantly more likely to become migrant workers when they are members of a household in receipt of a pension. Ranchod (2006) estimates the effect of the means tested South African Old Age Pension on labor supply among the elderly African subpopulation in South Africa, and finds a significant decrease in employment rates and the labor supply. Those who remain employed beyond pensionable age are more likely to work in jobs with flexible hours, and work even fewer hours than people in similar jobs who are not pension age eligible. Ardington et al. (2009) quantify the labor supply responses of prime-aged adults to the presence of pensioners in their households, and find large cash transfers to the elderly lead to increased employment among prime-aged adults, which occurs primarily through labor migration.[3]

Second, for Brazil, De Carvalho (2008) estimates the impact of social security benefits (1991 pension reform) on the retirement decisions of rural workers using the Difference in Difference in Difference (DDD) method. It is found that receiving old-age benefits increases the probability of not working by about thirty-eight percentage points and reduces total hours per week by 22.5 hours.

Third, for Mexico, Juarez (2010) studies the effect of the 2011 pension scheme on the labor supply of pensionable individuals and other family members based on the DDD method. It is found that the program has no significant effect on the time use of pensionable individuals; both men and women 18 to 59 years old increase their labor supply if they live with a pensionable man, but decrease hours worked if they live with a pensionable woman.[4]

Fourth, for India, Kaushal (2013) uses a regression model to estimate the effect of a recent expansion in India's National Old Age Pension Scheme, and finds that the public pension has a modest negative effect on the employment of elderly and near pensionable men with a primary or lower education but no effect on the employment of similar women.

The results of empirical studies for China are not consistent. Some results suggest that the NRPS reduces the labor supply, whereas some studies find that the NRPS does not affect the labor supply. For example, Cheng (2014) conducts an empirical study on the impact of the NRPS on labor force participation, using Shichuan Province survey data conducted in 2011 and an instrument variable (IV) method and probit regression model (IV-probit model). He indicates that the NRPS coverage (the pension enrollment) may decrease 10.3% of agriculture labor force participation probability, and 6.6% of total labor force participation probability (the total of agriculture and non-agriculture labor force participations). The pension receipt may decrease 13.6% of agriculture labor force participation probability, and 4.4% of total labor force participation probability. Zhang (2015) uses the 2011 CHARLS data and instrument variable and regression discontinuity design methods (IV-RDD methods) to investigate the NRPS effect, and points out that a pension from the NRPS significantly reduces the probability of labor force participation of the elderly aged around 60 years, but does not affect the hours worked. Liu et al. (2016) use the 2011 Rural Fixed Observatory Survey data (*Nongcun Guding Guanchadian Chouyang Diaocha*) conducted by the Ministry of Agriculture, and propensity score matching (PSM) Difference in Difference (DID) method, and find that even though the influence of participation in the NRPS on the probability of labor force participation is not statistically significant, the NRPS does reduce the total working hours, agriculture working hours, and migration working hours. Liu and Zeng (2016) use the 2013 CHARLS data and IV-probit and Tobit models, and find that participation in the NRPS can increase the probability of total labor force participation, and labor force participation in agriculture employed work and self-employed work, but reduces the probability of becoming a non-agriculture employed worker and self-employed. Moreover, NRPS can increase the total working hours, agriculture employed working hours, and self-employed working hours, but reduces the working hours for both non-agriculture employed workers and the self-employed. Liu (2017) uses the 2013 CHARLS data and OLS and probit regression models to estimate the effect of the NRPS. He indicates participation in the NRPS increases both the labor force participation and working hours (particularly, the total labor force participation and agriculture labor force participation, the total working hours, and agriculture working hours), whereas the pension account reduces both labor force participation and working hours. Whereas Zhang et al. (2014) use 2011 CHARLS data and RD-DID methods, and find pension receipt from the NRPS does not significantly affect the retirement and work hours. Xie (2015) uses the 2008 and 2012 CHARLS data and RD-DID methods to investigate the NRPS effect. Xie points out that pension receipt for the NRPS does not significantly affect the labor force participation and work hours. Ning et al. (2016) use the 2011 and 2013 CHARLS data and RD-DID methods to investigate the NRPS effect. Their results concur with Xie's (2015). One reason for the various findings may be that the survey datasets and the estimation method are different. Thus it is necessary to re-estimate using new survey data and methods. That is the intent of this chapter.

9.3.3 Contributions of This Study

Although published studies investigate the impact of NRPS on labor force participation in China, there remain some issues to consider.

First, CHRLS data and IV-probit, PSM, and RDD models are used in published studies, but empirical studies based on the quasi-natural experiment are scarce. This study uses longitudinal survey data of CHNS from 2000 to 2011 to construct a quasi-natural experiment dataset to investigate the effect of the NRPS on labor force participation of the rural elderly group. The estimation uses the new datasets and the quasi-natural experiment method provides new evidence.

Second, the impact of policy may change over time. Currently, there is no empirical study to consider the short-term and long-term effects of the NRPS. This study addresses this gap in research.

Third, because of the large regional disparity in China it is thought that labor market conditions differ by region. The study also analyses the policy effect in three regions: the Eastern, Central, and Western regions. The determinants of the decision to work differ by gender (for example, women may do more housework) and the labor market commitment is lower than for men. Therefore, we use a subsample of men and women to estimate the policy effects.

Lastly, this study uses various treatments, control group indexes, and various subsamples to take the analyses and compare these results in order to examine the estimation bias of variable setting and sample selection. This study uses a Placebo test to assess the propriety of the estimation model and the quasi-natural experiment design.

9.4 Methodology and Data

9.4.1 Model

The DID model for labor force participation can be represented as follows:

$$Y_{it} = a + \beta_Y \text{Year}_{it} + \beta_T \text{Treat}_{it} + \beta_{TY} \text{Treat}_{it} \times \text{Year}_{it} + \beta_X X_{it} + \varepsilon_{it} \qquad (9.1)$$

In Eq. (9.1), Y is the probability of labor force participation, i stands for the individual, t for years, *Year* for NRPS implementation years (2009, and 2011 in this study), *Treat* for the treatment group, X for the individual characteristics variables (e.g. age, education, health status, gender), family factors (e.g. family number, household income), the regional dummy variables, a is the constant term, and ε is the error term. β represents the estimated coefficient for each variable.

This study divides the years before the implementation of the NRPS (2000, 2004, and 2006) as the pre-policy period and the years of 2009 and 2011 as the post-policy period. The details of the treatment group are introduced in Sect. 9.4.2.

β_{TY} is estimated coefficient of DID item which is an interaction item of *Treat* and *Year*. When β_{TY} is a negative value, and it is statistically significant, it indicates that the NRPS implementation decreases labor force participation, and vice versa.

9.4.2 Data

This study employs five waves (2000, 2004, 2006, 2009, and 2011) of the CHNS data. For the detailed information on the CHNS, please see Section 2.3 in Chap. 2 of the book. Although the longitudinal survey began in 1989, the survey data around the implementation of the policy (from 2000 to 2011) is used because the NRPS was implemented from 2009. This study utilizes samples from 11 provinces covered in the longitudinal survey. They are Beijing, Liaoning, Heilongjiang, Shanghai, Jiangsu, Shandong, Hernan, Hubei, Hunan, Guangxi, and Guizhou. Because the NRPS covers the individual with rural registration in China, we select the samples with rural registration as the analyzed objects.

The independent variables of employment are two types: a binary variable for labor force participation and a category variable of employment status which includes regular worker, irregular worker, self-employed, and non-work.[5]

Year is a year dummy variable from the NRPS implementation period (2009 and 2011).

Treat represents a treatment group dummy variable. Even though we cannot gain the information for the kinds of pension receipt, because based on the regulations of the NRPS, participants older than 60 receive the pension benefit, we construct the treatment group as follows (see Table 9.1).

The DID item in Eq. (9.1) is the interaction term of the two variables used: the policy implementation year dummy and the treatment group dummy (Year × Treat).

To examine whether individual characteristics may affect labor force participation, family number, health status,[6] and male dummy variables are used. It is expected that the probability of labor force participation is greater for the larger family number group, the better health status group, and the male group. Moreover, Wu and Zhao (2010) and Li, Whalle, and Xing (2014) show that regional variables also affect individual labor force participation behavior, and therefore the Eastern, Central, and Western regional dummy variables are used to control the regional disparity.

9.5 Descriptive Statistics Results

First, Table 9.2 summarizes the variable means by pension receipt group and non-pension receipt groups and by age categories (the group aged 50–59, the group aged 60–70). It is observed that for both the group aged 50–59 years

Table 9.1 Treatment group and control group setting in the study

Types[a]	*Treatment group*	*Control group*	*Table number*
I[b]	Pension receipt, aged older than 60	Non-pension receipt, aged older than 60	Table 9.4, Table 9.5, Table 9.6, Table 9.7, Table 9.9
II[c]	Aged 60–64	Aged 55–59	Table 9.8(1)
III[d]	Aged 60–64	Aged 50–59	Table 9.8(2)
IV[e]	Aged 60–70	Aged 50–59	Table 9.8(3)
V[f]	Pension receipt, aged older than 50	Non-pension receipt, aged older than 50	Table 9.8(4)
VI[g]	Aged 55–59	Aged 50–54	Table 9.10

Source: Author

[a]Type I is used to conduct the basic analyses. Type II, Type III, Type IV, and Type V are used to conduct the robustness checks. Type VI is used to conduct the Placebo test

[b]The treatment group is constructed as those who did not receive pension benefit and older than 60 before 2009 and received pension benefit after 2009. The control group is constructed as those who did not receive the pension benefit and older than 60 before and after 2009 (Type I)

[c]The treatment group is constructed as those who did not receive pension benefit and aged 60–64 before 2009 and received pension benefit after 2009. The control group is constructed as those who did not receive the pension benefit and aged 55–59 before and after 2009 (Type II)

[d]The treatment group is constructed as those who did not receive pension benefit aged 60–64 before 2009 and received pension benefit after 2009. The control group is constructed as those who did not receive the pension benefit and aged 50–59 before and after 2009 (Type III)

[e]The treatment group is constructed as those who did not receive pension benefit and aged 60–70 before 2009 and received pension benefit after 2009. The control group is constructed as those who did not receive the pension benefit and aged 50–59 before and after 2009 (Type IV)

[f]The treatment group is constructed as those who did not receive pension benefit and older than 50 before 2009 and received pension benefit after 2009. The control group is constructed as those who did not receive the pension benefit and older than 50 before and after 2009 (Type V)

[g]The treatment group is constructed as those aged 55–59, and the control group is constructed as those aged 50–54 (Type VI)

and the group aged 60–70 years, the variable means differ by the pension receipt group and non-pension receipt group. For example, the proportion of higher education group is greater for the pension receipt group (2.8%, 6.1%) than for the non-pension receipt group (1.0%, 0.6%). The non-labor income is higher for the pension receipt group (42,370 yuan, 41,098 yuan) than for the non-pension receipt group (26,671 yuan, 24,296 yuan).

Second, does the disparity of the individual characteristics and income between the pension receipt group and non-pension receipt group affect the decision to work? Table 9.3 summarizes the labor force participation rate (LFPR)[7] by age group. In both the pre-policy period (2004, 2006) and post-policy period (2009, 2011), the LFPR is higher for the pension

Table 9.2 Descriptive statistics

	Total		*Pension = 1*				*Pension = 0*			
			50 ≤ Age < 60		*60 ≤ Age ≤ 70*		*50 ≤ Age < 60*		*60 ≤ Age ≤ 70*	
	Mean	*S.D.*	*Mean*	*S.D.*	*Mean*	*S.D.*	*Mean*	*S.D.*	*Mean*	*S.D.*
Pension	167	528	1256	900	1231	827	0	0	0	0
Pension coverage	0.134	0.341	1	0	1	0	0	0	0	0
LR	0.534	0.499	0.158	0.365	0.077	0.266	0.668	0.471	0.479	0.500
Age	59	5	55	3	65	3	55	3	64	3
Education										
Less than primary school	0.418	0.493	0.219	0.414	0.246	0.431	0.389	0.488	0.545	0.498
Primary school	0.271	0.445	0.211	0.408	0.259	0.439	0.276	0.447	0.277	0.448
Junior high school	0.204	0.403	0.320	0.467	0.248	0.432	0.224	0.417	0.136	0.343
Senior high school	0.069	0.253	0.153	0.360	0.067	0.251	0.085	0.279	0.025	0.156
Vocational school	0.025	0.155	0.070	0.255	0.118	0.322	0.016	0.125	0.010	0.100
College	0.013	0.115	0.028	0.164	0.061	0.240	0.010	0.098	0.006	0.076
Health	5.639	2.303	6.600	2.099	6.250	2.400	5.549	2.315	5.468	2.228
Male	0.584	0.493	0.624	0.485	0.682	0.466	0.565	0.496	0.587	0.492
Family number	3.844	1.714	3.455	1.607	3.432	1.706	3.924	1.628	3.876	1.851
No-earning income (yuan)	27,931	38,497	42,370	55,685	41,098	39,158	26,671	38,409	24,296	32,818
Regions										
East	0.361	0.480	0.563	0.496	0.525	0.500	0.355	0.479	0.295	0.456
Central	0.381	0.486	0.262	0.440	0.280	0.449	0.398	0.490	0.398	0.490
West	0.258	0.437	0.176	0.381	0.196	0.397	0.247	0.431	0.307	0.461
Survey year										
y2000	0.193	0.395	0.129	0.336	0.121	0.327	0.197	0.398	0.215	0.411
y2004	0.182	0.385	0.150	0.357	0.174	0.379	0.181	0.385	0.190	0.392
y2006	0.175	0.380	0.174	0.380	0.173	0.378	0.174	0.379	0.177	0.382

(*continued*)

Table 9.2 (continued)

	Total		*Pension = 1*				*Pension = 0*			
			50 ≤ Age < 60		*60 ≤ Age ≤ 70*		*50 ≤ Age < 60*		*60 ≤ Age ≤ 70*	
	Mean	*S.D.*	*Mean*	*S.D.*	*Mean*	*S.D.*	*Mean*	*S.D.*	*Mean*	*S.D.*
y2009	0.183	0.387	0.218	0.413	0.163	0.370	0.183	0.386	0.182	0.386
y2011	0.267	0.442	0.328	0.470	0.369	0.483	0.265	0.441	0.236	0.425
Observations	11,346		688		833		6235		3,590	

Source: Calculated based on CHNS from 2000 to 2011

Table 9.3 Labor force participation rate (LFPR) in rural China

	Pension (%)	*No-pension (%)*	*Pension–No-pension (%)*
2004			
55–59	18.2	68.1	−50.0
60-64	5.3	59.6	−55.0
65–69	5.3	46.2	−41.0
70+	5.2	21.9	−17.0
2006			
55–59	17.1	66.7	−50.0
60–64	11.1	59.0	−48.0
65–69	8.1	41.5	−34.0
70+	2.6	23.0	−20.0
2009			
55–59	20.9	71.4	−50.0
60–64	10.2	69.2	−59.0
65–69	9.8	50.7	−41.0
70+	1.3	28.3	−27.0
2011			
55–59	8.7	69.9	−61.0
60–64	8.9	60.2	−51.0
65–69	10.2	55.7	−46.0
70+	6.9	30.3	−23.0

Source: Calculated based on CHNS from 2000 to 2011

receipt group than for the non-pension receipt group. For example, for the group aged 65–69, the LFPR gap[8] is −41% in 2004, −34.0% in 2006, −41.0% in 2009, and −46.0% in 2011. Compared with the pre-policy period, the gap increased for the post-policy period. It indicates that the NRPS seems to affect the labor force participation. However, these calculations do not control the other factors which may affect the individual labor supply. A more rigorous econometric analysis is needed to investigate the impact of the NRPS on labor force participation and employment status.

9.6 Econometric Analysis Results

9.6.1 *The Impact of NRPS on Labor Force Participation*

Table 9.4 shows the results of the impact of the NRPS on labor force participation using the DID model. Two datasets composed of the period 2000 to 2009 (short term) and the period 2000 to 2011 (long term) are used to

Table 9.4 Results of the impact of NRPS on labor force participation

	(1)		*(2)*		*(3)*		*(4)*	
	Coeff.	*S.E.*	*Coeff.*	*S.E.*	*Coeff.*	*S.E.*	*Coeff.*	*S.E.*
Panel A: (2000–2009), Aged50–70								
After 2009	−0.176***	0.034	−0.193***	0.035	−0.197***	0.035	−0.193***	0.035
Treatment	−1.307***	0.058	−1.332***	0.063	−1.335***	0.063	−1.349***	0.063
DID	−0.351***	0.131	−0.360***	0.134	−0.358***	0.135	−0.362***	0.135
Age			−0.027	0.061	−0.026	0.062	−0.025	0.062
Age squared			−1.615E-04	0.001	−1.628E-04	0.001	−1.778E-04	0.001
Education (Less than primary school)								
Primary school			0.185***	0.035	0.183***	0.035	0.186***	0.035
Junior high school			0.314***	0.042	0.313***	0.042	0.302***	0.042
Senior high school			0.203***	0.062	0.198	0.062	0.209***	0.062
Vocational school			0.189*	0.110	0.165***	0.110	0.188*	0.110
College			0.454***	0.163	0.455***	0.163	0.476***	0.163
Health			0.005	0.006	0.006	0.006	−0.001	0.007
Male			−0.070**	0.029	−0.060**	0.030	−0.058*	0.030
Family number					0.013	0.009	0.009	0.009
No-earning income					7.080E-07*	0.000	5.520E-07	0.000
Regions (East)								
Central							−0.157***	0.035
West							0.021	0.040
Constants	0.322***	0.017	2.353	1.817	2.245	1.821	2.327	1.823
Observations	8,251		8,251		8,251		8,251	
Log likelihood	−5317.674		−5017.249		−4998.474		−4983.359	
Pseudo R^2	0.079		0.118		0.118		0.121	

(*continued*)

Table 9.4 (continued)

	(1)		*(2)*		*(3)*		*(4)*	
	Coeff.	*S.E.*	*Coeff.*	*S.E.*	*Coeff.*	*S.E.*	*Coeff.*	*S.E.*
Panel B: (2000–2011), Aged50–70								
After 2009	−0.190***	0.026	−0.217***	0.026	−0.216***	0.026	−0.225***	0.027
Treatment	−1.307***	0.058	−1.323***	0.062	−1.325***	0.063	−1.337***	0.063
DID	−0.328***	0.091	−0.316***	0.093	−0.322***	0.094	−0.322***	0.094
Age			−0.039	0.054	−0.038	0.054	−0.038	0.054
Age squared			−6.660E-05	0.000	−7.560E-05	0.000	−7.890E-05	0.000
Education (Less than primary school)								
Primary school			0.219***	0.031	0.213***	0.031	0.219***	0.031
Junior high school			0.300***	0.035	0.294***	0.035	0.288***	0.035
Senior high school			0.253***	0.054	0.246***	0.054	0.258***	0.054
Vocational school			0.174*	0.093	0.155*	0.093	0.176***	0.093
College			0.567***	0.125	0.563***	0.126	0.576*	0.126
Health			−0.012**	0.006	−0.012**	0.006	−0.016***	0.006
Male			−0.015	0.025	−0.009	0.026	−0.007	0.026
Family number					0.005	0.008	2.951E-04	0.008
No-earning income					3.260E-07	0.000	1.500E-07	0.000
Regions (East)								
Central							−0.146***	0.031
West							0.039	0.034
Constants	0.322***	0.017	2.774*	1.582	2.712*	1.585	2.830*	1.587
Observations	11,264		11,264		11,264		11,264	
Log likelihood	−7185.418		−6791.219		−6761.481		−6741.822	
Pseudo R^2	0.093		0.131		0.131		0.134	

Note:

*, **, ***: statistically significant levels are 10%, 5%, and 1%

take the analyses in order to consider the influence of the policy over various periods (e.g. a short term, or a long term after the policy is implemented). They are summarized in Panel A (2000–2009) and Panel B (2000–2011). The main findings follow.

The results in both Panel A and Panel B shows that the coefficients of the DD item are negative values, all of which are statistically significant. It indicates that the NRPS may negatively affect labor force participation, and that the pension decreases the probability of choosing to work and makes leisure time increase, which may contribute to an increase in the welfare of the elderly group in the rural region. However, the pension may decrease the elderly labor supply, which may result in a labor shortage for the agriculture industry in the future.

Second, to compare the coefficient values between Panel A and Panel B, the absolute value is greater for Panel A (from 0.351 to 0.362) than for Panel B (from 0.316 to 0.328). In the long term the negative effect of the NRPS on labor force participation becomes smaller. The estimation using the new longer survey data to investigate the NRPS effect should be conducted more in the future because now only data for 2011 is available.

Third, the coefficient values of the DID item in these models are similar: model1 (basic model which only uses three variables, after 2009 dummy, Treatment group dummy, and DID item), model2 (to add the individual characteristic variables to model1), model3 (to add family and income variables to model2), and model4 (to add region dummy variables to model3). It is clear that even though the individual characteristics, family factors, income factors, and regional factors may affect the work decision, the influence of these factors is small, and when these factors are controlled, the impact of the NRPS is still present.

9.6.2 *Results of Impact of NRPS on Employment Status*

It is thought the work conditions (e.g. working hours, wage) differ by employment status (e.g. regular worker, irregular worker, self-employed, no-work). The results of the impact of the NRPS on the probability of various employment statuses are summarized in Table 9.5.

The coefficient value of DID for the regular employed worker sector is positive, and it is statistically significant at the 10% level. It indicates that the NRPS may increase the probability of becoming a regular worker. However, the differences of probability between the irregular worker, the self-employed, and no-work are not statistically significant. It

Table 9.5 Results of impact of NRPS on employment status

	(1) Regular/non-work		*(2) Irregular/ non-work*		*(3) Self-employment/ non-work*	
	Coeff.	*S.D.*	*Coeff.*	*S.D.*	*Coeff.*	*S.D.*
After 2009	−0.285***	0.105	0.307***	0.107	−0.442***	0.047
Treatment	0.623***	0.232	−0.017	0.332	−1.265***	0.194
DID	0.651*	0.392	0.317	0.496	−0.054	0.360
Age	0.836***	0.263	0.377	0.249	0.035	0.097
Age squared	−0.008***	0.002	−0.004*	0.002	−0.001	0.001
Education (Less than primary school)						
Primary school	1.578***	0.188	1.002***	0.140	0.327***	0.054
Junior high school	2.627***	0.180	1.662***	0.140	0.476***	0.067
Senior high school	3.410***	0.201	1.516***	0.204	0.174	0.113
Vocational school	5.167***	0.333	1.932***	0.532	0.099	0.348
College	5.778***	0.436	3.307***	0.498	−0.375	0.576
Health	0.010	0.023	−0.029	0.023	−0.007	0.010
Male	0.132	0.104	0.096	0.106	−0.043	0.046
Family number	−0.065*	0.033	0.041	0.033	0.009	0.014
No-earning income	1.400E-06	0.000	−5.960E-06***	0.000	4.130E-07	0.000
Regions (East)						
Central	−1.313***	0.118	−1.661***	0.135	−0.098*	0.057
West	−1.193***	0.153	−0.953***	0.138	0.243***	0.062
Constants	−23.279***	7.551	−10.099	7.205	1.052	2.861
Observations			9,411			
Log likelihood			−8641.204			
Pseudo R^2			0.124			

Source: Calculated based on CHNS from 2000 to 2011

Note:

*, **, ***: statistically significant levels are 10%, 5%, and 1%

may be that the rural laborers can enter into the irregular worker sector and the self-employed sector easily, and therefore the influence of the NRPS on the labor force participation for these two sectors may be smaller. Why may the NRPS increase labor force participation in the regular worker sector? It can be explained as follows. First, the wage for the regular worker sector is higher than the wage for the other sectors, and therefore in order to gain more income, the worker may prefer to work as a regular worker even though he (she) receives the pension benefits. Second, even though the legal retirement age is between 50 and 60 years old in the public sector (e.g. government organizations, public organizations, SOEs), the retirement age for the owner or manager in the private sector (e.g. the private owned enterprises) may be older than 60 years, and thus some pension receipts can choose to continue to work as a regular worker. Third, there is no earning-test for pension receipt when a pensioner is working. The probability of choosing to become a regular worker may be high for the pensioner because the pension benefit from the NRPS is small.

9.6.3 *Results of Impact of NRPS on Labor Force Participation by Various Groups*

1. *Results of impact of NRPS on labor force participation by regional groups*

Because of the large regional disparity in China it is thought that the labor market situation may differ by region. This study investigates the impact of the NRPS in the Eastern, Central, and Western regions. The results are summarized in Table 9.6.

All coefficient values of DID item are negative: they are −0.272 for the Eastern region, −0.300 for the Central region, and −1.052 for the Western region. In addition, they are statistically significant at 5% for the Eastern and Western regions, and 10% for the Central region. It indicates that the impact of the NRPS is greatest for the Western region. This may be because the willingness to work, the family care for the elderly, and the standard of living differ between regions. For example, the living standard is lower for the Western region so even though the pension benefit is small, the impact of the NRPS may be greater for the Western region than for the Eastern and Central regions.

2. *Results of impact of NRPS on labor force participation by gender*

It is noted that responsibility for childcare, family care, and housework differs by gender (Gronau 1977; Becker 1985), and therefore the labor force participation behavior may differ between women and men. The results of the impact of the NRPS by women and men groups are summarized in Table 9.7.

Table 9.6 Results of impact of NRPS on labor force participation by regions

	(1) East		*(2) Central*		*(3) West*	
	Coeff.	*S.D.*	*Coeff.*	*S.D.*	*Coeff.*	*S.D.*
After 2009	−0.264***	0.046	0.042	−3.140	−0.330***	0.052
Treatment	−1.294***	0.090	−1.251***	0.112	−1.708***	0.155
DID	−0.272**	0.126	−0.300*	0.180	−1.052**	0.427
Age	−0.337***	0.092	0.176**	0.086	−0.030	0.108
Age squared	0.002***	0.001	−0.002***	0.001	−2.107E-04	0.001
Education (Less than primary school)						
Primary school	0.271***	0.055	0.261***	0.048	0.119*	0.062
Junior high school	0.271***	0.057	0.352***	0.060	0.285***	0.074
Senior high school	0.313***	0.086	0.349***	0.083	−0.088	0.130
Vocational school	0.192	0.149	0.348**	0.141	−0.177	0.241
College	0.709***	0.176	0.626***	0.207	0.022	0.390
Health	−0.003	0.011	−0.036***	0.008	−0.001	0.012
Male	−0.046	0.044	0.048	0.041	−0.030	0.051
Family number	−0.001	0.014	0.033	0.012	−0.044***	0.014
No-earning income	9.240E-07*	0.000	−3.010E-07**	0.000	−4.130E-07	0.000
Constants	11.457***	2.712	−3.775	2.536	3.157	3.205
Observations	4,074		4,280		2,910	
Log likelihood	−2347.401		−2655.822		−1685.235	
Pseudo R^2	0.168		0.104		0.155	

Source: Calculated based on CHNS from 2000 to 2011

Note:

*, **, ***: statistically significant levels are 10%, 5%, and 1%

The coefficient values of the DID item are negative values: they are −0.270 for men and −0.521 for women. In addition, they are statistically significant at the 5% level for men and 1% level for women. This indicates that the impact of the NRPS is greater for women than for men. The implementation of the NRPS decreases the labor supply of women more than that of men. It can be explained by the household role division based on the gender role segregation hypothesis (Gronau 1977; Becker 1985). When the income factor is consistent (e.g. the pension account is similar), the probability of doing the housework (or the probability of not doing market work) may be greater for women than for men.

Table 9.7 Results of impact of NRPS on labor force participation by gender

	(1) Male		*(2) Female*	
	Coeff.	*S.D.*	*Coeff.*	*S.D.*
After 2009	−0.163***	0.035	−0.312***	0.041
Treatment	−1.317***	0.081	−1.369***	0.101
DID	−0.270**	0.114	−0.521***	0.176
Age	−0.119*	0.070	0.081	0.083
Age squared	0.001	0.001	−0.001	0.001
Education (Less than primary school)				
Primary school	0.198***	0.041	0.249***	0.047
Junior high school	0.333***	0.047	0.222***	0.055
Senior high school	0.328***	0.070	0.150*	0.085
Vocational school	0.227**	0.113	0.071	0.166
College	0.516***	0.153	0.720***	0.227
Health	−0.023***	0.007	−0.008	0.009
Family number	0.010	0.010	−0.011	0.012
No-earning income	1.580E-07	0.000	8.030E-08	0.000
Regions (East)				
Central	−0.105***	0.039	−0.197***	0.049
West	0.045	0.045	0.033	0.051
Constants	5.132**	2.085	−0.560	2.456
Observations	6,580		4,684	
Log likelihood	−3919.903		−2806.312	
Pseudo R^2	0.140		0.130	

Source: Calculated based on CHNS from 2000 to 2011

Note:

*, **, ***: statistically significant levels are 10%, 5%, and 1%

9.6.4 Robustness Checks

1. *Results using various treatment and control groups*

To consider that the estimated results may vary according to the treatment and construction of control groups this study uses various treatment and control groups to investigate the policy effect. The results are summarized in Table 9.8. The main findings are as follows.

- First, the results using the various treatment and control group categories (see Type II, Type III, Type IV, and Type V in Table 9.1) indicate that even though the coefficients of DID items are not

Table 9.8 Results using various treatment groups

	(1)		*(2)*		*(3)*		*(4)*	
	Control: Aged55–59 group		*Control: Aged50–59 group*		*Control: Aged50–59 group*		*Control: No-pension group*	
	Treatment: Aged60–64 group		*Treatment: Aged60–64 group*		*Treatment: Aged60–70 group*		*Treatment: Pension receipt group*	
	Objects: Aged55–64		*Objects: Aged50–64*		*Objects: Aged50–70*		*Objects: Aged50+*	
	Coeff.	*S.D.*	*coeff.*	*S.D.*	*coeff.*	*S.D.*	*Coeff.*	*S.D.*
After 2009	−0.196***	0.048	−0.200***	0.048	−0.261***	0.033	−0.222***	0.033
Treatment	0.008	0.090	0.038	0.082	−0.027	0.057	−1.290***	0.057
DID	−0.048	0.073	−0.067	0.062	−0.021	0.051	−0.355***	0.125
Age	−0.429	0.355	−0.218	0.156	−0.121**	0.053	−0.026	0.021
Age squared	0.003	0.003	0.001	0.001	0.001	4.482E-04	−1.806E-04	1.620E-04
Education attainment (Less than primary school)								
Primary school	0.194***	0.043	0.146***	0.036	0.162***	0.031	0.170***	0.033
Junior high school	0.126**	0.050	0.031	0.043	0.148***	0.035	0.273***	0.040
Senior high school	0.146*	0.080	0.038	0.071	0.073	0.052	0.192***	0.060
Vocational school	−0.429***	0.129	−0.603***	0.110	−0.352***	0.085	0.039	0.100
College	−0.121	0.158	−0.152	0.131	0.109	0.110	0.517***	0.152
Health	−0.035***	0.008	−0.030***	0.007	−0.026***	0.006	−0.002	0.006
Male	−0.078**	0.037	−0.055*	0.031	−0.028	0.026	−0.037	0.027
Family number	0.036***	0.011	0.019**	0.009	0.020***	0.008	0.004	0.008
No-earning income	−1.820E-06***	5.180E-07	−1.690E-06***	4.520E-07	−1.140E-06***	3.230E-07	6.700E-07*	3.910E-07

(*continued*)

Table 9.8 (continued)

	(1)		*(2)*		*(3)*		*(4)*	
	Control: Aged55–59 group		*Control: Aged50–59 group*		*Control: Aged50–59 group*		*Control: No-pension group*	
	Treatment: Aged60–64 group		*Treatment: Aged60–64 group*		*Treatment: Aged60–70 group*		*Treatment: Pension receipt group*	
	Objects: Aged55–64		*Objects: Aged50–64*		*Objects: Aged50–70*		*Objects: Aged50+*	
	Coeff.	*S.D.*	*coeff.*	*S.D.*	*coeff.*	*S.D.*	*Coeff.*	*S.D.*
Regions (East)								
Central	0.061	0.044	−0.031	0.037	−0.055*	0.030	−0.132***	0.033
West	0.191***	0.048	0.121***	0.040	0.123***	0.033	0.055	0.037
Constants	14.570	10.524	8.565*	4.934	5.394***	1.586	2.410***	0.677
Observations	5036		7257		10,735		10,220	
Log likelihood	−3359.814		−4788.098		−6967.258		−5894.488	
Pseudo R^2	0.037		0.047		0.061		0.168	

Source: Calculated based on CHNS from 2000 to 2009

Note: *, **, ***: statistically significant levels are 10%, 5%, and 1%

statistically significant, these values are negative. It is again confirmed that the NRPS may negatively affect labor force participation.

- Second, the results shown in Table 9.4 are similar to the results shown in Table 9.8. This confirms that the NRPS negatively affects labor force participation by the elderly in rural China.

2. *Results using various samples*

There exists a double pension participation problem whereby migrants with rural registration may participate in both the NRPS and other pension schemes (e.g. the Urban Employment Social Pension Scheme and commercial pensions), particularly for the regular employed worker group. To explore the double pension participation phenomenon, this study investigates the impact of the NRPS using two datasets: the dataset excluding regular workers, and the dataset composed of only the self-employed and the no-work and excluding employed workers. These results are summarized in Table 9.9.

It is shown that the results in Tables 9.4 and 9.9 are similar. The coefficients of DID items are negative value (−0.276 in Estimation (1), −0.314 in Estimation (2)), and all of these values are statistically significant. It is confirmed again that the NRPS may decrease the probability of labor force participation for the rural elderly.

3. *Results of the Placebo test*

Finally, a placebo-controlled test is employed to test the propriety of the DID/DDD models used in the study. Specifically, because the legal age for receipt of the NRPS is older than 60 it is thought that the NRPS only affects the supply of workers older than 60. Therefore, when the group aged 50–54 years is used as the control group, and the group aged 55–59 years is used as the treatment group, the results should be different to the results shown in Table 9.4. The placebo-controlled test results are summarized in Table 9.10. It is found that the coefficient of DID items in (1), (2), (3), and (4) are positive values, and all values are not statistically significant. It is clear that these results are different to Table 9.4. This indicates the validity of the DID model and the treatment and control groups constructed in this study.

Table 9.9 Results using various samples

	(1) Excluding regular worker		*(2) Excluding employed worker*	
	Coeff.	*S.D.*	*Coeff.*	*S.D.*
After 2009	−0.233***	0.027	−0.277***	0.028
Treatment	−1.511***	0.073	−1.540***	0.078
DID	−0.276**	0.112	−0.314**	0.126
Age	−0.027	0.055	−0.037	0.056
Age squared	−1.399E-04	0.000	−3.730E-05	0.000
Education attainment (Less than primary school)				
Primary school	0.190***	0.031	0.165***	0.032
Junior high school	0.218***	0.037	0.163***	0.038
Senior high school	0.035	0.059	−0.037	0.062
Vocational school	−0.409***	0.130	−0.511***	0.139
College	0.026	0.184	−0.601**	0.270
Health	−0.014**	0.006	−0.013**	0.006
Male	−0.019	0.027	−0.030	0.027
Family number	0.003	0.008	0.002	0.008
No-earning income	−4.790E-08	0.000	3.090E-07	0.000
Regions (East)				
Central	−0.078**	0.032	0.015	0.033
West	0.113***	0.035	0.195***	0.036
Constants	2.357	1.635	2.517	1.671
Observations	10,629		10,156	
Log likelihood	−6333.621		−6026.630	
Pseudo R^2	0.140		0.143	

Sources: Calculated based on CHNS from 2000 to 2009

Note:

(1) *, **, ***: statistically significant levels are 10%, 5%, and 1%

(2) The model is similar to the Panel A in Table 9.4

(3) The employed worker includes the regular worker and irregular worker

9.7 Conclusions

The Chinese government implemented the NRPS in 2009 to expand public pension coverage in all of rural China. The NRPS participants receive their pension when they reach 60. Does the NRPS affect the labor supply of the rural elderly in China? Based on the natural experiment methods (DID method), using five waves (2000, 2004, 2006, 2009, and 2011) of longitudinal survey data of CHNS, this study employs an empirical study to provide useful evidence related to this issue.

Table 9.10 Placebo test results

	(1)		(2)		(3)		(4)	
	Coeff.	*S.E.*	*Coeff.*	*S.E.*	*Coeff.*	*S.E.*	*Coeff.*	*S.E.*
After 2009	−0.311***	0.049	−0.306***	0.050	−0.291***	0.050	−0.294***	0.050
Treatment	−0.314***	0.047	0.064	0.086	0.055	0.087	0.063	0.087
DID	0.084	0.068	0.081	0.069	0.071	0.069	0.062	0.069
Age			−0.208	0.323	−0.189	0.323	−0.190	0.324
Age squared			0.001	0.003	0.001	0.003	0.001	0.003
Education (Less than primary school)								
Primary school			0.226***	0.043	0.219***	0.043	0.221***	0.044
Junior High school			0.333***	0.046	0.333***	0.046	0.329***	0.047
Senior High school			0.189***	0.063	0.196***	0.063	0.210***	0.064
Vocational school			−0.012	0.119	0.011	0.119	0.026	0.120
College			0.652***	0.169	0.678***	0.169	0.693***	0.170
Health			−0.032***	0.007	−0.030***	0.008	−0.032***	0.008
Male			−0.032	0.035	−0.017	0.035	−0.012	0.035
Family number					0.033***	0.011	0.028***	0.011
No-earning income					−8.520E-07**	0.000	−9.370E-07**	0.000
Regions (East)								
Central							−0.101**	0.041
West							0.069	0.047
Constants	0.579***	0.033	8.083	8.825	7.350	8.846	7.488	8.856
Observations	5,645		5,645		5,645		5,645	
Log likelihood	3745.057		−3646.992		−3626.986		−3619.686	
Pseudo R^2	0.018		0.033		0.033		0.035	

Source: Calculated based on CHNS from 2000 to 2011

Note:

(1) *, **, ***: statistically significant levels are 10%, 5%, and 1%

(2) Treatment group is the group aged 55–59 years old, control group is the one aged 50–54 years old

Some major conclusions emerge. First, generally, the NRPS decreases the probability of labor force participation. Second, to compare with the policy effect in the short term (from 2000 to 2009), the negative effect becomes smaller over the long term (from 2000 to 2011). Third, the NRPS may increase the probability of becoming a regular worker. However, the differences of probability between the irregular worker, the self-employed, and no-work are not statistically significant. Fourth, even though the NRPS may decrease the labor force participation in the Eastern, Central, and Western regions, the impact of the NRPS is greater for the Western region than for the Eastern and Central regions. Fifth, even though the NRPS may decrease the labor force participation for both women and men, the impact of the NRPS is greater for women than for men. Finally, the robustness checks (e.g. using various treatment and control groups, using various datasets and Placebo test) confirms again that the NRPS may decrease the labor force participation of the rural elderly. These results are consistent with the previous studies (Cheng 2014; Ning et al. 2016).

These empirical study results suggest some policy implications could be considered. The results indicate that the NRPS may decrease the labor force participation of the rural elderly. The NRPS as a public pension system can improve the welfare of the rural elderly; it is also expected to reduce the social security gap between the rural and urban residents, and to reduce the poverty of the elderly. However, it should be noted that the public pension system might negatively affect labor force participation. With the aging population in China, the labor supply shortage problem is likely to become more serious in the future, and therefore when the government promotes reform and constructs the public pension system, both the welfare effect and the influence of the pension on the labor market should be considered.

In developed countries (e.g. Japan), the fulfilled national universal pension system provides a safety net for the elderly, and a set of problems for the government, for example the heavy pension burden. The Chinese government should ponder on these problems in order to construct a fair and sustainable public pension system for the whole of China. Even though the empirical study indicates that the NRPS may decrease the rural elderly labor supply, the government should not reduce the pension benefit for the rural elderly in the future. The problem is that the public pension system is a segmented system in China at present. Specifically, the Urban Employment Basic Pension (UEBP), the Civil Servant Pension (CSP), the Urban Resident Basic Pension

Scheme (URBPS), and the NRPS are operating simultaneously (Cai and Cheng 2014). The main eligible group for the UEBP and CSP are the working urban residents, the eligibility group for the URBPS is non-working urban residents, and the eligibility group for the NRPS is the working and non-work rural residents. The pension benefit, the pension premium payment, differs by these pension systems. The pension benefit is more for the CSP and UEBP than for NRPS. From August 2012 the URBPS and NRPS were integrated into the "Urban and Rural Resident Social Pension Scheme" (URRSPS), but the pension benefit differs between urban and rural groups: the pension benefit is smaller for the rural group than for the urban group. Thus, to integrate this public pension in order to reduce the social security inequality between the work sectors and *Hukou* system is an important issue for the Chinese government to address. At the same time, more should be done to evaluate the effect of the public pension scheme over the long term and from various perspectives.

Notes

1. In China, from the lowest level to the highest level, the hierarchy of government is the village government, township government, county government, municipal government, provincial government, and central government.
2. For developed countries, most previous studies indicate that the pension reduces the elderly labor supply and increases the probability of retirement. In other words, to decrease the pension benefit and to delay the pension receipt can increase the elderly labor supply. Please refer to Krueger and Pischke (1992), Samwick (1998), Blau and Goodstein (2010), and Vere (2011) for the U.S.; Oshi et al. (2009) and Shimizutani and Oshio (2013) for Japan; Kudrna and Woodland (2011) for Australia; Maloney (2000) for New Zealand; Martin and Marcos (2010) for Spain; Hernaes et al. (2016) for Norway; and Borsch-Supan (2000) for Germany.
3. Ardington, Case, and Hosegood (2009) explained the reason for the results as being that the pension's impact is attributable to the increase in household resources it represents, which can be used to support migrants until they become self-sufficient, and to the presence of pensioners who can care for small children, which allows prime-aged adults to look for work elsewhere.
4. Juarez (2010) explained the reason for the results as the income in the hands of elderly women being shared more with younger family members than income in the hands of elderly men.

5. Based on the questionnaire, the worker who works for another person or enterprise as permanent employee is a regular worker; the worker who is a contractor with other people or enterprise or a temporary worker is an irregular worker; the worker who is self-employed, the owner-manager with employees, self-employed, independent operator with no employees, the paid family worker, or the unpaid family worker is the self-employed; the one who is not working in the survey year is a non-working one.
6. Because the missing values for the subjective health status are more, the mental health score is used in this analysis. The health status is poor when the mental health score is higher. The analyses use the subjective health status variable and the results are similar to the mental health score. To maintain the observations in econometric analysis, the results use the mental health score variables present in Sect. 9.6.
7. Here, labor force participation rate is the proportion of workers in the total population by age groups.
8. Here, the LFPR gap is calculated by the equation as "LFPR of pension receipt group-LFPR of no-pension receipt group".

References

Ardington, C., Case, A., & Hosegood, V. (2009). Labor supply responses to large social transfers: Longitudinal evidence from South Africa. *American Economic Journal: Applied Economics, 1*(1), 22–48.

Becker, G. S. (1985). The allocation of effort, specific human capital, and the differences between men and women in earning and occupations. *Journal of Labor Economics, 3*(1), 33–58.

Bertrand, M., Mullainathan, S., & Miller, D. (2003). Public policy and extended families: Evidence from pensions in South Africa. *The World Bank Economic Review, 17*(1), 27–50.

Blau, D. M., & Goodstein, R. M. (2010). Can social security explain trends in labor force participation of older men in the United States? *Journal of Human Sources, 45*(2), 328–363.

Borsch-Supan, A. (2000). Incentive effects of social security on labor participation: Evidence in Germany and across Europe. *Journal of Population Economics, 78*, 25–49.

Cai, F., Giles, J., O'Keefe, P., & Wang, D. (2012). *The elderly and old age support in rural China: Challenges and prospects*. Washington, DC: World Bank.

Cai, F., & Wang, M. (2008). *Reports on China's population and labor No. 9: linking up Lewis and Kuznets turning points*. Beijing: Social Science Academic Press (In Chinese).

Cai, Y., & Cheng, Y. (2014). Pension reform in China: Challenges and opportunities. *Journal of Economic Survey, 28*(4), 636–651.

Cheng, J. (2014). The effect of old-age security on labor supply. *Economic Research, 10*, 60–73 (In Chinese).

De Carvalho, F. I. (2008). Old-age benefits and retirement decisions of rural elderly in Brazil. *Journal of Development Economics, 86*, 129–146.

Gronau, R. (1977). Leisure, home production, and work—The theory of the allocation of time revisited. *Journal of Political Economy, 85*(6), 1099–1123.

Hernaes, E., Markussen, S., Piggott, J., & Roed, K. (2016). Pension reform and labor supply. *Journal of Public Economics, 142*, 39–55.

Juarez, L. (2010). The effect of an old-age demogrant on the labor supply and time use of the elderly and non-elderly in Mexico. *The B.E. Journal of Economic Analysis & Policy, 10*(1). (Topics), Article 48.

Kaushal, N. (2013). How public pension affects elderly labor supply and well-being: Evidence from India. *World Development, 56*, 214–255.

Krueger, A. B., & Pischke, J. S. (1992). The effect of social security on labor supply: A cohort analysis of the Notch Generation. *Journal of Labor Economics, 10*(4), 412–437.

Kudrna, G., & Woodland, A. D. (2011). Implications of the 2009 age pension reform in Australia: A dynamic general equilibrium analysis. *Economic Record, 87*(277), 183–201.

Li, S., Whalle, J., & Xing, C. (2014). China's higher education expansion and unemployment of college graduates. *China Economic Review, 30*, 567–582.

Liu, H. (2017). Social security and labor supply of rural elderly: A research based on china health and retirement longitudinal study. *Labor Economic Research, 5*(2), 96–111 (In Chinese).

Liu, L., & Zeng, Y. (2016). Effect of the new rural pension scheme on rural household labor supply. *Agriculture Technology Economics, 6*, 56–67 (In Chinese).

Liu, Y., Zhong, P., & Wang, Y. (2016). The effect of the new rural pension scheme on working hours of the elderly. *Population and Economics, 5*, 114–126 (In Chinese).

Maloney, T. (2000). The impact of welfare reform on labor supply behaviour in New Zealand. *Labor Economics, 7*, 427–448.

Martin, A. R. S., & Marcos, V. S. (2010). Demographic change and pension reform in Spain: An assessment in a two-earner OLG model. *Fiscal Studies, 31*(3), 405–452.

Ning, M., Gong, J., Zheng, X., & Zhuang, J. (2016). Does new rural pension scheme decrease elderly labor supply? Evidence from CHARLS. *China Economic Review, 41*, 315–330.

Oshi, T., Oishi, A., & Shimizutani, S. (2009). Social security reforms and labor force participation of the elderly in Japan. *Japanese Economic Review, 62*(2), 248–271.

Posel, D., Fairburn, J. A., & Lund, F. (2006). Labour migration and households: A reconsideration of the effects of the social pension on labour supply in South Africa. *Economic Modelling, 23*, 836–853.
Ranchod, V. (2006). The effect of the South Africa old age pension on labor supply of the elderly. *South African Journal of Economics, 74*(4), 725–744.
Samwick, A. A. (1998). New evidence on pension, social security, and the timing of retirement. *Journal of Public Economics, 70*, 207–236.
Shimizutani, S., & Oshio, T. (2013). Revisiting the labor supply effect of social security earnings test: New evidence from elimination and reinstatement in Japan. *Japan and the World Economy, 28*, 99–111.
Vere, J. P. (2011). Social security and elderly labor supply: Evidence from the health and retirement study. *Labor Economics, 18*, 676–686.
Wu, Y., & Zhao, Q. (2010). Higher education expansion and employment of university graduates. *Economic Research, 9*, 93–108 (In Chinese).
Xie, E. (2015). The influences of New Pension Scheme on elderly labor supply and well-being in rural areas. *Journal of Finance and Economic, 41*(8), 39–49.
Zhang, C. (2015). Pension income and labor supply of the elderly: An analysis based on RD method. *World Economic Papers, 6*, 76–89 (In Chinese).
Zhang, C., Giles, J., & Zhao, Y. (2014). Policy evaluation of China's new rural pension program. *China Economic Quarterly, 14*(1), 203–230 (In Chinese).

CHAPTER 10

Impact of Social Insurance Contributions on Wages

10.1 Introduction

In China, during the planned economy period, the government managed the whole enterprise in the urban regions, and therefore the social security systems were managed by the government. Under the economic transition period, the social security systems reforms occurred along with the state-owned enterprises (SOEs) reforms. The government security systems changed into the social security systems for the SOEs. At the same time, the privately owned enterprises (POEs) and foreign-owned enterprises (FOEs) were developed. The social security systems cover the enterprises including both the public sector and private sector from the 1990s. Even though the social security systems can provide the security for the elderly living, health care, and work injury, because the social insurance contributions are usually paid by enterprises, when the social insurance premium is high for an enterprise, the enterprise may transfer the social insurance contributions to workers throughout reducing the worker's wage level. Actually, in China, the data from the Ministry of Human Resources and Social Security of the People's Republic of China (PRC) show the ratio of total social insurance contributions charged by enterprises to total wage bills is around 40% in 2015. It is thought the enterprise might transfer these social insurance contributions to workers.

X. Ma, *Economic Transition and Labor Market Reform in China*,
https://doi.org/10.1007/978-981-13-1987-7_10

The social insurance contributions can be thought as a kind of payroll tax for the wage. It is usually argued the higher taxes for the enterprise may cause the enterprise's taxes burden transfer behavior—the enterprise may transfer the taxes burden to worker by decreasing the wage level, or transfer to consumer by rising the good price. Thus to investigate the impact of the social insurance contributions on wage is an important issue. Most previous studies indicated that the social insurance contributions may decrease the worker's wage (Hamermesh 1979; Gruber 1994; Fishback and Kantor 1995; Anderson and Meyer 2000; Kugler and Kugler 2003; Yiwamoto and Hamaaki 2006; Sakei and Kazegami 2007), whereas Gruber and Krueger (1991), Gruber (1994, 1997), and Tachibanaki and Yokoyama (2008) found that the impacts of the social insurance contributions on wage are not statistically significant. Yiwamoto and Hamaaki (2006) even found the wage is higher for the workers in the enterprise with the higher health care social insurance contributions.

Although published studies investigate the impact of social insurance contributions on wage, there remain some issues to consider. First, as the largest economic transition country, along with the market-oriented reform, government reformed the social security system, and the social insurance contributions became high in China. However, the issue on the impact of social insurance contributions on wage for China is not analyzed. This study can fill the shortage. Second, even though the previous studies analyzed the issue by various groups, there is no study to focus on the labor market segmentation by the private sector and public sector, which is the largest feature for economic transition countries, particularly for the country that carried out the reforms by the progressive reform pattern. This study analyzes the issue to consider the various ownership types. To address the heterogeneity, initial dependent and endogeneity problems, the fixed-effects model, the random-effects model, and the Generalized Method of Moments (GMM) are used.

This study is structured as follows. Section 10.2 introduces the public social security system reform and the social insurance contributions based on rules in Chinese enterprises, and Sect. 10.3 introduces the channels in which the social insurance contributions may influence the worker's wage, and previous empirical studies for the developed countries on the issue. Section 10.4 gives the framework for the empirical analysis, including models and datasets. Section 10.5 presents estimated results and explains these results. Section 10.6 summarizes the conclusions.

10.2 The Social Security System and Social Insurance Premium for Enterprises in China

In 1951, during the planned economy period (1949–1977), the PRC enacted its first social security law, entitled *LaoDong BaoXian TiaoLi*, to provide social security for SOEs and collective-owned enterprises (COEs). The social security systems included (a) pension insurance, (b) health care insurance, (c) workers compensation insurance (work injury insurance), and (d) maternity insurance. These social security systems were managed by the government, and the whole insurance fund was supported by government.

During the economic transition period, the government reformed the social security systems in the public sector along with the SOEs reform. To reduce the social security financial burden, the government security systems changed into social security systems, in which the social security funds were established by government, enterprises, and workers. The enterprises and workers mainly bear the funds by paying the insurance premium based on wage. For example, the total pension insurance premium is 28% of wage, it is 20% for the enterprise, and it is 8% for individual worker. Table 10.1 summarizes the insurance premiums of the social insurance systems in China in 2015. Based on the regulations for social security systems, during the 2000s, the social security system is composed of six kinds of system: (a) pension insurance, (b) health care insurance, (c)

Table 10.1 Social security systems and insurance premium by enterprise and individual worker in China (2015)

	Total (%)	*Enterprise*	*Worker*
a. Pension	28	20%	8%
b. Health care	8	6%	2%
c. Unemployment	2–3	Regional disparity	Regional disparity
d. Injury	0.75	0.75%	0%
e. Maternity	0.50	0.50%	0%
Total	39.25	27.25% (+unemployment insurance premium)	10% (+unemployment insurance premium)
(a + b + c + d + e)			
f. Housing	10–24	5–12%	5–12%

Source: Author

Note: Data based on Chinese government regulations

unemployment insurance, (d) worker compensation insurance (work injury insurance), (e) maternity insurance, and (f) housing fund insurance. Except the unemployment insurance and worker compensation insurance, the other insurance premiums are charged by enterprise and worker individual based on wage. The lowest wage level for the insurance premium is 60%[1] of the regional average wage level in the prior year, while the highest wage level is 300% of the regional average wage level in the prior year. It is clear that the total insurance premium charged by enterprises is around 30–40% of the wage. Actually, it should be noted that the insurance premiums summarized in Table 10.1 are based on the central government regulations, they are different by regions.

To reduce the enterprise insurance contribution burden, the Chinese government published a set of regulations recently. For example, the government published the regulation in May 2016. Based on the regulation, when the pension insurance premium of enterprise is higher than 20% of wage, it should be reduced to 20% within two years, to decrease the total unemployment insurance premium to 1–1.5%, and to reduce the worker's unemployment insurance premium to be lower than 0.5%. Even though the government made an effort to reduce the insurance contribution burden for enterprises and workers, it is clear that the insurance contribution is still high for Chinese enterprises.

10.3 Empirical Studies on the Issue

10.3.1 The Channels for the Impact of Social Insurance Contributions on Wage

Based on the partial equilibrium model, the channel of the impact of social insurance contributions on wage can be shown by Fig. 10.1.

First, when the social insurance contributions are zero, the equilibrium wage and employment is W_0 and L_0.

Second, when the insurance contribution based on worker's wage (here, it is named as social insurance contributions) become t, if the insurance contribution charged by the enterprise is t (which means the enterprise charges the whole social insurance contributions), the labor demand will shift from D(W) to $D(W_1+t)$. Based on the new equilibrium model, worker's wage will decrease from W_0 to W_1, and employment will decrease from L_0 to L_1; labor cost for the enterprise will increase from W_0 to W_1+t, which is higher than W_0 in the prior period. It is shown that the social insurance contributions (t: AC) will be shared by the enterprise (AB) and workers (BC). It is pointed out that the share of the enterprise

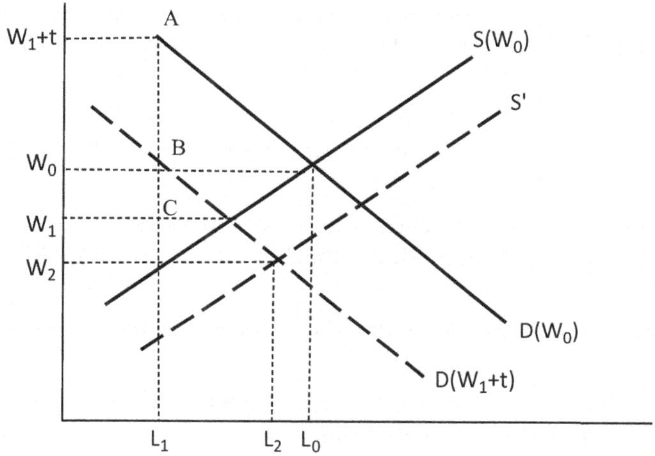

Fig. 10.1 The impact of social insurance contributions on wage based on the partial equilibrium model. *Source*: By author based on Kotlikoff and Summer (1987), Gruber (1997), Bojas (2004), and Adhikari et al. (2009)

and workers is determined by the wage elasticity of labor demand and labor supply (Hamermesh 1979; Kotlikoff and Summer 1987; Gruber and Krueger 1991; Gruber 1997; Bojas 2004; Adhikari et al. 2009).

Third, Summers (1989) indicated that when the workers consider the social insurance contributions benefit, for example, from a lifecycle perspective, the workers consider the social insurance contributions (e.g. pension insurance contribution) is a part of payment in the future (when they are senior citizens). The labor supply should shift from $S(W_0)$ to S', which will cause the wage decrease to W_2 which is lower than W_1, and the employment will become L_2 which means the employment decrease will become smaller.

Because the labor supply and labor demand situations and the worker's cognition or preference for the social insurance contributions differ by various groups, the impact of social insurance contributions on wage is not clearly based on the partial equilibrium model, and it should be investigated by the empirical study.

To consider the model[2] about the impact of social insurance contributions on wage, the labor demand depends on wage and social insurance contributions based on wage (t_e) which charged by the enterprise can be expressed by Eq. (10.1):

$$D = D\left(W\left(1+t_e\right)\right) \tag{10.1}$$

The labor supply depends on wage and social insurance contributions based on wage (t_w) which charged by the worker can be expressed by Eq. (10.2):

$$S = S\left(W\left(1 - at_w\right) + qWt_e\right) \tag{10.2}$$

To differentiate the function when labor demand is equal to labor demand in the partial equilibrium model, it can be shown by Eq. (10.3)

$$\left[n^d\left(1+t_e\right) - n^s\left(1 - at_w + qt_e\right)\right] dw / w = \left(-n^d + n^s q\right) dt_e - n^s a dt_w \tag{10.3}$$

In Eq. (10.3), n^d stands for the wage elasticity of labor demand and n^s is the wage elasticity of labor supply.

When the social insurance contributions change (for example, the insurance premium rises), the change of the labor cost which determines the enterprises' labor demand can be expressed by Eq. (10.4); the influence of the social insurance contributions charged by the enterprise on wage can be expressed by Eq. (10.5).

$$dw\left(1+t_e\right) / w\left(1+t_e\right) = dw / w + dt_e / \left(1+t_e\right) \tag{10.4}$$

$$\left(dw / w\right) / dt_e = \left(-n^d + n^s q\right) / \left[n^d\left(1+t_e\right) - n^s\left(1 - at_w + qt_e\right)\right] \tag{10.5}$$

In most previous studies, for the issue about the social insurance contributions on wage, based on Eq. (10.5), the wage function is estimated as follows:

$$\ln W = a + t_e \text{Insurance} + \beta X + \delta \tag{10.6}$$

In Eq. (10.6), *Insurance* stands for enterprise's social insurance contributions (social insurance contributions), X for the factors which can affect wage level, a is the constant term, and δ is the error term. t_e and β represent the estimated coefficient for variables.

10.3.2 Empirical Studies on the Impact of Social Insurance Contributions on Wage

There are a number of empirical studies on the impacts of the social insurance contributions (social insurance contributions) on wage.

First, in the early period, the estimations based on inductive type wage function were employed. The social insurance contributions rate, which is the ratio of social insurance contributions to wage, is utilized as an independent variable. Most empirical studies found the social insurance contributions negatively affect wage, which means the enterprise may transfer the social insurance burden to workers. For example, Hamermesh (1979) found the enterprise transfer 33% social insurance contribution burden to workers immediately in the U.K. Holmlund (1983) utilized the Swedish time series data to analyze influence of the social insurance contributions reform which lead to the social insurance contributions rate increasing from 14% to 40% on wage, and it is found that the enterprises transfer a half of social insurance contributions burden to workers.

Second, for these empirical studies based on cross-section data analysis methods, Triplett (1983), Smith and Ehrenberg (1983), Asher (1984), and Yiwamoto and Hamaaki (2006) argued that there may remain an endogeneity problem. To address the problem, the instrument variable method and difference in difference (DID) method based on a natural experiment are utilized in empirical studies from the 1990s. For example, Gruber and Krueger (1991), Gruber (1994), Fishback and Kantor (1995), Anderson and Meyer (2000), Gruber (1997), and Sakei and Kazegami (2007) utilized the change of Worker Compensation Insurance (Gruber and Krueger 1991), Health Care Insurance (Gruber 1994), Worker Injury Compensation Law (Fishback and Kantor 1995), Employment Insurance (Anderson and Meyer 2000) for the USA, Health Care Insurance for Japan (Sakei and Kazegami 2007), total social insurance for Chile (Gruber 1997), and total social insurance for Columbia (Kugler and Kugler 2003) as the quasi-natural experiment and investigate the social insurance contributions on wage based on the DID model. However, these empirical study results are not consistent. For example, Fishback and Kantor (1995), Anderson and Meyer (2000), Kugler and Kugler (2003), and Sakei and Kazegami (2007) indicated that the social insurance contributions decrease the wage levels, whereas Gruber and Krueger (1991) and Gruber (1994, 1997) found that the impact of the social insurance contributions on wage are not statistically significant.

10.3.3 Two Hypotheses Setting

To the author's knowledge, there is not an empirical study on the issue for China, and this study is expected to provide new evidence from China, which is an economic transition country. Based on the economic theory and these previous studies, two hypotheses are constructed as follows.

H1 : The enterprise's social insurance contributions negatively affect worker's wage in China.

Based on the partial equilibrium model shown in Fig. 10.1, the impact of social insurance contributions on wage is determined by the elasticity of labor supply and demand to wage. Because there remains surplus labor in rural China (Minami and Ma 2010, 2014), it can be thought the wage elasticity of labor supply is not great. Whereas because the collective bargaining influence of the labor group (e.g. the union) on wage is small, the influence of enterprise for the wage and employment determination is relatively greater. Thus when the social insurance contributions increase, the enterprises may transfer the social insurance contributions to workers, which cause the worker's wage to decrease. Therefore, there may remain a negative relation between the social insurance contributions and wage (*H1*).

H2 : The negative influence of enterprise's social insurance contributions on wage is greater for the private sector than for the public sector in China.

To consider Hypothesis 2, two reasons can explain it. First, it may be because the management purpose differs by sectors. Concretely, as it is investigated in Chaps. 3 and 5 in the book, the Chinese labor market is segmentation by the public sector (SOEs) and private sector (POEs, FOEs, and COEs). Enterprises in the public sector may make an effort to achieve the government political purpose, for example to reduce income inequality and to maintain employment security and country safety, whereas the private sector pursues the profit maximum to keep alive in the competitive market. Therefore, to maintain the maximum profit, the probability to transfer the enterprise's social insurance contributions burden to worker is higher for the private sector than the public sector. Second, the function of market mechanism on the wage and employment determination is greater for the private sector than the public sector. Therefore, when the enterprise's social insurance contributions become high, the enterprises in the private sector will adjust the resource allocation immediately, for example to reduce the labor cost which causes the wage decrease. For these two reasons, it can be thought that the negative influence of enterprise's social insurance contributions on wage may be greater for the private sector than for the public sector (*H2*).

10.4 Methodology and Data

10.4.1 Model

In this study, to investigate the impact of the enterprise's social insurance contributions on wage, four kinds of estimated models are utilized in the study. We employ the test to confirm which model is proper.

First, the model based on the ordinary least squares (OLS) regression is shown as follows:

$$\ln W_i = a + \beta_I \text{Insurance}_i + \beta_H H_i + v_i \tag{10.7}$$

In Eq. (10.7), ln (see the above equation 10.7) W is the logarithm of wage, *i* stands for the enterprise, *Insurance* for enterprise's average social insurance contributions for each worker, and *H* for the enterprise characteristics variables (e.g. K/L, export ratio, firm size, ownership type, industry sector) and survey year dummy variables. *a* is the constant term, and *v* is the error term. *β* represents the estimated coefficient for each variable.

Second, it is argued that there exist the time invariant factors such as unobserved characteristic (unobserved ability, psychological factors, special behavior pattern) which may affect the wage, and it is thought that there remains the bias by the heterogeneity problem. To address this problem, the fixed-effects model (FE) and random-effects model (RE) are utilized, which is expressed as follows:

$$Y_{it} = a + \beta_I \text{Insurance}_{it} + \beta_H H_{it} + \varepsilon_i + u_{it} \tag{10.8}$$

In Eq. (10.8), *i* stands for the individual and *t* for years. *ε* stands for the unobserved enterprise characteristic, and *u* is the real error term. The definitions of *β*, *Insurance*, and *H* are similar to those in Eq. (10.8).

Third, even though the fixed-effects model and random-effects model can address the heterogeneity problem, there may remain the initial dependent problem and the endogeneity problem. The GMM can be utilized to address these econometric problems, which produce consistent parameter estimates for a finite number of time periods (t), and a large cross-sectional dimension (n) (see e.g. Arellano and Bond 1991; Arellano and Bover 1995; Blundell and Bond 1998). Based on Arellano and Bond (1991), the GMM model can be represented as follows:

$$\frac{1}{n}\sum_{n}^{i=1} Y_{is} \begin{bmatrix} \left(Y_{it} - Y_{i,t-1}\right) - \left(Y_{i,t-1} - Y_{i,t-2}\right)' \gamma - \\ \left(X_{i,t-1} - X_{i,t-2}\right)' \beta \end{bmatrix} = 0, \quad s = 0,1,\ldots,t-2; \quad t = 2,3,\ldots,T \tag{10.9}$$

When the lagged dependent variable increases, the instrument variables (Y_{i1}, $Y_{i2,\ldots,}$ Y_{iT-2}) will become more, and the matrix can be expressed as Eq. (10.10):

$$W_i = \begin{pmatrix} [Y_{i1}] & 0 & \ldots & 0 \\ 0 & [Y_{i1}, Y_{i2}] & \ldots & 0 \\ 0 & 0 & \ldots & 0 \\ 0 & 0 & \ldots & [Y_{i1,} Y_{iT-2}] \end{pmatrix} \tag{10.10}$$

When the lagged dependent variables as instrument variables are not correlated with lagged *u*, which can be expressed as $E\left(W_i' \Delta u_i\right) = 0$, then the dynamic panel data analyzed model can be expressed as follows:

$$\begin{aligned} &\left(Y_{it} - Y_{i,t-1}\right) = \left(Y_{i,t-1} - Y_{i,t-2}\right)' \gamma - \left(X_{i,t-1} - X_{i,t-2}\right)' \beta + \left(u_{it} - u_{i,t-1}\right) \\ &\Delta Y_{it} = \Delta Y_{it-1}' \gamma + \Delta X_{i,t-1}' + \Delta u_i, \quad i = 1,2,\ldots,N \end{aligned} \tag{10.11}$$

The instrument variables shown in Eq. (10.10) and dynamic panel analyzed method shown in Eq. (10.11) are utilized in the GMM.

In Eqs. (10.9–10.11), *X* includes *Insurance* and *H* variables in Eqs. (10.7 and 10.8). The coefficients of *Insurance* variable should be noted in the results based on the GMM model. Because the dataset is four waves panel data, which means *T* is short, we utilized the one-step GMM method in this study.

When the coefficient of *Insurance* has a negative value and is statistically significant, it is shown that the social insurance contributions negatively affect worker wage, and therefore H1 is supported.

To test H2, subsamples for the public sector and private sector are utilized. When the coefficient value of *Insurance* is greater for the private sector and it is statistically significant, H2 is supported.

10.4.2 Data

The firm-level data is derived from the Chinese Large and Medium-size Manufacturing Enterprises (CLMME) dataset from 1998 to 2007 conducted by the National Bureau of Statistics (NBS). The unit of observation is a firm, which is defined as a legal unit (*Faren Danwei*). The dataset comprises all state-owned enterprises (SOEs) as well as non-state-owned enterprises (non-SOEs) with sales exceeding 5 million RMB. In census years, all industrial firms, irrespective of size, are sampled. The NBS firm-level data is available as early as from 1992, when all firms with independent accounting were covered, with an amount of 350,000 firms. In 1998, the NBS changed the coverage of the annual survey so that all SOEs and only the above-scale non-SOEs were included. Hence, firms can be easily linked from 1998 onwards and most studies start their sample in that year. The survey has been conducted in the following years, but to the best of our knowledge the latest year with reliable data available is 2007. Because only the dataset from 2004 to 2007 includes the social security fee information, we focus on the period of 2004–2007. The full sample covers all industrial firms, which consists of mining, manufacturing, and public utilities; nevertheless, many studies limit themselves to the manufacturing sector. Thus, we also choose the firm in manufacturing industry sector. The sample utilized in this study is 263,862 in 2004, 257,991 in 2005, 282,064 in 2006, and 312,207 in 2007. The ownership types are classified into five kinds based on the dataset: state-owned enterprises (SOE); collectively owned enterprises (COE); POE; foreign-owned enterprise (FOE); Hong Kong and Taiwan-owned enterprise (HTOE), and other types of enterprise (Other). The public sector comprises SOEs and the private sector includes COE, POE, FOE, and HTOE. The proportions by ownership types in the analyzed sample dataset is 8.2% for SOE, 4.6% for COE, 37.4% for POE, 4.7% for FOE, 4.8% for HTOE, and 40.3% for Other. Even though it is thought that the firm size is larger for the SOEs, because our dataset only focuses on the non-listed Chinese enterprises which include more enterprises in the private sector, it is shown that the proportion of small and middle-sized enterprises is higher for the SOEs than the FOEs and HTOEs among the non-listed Chinese enterprises (see Table 10.2).

Table 10.2 Descriptive statistics

	Total	*SOE*	*COE*	*POE*	*FOE*	*HTOE*
ln *w*	2.581	2.707	2.673	2.607	3.071	2.867
Insurance	0.126	0.346	0.170	0.103	0.149	0.111
K/L	356.270	933.134	397.480	281.277	596.592	392.986
Export	0.165	0.040	0.071	0.103	0.419	0.441
Profit	24.016	37.780	28.839	25.597	46.285	23.366
Firm size						
Small	0.332	0.361	0.286	0.314	0.158	0.201
Middle	0.334	0.211	0.324	0.358	0.293	0.333
Large	0.334	0.428	0.390	0.327	0.550	0.466
Ownership types						
SOE	0.082					
COE	0.046					
POE	0.374					
HTOE	0.047					
FOE	0.048					
Other	0.403					
Industry sector						
Industry1	0.041	0.061	0.099	0.046	0.003	0.007
Industry2	0.080	0.088	0.065	0.086	0.080	0.047
Industry3	0.128	0.039	0.069	0.130	0.142	0.191
Industry4	0.028	0.004	0.013	0.026	0.040	0.059
Industry5	0.032	0.012	0.014	0.037	0.031	0.035
Industry6	0.056	0.056	0.054	0.053	0.048	0.073
Industry7	0.154	0.118	0.166	0.157	0.143	0.149
Industry8	0.071	0.065	0.091	0.078	0.040	0.039
Industry9	0.095	0.055	0.103	0.104	0.068	0.075
Industry10	0.159	0.174	0.172	0.165	0.168	0.106
Industry11	0.124	0.088	0.106	0.106	0.218	0.204
Industry12	0.033	0.240	0.048	0.012	0.017	0.016
Observations	1,112,493	91,415	50,971	416,347	52,957	52,835

Source: Calculated based on Chinese Large and Medium-size Manufacturing Enterprises (CLMME) database from 2004 to 2007

Note:

(1) SOE: state-owned enterprise; POE: privately owned enterprise; FOE: foreign-owned enterprise excluding the Hong Kong and Taiwan enterprises; HTOE: Hong Kong and Taiwan-owned enterprise

(2) The industry sectors from 1 to 12 are as follows: Mining, Food, Textile, Leather, Timber, Cultural goods, Chemical, Building products, Metal, Equipment, Electrical appliance manufacturing industries and Energy industry

The independent variable is a logarithm of average wage which is calculated by the total wage bill divided by the number of workers in the enterprise.

Insurance is the ratio of total social insurance contributions charged by enterprises to worker's total wage. Based on the dataset, social insurance includes the pension insurance, unemployment insurance, and housing fund insurance.

The other controlled variables are also constructed. (1) *K/L* is calculated by the asset divided by the number of workers. We use the K/L to control the disparity on enterprise capital (or technology, skill). (2) Global business may affect the wage level, and we construct the *Export* variable (the ratio of export good value to total revenue) to control the global business influence on wage. (3) The enterprise's *profit* is calculated by the total revenue minus cost. Because wage is a part of the labor cost, it is thought the profit may influence the wage level. In the perfect competitive market, when the other factors are constant, the wage should be low for the enterprises with higher profit. (4) Based on the economies of scale, firm size may affect the revenue, or profit, and therefore it may affect worker's wage. We construct the *firm size* dummy variables based on the worker numbers, from the first (small firm) to the third quintiles (large firm). (5) It can be thought that the wage level differs by the industry sectors. Based on the dataset and National Economic Industry Classification Code published in 2002 and 2011, we constructed twelve kinds of *industry sector* dummy variables to control the industry sector disparities: Mining, Food, Textile, Leather, Timber, Cultural goods, Chemical, Building products, Metal, Equipment, Electrical appliance manufacturing industries, and Energy industry. (6) *Year* dummy variables for 2004–2007 are also utilized to control the macroeconomic and policy influence on wage.

The descriptive statistics of variables are summarized in Table 10.2. First, the average worker wage level and enterprise's insurance contribution ratio differs by ownership type enterprise. The wage level is highest for FOE and lowest for COE; the enterprise insurance contribution ratio is highest for the SOEs (34.6%) and is lowest for POE (10.3%). It seems that there is no negative relation between the enterprise's insurance contribution ratio and worker's wage, which is shown in the previous studies.

Second, the enterprise's characteristics are different between various ownership type groups. For example, the K/L is higher for the public sector (SOE) than the private sector (POE, FOE, HTOE), and it is indicated that the capital investment is more for the public sector than the private sector. This may be caused by the government public investment mainly supporting the SOEs; the export ratio is higher for FOE and HTOE, and it is shown that the global business is more developed in the FOEs and HTOE. To compare with the POEs, the proportions of large enterprises is higher for the FOE, HTOE, and SOE enterprises. The distribution of industry sectors differs by various ownership type enterprise groups. For example, the proportion of industry 1 (Mining manufacturing industry) is higher for SOEs (6.1%) than POEs (4.6%), FOEs (0.3%), and HTOEs (0.7%). It can be thought that these different enterprise characteristics may influence the wage level.

Even though the descriptive statistics results in Table 10.2 show that it seems like that the enterprise's social insurance contributions does not negatively affect the worker's wage, it should be noted that they are the results which are not controlled by the other factors that may affect the wage level (such as capital, global business, firm size, global business, industry sector). The detailed econometric analyzed results will be introduced in Sect. 10.5.

10.5 Econometric Analysis Results

10.5.1 Results of Impact of Social Insurance Contribution on Wage

Table 10.3 shows the results of the impact of the social insurance contributions in the survey on wage using the OLS, fixed-effects model (FE), random-effects model (RE), and one-step general method of moments (GMM).

First, the *F*-test and the Breusch and Pagan Lagrangian multiplier test results indicate both the fixed-effects model and random-effects model are more proper than the OLS, and the Hausman test results show that the fixed-effects model is superior to the random-effects model. Based on the fixed-effects model, the coefficient of total insurance contribution ratio paid by enterprises is −0.009, and it is statistically significant at 1%.

Second, the results based on the GMM method show that the coefficient of total insurance contribution ratio charged by enterprises is −0.009, and it is statistically significant at 1%.

These results indicate that the enterprise's social insurance contributions negatively affect the wage, which indicates that the enterprise's social insurance contributions rise may cause the wage to decrease; the enterprise may transfer the enterprise's social insurance contributions burden to the worker. Based on these results, H1 (the enterprise's social insurance contributions negatively affect worker's wage in China) is supported. The results in this study are consistent with Hamermesh (1979), Gruber (1994), Fishback and Kantor (1995), Anderson and Meyer (2000), Kugler and Kugler (2003), Komamura and Yamada (2004), Yiwamoto and Hamaaki (2006), and Sakei and Kazegami (2007) for the developed countries (the USA and Japan), and

Table 10.3 Results of the impact of social insurance contributions on wage

	OLS		*FE*		*RE*		*One-step GMM*	
	Coef.	t *value*	*Coef.*	t *value*	*Coef.*	t *value*	*Coef.*	t *value*
ln w_t_1							0.161***	49.00
Insurance	−0.004***	−7.33	−0.009***	−21.50	−0.008***	−18.87	−0.009***	−14.59
K/L	0.006***	49.60	0.003***	16.36	0.005***	37.74	0.003***	8.12
Export	0.052***	35.38	0.005**	2.21	0.053***	32.55	−0.002	−0.53
Profit	−0.008***	−8.01	0.043***	16.25	0.006***	4.11	0.019***	3.33
Ref (small firm)								
Middle	0.131***	107.84	0.101***	67.42	0.125***	106.1	0.069***	26.97
Large	0.286***	232.00	0.202***	95.97	0.265***	187.1	0.134***	37.64
Ref (SOE)								
COE	−0.102***	−33.03	−0.002	−0.36	−0.057***	−18.03	−0.007	−1.05
POE	−0.167***	−69.71	0.002	0.39	−0.086***	−33.45	−0.006	−0.87
HTOE	0.036***	11.28	0.025***	5.40	0.013***	3.94	0.024***	3.27
FOE	0.207***	63.78	−0.001	−0.15	0.067***	20.72	0.002	0.27
Other	−0.083***	−35.70	−0.012***	−2.67	−0.061***	−23.2	−0.015**	−2.03
Industry	Yes		Yes		Yes		Yes	
Year	Yes		Yes		Yes		Yes	
Constants	2.372***	757.32	2.296	171.83	2.344***	605.3	2.082***	82.95
Observations	1,112,934		1,112,934		1,112,934		386,715	
Groups			407,715		407,715		219,666	
Within			0.200		0.193			
Between			0.076		0.144			
Overall			0.115		0.1677			
Adj R-squared	0.175							
Prob > *F*			0.000					

(*continued*)

Table 10.3 (continued)

	OLS		*FE*		*RE*		*One-step GMM*	
	Coef.	t *value*	*Coef.*	t *value*	*Coef.*	t *value*	*Coef.*	t *value*
Breusch and Pagan Lagrangian multiplier test					chibar2(01) = 3.0e+05 Prob > chibar2 = 0.0000			
Hausman test			chi2(25) = 18147.23 Prob > chi2 = 0.000				Prob > chi2 = 0.000	

Source: Calculated based on Chinese Large and Medium-size Manufacturing Enterprises (CLMME) database from 2004 to 2007

Note:

(1) *, **, ***: statistically significant levels are 10%, 5% and 1%

(2) ln w_t_1 shows the logarithms of wage in the prior survey year

(3) To express clearly, K/L and profit utilized in analyses are actual values divided by 1000

(4) Industry sector, and year dummy variables are estimated, these results are not expressed in Table 10.3

(5) OLS: ordinary least squares regression; FE: fixed-effects model; RE: random-effects model: GMM: generalized method of moments

developing countries (Chile). China is both a developing country and economic transition country, and these results can provide the new evidence for the issue.

10.5.2 *Results of Impact of Social Insurance Contributions on Wage by Ownership Types*

To prove H2, estimations by using subsamples are employed, and these results are summarized in Table 10.4 (SOE and COE), Table 10.5 (POE and FOE), Table 10.6 (HTOE), and Fig. 10.2.

First, based on the fixed-effects model, the coefficients of enterprise's insurance contribution ratio for their workers are −0.007 (SOE), −0.0004 (COE), −0.012 (POE), −0.054 (FOE), and −0.085 (HTOE), and are statistically significant at 1% based on the fixed-effects model. They are −0.004 (SOE), −0.033 (COE), −0.012 (POE), −0.082 (FOE), and −0.057 (HTOE) and statistically significant at 1% based on the GMM model. Except the results of SOEs based on the one-step GMM method, all the other estimated values are negative, and it is found that the enterprise's insurance contribution rise may decrease the worker wage level, which means when the government increases the enterprise's insurance contribution insurance premium, enterprises may transfer the social insurance contributions to the workers in either private sector or private sector. It indicates that the enterprises may adjust the resource allocation to address the insurance contribution rise, for example, to reduce the worker's wage in both public sector and private sector. The results can be explained as follows. In the 2000s, the market-oriented reform caused the function of market mechanism to increase, and therefore either the public sector or the private sector tried to pursue the profit maximum; thus when the other factors are constant (or not changed), in order to retain the profit maximum, the enterprise may choose to reduce the labor cost to deal with the insurance contribution rise for both public sector and private sector.

Second, it is clear that the negative effects differ by ownership type. It is found that the negative effect is greater for the private sector (FOEs, HTOEs, POEs, and COEs) than for the public sector (SOEs). Based on the GMM method results, the negative effect is highest for the FOEs (−0.082) and lowest for the SOEs (−0.004). Based on these results, H2 is supported. As above, these results can be explained as follows. It may be caused by the different management purposes between these two sectors. For example, the SOEs are not only for the profit maximum, they also respond to the government's policy purpose (e.g. to produce the goods for national secu-

Table 10.4 Results of the impact of social insurance contributions on wage for SOEs and COEs

	SOE				*COE*			
	FE		*one-step GMM*		*FE*		*one-step GMM*	
	Coef.	t *value*	*Coef.*	t *value*	*Coef.*	t *value*	*Coef.*	t *value*
ln w_t_1			0.165***	12.06			0.167***	13.77
Insurance	−0.007***	−13.16	−0.004	−5.28	−4.027E-04	−0.250	−0.033***	−8.76
K/L	0.003***	18.76	−0.002***	−3.78	0.054***	24.380	0.016***	5.49
Export	0.037***	3.53	−0.038**	−2.34	0.028***	2.700	0.012	0.65
Profit	0.001	0.79	−0.013*	−1.62	0.055***	4.760	0.064***	4.87
Ref (small firm)								
Middle	0.240***	42.3	0.052***	4.73	0.136***	21.730	0.102***	11.75
Large	0.494***	81.52	0.127***	8.63	0.238***	35.880	0.181***	14.57
Industry	Yes		Yes		Yes		Yes	
Year	Yes		Yes		Yes		Yes	
Constants	2.208***	179.62	2.486***	32.99	2.575***	200.470	2.096***	28.5
Observations	91,475		33,917		50,971		32,973	
Groups	37,055		20,714		31,717		20,533	
Within	0.147				0.108			
Between	0.224				0.111			
Overall	0.185				0.110			
Adj R-squared								
Prob > *F*	0.000				0.000			
Breusch and Pagan Lagrangian multiplier test	chibar2(01) = 35382.17				chibar2(01) = 6740.64			

(*continued*)

Table 10.4 (continued)

	SOE				*COE*			
	FE		*one-step GMM*		*FE*		*one-step GMM*	
	Coef.	t *value*	*Coef.*	t *value*	*Coef.*	t *value*	*Coef.*	t *value*
Hausman test	Prob > chibar2 = 0.0000 chi2(20) = 1847.95 Prob > chi2 = 0.000				Prob > chibar2 = 0.0000 chi2(20) = 475.74 Prob > chi2 = 0.000			
Prob > chi2			0.000				0.000	

Source: Calculated based on Chinese Large and Medium-size Manufacturing Enterprises (CLMME) database from 2004 to 2007

Note:

(1) *, **, ***: statistically significant levels are 10%, 5% and 1%

(2) ln w_t_1 shows the logarithms of wage in the prior survey year

(3) To express clearly, K/L and profit utilized in analyses are actual values divided by 1000

(4) Industry sector, and year dummy variables are estimated, these results are not expressed in Table 10.4

(5) FE: fixed-effects model; GMM: generalized method of moments

Table 10.5 Results of the impact of social insurance contributions on wage for POEs and FOEs

	POE				*FOE*			
	FE		*one-step GMM*		*FE*		*one-step GMM*	
	Coef.	t *value*	*Coef.*	t *value*	*Coef.*	t *value*	*Coef.*	t *value*
ln w_t_1			0.135***	36.7			0.304***	27.10
Insurance	−0.012***	−9.91	−0.012***	−10.2	−0.054***	−11.32	−0.082***	−15.95
K/L	0.035***	21.91	0.051***	28.40	0.035***	11.39	0.057***	15.40
Export	−0.001	−0.19	−0.001	−0.19	0.007	1.44	−0.006***	−0.55
Profit	0.084***	8.55	0.256***	18.62	−0.099***	−5.38	−0.015***	−0.84
Ref (Small firm)								
Middle	0.103***	31.79	0.067***	22.55	0.066***	5.57	0.049***	4.30
Large	0.211***	46.06	0.130***	30.95	0.132***	8.87	0.105***	7.35
Industry	Yes		Yes		Yes		Yes	
Year	Yes		Yes		Yes		Yes	
Constants	2.294***	9.80	2.150***	70.94	2.635***	8.88	1.967***	20.13
Observations	416,347		245,140		52,957		37,154	
Groups	252,799		142,698		32,203		21,957	
Within	0.137				0.114			
Between	0.038				0.012			
Overall	0.056				0.020			
Adj R-squared								
Prob > *F*	0.000				0.000			
Breusch and Pagan Lagrangian multiplier test	chibar2(01) = 32549.24				chibar2(01) = 6969.94			
	Prob > chibar2 = 0.0000				Prob > chibar2 = 0.0000			

(continued)

Table 10.5 (continued)

	POE				*FOE*			
	FE		*one-step GMM*		*FE*		*one-step GMM*	
	Coef.	t *value*	*Coef.*	t *value*	*Coef.*	t *value*	*Coef.*	t *value*
Hausman test	chi2(20) = 966.97 Prob > chi2 = 0.000				chi2(20) = 433.76 Prob > chi2 = 0.000			
Prob > chi2			0.000				0.000	

Note and *Source*: see Table 10.4

Table 10.6 Results of the impact of social insurance contributions on wage for HTOEs

	HTOE			
	FE		*One-step GMM*	
	Coef.	t *value*	*Coef.*	t *value*
ln w_t_1			0.201***	18.91
Insurance	−0.085***	−10.59	−0.057***	−9.77
K/L	0.003***	4.53	0.004***	5.80
Export	0.038***	3.19	0.005	0.62
Profit	0.053**	2.37	0.048*	1.69
Ref (Small firm)				
Middle	0.113***	10.30	0.074***	7.89
Large	0.202***	14.11	0.136***	11.13
Industry	Yes		Yes	
Year	Yes		Yes	
Constants	2.707***	9.08	2.239***	24.03
Observations	52,835		37,543	
Groups	32,484		22,138	
Within	0.114			
Between	0.040			
Overall	0.043			
Adj R-squared				
Prob > *F*	0.000			
Breusch and Pagan Lagrangian multiplier test	chibar2(01) = 4863.57			
	Prob > chibar2 = 0.0000			
Hausman test	chi2(20) = 1819.07			
Prob > chi2			0.000	

Note and *Source*: see Table 10.4

rity, to enlarge the employment for the social security), and the government invests the majority public financial support in the SOEs. Thus the SOEs do not need to adjust the worker's wage level to respond to the social insurance contributions rise. In addition, to compare with the private sector, the influence of market mechanism on wage is smaller for the enterprises in the public sector, for example, the basic wage and employment in the public sector are still managed and controlled by the government during the 2000s (see Chap. 2 in the book), and thus the wage adjustment to address the social insurance contributions rise cannot be employed immediately in the public sector. Whereas, in order to retain the profit maximum, enterprises in the private sector may choose to transfer the social insurance contributions rise burden to workers immediately.

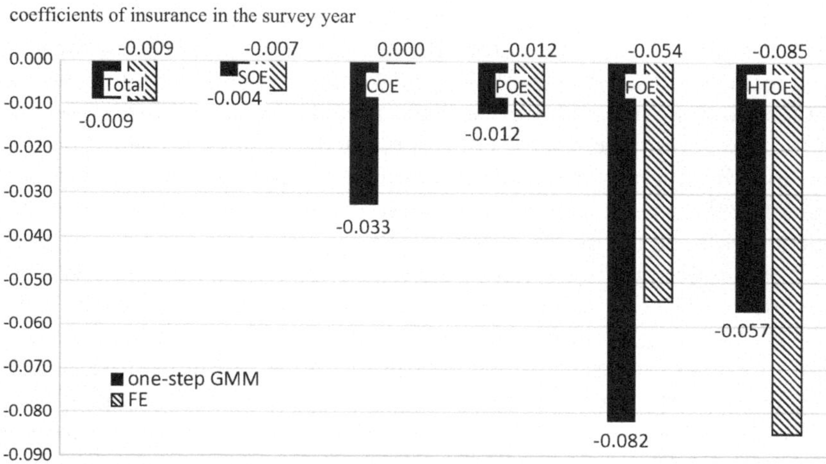

Fig. 10.2 Summary of the results of the impact of social insurance contributions on wage. *Note*: (1) Estimated coefficients of social insurance contributions are expressed in the figure. Logarithms of wage in the prior survey year, K/L, export, profit, firm size, industry sector, survey year dummy variables are controlled in these analyses. (2) GMM: generalized method of moments; FE: fixed-effects model. *Source*: Calculated based on CLMME database from 2004 to 2007

10.6 Conclusions

The Chinese government enforced the public security system reform during the economic transition period; the social insurance contributions, which can be thought of as a kind of social insurance contributions, is nearly 40% of total wage. It is thought the enterprises may transfer the social insurance contributions to a worker by reducing the worker's wage. Do the social insurance contributions influence wage? This chapter employs an empirical study using the enterprise panel survey data-2004–2007 CLMME database to prove two hypotheses on the issue. The fixed-effects model, random-effects model, and the GMM method are used to address the heterogeneity, and prior dependent and endogenous problems. The main findings are as follows.

First, in general, it is clear that the social insurance contributions negatively affect the worker's wage level, and the enterprise may transfer the social insurance contributions rise to the worker. Therefore, H1 is supported.

Second, the effect of the social insurance contributions on wage differs by various ownership type groups, and it is found that even though the social insurance contributions rise may decrease the worker wage level for both the public and private sectors, the negative effect is greater for the private sector (FOEs, HTOEs, POEs, and COEs) than for the public sector (SOEs), and the negative effect is highest for the FOEs and lowest for the SOEs. Based on these results, H2 is supported. It can be explained by the fact that the enterprise management purpose and the influence of the function of market mechanism on wage determination are different between the public sector and the private sector.

These empirical study results suggest some policy implications could be considered. The results indicate that the insurance premium rise may negatively affect wage, and the enterprises might transfer the insurance burden to workers (particularly the enterprises in the private sector), which may decrease the wage, and decrease the good consumption which may cause the economic growth decrease. To address the aging population problem, the Chinese government reformed the public security systems. Along with these reforms, the insurance premium increased for both workers and enterprises. How to balance the responsibilities of the government, enterprises, and workers is an important issue to be discussed. Because there still remain surplus laborers in the rural regions, and the influence of the union collective bargaining on wage is not great in China, the influence of labor demand side (enterprise) on the wage determination is greater than for labor supply side (worker). It can be thought that when the wage elasticity of labor supply is small, the enterprise can transfer the social insurance contributions to workers. Therefore, government should consider retaining or increasing the social insurance fund by ways other than raising the social insurance contributions. Moreover, the labor market segmentation by the public sector and private sector lead to different results on the impact of social insurance contributions on wage. It should be noted that the social security coverage scale spreading from the public sector to the private sector may increase the welfare of workers in the private sector, whereas the harm by the social security system reform is greater for the workers in the private sector than those in the public sector. This is a new inequality problem which should be considered.

Finally, for the enterprise panel data limited, we only analyzed the impact of social insurance contributions on wage enterprise from 2004 to 2007. As it is described in Sect. 10.2, the Chinese government decreased the social insurance contributions from 2015; a detailed analysis utilizing long-term panel data should be done, and the natural-experiment method should be utilized based on more appropriate long-term survey data in the future. This study only analyzed the impact of social insurance contributions on wage, and it can be that the enterprise may adjust the employment to address the social insurance contributions rise, for example, to reduce the low-skilled worker employment or to increase the production price. These issues should be studied in future research. The influence of the regional disparities on the implementation situations of social security systems should also be considered, and more empirical studies should be done on the issue.

Notes

1. The lowest wage level for the social insurance contributions differs by the regions. For example, it is 40% of the prior year average wage in Beijing.
2. This part has referenced Kotlikoff and Summer (1987), Gruber (1997), Bojas (2004), Yiwamoto and Hamaaki (2006), Sakei and Kazegami (2007), and Adhikari et al. (2009).

References

Adhikari, D. R., Everson, W., & Gray, L. (2009). Effect of unemployment insurance tax on wages and reallocation of labour. *Applied Economics Letters, 16*(2), 147–150.

Anderson, P., & Meyer, B. (2000). The effects of the unemployment insurance payroll tax on wages, employment, claims and denials. *Journal of Public Economics, 78*, 81–106.

Arellano, M., & Bond, S. (1991). Some tests of specification for panel data: Monte Carlo evidence and an application to employment equations. *Review of Economic Studies, 58*, 277–298.

Arellano, M., & Bover, O. (1995). Another look at the instrumental variable estimation of error-components models. *Journal of Econometrics, 68*, 29–51.

Asher, M. A. (1984). On the estimation of payroll tax incidence: Comments. *Southern Economic Journal, 50*(4), 1224–1230.

Blundell, R., & Bond, S. (1998). Initial conditions and moment restrictions in dynamic panel data models. *Journal of Econometrics, 87*, 115–143.

Bojas, G. (2004). *Labor economics* (3rd ed.). New York and London: McGraw-Hill/Irwin.

Fishback, P., & Kantor, S. E. (1995). Did workers pay for the passage of Workers' Compensation Law? *Quarterly Journal of Economics, 110*(3), 713–742.

Gruber, J. (1994). The incidence of mandated maternity benefits. *American Economic Review, 84*(3), 622–641.

Gruber, J. (1997). The incidence of payroll taxation: Evidence from Chile. *Journal of Labor Economics, 15*(3), 72–101.

Gruber, J., & Krueger, A. (1991). The incidence of mandated employer-provided insurance: Lessons from workers' compensation insurance. In D. Bradford (Ed.), *Tax policy and the economy* (Vol. 5, pp. 111–144). Cambridge, MA: MIT Press.

Hamermesh, D. (1979). New estimates of the incidence of the payroll Tax. *Southern Economic Journal, 45*, 1208–1219.

Holmlund, B. (1983). Payroll taxes and wage inflation: The Swedish experience. *Scandinavian Journal of Economics, 85*(1), 1–15.

Komamura, K., & Yamada, A. (2004). Who bears the burden of social insurance? Evidence from Japanese health and long-term care insurance data. *Journal of the Japanese and International Economies, 18*, 565–581.

Kotlikoff, L., & Summer, L. (1987). Tax incidence. In A. Auerbach & M. Feldstein (Eds.), *Handbook of public economics, vol. 2* (pp. 1043–1092). Amsterdam and Oxford: Elsevier.

Kugler, A., & Kugler, M. (2003). The labor market effects of payroll taxes in a middle-income country: Evidence from Colombia. *CEPR Discussion Paper*, No. 4046.

Minami, R., & Ma, X. (2010). The Lewisian turning point of Chinese economy: Comparison with Japanese experience. *China Economic Journal, 3*(2), 165–181.

Minami, R., & Ma, X. (2014). Labor market and Lewisian turning point in China. In R. Minami, F. Makino, & K. Kim (Eds.), *Lewisian turning point in the Chinese economy* (Chapter 5, pp. 76–100). Palgrave Macmillan.

Sakei, M., & Kazegami, S. (2007). An analysis on the burden of health care insurance. *Health and Social, 42*(3), 235–248 (In Japanese).

Smith, R. S., & Ehrenberg, R. G. (1983). Estimation wage-fringe trade-offs: Some data problems. In J. E. Triplett (Ed.), *The measurement of labor cost.* Chicago: University of Chicago Press.

Summer, L. H. (1989). Some simple economics of mandated benefits. *American Economic Review, 79*(2), 177–183.

Tachibanaki, T., & Yokoyama, Y. (2008). The estimation of the incidence of employer contribution to social security in Japan. *Japanese Economic Review, 59*(1), 75–83.

Triplett, J. E. (1983). *The measurement of labor cost.* Chicago: University of Chicago Press.

Yiwamoto, Y., & Hamaaki, J. (2006). An analysis on the burden of social insurance: From economics perspective. *Social Security Studies, 42*(3), 204–218 (In Japanese).

Index

X. Ma, *Economic Transition and Labor Market Reform in China*,
https://doi.org/10.1007/978-981-13-1987-7

The manufacturer's authorised representative in the EU is Springer Nature Customer Service Centre GmbH, Europaplatz 3, 69115 Heidelberg, Germany. If you have any concerns regarding our products, please contact ProductSafety@springernature.com

Printed and bound by CPI Group (UK) Ltd, Croydon, CR0 4YY
25/09/2026
02222897-0011